TRANSLATING 1 JOHN

CLAUSE BY CLAUSE

EBOOKS FOR TRANSLATING THE NEW TESTAMENT
Herbert W. Bateman IV, series editor

Translating Jude Clause by Clause: An Exegetical Guide (2013)
Herbert W. Bateman IV

Translating 2 and 3 John Clause by Clause: An Exegetical Guide (2014)
Aaron C. Peer and Herbert W. Bateman IV

Translating Ephesians Clause by Clause: An Exegetical Guide (2015)
Benjamin I. Simpson

Translating Philippians Clause by Clause: An Exegetical Guide (2015)
Thomas S. Moore

Translating Colossians Clause by Clause: An Exegetical Guide (2016)
Adam Copenhaver

Translating 2 Timothy Clause by Clause: An Exegetical Guide (2016)
Phillip A. Davis

Translating Titus Clause by Clause: An Exegetical Guide (2016)
J. Michael McKay Jr.

Translating 1 Timothy Clause by Clause: An Exegetical Guide (2017)
Charles Martin

Translating James Clause by Clause: An Exegetical Guide (2017)
William C. Varner

Translating 1 John Clause by Clause: An Exegetical Guide (2017)
Herbert W. Bateman IV and Aaron C. Peer

Expectations for 2018–2020

Translating Romans Clause by Clause: An Exegetical Guide
William Johnston

Translating 1 Corinthians Clause by Clause: An Exegetical Guide
Michael H. Burer

Translating 2 Corinthians Clause by Clause: An Exegetical Guide
Michael H. Burer

Translating Galatians Clause by Clause: An Exegetical Guide
James MaGahey

Translating 1 Thessalonians Clause by Clause: An Exegetical Guide
William C. Varner

Translating Hebrews Clause by Clause: An Exegetical Guide
Herbert W. Bateman IV

Translating 2 Peter Clause by Clause: An Exegetical Guide
Herbert W. Bateman IV

EBOOKS FOR TRANSLATING THE NEW TESTAMENT

TRANSLATING 1 JOHN
CLAUSE BY CLAUSE

An Exegetical Guide

Herbert W. Bateman IV

Aaron C. Peer

Cyber-Center for Biblical Studies Publication

Translating 1 John Clause by Clause: An Exegetical Guide
© 2017 by Herbert W. Bateman IV and Aaron C. Peer

Published by Cyber-Center for Biblical Studies, 4078 E. Oldfield Drive, Leesburg, IN.

EBooks for Translating the New Testament © 2014 by Cyber-Center for Biblical Studies.

The Greek Text is original based upon text critical comparisons and evaluations of Nestle-Aland's *Novum Testamentum Graece* 26th & 27th & 28th edition, (Stuttgart, Germany: Deutsche Bibelgesellschaft, 1979, 1993, 2012); Zane C. Hodges and Arthur L. Farstad, *The Greek New Testament According to the Majority Text* (Nashville: Thomas Nelson, 1985), 720-21; Marice A. Robinson and William G. Pierpont, *The New Testament in the Original Greek: Byzantine Textform 2005* (Southborough, MA: Chilton, 2005), 351-52; Michael W. Holmes, *The Greek New Testament SBL Edition*, Society of Biblical Literature (Atlanta, GA: Society of Biblical Literature and Bellingham, Washington: Logos Bible Software, 2010).

Nestle–Aland, Novum Testamentum Graece, 28th Revised Edition, edited by Barbara and Kurt Aland, Johannes Karavidopoulos, Carlo M. Martini, and Bruce M. Metzger in cooperation with the Institute for New Testament Textual Research, Münster/Westphalia, © 2012 Deutsche Bibelgesellschaft, Stuttgart. Used by permission.

The Greek font GraecaU is available from www.linguistsoftware.com/lgku.htm, +1-425-775-1130.

ISBN-13: 978-0-9907797-7-3

Contents

Preface to the Series iii

Acknowledgement of the Author iv

Charts and Abbreviations vi

Consulted Sources vii

Introduction

Contextual Orientation 1

Greek Text for Verbal Recognition 1

Clausal Outlines for Translating 1 John 4

Independent Clauses 5

Dependent Clauses 10

Tips for Translating 1 John 15

Clausal Outlines Translated and Explained 19

Clausal Outlines for Translation

1 John 1:11–4 Prologue 18

1 John 1:5–2:2 20

1 John 2:3–11. 23

1 John 2:12–17 26

1 John 2:18–29 28

1 John 3:1–10 32

1 John 3:11–17 36

1 John 3:18–24 39

1 John 4:1–6 41

1 John 4:7–10 43

1 John 4:11–16c 45

1 John 4:16d–21 47

1 John 5:1–4 50

1 John 5:5–12 51

1 John 5:13–21 54

Clausal Outlines Translated and Syntax Explained

1 John 1:11–4 Prologue 57

1 John 1:5–2:2 66

1 John 2:3–11 78

1 John 2:12–17 91

1 John 2:18–29 100

1 John 3:1–10 122

1 John 3:11–17 137

1 John 3:18–24 148

1 John 4:1–6 160

1 John 4:7–10 170

1 John 4:11–16c 177

1 John 4:16d–21 186

1 John 5:1–4 195

1 John 5:5–12 203

1 John 5:13–21 214

First John Translated 228

Selected Bibliography for Further Study 232

Preface to the Series

Time. It is a precious commodity. Pertinent for survival in today's world involves discovering shortcuts to save time and developing skills at working smarter and not harder. This is certainly true in translating and interpreting the New Testament Greek text in preparation for teaching and preaching. Although many people aspire to learning biblical Greek, it takes time — far more time than some seminaries today wish to devote to teaching people how to study the Bible in its original language. More and more language departments today seem to be forced to settle on providing one year to learn the basics of elementary Greek, and then expect software programs like Accordance, Bible Works, and Logos to do the rest. Unfortunately students only learn how to translate and parse verbs without knowing about and thereby appreciating how a biblical author may string together his argument through his use of words, phrases, and clauses.

Better seminaries provide students opportunities to advance to the next level so that their students may learn how to wrestle with the syntax and semantics of a text and thereby appreciate and critically evaluate the differences between the numerous English translations and interact with commentaries with some degree of competence. Students learn the joy that comes with wrestling with the text, to sit and ponder the text, and to absorb the text so that it impacts the way they might live and perhaps even how they might teach and preach it. Naturally, this sort of grappling with the biblical text takes time. Are there any shortcuts? Are there any tools that help a student, a teacher, or a pastor to work smarter and not harder in their struggle to translate and interpret the biblical text?

This series, eBooks for Translating the New Testament provides students, teachers, and pastors, guides for translating and interpreting the books of the New Testament. Customized to save time, they underscore the specific stylistic features favored by an author that are evident in their writings. Designed to help a person work smarter — not harder they provide a visual vital for illustrating the syntactical relationships between clauses that may be compared, contrasted, and critically evaluated with comprehension upon further investigation when using the variety of commentaries and English translations available today.

Needless to say, any translation and syntactical understanding of the biblical text takes time and effort. Nevertheless, eBooks for Translating the New Testament is customized to save time, designed to help a student, teacher or pastor work smarter — not harder, and intended to move people to ponder, absorb, and eventually share what is learned in a given New Testament book with others.

HERBERT W. BATEMAN IV
SERIES EDITOR

Acknowledgement of the Authors

ENGLISH GRAMMAR is not the most exciting subject to study and learn and yet grammar and syntax is a vital skill for interpreting the Bible whether in an English translation or a Greek New Testament text. Consequently, I'm indebted to several people who throughout my training emphasized the importance of grammar and syntax for interpreting the Bible.

WHILE AT CAIRN UNIVERSITY, Janice Okulski required all her students to create a grammatical diagram for the NIV translation of Philippians, and Dr. McGormick expected his students to structurally outline an English translation of Galatians in order to trace Paul's train of thought. Special attention was always given to connecting words like "so that" (= result), "in order that" (= purpose), "therefore" (= inferential), "because" (= reason), etc. Both professors prepared me for later study in the Greek New Testament and to whom I owe a great debt of gratitude. And though professor Okulski and McGormick provided a sound foundation for studying the English Bible, Dallas Theological Seminary expanded that groundwork when I began working in the New Testament Greek text.

WHILE AT DALLAS THEOLOGICAL SEMINARY, Darrell Bock, Buist Fanning, John Grassmick, and other New Testament faculty members were instrumental in teaching me skills of translation, syntax, and exegesis. Naturally, skills take time to master and shortcuts were later developed while teaching others how to learn and work in the New Testament Greek text. While tutoring students as a teacher's assistant at Dallas Theological Seminary during the latter 80s, the chart "Indicatives: Distinguishing Tenses" (see page 3) was a tool initially developed to help students recognize verbal tenses while learning elementary Greek.

LATER AS A PROFESSOR, my pedagogical skills were challenged and eventually sharpened as I was learning how to help students study as painlessly as possible two languages: English and New Testament Greek. Some of the results are evident in this eBook for Translating the New Testament. While teaching New Testament Greek during the latter 90s, I developed a code for coloring verb tenses (see page 2) so that students might turn their Greek New Testament into a user friendly tool to return to time and again after graduation and in ministry. While working on the final stages of *A Workbook for Intermediate Greek: Grammar, Exegesis, and Commentary on 1–3 John*, ways to distinguish substantival subject and direct object clauses within an independent clausal outline sorted itself out for easier visual recognition.

CONSEQUENTLY, I AM INDEBTED TO THREE GROUPS OF PEOPLE who have shaped this book *Translating Jude Clause by Clause*: two undergraduate professors from Cairn University, the New Testament department at Dallas Theological Seminary, and the numerous students whom I have tutored and taught since 1986.

HERBERT W. BATEMAN IV

WHEN I WAS A KID, we would often visit the home of my maternal grandparents, Joe and Goldie Oklak. As much as I loved them, there was not much to do at their home, except puzzles. They had puzzles in their drawers, on their tables, and even in their basement. Every time I would go to their home, even when I was three years old, I felt myself drawn to their puzzles. If I had to pinpoint a moment where my fondness for grammar began, I guess it would be those formative puzzle-seeking moments at my grandparent's card table. Grammar, whether English or Greek, is just a puzzle to solve, but as we put together the syntactical pieces of the Greek text of the New Testament, the solution ends up being God's very words to mankind.

MY SOPHOMORE YEAR OF COLLEGE I started taking Greek with Dr. Herbert W. Bateman IV. I remember him being fairly hard-nosed, if I am to be honest. One thing I quickly learned from Herb was how little I really knew about grammar. I believe that my early English teachers thought that we would just absorb grammar by osmosis through reading. I do not think that philosophy holds up in my experience. Herb helped me learn grammar by challenging me to actually do grammar and to verbally explain the grammar of a biblical text. I have never been one to back down from a challenge, so I threw myself into studying Greek. I quickly discovered that I actually enjoyed it.

AFTER TWO YEARS OF GREEK, Herb asked me to be his Teaching Assistant, and we have been teaching or working together in some capacity ever since. While teaching with Herb, we noticed that pastoral students were not getting the skills they needed to adequately use their Greek text. They might know some grammar and have a little bit of exegetical knowledge, but there was a glaring missing piece, syntax. For years Herb has poured his life into helping pastors learn basic syntax, so that they can trace a biblical author's flow of thought, and along with his intermediate Grammar, this series is a product of that quest. During this process, Herb has become a dear friend, and without his vision and pavement-pounding dedication, this series would not exist.

IN SHORT, I owe my love for puzzles to my Grandma and Grandpa Oklak, and my love for the puzzle that is the Greek grammar and syntax of the New Testament to Herb Bateman.

Dedication

I would like to dedicate this work to my beautiful, kind, brilliant, and thoughtful wife, Shannon Peer. She is the one who listens to me drone on about stuff that she does not care about, because she knows I do. She is the one who sacrifices and takes care of six kids, while I spend a great deal of my time in meetings and researching, teaching, writing, and preaching. She is the one who pours over my words as a careful editor, when she probably has twenty others things that she would rather be doing. I dedicate this work to her, even though a book dedication could never contain the amount of love and affection I have for her.

AARON C. PEER

Charts and Abbreviations

Charts

Number of Words in 1 John . . . . , 1

Key for Color Coding 1 John 2

Indicatives: Distinguishing Tenses 4

Independent Conjunctive Clauses 7

Types of Independent Clauses in 1 John 9

Types of Dependent Clauses in 1 John 14

Hapax Legomena in 1 John 16

Abbreviations

ASV	American Standard Version (1901 edition)
BDAG	*A Greek-English Lexicon of the New Testament and Other Early Christian Literature*
BDF	*A Grammar of the New Testament* by Blass, Debrunner, and Funk
CEB	Common English Bible
CNT	Comprehensive New Testament
CSB	Christian Standard Bible
ESV	English Standard Version
KJV	King James Version
MT	Majority Text Greek Text
NA	Nestle-Aland Greek Text
NAV	New American Version
NASB	New American Standard Bible (1995 edition)
NET	New English Translation
NIV	New International Version (1984 edition)
NKJV	New King James Version
NLT	New Living Translation (second edition)
NRSV	New Revised Standard Version
RP	Robinson-Pierpont Greek Text
RSV	Revised Standard Version
SBL	Society of Biblical Literature Greek Text
TNIV	Today's New International Version
WEB	World English Bible

Consulted Sources

Bateman IV, Herbert W. *Interpreting the General Letters*. Handbook for New Testament Exegesis, edited by John D. Harvey. Grand Rapids: Kregel, 2013.

_____. *A Workbook for Intermediate Greek: Grammar, Exegesis, and Commentary on 1–3 John*. Grand Rapids: Kregel, 2008.

Bauer, Walter, Frederick W. Danker, William F. Arndt, and F. Wilbur Gingrich. *A Greek–English Lexicon of the New Testament and Other Early Christian Literature*. Third Edition. Chicago and London: University of Chicago Press, 2000.

Blass, F., and Debrunner, A. *A Greek Grammar of the New Testament and Other Early Christian Literature*. Translation and revision of the 9th–10th German edition, by Robert W. Funk. Chicago: University of Chicago Press, 1961.

Brown, Raymond E. *The Epistles of John*. The Anchor Bible. Garden City, NY: Doubleday, 1982.

Bullinger, E. W. *Figures of Speech Used in the Bible: Explained and Illustrated*. Grand Rapids: Baker, 1968; tenth 1984.

Burer, Michael H. and Jeffery E. Miller. *A New Reader's Lexicon of the Greek New Testament*. Grand Rapids: Kregel, 2008.

Culy, Martin M. *I, II, III John: A Handbook on the Greek Text*. Waco, TX: Baylor University Press, 2004.

Fanning, Buist. *Verbal Aspect in the New Testament*. Edinburgh: T&T Clark, 1991.

Funk, Robert W. "Form and Structure of II John and III John." *Journal of Biblical Literature* 86.4 (1967): 424-30.

Guthrie George H. and J. Scott Duvall *Biblical Greek Exegesis: A Guided Apporach to Learning Intermediate and Advanced Greek*. Grand Rapids: Zondervan, 1988.

Hodges, Zane C, and Arthur L. Farstad. *The Greek New Testament According to the Majority Text*. Nashville, TN: Thomas Nelson, 2nd ed. 1985.

Holmes, Michael W. *The Greek New Testament SBL Edition*, Society of Biblical Literature. Atlanta, GA: Society of Biblical Literature and Bellingham, Washington: Logos Bible Software, 2010.

Kruse, Colin G. *The Letters of John*. The Pillar New Testament Commentary. Grand Rapids: Eerdmans, 2000.

Lieu, Judith M. *I, II, III John: A Commentary*. The New Testament Library. Louisville, KY: Westminster John Knox Press, 2008.

MacDonald, William G. *Greek Enchiridion: A Concise Handbook of Grammar for Translation and Exegesis*. Peabody, MA: Hendrickson, 1979.

Metzger, Bruce M. *A Textual Commentary on the Greek New Testament* (New York: United Bible Society, 2nd edition, 1994.

Mounce, William D. *Basics of Biblical Greek Grammar*, Third edition. Grand Rapids: Zondervan, 2009.

_____. *A Graded Reader of Biblical Greek*. Grand Rapids: Zondervan, 1996.

Moule, C. F. D. *An Idiom Book of New Testament Greek*. 2nd edition. Cambridge University Press, 1959.

Moulton, James Hope. *A Grammar of New Testament Greek*, Volume 1, *Prolegomena*. Edinburgh: T & T Clark, 1906, 3rd ed. 1957.

Nestle, Eberhard, editor. *Greek New Testament: Edited with Critical Apparatus*. New York: American Bible Society, 1816.

Nestle–Aland 26th edition of *Novum Testamenum Graece*. Stuttgart, Germany: Deutsche Bibelgesellschaft, 1979.

Nestle–Aland 27th edition of *Novum Testamenum Graece*. Stuttgart, Germany: Deutsche Bibelgesellschaft, 1993.

Nestle–Aland 28th edition of *Novum Testamenum Graece*. Stuttgart, Germany: Deutsche Bibelgesellschaft, 2012.

Pierpont, William G. and Maurice A. Robinson. *The New Testament in the Original Greek: Byzantine Textform 2005*. Southborough, MA: Chilton Book, 2005.

Porter, Stanley E. *Idioms of the Greek New Testament*. Sheffield, England: JSOT Press, 1992.

Robertson, A. T. *A Grammar of the Greek New Testament in the Light of Historical Research*. Nashville: Broadman Press, 1934.

Rogers Jr, Cleon L. and Cleon L. Rogers III. *The New Linguistic and Exegetical Key to the Greek New Testament*. Grand Rapids: Zondervan, 1998.

Stanley K. Stowers. *Letter Writing in Greco-roman Antiquity*. Philadelphia: The Westminster Press, 1986.

Turner, Nigel. *A Grammar of New Testament Greek, Volume 3: Syntax*. Edinburgh: T & T Clark, 1964.

Wallace, Daniel B. *Greek Grammar Beyond the Basics: An Exegetical Syntax of the New Testament*. Grand Rapids, MI: Zondervan Publishing House, 1996.

Yarbrough, Robert W. *1–3 John*. Baker Exegetical Commentary on the New Testament. Grand Rapids: Baker Academic, 2008.

Zerwick, Maximilian. *Biblical Greek: Illustrated by Examples*. Translated and adapted by Joseph Smith. Rome: Scripta Pontificii Instituti Biblici, 1963.

Introduction

ANYONE WHO ASPIRES to sit down, open their New Testament Greek text, and begin translating any given New Testament book reveals a noble desire. Sometimes that noble desire deteriorates into a tedious task. Other times translating is a joy because some books in the New Testament are easier than others to translate. First John is one of those easier books because the vocabulary is simple and familiar. Yet John's style of writing and his syntax can be challenging. This first section, "Introduction." familiarizes you with elements found in sections one and two of *Translating 1 John Clause by Clause* as well as provides tips for translating 1 John.

Section Two, "Clausal Outline for Translation," guides you in translating 1 John. John's letter is presented in fifteen manageable units of thought. Each unit has three components: a contextual orientation, a Greek text for verbal recognition, and a clausal outline.

Section three, "Clausal Outlines Translated and Syntax Explained," re-presents the Greek text with verbs and verbals colored for easy tense recognition. Clausal outlines are also re-presented but with an interpretive translation. Finally a detailed syntactical explanation appears for each verb, verbal, and major connecter explaining the interpretive structural outline.

Contextual Orientation

"Contextual Orientation" in section two provides a summary for each unit to be translated. Often the translation of any given book of the New Testament involves isolating every Greek word in order to decline, parse, and translate them into English. Efforts spent translating individual words can cause a person to miss the author's big picture. And yet knowing something about the big picture helps in the translation process. So every unit in *Translating 1 John Clause by Clause* begins with a summary statement based upon John's flow of thought that orients you to the Greek paragraph to be translated. To put it another way, we give you a picture of the forest before you get lost among the trees.

Greek Text for Verbal Recognition

"Greek Text for Verbal Recognition" in section two provides manageable portions of 1 John to practice tense recognition of all verbs and verbals (i.e., participles and infinitives). But before explaining the purpose and process for verbal recognition, something must be said about John's Greek text. Depending on the New Testament Greek text used, 1 John may consist of 2,134 Greek words (NA^{28}), 2,138 Greek words (SBL Text), 2,151 Greek words (RP^{2005} Text), or 2,150 Greek words

Number of Words in 1 John				
Chapter	NA28	SBL	RP^{2005}	MT
One	206	207	207	207
Two	587	584	581	580
Three	468	469	472	472
Four	449	449	453	452
Five	424	429	438	439

(Majority Text = MT).[1] Nevertheless the New Testament Greek text in *Translating 1 John Clause by Clause* mirror's Nestle-Alands 28th edition, but there are differences.

The reason for the "Greek Text for Verbal Recognition" section is twofold. First, it presents a controllable number of verses you can conquer relatively quickly rather than feeling overwhelmed by one hundred five (105) verses all at once.

Second, it provides an opportunity to locate and color all verbs and verbals (e.g., participles and infinitives) according to their tense. Rather than parse immediately all verbs and verbals (the act of parsing occurs later in the translation process), the exercise encourages recognition of verb and verbal tenses. Once the tense is determined, use a colored pencil to identify the tense. For

Key for a 3 X 5 card for students to place in the student's Greek text.				
Tense	Indicative	Participle	Infinitive	Imperative
Present	▭	⬭	▬	[▭]
Aorist	▬	⬭	▬	[▬]
Imperfect	▬	⬭	▬	[▬]
Perfect	▬	⬬	▬	[▬]
Pluperfect	▬	⬭	▬	[▬]
Future	▬	⬭	▬	[▬]

the present tense verbs and verbals use yellow, for aorists light blue, for the imperfects light green, for perfects light red, for the pluperfects orange, and futures light brown. You check how well you did in section three, "Clausal Outlines Translated and Syntax Explained," where correct tense coloring of the verbs and verbals is found.

You may create other clues for distinguishing indicatives from verbals. For instance, adverbial participles may be colored to identify tense but then circled with a black pen for quick recognition of its adverbial usage. Adverbial infinitives, on the other hand, might be colored to identify tense and then underlined. Imperatives might be colored and then placed in [brackets]. The following chart "Indicatives: Distinguishing Tense" will help steer you to recognize the tense of any given indicative verb by isolating a tense formative Greek letter or letters.[2]

---

[1] Nestle-Aland's *Novum Testamentum Graece* 28th edition, (Stuttgart, Germany: Deutsche Bibelgesellschaft, 1979, 1993, 2012); Zane C. Hodges and Arthur L. Farstad, *The Greek New Testament According to the Majority Text* (Nashville: Thomas Nelson, 1985); Marice A. Robinson and William G. Pierpont, *The New Testament in the Original Greek: Byzantine Textform 2005* (Southborough, MA: Chilton, 2005); Michael W. Holmes, *The Greek New Testament SBL Edition*, Society of Biblical Literature (Atlanta, GA: Society of Biblical Literature and Bellingham, Washington: Logos Bible Software, 2010).

[2] If you recall from elementary Greek grammar, a tense formative is a Greek letter or couple of letters inserted between a tense stem and the connecting vowel. Naturally, the charts provided in this chapter identify the tense formative letters for you. A "Master Verb Chart" and "Master Participle Chart" listing tense formatives appears in William D. Mounce, *Basics of Biblical Greek Grammar*, 3rd ed. (Grand Rapids: Zondervan, 2009), 354-56.

Indicatives: Distinguishing Tense[3]

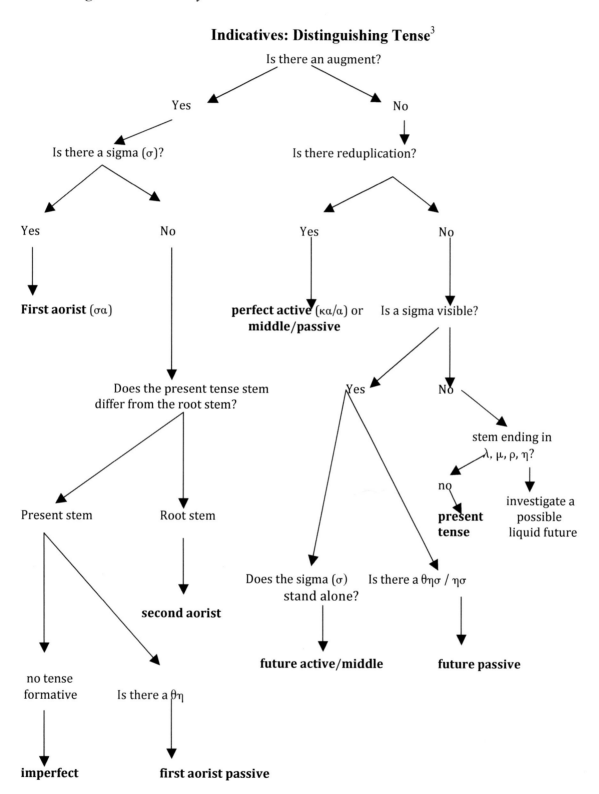

Is there an augment?

Yes — Is there a sigma (σ)?

No — Is there reduplication?

Is there a sigma (σ)?
- Yes → **First aorist** (σα)
- No → Does the present tense stem differ from the root stem?

Is there reduplication?
- Yes → **perfect active** (κα/α) or **middle/passive**
- No → Is a sigma visible?

Does the present tense stem differ from the root stem?
- Present stem
- Root stem → **second aorist**

Present stem
- no tense formative → **imperfect**
- Is there a θη → **first aorist passive**

Is a sigma visible?
- Yes
- No → stem ending in λ, μ, ρ, η?

stem ending in λ, μ, ρ, η?
- no → **present tense**
- → **investigate a possible liquid future**

Does the sigma (σ) stand alone? → **future active/middle**

Is there a θησ / ησ → **future passive**

_____

[3] This chart was first published in Herbert W. Bateman IV, *A Workbook for Intermediate Greek: Grammar, Exegesis, and Commentary on 1–3 John* (Grand Rapids: Kregel, 2008), 589.

Clausal Outline for Translating

Section two, "Clausal Outline for Translation," also provides a structural outline that visualizes the *coordination* and *subordination* of all four hundred twenty-five (425) Greek clauses in 1 John.[4] Not only does it simplify the translation process, it traces John's flow of thought, and provides a visual tool to refer to whenever you teach or preach the letter. By nature, a clause has a subject and a predicate, which may be a verb, a participle, or an infinitive. They may be independent or dependent clauses.[5] Whereas independent clauses can stand alone, dependent clauses have a subordinate relationship to another clause. The purpose of a clausal outline is to visualize the relationship clauses have to one another in order to trace John's thought. The following chart summarizes the types of independent and dependent clauses found in 1 John.

Types (Classifications) of Independent and Dependent Clauses[6]	
Three Types of Independent Clauses	Four Types of Dependent Clauses

Conjunctive clauses are introduced by
 	
    simple connective (καί or δέ),
 	
    contrastive conjunction (δέ, πλὴν),
 	
    correlative conjunction (μέν...δέ or καί...καί)
 	
    explanatory conjunction (γάρ),
 	
    inferential conjunction (ἄρα, διό, οὖν, γάρ),
 	
    transitional conjunction (δέ or οὖν).
	Pronominal clauses are introduced by
	
	    a relative pronoun (ὅς),
	
	    a relative adjective (οἷος, *such as*; ὅσος, *as much/many as*),
	
	    a relative adverb (ὅπου, *where*; ὅτε, *when*).
	
	    a demonstrative pronoun (οὗτος)

Prepositional clauses are introduced by
 	
    "for this reason" (διὰ τοῦτο)
 	
    "for this reason" (ἐπὶ τοῦτο)
 	
    "as a result of this" (ἐκ τοῦτο)
 	
    "why" (εἰς τίνα)
 	
    "in this" (ἐν τοῦτο)
	Conjunctive clauses are introduced by a subordinate conjunction that denote semantical concepts such as time (ὅτε, ὅτον); reason and cause (διό, ὅτι, ἐπεί); purpose and result (ἵνα, ὥστε); comparison (καθώς, ὡς, ὡσεί, ὥσπερ); etc.

	Participial clauses are introduced by participles
Asyndeton clauses are not introduced by a conjunctive word or phrase.	Infinitival clauses are introduced by infinitives

---

[4] Other terminology exists for this same process. Mounce calls it "phrasing," Guthrie calls it "grammatical diagram," and MacDonald calls it "textual transcription." Nevertheless, another difference is that I concentrate predominately on the clause level whereas the others will tend to break sentences into smaller units. William D. Mounce, *A Graded Reader of Biblical Greek* (Grand Rapids: Zondervan, 1996), xvi-xxiii; George H. Guthrie and J. Scott Duvall, *Biblical Greek Exegesis: A Guided Approach to Learning Intermediate and Advanced Greek* (Grand Rapids: Zondervan, 1988), 27-42; William G. MacDonald, *Greek Enchiridion: A Concise Handbook of Grammar for Translation and Exegesis* (Peabody, MA: Hendrickson, 1979), 5-52.

[5] Unlike MacDonald, Mounce, and Guthrie who encourage breaking a sentence into clauses and phrases (whose works are mentioned above), the approach in the pages to follow isolates only, with a few exceptions, the clauses of a sentence.

[6] Chart is adapted from Daniel B. Wallace, *Greek Grammar Beyond the Basics* (Grand Rapids: Zondervan, 1996), 656-65.

There is a wealth of material available for people wishing to translate the New Testament. The following four sources are just a few recommended helps to use in completing the translation of 1 John.

>   Bateman IV, Herbert W. *A Workbook for Intermediate Greek: Grammar, Exegesis, and Commentary on 1–3 John*. Grand Rapids: Kregel, 2008.

>   Bauer, Walter, Frederick W. Danker, William F. Arndt, and F. Wilbur Gingrich. *A Greek–English Lexicon of the New Testament and Other Early Christian Literature*. Third Edition. Chicago and London: University of Chicago Press, 2000. (Abbreviation: BDAG)

>   Burer, Michael H. and Jeffery E. Miller. *A New Reader's Lexicon of the Greek New Testament*. Grand Rapids: Kregel, 2008.

>   Culy, Martin M. *I, II, III John: A Handbook on the Greek Text*. Waco, TX: Baylor University Press, 2004.[7]

Before delving into translating 1 John clause by clause, it may be helpful to define and illustrate the different types of clauses typically found in 1 John.

Independent Clauses

INDEPENDENT CLAUSES ARE RATHER IMPORTANT in determining John's main thought of a given sentence. There are ***three types of independent clauses*** found in the Greek New Testament: (1) conjunctive, (2) prepositional, and (3) asyndeton. All three types of independent clauses appear in the one hundred ninety (190) independent clauses found in 1 John. Forty-nine percent (49%) are conjunctive, six percent (6%) are prepositional, and forty-five percent (45%) are asyndeton independent clauses.

THE FIRST AND MOST COMMON TYPE OF INDEPENDENT CLAUSE in the New Testament is the ***conjunctive independent clause*** whereby the clause is introduced by a conjunction (καί, δέ, γάρ, ἄρα, διό, οὖν, πλήν, ὅθεν). Sometimes the conjunction starts the clause. Other times it appears in a post-positive position. As in other New Testament letters, the conjunctive independent clause dominates in 1 John. In fact, independent conjunctive clauses appear in 1 John *at least* ninety-three (93) times. The following are a few representative samples worthy of mention.

---

[7] Culy, though helpful at times, struggles with syntactical and semantical labels. For instance, he does not provide semantical labels for verb tenses. "I continue to believe," he says, "that such tense labels should be abandoned since the phenomena they describe are at best only partially related to the Greek verb tenses themselves and frequently lead exegetes to think erroneously that an aorist verb, for example, *emphasizes* the beginning of an action." Culy, *I, II, III John* [2004], xxii-xxiii. Consequently, Culy will not entertain semantical classifications of verb tenses. Yet he does recognize the relevance of other syntactical and semantical labels and does engage the text in helpful ways. He is, however, at odds with other intermediate grammarians like Daniel B. Wallace, *Greek Grammar Beyond the Basics*. This translation guide, however, is more in keeping Wallace and others like him when it comes to classifying verb tenses and entertaining other syntactical and semantical classifications.

$^{2:5a}$ **Καὶ** ἔστιν αὕτη ἡ ἀγγελία
$^{2:5a}$ **Now** this is the gospel message

$^{2:11a}$ ὁ **δὲ** μισῶν τὸν ἀδελφὸν αὐτοῦ ἐν τῇ σκοτίᾳ ἐστὶν
$^{2:11a}$ **But** the one who hates his brother is in the darkness

$^{2:18d}$ **ὅθεν** γινώσκομεν ὅτι ἐσχάτη ὥρα ἐστίν
$^{2:18d}$ **Therefore** we know that it is the last hour

$^{3:24a}$ **καὶ** ὁ τηρῶν τὰς ἐντολὰς αὐτοῦ ἐν αὐτῷ μένει
$^{3:24a}$ **and** the one who keeps his commandments abides with God

$^{4:18b}$ **ἀλλ'** ἡ τελεία ἀγάπη ἔξω βάλλει τὸν φόβον
$^{4:18b}$ **but** perfect love casts out fear

$^{4:20d}$ ὁ **γὰρ** μὴ ἀγαπῶν τὸν ἀδελφὸν αὐτοῦ . . . , τὸν θεὸν . . . οὐ δύναται ἀγαπᾶν
$^{4:20d}$ **for** the one who does not love his brother . . . is unable to love God

$^{5:4b}$ **καὶ** αὕτη ἐστὶν ἡ νίκη ἡ νικήσασα τὸν κόσμον, ἡ πίστις ἡμῶν
$^{5:4b}$ **And** this is the conquering power, our faith

$^{5:7}$ **ὅτι** τρεῖς εἰσιν οἱ μαρτυροῦντες, ^{8}τὸ πνεῦμα καὶ τὸ ὕδωρ καὶ τὸ αἷμα
$^{5:7}$ **For** there are three that testify, ^{8}the Spirit and the water and the blood

Naturally, these clauses are independent because they contain a subject and predicate, present a complete thought, and can stand-alone. Nevertheless, each of these independent clauses begins with conjunction that makes some sort of connection with a previous clause or clauses. As you can see from the selected samples, conjunctions sometimes appear in the post-positive position (2:11a; 4:20d) but not always (2:5a, 18d; 3:24a, 18b; 5:4b, 7).

The most frequent conjunctive independent clauses appearing in 1 John are those introduced with καί. Of the ninety-three (93) conjunctive independent clauses, seventy-five percent (75%) begin with "and" (καί). John's favored usage of "and" (καί) is that of a coordinating conjunction, fifty-one (51) times. Yet, καί is also interpreted twice as an ascensive (2:18c, 28a), three time as contrastive (2:20a; 4:3a; 5:17b), twice as emphatic (3:1c, 4b), once as explanatory (1:2a), seven times as inferential (1:4a; 2:11b, 3:13a, 19a, 22a; 4:11b, 16a), and four times as transitional a conjunction (1:5a; 2:3a, 25a, 27a).

And while John's favored conjunction used is καί, six other conjunctions also appear in John's letters: ἀλλά, δέ, ὅτι, γάρ, and πάλιν. The following chart not only lists the conjunction and where they appear in 1 John, it identifies how the conjunction has been interpreted.

	καί	ἀλλά	δέ	ὅτι	γάρ	πάλιν
Ascensive The conjunction provides a point of focus "even"	2:18c, 28a					
Connective or **Coordinate** The conjunction adds an additional element to the discussion "and, also"	1:2b, 2c, 2d, 3b, 6d, 7d, 8c, 10c 2:2a, 2b, 4b, 10b, 11c, 17a, 20b, 24c, 27c, 27f 3:2b, 3a, 5a, 5c, 9c, 12c, 15b, 23a, 24a, 24b, 24c 4:3c, 4b, 5c, 7c, 7d, 12d, 14, 15c, 16b, 16e, 16f, 21a 5:1b, 3c, 4b, 6d, 8b, 11a, 11c, 14a, 16c, 20d		1:3d 5:20a			
Contrastive or **Adversative** The conjunction provides an opposing thought to the idea to which it is connected "but, yet"	2:20a 4:3a 5:17b	2:2c, 7b, 16b, 19b, 19e, 21c, 27e 3:18b 4:1b, 18b 5:6c	2:11a, 17b 3:12e			2:8a
Emphatic The conjunction intensifies the discussion "indeed"	3:1c, 4b					
Explanatory Following verbs of emotion, the conjunction provides additional information "for"	1:2a			2:16a 3:11a 5:7	4:20d 5:3a	
Inferential The conjunction signals a conclusion or summary of a discussion "therefore, thus"	1:4a 2:11b 3:13a, 19a, 22a 4:11b, 16a					
Transitional The conjunction moves the discussion in a new direction "now"	1:5a 2:3a, 25a, 27a		5:5a			

THE SECOND TYPE OF INDEPENDENT CLAUSE is the ***prepositional independent clause*** introduced by a preposition (διὰ τοῦτο, εἰς τοῦτο, ἐπὶ τοῦτο, ἐκ τοῦτο, ἐν τοῦτο). As it was the case for conjunctive independent clause, each prepositional independent clause has a subject and predicate, presents a complete thought, and can stand-alone. What differs is that these independent clauses begin with a preposition. There are *at least* twelve (12) independent clauses in 1 John introduced with a preposition. Five representative examples are worthy of mention.

> 3:1d **διὰ τοῦτο** ὁ κόσμος οὐ γινώσκει ἡμᾶς
> 3:1d **For this reason**, the world does not know us

> 3:8c **εἰς τοῦτο** ἐφανερώθη ὁ υἱὸς τοῦ θεοῦ
> 3:8c **for this reason** the Son of God was revealed

> 4:5b **διὰ τοῦτο** ἐκ τοῦ κόσμου λαλοῦσιν
> 4:5b **Therefore they speak** from the world's perspective

> 4:9a **ἐν τούτῳ** ἐφανερώθη ἡ ἀγάπη τοῦ θεοῦ ἐν ἡμῖν
> 4:9a **By this** the love of God has been revealed in us

> 4:13a **Ἐν τούτῳ** γινώσκομεν ὅτι ἐν αὐτῷ μένομεν καὶ αὐτὸς [μένομεν] ἐν ἡμῖν
> 4:13a **By this** we know that we abide in God and he [*abides*] in us

While some of these conclude John's thought, more often the "by this" and "for this reason" raises interpretive challenges. Interpreters are left asking: "To what does the prepositional phrase refer?" So whenever the prepositional phrase "by this" (ἐν τούτῳ) or "for this reason" (διὰ τοῦτο, εἰς τοῦτο) appears in 1 John, you must always ask yourself does this phrase refer to the preceding statement or to the statement that follows? More will be said about interpreting these sorts of clauses when we discuss "Tips for Translating John."

THE THIRD TYPE OF INDEPENDENT CLAUSE is the ***asyndeton independent clause*** whereby an independent clause has neither an introductory conjunction nor an opening prepositional phrase. There are at least eighty-five (85) examples of the asyndeton independent clause. Eight examples are worthy of mention because they appear consistently throughout the letter:

> 2:1d παράκλητον **ἔχομεν** πρὸς τὸν πατέρα, Ἰησοῦν Χριστὸν δίκαιον
> 2:1d **we have** an advocate with the Father, Jesus who is the Christ, the righteous one

> 2:15a Μὴ **ἀγαπᾶτε** τὸν κόσμον μηδὲ τὰ ἐν τῷ κόσμῳ
> 2:15a Do not **love** the world nor the things in the world

> 3:4a Πᾶς ὁ ποιῶν τὴν ἁμαρτίαν καὶ τὴν ἀνομίαν **ποιεῖ**
> 3:4a Everyone who makes it a practice to sin also **practices** lawlessness

4:6b ὁ γινώσκων τὸν θεὸν **ἀκούει** ἡμῶν
4:6a the person who knows God **listens** to us

4:12a θεὸν οὐδεὶς πώποτε **τεθέαται**
4:12a No one **has seen** God at any time

4;16d Ὁ θεὸς ἀγάπη **ἐστίν**,
4:16d God **is** love,

5:1a Πᾶς ὁ πιστεύων (**ὅτι** Ἰησοῦς **ἐστιν** ὁ Χριστὸς) ἐκ τοῦ θεοῦ **γεγέννηται**,
5:1a Everyone who believes (**that** Jesus **is** the Christ) **has been fathered** by God,

5:12b ὁ μὴ ἔχων τὸν υἱὸν τοῦ θεοῦ τὴν ζωὴν οὐκ **ἔχει**.
5:12b the one who does have the Son of God does not **have** this eternal life.

Once again, these clauses are independent because they contain a subject and predicate, present a complete thought, and can stand-alone. Yet they differ from one another. To begin with, four of these clauses speak of a generic person: "Everyone" (3:4a, 5:1a) or "the one who" (4:6b, 5:12b). They express a gnomic or timeless proverbial like truth. Some merely state a fact: "we have an advocate" (2:1b), "no one has seen God" (4:12a), or "God is love" (4:16b). One is a command: "do not love the world" (2:15a). These are representative independent asyndeton clauses you can expect to encounter when studying 1 John.

IN SUMMARY, independent clauses are rather important in determining the main thought of a given sentence. The predominant types of independent clauses are the conjunctive independent clause with ninety-three (93) occurrences, the prepositional independent clause with twelve (12) occurrences, and the asyndeton independent clause with eighty-five (85) occurrences in 1 John.

Chapter	Conjunctive Independent Clauses	Prepositional Independent Clauses	Asyndeton Independent Clauses
One	2a, 2b, 2c, 2d, 3b, 3d, 4a, 5a, 6d, 7d, 8c, 10c		6c, 7c, 8b, 9b, 10b
Two	2a, 2b, 2c, 3a, 4b, 7b, 8a, 10b, 11a, 11b, 11c, 16a, 16b, 17a, 17b, 18c, 19b, 19e, 20a, 20b, 21c, 24c, 25a, 27a, 27c, 27e, 27f, 28a	5c	1a, 1d, 4a, 5b, 6a, 7a, 7d, 9, 10a, 12, 13a, 13b, 14a, 14b, 14c, 15a, 15c, 18a, 19a, 19d, 21a, 22a, 22c, 23a, 23b, 24a, 26, 27i, 29b
Three	1c, 2b, 3a, 4b, 5a, 5c, 9c, 11a, 12c, 12e, 13a, 15b, 18b, 19a, 22a, 23a, 24a, 24b, 24c	1d, 8c, 10a, 16a	1a, 2a, 2c, 4a, 6a, 6b, 7a, 7b, 8a, 9a, 10b, 14a, 14c, 15a, 17d, 18a, 21b
Four	1b, 3a, 3c, 4b, 5c, 7c, 7d, 11b, 12d, 14, 15c, 16a, 16b, 16e, 16f, 18b, 20d, 21a	5b, 6d, 9a, 10a, 13a, 17a	1a, 2b, 4a, 5a, 6a, 6b, 6c, 7a, 8a, 12a, 12c, 15b, 16d, 18a, 19a, 20c
Five	1b, 3a, 3c, 4b, 5a, 6c, 6d, 7, 8b, 11a, 11c, 14a, 16c, 17b, 20a, 20d	2a	1a, 6a, 6b, 8a, 9b, 10a, 10b, 12a, 12b, 13a, 15c, 16b, 16d, 16e, 17a, 18a, 19a, 20e, 21

These one hundred ninety (190) independent clauses always appear to the left of the clausal outline with all respective verbs **highlighted** and **underlined**. Consequently independent clauses always appear to the extreme left of the page as illustrated above. Just as there are different types of independent clauses, there are various types of dependent clauses in John's letters worthy of some introduction.

Dependent Clauses

THERE ARE *FOUR TYPES OF DEPENDENT CLAUSES*: (1) pronominal clauses are introduced by a relative pronoun (ὅς, ἥ, ὅ), relative adjective (οἷος, *such as*; ὅσος, *as much/many as*), relative adverb (ὅπου, *where*; ὅτε, *when*), or sometimes a demonstrative pronoun (οὗτος), (2) conjunctive clauses are introduced by a subordinate conjunction (ἵνα, ὅτι, καθώς, εἰ, ἐάν, etc.), (3) participial clauses are introduced by a participle, and (4) infinitival clauses are introduced by certain infinitives or infinitives with a preposition (e.g., διὰ, μετα, εἰς + infinitive). There are two hundred thirty-five (235) dependent clauses in 1 John. Fifteen percent (15%) are pronominal, sixty-five percent (65%) are conjunctive, and twenty percent (20%) are participial clauses.

Procedurally, identifying *the type of dependent clause* occurs first, and then the relationship of the dependent clause to words in other clauses (i.e., the *syntactical function*) is determined. The syntactical function of a clause may either be *adverbial*, *adjectival*, or *substantival*. Once the syntactical relationship of a dependent clause is determined, it is positioned in either above or under the word in modifies for easy identification. If *adverbial*, the first word of the clause is positioned either above or under the verb or verbal it modifies. If *adjectival*, the first word of the clause is positioned either above or under the noun or pronoun it modifies. If *substantival*, the clause is placed in parenthesis. The following examples of dependent clauses can be expected in 1 John.

THE FIRST TYPE OF DEPENDENT CLAUSE is the pronominal. There are *at least* thirty-six (36) **dependent pronominal clauses** in 1 John. All begin with either a relative or indefinite relative pronoun. Sixty-nine percent (69%) are *adjectival*. Thirty-one percent (31%) function *substantivally*. All fifty-five (55) *adjectival* relative clauses are positioned under the noun or pronoun they modify and all twenty-one (21) *substantival* relative clauses are placed in parenthesis. Ten examples are worthy of mention. All of the relative pronouns are underlined and in bold with their respective verbs.

^{1:5a} Καὶ ἔστιν αὕτη ἡ ἀγγελία
^{1:5a} Now this is the *gospel* message

|

^{1:5b} **ἣν ἀκηκόαμεν** ἀπ᾽ αὐτοῦ
^{1:5b} **which we have heard**

|

^{1:5c} καὶ [ἣν] **ἀναγγέλλομεν** ὑμῖν,
^{1:5c} and **which we announce** to you

^{2:5a} ὃς δ' ἂν **τηρῇ** αὐτοῦ τὸν λόγον,
^{2:5a} But **whoever keeps** his word,

|

^{2:5b} ἀληθῶς ἐν τούτῳ ἡ ἀγάπη τοῦ θεοῦ τετελείωται.
^{2:5b} truly, in this person, God's love has been perfected.

^{3:17a} ὃς δ' ἂν **ἔχῃ** τὸν βίον τοῦ κόσμου
^{3:17a} but **whoever has** the livelihood of the world

|

^{3:17b} καὶ [ὃς] θεωρῇ τὸν ἀδελφὸν αὐτοῦ χρείαν **ἔχοντα**
^{17b} and [*whoever*] **sees** his brother in need

|

^{3:17c} καὶ [ὃς] **κλείσῃ** τὰ σπλάγχνα αὐτοῦ ἀπ' αὐτοῦ,
^{3:17c} and [*whoever*] **closes** his heart against him,

|

^{3:17d} πῶς ἡ ἀγάπη τοῦ θεοῦ μένει ἐν αὐτῷ;
^{3:17d} How does the love of God remain in him?

^{4:6b} (ὃς οὐκ **ἔστιν** ἐκ τοῦ θεοῦ) οὐκ ἀκούει ἡμῶν.
^{4:6b} (**whoever is** not from God) does not listen to us.

^{4:15a} ὃς ἐὰν **ὁμολογήσῃ** (ὅτι Ἰησοῦς **ἐστιν** ὁ υἱὸς τοῦ θεοῦ),
^{4:15a} Whoever confesses (that Jesus is the Son of God),

|

^{4:15b} ὁ θεὸς ἐν αὐτῷ μένει
^{4:15b} God abides in him,

^{5:15a} καὶ ἐὰν οἴδαμεν (ὅτι ἀκούει ἡμῶν)
^{5:15a} and if we know (that he hears us)

|

^{5:15b} ὃ ἐὰν **αἰτώμεθα**,
^{5:15b} **whatever we ask**,

|

^{5:15c} οἴδαμεν (ὅτι ἔχομεν τὰ αἰτήματα)
^{5:15c} we know (that we have the requests)

|

^{5:15d} ἃ **ᾐτήκαμεν** ἀπ' αὐτοῦ.
^{5:15d} **that we have** asked from him

Although only ten relative clauses are listed above, they are representative of what to expect in 1 John. On the one hand, 1 John 1:5b-c and 5:15c exemplify relative pronouns modifying nouns: "the gospel" (ἡ ἀγγελία) and "the requests" (τὰ αἰτήματα) respectively. 1 John 3:17a-c, 4:15a, 5:15d exemplify relative pronouns that modify pronouns "in him" (ἐν αὐτῷ) or "us" (ἡμῶν). 1

John 2:5a exemplify an indefinite relative pronoun modifying "in this" (ἐν τούτῳ). On the other hand, 1 John 4:6b exemplify a substantival relative pronoun that is the subject of the independent clause.

THE SECOND TYPE OF DEPENDENT CLAUSE is the conjunctive. There are *at least* one hundred fifty-two (152) examples of ***dependent conjunctive clauses*** in 1 John. Of these conjunctive clauses, fifty-five (36%) are substantival, twenty-one (14%) are adjectival, and seventy-six (50%) are adverbial. Those that are substantival are often embedded in an independent or dependent clause and appear in parenthesis. The following are a few representative samples worthy of mention.

^{1:8a} **ἐὰν εἴπωμεν** (ὅτι ἁμαρτίαν οὐκ ἔχομεν),
^{1:8a} **if we say**, ("We have no sin"),

|

^{1:8b} ἑαυτοὺς πλανῶμεν
^{1:8b} we deceive ourselves

^{2:19c} **εἰ** γὰρ ἐξ ἡμῶν **ἦσαν**,
^{2:19c} for **if they had been** of us,

|

^{2:19d} μεμενήκεισαν ἂν μεθ' ἡμῶν·
^{2:19d} they would have remained with us;

^{2:19e} ἀλλ' [ἐξῆλθαν]
^{2:19e} but [*they went out*],

|

^{2:19f} **ἵνα φανερωθῶσιν** (ὅτι οὐκ εἰσὶν πάντες ἐξ ἡμῶν).
^{2:19f} **so that it would be shown** (that they all are not of us).

^{4:10a} ἐν τούτῳ ἐστὶν ἡ ἀγάπη,
^{4:10a} In this is love,

|

^{4:10b} οὐχ **ὅτι** ἡμεῖς **ἠγαπήκαμεν** τὸν θεόν,
^{4:10b} not **that we have loved** God,

|

^{4:10c} ἀλλ' **ὅτι** αὐτὸς **ἠγάπησεν** ἡμᾶς
^{4:10c} but **that he loved** us

|

^{4:10d} καὶ [**ὅτι**] **ἀπέστειλεν** τὸν υἱὸν αὐτοῦ ἱλασμὸν περὶ τῶν ἁμαρτιῶν ἡμῶν.
^{4:10d} and [*that*] **he sent** his Son to be the atoning sacrifice for our sins.

Of these examples, two are embedded in another dependent clause as its direct object and thereby placed in parenthesis (1:8a, 2:19f). Three are adverbial (1:8a, 2:19a, 2:19f). First John

1:8a and 2:19c are third and second class conditional clauses modifying the verbs "we decieve" (πλανῶμεν) and "they would have remained" (μεμενήκεισαν). First John 2:19f is an adverbial clause modifying "they went out" (ἐξῆλθαν). Three are adjectival (4:10b-d) modyfying "in this" (ἐν τούτῳ). Due to the large number of conjunctive clauses (147 out-of 185), they are extremely important for tracing John's flow of thought in any New Testament book.

THE THIRD TYPE OF DEPENDENT CLAUSE is the participial clause. There are forty-seven (47) **dependent participial clauses** in 1 John. They are all substantival participles. Five (5) substantival participial clauses are worthy of mention.

> 3:4a Πᾶς ὁ ποιῶν τὴν ἁμαρτίαν καὶ τὴν ἀνομίαν ποιεῖ,
> 3:4a Everyone who makes it a practice to sin also practices lawlessness

> 4:16e καὶ ὁ μένων ἐν τῇ ἀγάπῃ ἐν τῷ θεῷ μένει
> 4:16e and the one who abides in love abides in God

> 5:13a Ταῦτα ἔγραψα ὑμῖν . . . (τοῖς πιστεύουσιν εἰς τὸ ὄνομα τοῦ υἱοῦ τοῦ θεοῦ).
> 5:13a I have written these things to you . . . (*namely* you who believe in the name of the Son of God).

> 5:5a τίς [δέ] ἐστιν ὁ νικῶν τὸν κόσμον
> 5:5a Now who is the who overcomes the world

A favored substantival particle is participial clause that functions as the subject of the independent clause (3:4a, 4:16c). Of the forty-seven participial clauses, forty-one (87%) function as the subject of a clause. Two less frequently used subtantivial particles are those in apposition to another noun or pronoun (5:13a) and those functioning as a predicate nominative (5:5a).

THE FOURTH TYPE OF DEPENDENT CLAUSE is the infinitival clause. There are no **dependent infinitival clauses** in 1 John.

IN SUMMARY, there are four types of dependent clauses: pronominal, conjunctive, participial, and infinitival. The most frequent type of dependent clauses in 1 John are the **dependent conjunctive clauses** with *at least* two hundred thirty-five (235) examples. Fifteen percent (15%) are pronominal, sixty-five percent (65%) are conjunctive, and twenty (20%) are participial participal.

Dependent clauses are extremely important because they provide additional information about the stated subject within the independent clause and they help trace John's flow of thought. The following chart lists the types of dependent clauses in 1 John and their syntactical function.

Syntactical Function	Four Types of Dependent Clauses in 1 John	
Substantival Clauses	Pronominal	Relative Pronoun Subject: **2**:24a, 24b; **4**:6c
		Relative Pronoun Direct Object: **1**:1a, 1b, 1c, 1d, 1e, 3a
		Indefinite Pronoun Subject: **3**:22a; **5**:15b
	Conjunctive	ὅτι Direct Object: **1**:6a, 8a, 10a; **2**:3a, 4a, 5c, 12, 13a, 13b, 14a, 14b, 14c, 14d, 14e, 18b, 18d, 19f, 21e, 22b, 29a, 29b; **3**:2c, 5a, 5c, 14a, 15b, 19a, 19b, 24c; **4**:3d, 13a, 14, 15a, 20a; **5**:1a, 2a, 5b, 13b, 15a, 15c, 18a, 18b, 18c, 19a, 19b, 20a, 20b
		ἵνα Appositional: **3**:8d, 11c, 23b, 23c; **4**:21b; **5**:3b
		ἵνα Direct Object: **5**:16c
		εἰ Direct Object: **3**:13a
	Participial	None but the following substantival ptc. phrases are important in 1 John
		πᾶς + ptc. subject: **2**:23a, 29b; **3**:3a, 4a, 6a, 6b [2 times], 9a, 10b, 15a; **4**:7c, 7d; **5**:1a, 1b, 4a, 18a
		Subject: **2**:4a, 6a, 9 (twice), 10a, 11a, 17b, 23b; **3**:7b, 8a, 10c, 14c, 24a; **4**:6b, 8a, 16e, 18d, 20d, 21b; **5**:5b, 7, 10a, 10b, 12a, 12b, 18b
		Predicate nominative: **5**:5a, 6a, 6d
		Appositional: **2**:22c; **5**:13a, 16c
	Infinitive	None
Adjectival Clauses	Pronominal	Relative Adjectival Pronoun: **1**:2e, 5b, 5c; **2**:7c, 7e, 8b, 25b, 27b; **3**:11b, 24d; **4**:2c, 3b, 3d, 3e, 16c, 20e, 20f; **5**:10d, 14b, 15d
		Indefinite Adjectival Pronoun: 2:5a; 4:15a
	Conjunctive[8]	ὅτι Epexegetical: **1**:5d; **3**:1e, 16b, 16c, 20a, 20b, 20c; **4**:9b, 10b, 10c, 10d, 13c; **5**:9d, 11b, 14c
		ἵνα Epexegetical: **2**:27d; **3**:1b
		ὅταν Epexegetical: 5:2b, 2c
		καί Epexegetical: 3:10c
	Participial	None
Adverbial Clauses	Conjunctive	ὅτι + Indicative Mood: **2**:8c, 8d, 11d, 21b, 21d, 21e; **3**:2e, 8b, 9b, 9d, 12d, 14b, 22b, 22c; **4**:1d, 4c, 7b, 8b, 17c, 18c, 18d, 19b; **5**:4a, 6e, 9c, 10c
		ἵνα + Subjunctive Mood: **1**:3c, 4b, 9c, 9d; **2**:1b, 19f, 28b, 28d; **3**:5b; **4**:9c, 17b; **5**:13b, 20c
		καθώς; ὡς: **1**:7b; **2**:6b, 18b, 27g, 27h; **3**:2f, 3b, 7b, 12a, 23d; **4**:17d

---

[8] While Brown tends to view the ὅτι and ἵνα as epexegetical, Culy interprets the ὅτι and ἵνα as appositional. Wallace seems to interpret the as ἵνα appositional (**3**:8d, 11c, 23b, 23c; **4**:21b; **5**:3b) and as ὅτι epexegetical (**1**:5d; **3**:1e, 16b, 16c, 20a, 20b, 20c; **4**:9b, 10b, 10c, 10d, 13c; **5**:9d, 11b, 14c). We too interpret the as ἵνα appositional and as ὅτι epexegetical.

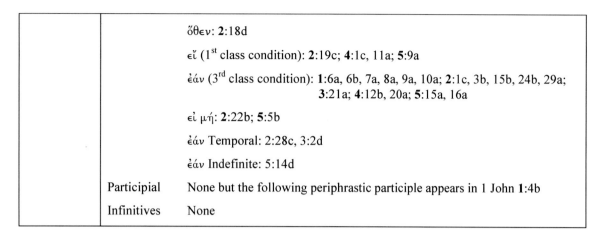

		ὅθεν: **2**:18d
		εἴ (1st class condition): **2**:19c; **4**:1c, 11a; **5**:9a
		ἐάν (3rd class condition): **1**:6a, 6b, 7a, 8a, 9a, 10a; **2**:1c, 3b, 15b, 24b, 29a; **3**:21a; **4**:12b, 20a; **5**:15a, 16a
		εἰ μή: **2**:22b; **5**:5b
		ἐάν Temporal: 2:28c, 3:2d
		ἐάν Indefinite: 5:14d
	Participial	None but the following periphrastic participle appears in 1 John **1**:4b
	Infinitives	None

Tips for Translating 1 John

EVERY AUTHOR OF THE NEW TESTAMENT has a writing style that exhibits features readily repeated or perhaps even unique to their letters. Speaking very simplistically Hebrews likes chiastic structures, Peter uniquely employs imperatival participles, Jude favors the use of adjectival participles, and the adverbial participle abounds in Paul. Although there are other stylistic issues that could be listed for each of these authors, the point to be made here is that 1 John also exhibits several stylistic features worth highlighting.

FIRST, THE FREQUENT USE OF THE PREPOSITIONAL PHRASE "in this" (ἐν τοῦτο). It occurs fourteen (14) times in 1 John (2:3, 4, 5 [2x]; 3:10, 16, 19, 24; 4:2, 9, 10, 13, 17; 5:2). It is, as Raymond Brown declares, "a frequent and most troublesome Johannine idiom." To what does the prepositional phrase refer? Thus whenever the prepositional phrase appears, you must always ask yourself this question: Does "in this" (ἐν τοῦτο) refer to the preceding statement (anaphoric) or to the statement that follows (cataphoric)? John appears, however, to follow a specific syntactical pattern that helps us answer our question. In cases where a subsequent subordinate clause is introduced by "that" (ὅτι + indicative mood clause), "in order that" (ἵνα + subjunctive mood clause), "if" (ἐάν + subjunctive mood clause), "whenever" (ὅταν), or "from" (ἐκ), then the prepositional phrase "in this" (ἐν τοῦτο) will generally point to and thereby be defined in *what follows in the subordinate clause*. This is an extremely important rule to remember when interpreting 1 John.

SECOND, THE SUBSTANTIVAL PARTICIPLE is a rather important stylistic feature of 1 John that warrants special attention. On the one hand, there is the typical substantival participle like "the one who does" (ὁ ποιῶν) and "the one who keeps" (ὁ τηρῶν) versus "the one who does not love" (ὁ μὴ ἀγαπῶν) and "the one who does not have" (ὁ μὴ ἔχων). On the other hand, the informal Greek construction "everyone" (πᾶς) + the article (ὁ) + a participle frequently speaks of one of two contrasting groups or generic groups of people. This latter construction occurs sixteen (16) times in 1 John (2:23a, 29b; 3:3a, 4a, 6b [2 times], 9a, 10b, 15a; 4:7c, 7d; 5:1a, 1b, 4a, 18a).

John's fondness of the substantival participle serves to divide people into one of two categories: "everyone who does this" as opposed to "everyone who does the opposite." Furthermore, these generic utterances nearly always involve a gnomic idea. John often provides theologically driven timeless truths throughout his letter by way of these substantival participles.

^{5:1a} Πᾶς ὁ πιστεύων (ὅτι Ἰησοῦς ἐστιν ὁ Χριστὸς) ἐκ τοῦ θεοῦ γεγέννηται
^{5:1a} Everyone who believes (that Jesus is the Christ) has been fathered by God

^{5:12a} ὁ ἔχων τὸν υἱὸν ἔχει τὴν ζωήν·
^{5:12a} The one who has the Son has eternal life;

^{5:12b} ὁ μὴ ἔχων τὸν υἱὸν τοῦ θεοῦ τὴν ζωὴν οὐκ ἔχει.
^{5:12b} the one who does not have the Son of God does not have eternal life.

The πᾶς plus the ὁ πιστεύων creates an gnomic statement that identifies an eternal truth: any person who believes the teaching about the messiahship of Jesus has a relationship with God. Any person who has or who believes in Jesus has eternal life, those who don't, don't.

THIRD, THE APPOSITIONAL USE OF ἵνα is almost idiomatic of John. The appositional use of ἵνα seldom appears in the New Testament yet it appears frequently in Johannine literature. There are six (6) occurrences in 1 John (**3:8d, 11c, 23b, 23c; 4:21b; 5:3b**). In every occurrence they clarify the demonstrative pronoun "this" (αὕτη) in the previous clause.

^{5:3a} **αὕτη** γάρ ἐστιν ἡ ἀγάπη τοῦ θεοῦ,
^{5:3a} For <u>this</u> is the love *for* God,
|
^{5:3b} **ἵνα** τὰς ἐντολὰς αὐτοῦ τηρῶμεν·
^{5:3b} *namely* **that** we keep his commandments

FINALLY, SOME WORDS IN 1 JOHN ARE UNIQUE and will not be found elsewhere in the New Testament. The following chart identifies the *hapax legomena* in 1 John.

	Hapax Legomena in 1 John			
1 John	***Hapax Legomena***	**English Translations**	**Lexical Form**	**Lexical Meaning**
1:5 2:11	ἀγγελία	message	ἀγγελία	
2:2 4:10	ἱλασμός	expiation, propitiation	ἱλασμός	expiation, propitiation

2:18, 22 4:3	ἀντίχριστος	antichrist	ἀντίχριστος	antichrist
2:20, 27	χρῖσμα	anointing, unction	χρῖσμα	anointing, unction
5:4	νικᾷ	victory	νικᾷ	victory

IN SUMMARY, several tips for translating 1 John begins with remembering that John likes the prepositional phrase "in this" (ἐν τοῦτο). It occurs fourteen (14) times in 1 John (2:3, 4, 5 [2x]; 3:10, 16, 19, 24; 4:2, 9, 10, 13, 17; 5:2). Remember to ask does the phrase anaphoric or cataphoric. Furthermore, John also likes the substantival participle. It is a rather important stylistic feature of 1 John not because of its frequent occurrence (only 20%) but because John uses substantive participles to divide people into one of two categories, those who follow Jesus and those who do not. It is also important because they tend to be generic utterances that provide theologically driven and timeless truths. Third, the appositional use of ἵνα is almost idiomatic of John. Finally, there are five *hapax legomena* in 1 John for which to be on the alert.

Clausal Outlines Translated and Syntax Explained

THE CLAUSAL OUTLINE PRESENTED FOR 1 JOHN reflects many interpretive decisions. This section entitled "Clausal Outlines Translated and Syntax Explained" was added for inquiring minds that might like to know why certain decisions were made and the significance of those decisions for interpretation. Naturally, *Translating 1 John Clause by Clause* is not a commentary, it is a tool designed to help you translate and visualize John's train of thought. Nevertheless, it makes commentary *like* remarks throughout the section described as "Syntactical Explanations." These clarifying remarks serve to justify the manner in which clauses have been structurally outlined. Three terms are typically used to describe the clausal decisions: grammatical function, syntactical function, and semantical function.

> **Grammatical Function**: Grammatical function concerns how a *word* or a *dependent clause* functions grammatically: subject, verb, or direct object.

> **Syntactical Function**: Syntactical function concerns how a *dependent clause* functions syntactically within a sentence: substantivally, adjectivally, and adverbially.

> **Semantical Function**: Semantical function concerns how a word functions in its literary context, which are listed and defined in syntax grammars, discussed in critical commentaries, and evident in all English Bible translations.

Once again, numerous interpretive decisions are reflected throughout the process. So when comparing the explanations below with English translations and commentaries, remember to think critically. We take no offense, if you differ with us. We do, however, take offense, if you just accept at face value our interpretive renderings. Please feel free to wrestle with the Greek text for 1 John and have fun.

Conclusion

REALIZING THE GREEK WORDS IN THE LETTERS OF 1 JOHN ARE RATHER EASY, *Translating 1 John Clause by Clause* focuses attention on tracing the flow of thought throughout the letter. Determining and *visualizing* the flow of thought of 1 John takes place by reproducing the exact word order of the Greek text in clausal outlines. There are several places in these letters where the syntax is less than clear. Nevertheless, an attempt is made to make as much sense as possible when syntax is less than clear.

In the pages that follow, three essential steps are generally taken to *visualize* the syntactical relationship of clauses within these letters. In section two, 1 John is broken into fourteen (14) units of thought. Every unit supplies a Greek text to practice verbal tense recognition. Every unit offers a contextual orientation for the verses to be translated. Every unit distinguishes independent clauses from dependent clauses. Independent clauses (the main thought) are placed farthest to the left of the page. Dependent clauses that directly modify a word in another clause are indented and positioned under (or above if necessary) the word it modifies for easy identification. Once clauses are positioned in an outline *they portray subordination and co–ordination of thought*, and as a result we are more apt to recognize the main point of any verse or group of verses. Finally, all key structural markers that help distinguish differing types of independent and dependent clauses are **highlighted** and <u>underlined</u>. Consequently, the clausal outlines throughout this exegetical guide are intended to help you to not only *translate* the Greek text of 1 John into English but also to *visualize* the basic grammatical and syntactical relationships, parallelisms, and emphases of the text. The clauses are re-presented, translated, and explained later in the book as a means to assist in the translation process of these letters.

Clausal Outline for Translation

Having introduced *Translating 1 John Clause by Clause* and providing some tips for translating 1 John, we now move to Section Two, "Clausal Outline for Translation." It is in this section that we begin translating the text. It would be helpful, however, to keep in mind that 1 John is a letter written to a community of believers who are currently facing a crisis, a crisis underscored by those who are causing dissention among believers. These disrupters are questioning the humanity of Jesus, the messiahship of Jesus, and the commands of God to love one another.

1 John 1:1–4

Contextual Orientation

John's opening four verses are an appraisal of those who proclaimed the message about Jesus. They were eyewitnesses (of whom John is an authoritative representative) who had experienced firsthand and had personal contact with the person, words, and deeds of Jesus during his earthly ministry (v. 1). They proclaimed (ἀπαγγέλλομεν) the revelations of Jesus's person, message, and work with a twofold intention. First, the message is proclaimed in order that (ἵνα) followers of Jesus might partner together in their communion with God and God's son, Jesus (vv. 2–3). Second, the proclaimed message is presently being written in order that (ἵνα) his joy, namely, communion with God, might be realized (v. 4).

Greek Text for Verbal Recognition for 1 John 1:1–4

¹Ὃ ἦν ἀπ' ἀρχῆς, ὃ ἀκηκόαμεν, ὃ ἑωράκαμεν τοῖς ὀφθαλμοῖς ἡμῶν, ὃ ἐθεασάμεθα καὶ αἱ χεῖρες ἡμῶν ἐψηλάφησαν, περὶ τοῦ λόγου τῆς ζωῆς – ²καὶ ἡ ζωὴ ἐφανερώθη, καὶ ἑωράκαμεν καὶ μαρτυροῦμεν καὶ ἀπαγγέλλομεν ὑμῖν τὴν ζωὴν τὴν αἰώνιον ἥτις ἦν πρὸς τὸν πατέρα καὶ ἐφανερώθη ἡμῖν – ³ὃ ἑωράκαμεν καὶ ἀκηκόαμεν ἀπαγγέλλομεν καὶ ὑμῖν, ἵνα καὶ ὑμεῖς κοινωνίαν ἔχητε μεθ' ἡμῶν. καὶ ἡ κοινωνία δὲ ἡ ἡμετέρα μετὰ τοῦ πατρὸς καὶ μετὰ τοῦ υἱοῦ αὐτοῦ Ἰησοῦ Χριστοῦ. ⁴καὶ ταῦτα γράφομεν ἡμεῖς ἵνα ἡ χαρὰ ἡμῶν ᾖ πεπληρωμένη.

Clausal Outline for Translating 1 John 1:1–4

1:1a (<u>Ὃ</u> <u>ἦν</u> ἀπ' ἀρχῆς),

1:1b (<u>ὃ</u> <u>ἀκηκόαμεν</u>),

1:1c (<u>ὃ</u> <u>ἑωράκαμεν</u> τοῖς ὀφθαλμοῖς ἡμῶν),

1:1d (<u>ὃ</u> <u>ἐθεασάμεθα</u>)

1:1e (<u>καὶ</u> [<u>ὃ</u>] αἱ χεῖρες ἡμῶν <u>ἐψηλάφησαν</u> περὶ τοῦ λόγου τῆς ζωῆς)

1:2a <u>καὶ</u> ἡ ζωὴ <u>ἐφανερώθη</u>,

1:2b καὶ <u>ἑωράκαμεν</u>

1:2c καὶ <u>μαρτυροῦμεν</u>

1:2d καὶ <u>ἀπαγγέλλομεν</u> ὑμῖν τὴν ζωὴν τὴν αἰώνιον

$$\overset{\displaystyle |}{^{1:2e}\underline{\mathring{\eta}\tau\iota\varsigma}\ \mathring{\eta}\nu\ \pi\rho\grave{o}\varsigma\ \tau\grave{o}\nu\ \pi\alpha\tau\acute{\epsilon}\rho\alpha\ \kappa\alpha\grave{\iota}\ \underline{\mathring{\epsilon}\phi\alpha\nu\epsilon\rho\acute{\omega}\theta\eta}\ \mathring{\eta}\mu\mathring{\iota}\nu\ ---}$$

$$^{1:3a}(\underline{\mathring{o}}\ \underline{\mathring{\epsilon}\omega\rho\acute{\alpha}\kappa\alpha\mu\epsilon\nu}\ \kappa\alpha\grave{\iota}\ \underline{\mathring{\alpha}\kappa\eta\kappa\acute{o}\alpha\mu\epsilon\nu})$$

$$^{1:3b}\underline{\mathring{\alpha}\pi\alpha\gamma\gamma\acute{\epsilon}\lambda\lambda o\mu\epsilon\nu}\ \kappa\alpha\grave{\iota}\ \mathring{\upsilon}\mu\mathring{\iota}\nu,$$

$$\overset{\displaystyle |}{^{1:3c}\underline{\mathring{\iota}\nu\alpha}\ \kappa\alpha\grave{\iota}\ \mathring{\upsilon}\mu\epsilon\mathring{\iota}\varsigma\ \kappa o\iota\nu\omega\nu\acute{\iota}\alpha\nu\ \underline{\mathring{\epsilon}\chi\eta\tau\epsilon}\ \mu\epsilon\theta'\ \mathring{\eta}\mu\mathring{\omega}\nu.}$$

$$^{1:3d}\kappa\alpha\grave{\iota}\ \mathring{\eta}\ \kappa o\iota\nu\omega\nu\acute{\iota}\alpha\ \underline{\delta\grave{\epsilon}}\ \mathring{\eta}\ \mathring{\eta}\mu\epsilon\tau\acute{\epsilon}\rho\alpha\ [\underline{\mathring{\epsilon}\sigma\tau\iota\nu}]\ \mu\epsilon\tau\grave{\alpha}\ \tau o\mathring{\upsilon}\ \pi\alpha\tau\rho\grave{o}\varsigma\ \kappa\alpha\grave{\iota}\ \mu\epsilon\tau\grave{\alpha}\ \tau o\mathring{\upsilon}\ \upsilon\mathring{\iota}o\mathring{\upsilon}\ \alpha\mathring{\upsilon}\tau o\mathring{\upsilon}\ \mathring{I}\eta\sigma o\mathring{\upsilon}\ X\rho\iota\sigma\tau o\mathring{\upsilon}.$$

$$^{1:4a}\underline{\kappa\alpha\grave{\iota}}\ \tau\alpha\mathring{\upsilon}\tau\alpha\ \underline{\gamma\rho\acute{\alpha}\phi o\mu\epsilon\nu}\ \mathring{\eta}\mu\epsilon\mathring{\iota}\varsigma$$

$$\overset{\displaystyle |}{^{1:4b}\underline{\mathring{\iota}\nu\alpha}\ \mathring{\eta}\ \chi\alpha\rho\grave{\alpha}\ \mathring{\eta}\mu\mathring{\omega}\nu\ \mathring{\mathring{\eta}}\ \underline{\pi\epsilon\pi\lambda\eta\rho\omega\mu\acute{\epsilon}\nu\eta}.}$$

1 John 1:5–2:2

Contextual Orientation

John advances (καί) from an appraisal of the messengers (vv. 1–4) to a portrayal of God (ἔστιν αὕτη ἡ ἀγγελία) and an assessment of those who claim to have a relationship with God (1:5–2:2). Beginning with the message preached by John and others about God, John underscores (ὅτι) their proclamation to be founded upon God's ethical purity grounded in love (vv. 1–5).

He then assesses several claims (ἐὰν εἴπωμεν) of people who profess to know this gospel message about God that contradict the message. Whereas some people *claim* (ἐὰν εἴπωμεν) to have a relationship with God, other people (ἐὰν δέ) *live* a life that demonstrates they have *a relationship with God and others* (vv. 6-7). Whereas some people *claim* (ἐὰν εἴπωμεν) they do not sin, other people (ἐὰν [ἀλλά]) *confess their sin to God*, which results in God's pardon (vv. 8–9). Whereas some people *claim* (ἐὰν εἴπωμεν) they have never sinned, the author's intention (ἵνα) for writing this letter is so that people might *know that through Jesus forgiveness* of sin exists for all people (1:10–2:2).

Greek Text for Verbal Recognition for 1 John 1:5–2:2

⁵Καὶ ἔστιν αὕτη ἡ ἀγγελία ἣν ἀκηκόαμεν ἀπ' αὐτοῦ καὶ ἀναγγέλλομεν ὑμῖν, ὅτι ὁ θεὸς φῶς ἐστιν καὶ σκοτία ἐν αὐτῷ οὐκ ἔστιν οὐδεμία.

⁶Ἐὰν εἴπωμεν ὅτι κοινωνίαν ἔχομεν μετ' αὐτοῦ καὶ ἐν τῷ σκότει περιπατῶμεν, ψευδόμεθα καὶ οὐ ποιοῦμεν τὴν ἀλήθειαν· ⁷ἐὰν δὲ ἐν τῷ φωτὶ περιπατῶμεν ὡς αὐτός ἐστιν ἐν τῷ φωτί, κοινωνίαν ἔχομεν μετ' ἀλλήλων καὶ τὸ αἷμα Ἰησοῦ τοῦ υἱοῦ αὐτοῦ καθαρίζει ἡμᾶς ἀπὸ πάσης ἁμαρτίας. ⁸ἐὰν εἴπωμεν ὅτι ἁμαρτίαν οὐκ ἔχομεν, ἑαυτοὺς πλανῶμεν καὶ ἡ ἀλήθεια οὐκ ἔστιν ἐν ἡμῖν. ⁹ἐὰν ὁμολογῶμεν τὰς ἁμαρτίας ἡμῶν, πιστός ἐστιν καὶ δίκαιος ἵνα ἀφῇ ἡμῖν τὰς ἁμαρτίας καὶ καθαρίσῃ ἡμᾶς ἀπὸ πάσης ἀδικίας. ¹⁰ἐὰν εἴπωμεν ὅτι οὐχ ἡμαρτήκαμεν, ψεύστην ποιοῦμεν αὐτὸν καὶ ὁ λόγος αὐτοῦ οὐκ ἔστιν ἐν ἡμῖν.

²·¹Τεκνία μου, ταῦτα γράφω ὑμῖν ἵνα μὴ ἁμάρτητε. καὶ ἐάν τις ἁμάρτῃ, παράκλητον ἔχομεν πρὸς τὸν πατέρα, Ἰησοῦν Χριστὸν δίκαιον· ²καὶ αὐτὸς ἱλασμός ἐστιν περὶ τῶν ἁμαρτιῶν ἡμῶν, οὐ περὶ τῶν ἡμετέρων δὲ μόνον ἀλλὰ καὶ περὶ ὅλου τοῦ κόσμου.

Clausal Outline for Translating 1 John 1:5–2:2

¹·⁵ᵃ<u>Καὶ ἔστιν</u> αὕτη ἡ ἀγγελία
|
¹·⁵ᵇ<u>ἣν ἀκηκόαμεν</u> ἀπ' αὐτοῦ

|
¹·⁵ᶜ<u>καὶ [ἣν] ἀναγγέλλομεν</u> ὑμῖν,

|
¹·⁵ᵈ<u>ὅτι</u> ὁ θεὸς φῶς <u>ἐστιν</u>

|
¹·⁵ᵉ<u>καὶ [ὅτι]</u> σκοτία ἐν αὐτῷ οὐκ <u>ἔστιν</u> οὐδεμία.

¹·⁶ᵃ<u>Ἐὰν εἴπωμεν</u> (<u>ὅτι</u> κοινωνίαν <u>ἔχομεν</u> μετ' αὐτοῦ)

^{1:6b} <u>καὶ</u> [ἐὰν] ἐν τῷ σκότει <u>περιπατῶμεν</u>,

^{1:6c} <u>ψευδόμεθα</u>

^{1:6d} καὶ οὐ <u>ποιοῦμεν</u> τὴν ἀλήθειαν·

^{1:7a} <u>ἐὰν</u> δὲ ἐν τῷ φωτὶ <u>περιπατῶμεν</u>

^{1:7b} <u>ὡς</u> αὐτός <u>ἐστιν</u> ἐν τῷ φωτί,

^{1:7c} κοινωνίαν <u>ἔχομεν</u> μετ᾽ ἀλλήλων

^{1:7d} <u>καὶ</u> τὸ αἷμα Ἰησοῦ τοῦ υἱοῦ αὐτοῦ <u>καθαρίζει</u> ἡμᾶς ἀπὸ πάσης ἁμαρτίας.

^{1:8a} <u>ἐὰν εἴπωμεν</u> (ὅτι ἁμαρτίαν οὐκ ἔχομεν),

^{1:8b} ἑαυτοὺς <u>πλανῶμεν</u>

^{1:8c} καὶ ἡ ἀλήθεια οὐκ <u>ἔστιν</u> ἐν ἡμῖν.

^{1:9a} <u>ἐὰν</u> [ἀλλὰ] <u>ὁμολογῶμεν</u> τὰς ἁμαρτίας ἡμῶν,

^{1:9b} πιστός <u>ἐστιν</u> καὶ δίκαιος

^{1:9c} <u>ἵνα ἀφῇ</u> ἡμῖν τὰς ἁμαρτίας

^{1:9d} <u>καὶ</u> [<u>ἵνα</u>] <u>καθαρίσῃ</u> ἡμᾶς ἀπὸ πάσης ἀδικίας.

^{1:10a} <u>ἐὰν</u> <u>εἴπωμεν</u> (ὅτι οὐχ <u>ἡμαρτήκαμεν</u>),

^{1:10b} ψεύστην <u>ποιοῦμεν</u> αὐτὸν

^{1:10c} <u>καὶ</u> ὁ λόγος αὐτοῦ οὐκ <u>ἔστιν</u> ἐν ἡμῖν.

^{2:1a} Τεκνία μου, ταῦτα <u>γράφω</u> ὑμῖν

^{2:1b} <u>ἵνα</u> μὴ <u>ἁμάρτητε</u>.

^{2:1c} <u>καὶ</u> <u>ἐάν</u> τις [<u>ἐστιν</u>] <u>ἁμάρτῃ</u>,

^{2:1d} παράκλητον <u>ἔχομεν</u> πρὸς τὸν πατέρα, Ἰησοῦν Χριστὸν δίκαιον·

^{2:2a} καὶ αὐτὸς ἱλασμός <u>ἐστιν</u> περὶ τῶν ἁμαρτιῶν ἡμῶν,

^{2:2b} [καὶ αὐτὸς ἱλασμός <u>ἐστιν</u>] οὐ περὶ τῶν ἡμετέρων δὲ μόνον

^{2:2c} ἀλλὰ [αὐτὸς ἱλασμός <u>ἐστιν</u>] καὶ περὶ ὅλου τοῦ κόσμου.

1 John 2:3–11

Contextual Orientation

John transitions (καί) from his first litany of claims and contradictory lifestyles (1:5–2:2) to another list of claims to demonstrate a true relationship with God grounded in obedience to God's command to love (vv. 3–11). John begins with a simple statement of fact: People who

Translating 1 John Clause by Clause

obey (τηρῶμεν) God's command to love know (γινώσκομεν) they have a relationship with God (2:3).

Once again, John assesses several claims (ὁ λέγων) of people who profess to know God. Whereas some people claim (ὁ λέγων) to have a relationship with God, others demonstrate their relationship with God via their obedience in loving others (vv. 4–6). Whereas the command to love is not new, an aspect of it is, because hatred is diminishing and love is increasing (vv. 7–8). Whereas some people (ὁ λέγων) claim to be loving, while being hateful, others demonstrate obedience to God's command by extending love toward other true believers and thereby manifest that they are truly loving members of God's community (vv. 9-11).

Greek Text for Verbal Recognition for 1 John 2:3–11

³Καὶ ἐν τούτῳ γινώσκομεν ὅτι ἐγνώκαμεν αὐτόν, ἐὰν τὰς ἐντολὰς αὐτοῦ τηρῶμεν. ⁴ὁ λέγων ὅτι Ἔγνωκα αὐτόν, καὶ τὰς ἐντολὰς αὐτοῦ μὴ τηρῶν, ψεύστης ἐστίν, καὶ ἐν τούτῳ ἡ ἀλήθεια οὐκ ἔστιν· ⁵ὃς δ' ἂν τηρῇ αὐτοῦ τὸν λόγον, ἀληθῶς ἐν τούτῳ ἡ ἀγάπη τοῦ θεοῦ τετελείωται. ἐν τούτῳ γινώσκομεν ὅτι ἐν αὐτῷ ἐσμεν· ⁶ὁ λέγων ἐν αὐτῷ μένειν ὀφείλει καθὼς ἐκεῖνος περιεπάτησεν καὶ αὐτὸς περιπατεῖν.

⁷Ἀγαπητοί, οὐκ ἐντολὴν καινὴν γράφω ὑμῖν, ἀλλ' ἐντολὴν παλαιὰν ἣν εἴχετε ἀπ' ἀρχῆς· ἡ ἐντολὴ ἡ παλαιά ἐστιν ὁ λόγος ὃν ἠκούσατε. ⁸πάλιν ἐντολὴν καινὴν γράφω ὑμῖν, ὅ ἐστιν ἀληθὲς ἐν αὐτῷ καὶ ἐν ὑμῖν, ὅτι ἡ σκοτία παράγεται καὶ τὸ φῶς τὸ ἀληθινὸν ἤδη φαίνει. ⁹ὁ λέγων ἐν τῷ φωτὶ εἶναι καὶ τὸν ἀδελφὸν αὐτοῦ μισῶν ἐν τῇ σκοτίᾳ ἐστὶν ἕως ἄρτι. ¹⁰ὁ ἀγαπῶν τὸν ἀδελφὸν αὐτοῦ ἐν τῷ φωτὶ μένει, καὶ σκάνδαλον ἐν αὐτῷ οὐκ ἔστιν· ¹¹ὁ δὲ μισῶν τὸν ἀδελφὸν αὐτοῦ ἐν τῇ σκοτίᾳ ἐστὶν καὶ ἐν τῇ σκοτίᾳ περιπατεῖ, καὶ οὐκ οἶδεν ποῦ ὑπάγει, ὅτι ἡ σκοτία ἐτύφλωσεν τοὺς ὀφθαλμοὺς αὐτοῦ.

Clausal Outline for Translating 1 John 2:3–11

²:³ᵃ **Καὶ** ἐν τούτῳ **γινώσκομεν** (ὅτι ἐγνώκαμεν αὐτόν),

|
²:³ᵇ ἐὰν τὰς ἐντολὰς αὐτοῦ **τηρῶμεν**.

²:⁴ᵃ ὁ λέγων (ὅτι Ἔγνωκα αὐτόν), καὶ τὰς ἐντολὰς αὐτοῦ μὴ τηρῶν, ψεύστης **ἐστίν**,

^{2:4b} <u>καὶ</u> ἐν τούτῳ ἡ ἀλήθεια οὐκ <u>ἔστιν</u>·

^{2:5a} <u>ὃς</u> δ' ἂν <u>τηρῇ</u> αὐτοῦ τὸν λόγον,

|
^{2:5b} ἀληθῶς ἐν τούτῳ ἡ ἀγάπη τοῦ θεοῦ <u>τετελείωται</u>.

^{2:5c} ἐν τούτῳ <u>γινώσκομεν</u> (<u>ὅτι</u> ἐν αὐτῷ <u>ἐσμεν</u>)·

^{2:6a} ὁ λέγων ἐν αὐτῷ μένειν <u>ὀφείλει</u> . . . καὶ αὐτὸς <u>περιπατεῖν</u>.

|
^{2:6b} <u>καθὼς</u> ἐκεῖνος <u>περιεπάτησεν</u>

^{2:7a} Ἀγαπητοί, οὐκ ἐντολὴν καινὴν <u>γράφω</u> ὑμῖν,

^{2:7b} <u>ἀλλ'</u> ἐντολὴν παλαιὰν [γράφω]

|
^{2:7c} <u>ἣν</u> <u>εἴχετε</u> ἀπ' ἀρχῆς·

^{2:7d} ἡ ἐντολὴ ἡ παλαιά <u>ἐστιν</u> ὁ λόγος

|
^{2:7e} <u>ὃν</u> <u>ἠκούσατε</u>.

|_____|
|
^{2:8b} <u>ὅ</u> <u>ἐστιν</u> ἀληθὲς ἐν αὐτῷ καὶ ἐν ὑμῖν,

^{2:8a} <u>πάλιν</u> ἐντολὴν καινὴν <u>γράφω</u> ὑμῖν,

|
2:8c ὅτι ἡ σκοτία **παράγεται**

|
2:8d καὶ [ὅτι] τὸ φῶς τὸ ἀληθινὸν ἤδη **φαίνει**.

2:9 ὁ λέγων ἐν τῷ φωτὶ εἶναι καὶ τὸν ἀδελφὸν αὐτοῦ μισῶν ἐν τῇ σκοτίᾳ **ἐστὶν** ἕως ἄρτι.

2:10a ὁ ἀγαπῶν τὸν ἀδελφὸν αὐτοῦ ἐν τῷ φωτὶ **μένει**,

2:10b καὶ σκάνδαλον ἐν αὐτῷ οὐκ **ἔστιν**·

2:11a ὁ **δὲ** μισῶν τὸν ἀδελφὸν αὐτοῦ ἐν τῇ σκοτίᾳ **ἐστὶν**

2:11b καὶ ἐν τῇ σκοτίᾳ **περιπατεῖ**,

2:11c καὶ οὐκ **οἶδεν** ποῦ ὑπάγει,

|
2:11d ὅτι ἡ σκοτία **ἐτύφλωσεν** τοὺς ὀφθαλμοὺς αὐτοῦ.

1 John 2:12–17

Contextual Orientation

John's mood shifts from one of assessment (2:3–11) to one of affection (2:12–17). John affectionately (τεκνία) writes to *affirm* (γράφω . . . ὅτι) followers of Jesus about their relationship with God, their resilience, and their victory over the devil (2:12–14) as well as to *warn* them not to develop an intimate relationship (μὴ ἀγαπᾶτε) with the world (2:15), because (ὅτι) the world and its negative behavior will not last in contrast with followers of Jesus who will enter an eternity with God (2:16-17).

Greek Text for Verbal Recognition for 1 John 2:3–11

³Καὶ ἐν τούτῳ γινώσκομεν ὅτι ἐγνώκαμεν αὐτόν, ἐὰν τὰς ἐντολὰς αὐτοῦ τηρῶμεν. ⁴ὁ λέγων ὅτι Ἔγνωκα αὐτόν, καὶ τὰς ἐντολὰς αὐτοῦ μὴ τηρῶν, ψεύστης ἐστίν, καὶ ἐν τούτῳ ἡ ἀλήθεια οὐκ ἔστιν· ⁵ὃς δ' ἂν τηρῇ αὐτοῦ τὸν λόγον, ἀληθῶς ἐν τούτῳ ἡ ἀγάπη τοῦ θεοῦ τετελείωται. ἐν τούτῳ γινώσκομεν ὅτι ἐν αὐτῷ ἐσμεν· ⁶ὁ λέγων ἐν αὐτῷ μένειν ὀφείλει καθὼς ἐκεῖνος περιεπάτησεν καὶ αὐτὸς περιπατεῖν.

⁷Ἀγαπητοί, οὐκ ἐντολὴν καινὴν γράφω ὑμῖν, ἀλλ' ἐντολὴν παλαιὰν ἣν εἴχετε ἀπ' ἀρχῆς· ἡ ἐντολὴ ἡ παλαιά ἐστιν ὁ λόγος ὃν ἠκούσατε. ⁸πάλιν ἐντολὴν καινὴν γράφω ὑμῖν, ὅ ἐστιν ἀληθὲς ἐν αὐτῷ καὶ ἐν ὑμῖν, ὅτι ἡ σκοτία παράγεται καὶ τὸ φῶς τὸ ἀληθινὸν ἤδη φαίνει. ⁹ὁ λέγων ἐν τῷ φωτὶ εἶναι καὶ τὸν ἀδελφὸν αὐτοῦ μισῶν ἐν τῇ σκοτίᾳ ἐστὶν ἕως ἄρτι. ¹⁰ὁ ἀγαπῶν τὸν ἀδελφὸν αὐτοῦ ἐν τῷ φωτὶ μένει, καὶ σκάνδαλον ἐν αὐτῷ οὐκ ἔστιν· ¹¹ὁ δὲ μισῶν τὸν ἀδελφὸν αὐτοῦ ἐν τῇ σκοτίᾳ ἐστὶν καὶ ἐν τῇ σκοτίᾳ περιπατεῖ, καὶ οὐκ οἶδεν ποῦ ὑπάγει, ὅτι ἡ σκοτία ἐτύφλωσεν τοὺς ὀφθαλμοὺς αὐτοῦ.

Clausal Outline for Translating 1 John 2:12–17

²⁺¹²**Γράφω** ὑμῖν, τεκνία, (<u>ὅτι</u> <u>ἀφέωνται</u> ὑμῖν αἱ ἁμαρτίαι διὰ τὸ ὄνομα αὐτοῦ).

²⁺¹³ᵃ**γράφω** ὑμῖν, πατέρες, (<u>ὅτι</u> <u>ἐγνώκατε</u> τὸν ἀπ' ἀρχῆς).

²⁺¹³ᵇ**γράφω** ὑμῖν, νεανίσκοι, (<u>ὅτι</u> <u>νενικήκατε</u> τὸν πονηρόν).

²⁺¹⁴ᵃ**ἔγραψα** ὑμῖν, παιδία, (<u>ὅτι</u> <u>ἐγνώκατε</u> τὸν πατέρα).

²⁺¹⁴ᵇ**ἔγραψα** ὑμῖν, πατέρες, (<u>ὅτι</u> <u>ἐγνώκατε</u> τὸν [πατέρα] ἀπ' ἀρχῆς).

²⁺¹⁴ᶜ**ἔγραψα** ὑμῖν, νεανίσκοι, (<u>ὅτι</u> ἰσχυροί <u>ἐστε</u>

²⁺¹⁴ᵈκαὶ [<u>ὅτι</u>] ὁ λόγος τοῦ θεοῦ ἐν ὑμῖν <u>μένει</u>

$^{2:14e}$καὶ [ὅτι] νενικήκατε τὸν πονηρόν).

$^{2:15a}$Μὴ ἀγαπᾶτε τὸν κόσμον μηδὲ τὰ ἐν τῷ κόσμῳ.

$^{2:15b}$ἐάν τις ἀγαπᾷ τὸν κόσμον,

$^{2:15c}$οὐκ ἔστιν ἡ ἀγάπη τοῦ πατρὸς ἐν αὐτῷ·

$^{2:16a}$ὅτι πᾶν τὸ ἐν τῷ κόσμῳ, . . . οὐκ ἔστιν ἐκ τοῦ πατρὸς

ἡ ἐπιθυμία τῆς σαρκὸς

καὶ ἡ ἐπιθυμία τῶν ὀφθαλμῶν

καὶ ἡ ἀλαζονεία τοῦ βίου,

$^{2:16b}$ἀλλὰ ἐκ τοῦ κόσμου ἐστίν.

$^{2:17a}$καὶ ὁ κόσμος παράγεται καὶ ἡ ἐπιθυμία αὐτοῦ,

$^{2:17b}$ὁ δὲ ποιῶν τὸ θέλημα τοῦ θεοῦ μένει εἰς τὸν αἰῶνα.

1 John 2:18–29

Contextual Orientation

After his somewhat emotive proclamation (Παιδία . . . ἐστίν) about living in the end times (v. 18), John contrasts (ἀλλ') his community of Jesus followers with those who have left their community (vv. 19). He heightens this initial contrast with yet another set of contrasts (ἀλλ'). Followers of Jesus who have the Holy Spirit given by Jesus contrast the liar, the antichrist, and the secessionists (vv. 20–23). He then exhorts (μενέτω) his readers to hold fast to the teaching of the eyewitnesses and resist the secessionists (vv. 24–25) before offering a summary (καί) of his thoughts about God's affirming Spirit (vv. 26–27) and the resulting (ἵνα) confidence for those who remain in Jesus (καὶ νῦν... μένετε; 2:28–29).

Greek Text for Verbal Recognition for 1 John 2:12–17

¹²Γράφω ὑμῖν, τεκνία, ὅτι ἀφέωνται ὑμῖν αἱ ἁμαρτίαι διὰ τὸ ὄνομα αὐτοῦ. ¹³γράφω ὑμῖν, πατέρες, ὅτι ἐγνώκατε τὸν ἀπ᾽ ἀρχῆς. γράφω ὑμῖν, νεανίσκοι, ὅτι νενικήκατε τὸν πονηρόν. ¹⁴ἔγραψα ὑμῖν, παιδία, ὅτι ἐγνώκατε τὸν πατέρα. ἔγραψα ὑμῖν, πατέρες, ὅτι ἐγνώκατε τὸν ἀπ᾽ ἀρχῆς. ἔγραψα ὑμῖν, νεανίσκοι, ὅτι ἰσχυροί ἐστε καὶ ὁ λόγος τοῦ θεοῦ ἐν ὑμῖν μένει καὶ νενικήκατε τὸν πονηρόν.

¹⁵Μὴ ἀγαπᾶτε τὸν κόσμον μηδὲ τὰ ἐν τῷ κόσμῳ. ἐάν τις ἀγαπᾷ τὸν κόσμον, οὐκ ἔστιν ἡ ἀγάπη τοῦ πατρὸς ἐν αὐτῷ· ¹⁶ὅτι πᾶν τὸ ἐν τῷ κόσμῳ, ἡ ἐπιθυμία τῆς σαρκὸς καὶ ἡ ἐπιθυμία τῶν ὀφθαλμῶν καὶ ἡ ἀλαζονεία τοῦ βίου, οὐκ ἔστιν ἐκ τοῦ πατρὸς ἀλλὰ ἐκ τοῦ κόσμου ἐστίν. ¹⁷καὶ ὁ κόσμος παράγεται καὶ ἡ ἐπιθυμία αὐτοῦ, ὁ δὲ ποιῶν τὸ θέλημα τοῦ θεοῦ μένει εἰς τὸν αἰῶνα.

Clausal Outline for Translating 1 John 2:18–29

²:¹⁸ᵃΠαιδία, ἐσχάτη ὥρα **ἐστίν**,

> ²:¹⁸ᵇ**καὶ καθὼς ἠκούσατε** (ὅτι ἀντίχριστος **ἔρχεται**),

|

²:¹⁸ᶜ**καὶ νῦν** ἀντίχριστοι πολλοὶ **γεγόνασιν**·

|

²:¹⁸ᵈ**ὅθεν γινώσκομεν** (ὅτι ἐσχάτη ὥρα **ἐστίν**).

²:¹⁹ᵃἐξ ἡμῶν **ἐξῆλθαν**,

²:¹⁹ᵇ**ἀλλ᾽** οὐκ **ἦσαν** ἐξ ἡμῶν·

²:¹⁹ᶜ**εἰ** γὰρ ἐξ ἡμῶν **ἦσαν**,

2:19d **μεμενήκεισαν** ἂν μεθ᾽ ἡμῶν·

2:19e **ἀλλ᾽** [ἐξῆλθαν]

2:19f **ἵνα φανερωθῶσιν** (ὅτι οὐκ **εἰσὶν** πάντες ἐξ ἡμῶν).

2:20a **καὶ** ὑμεῖς χρῖσμα **ἔχετε** ἀπὸ τοῦ ἁγίου,

2:20b καὶ **οἴδατε** πάντα.

2:21a οὐκ **ἔγραψα** ὑμῖν

2:21b **ὅτι** οὐκ **οἴδατε** τὴν ἀλήθειαν,

2:21c **ἀλλ᾽** [ἔγραψα ὑμῖν]

2:21d **ὅτι οἴδατε** αὐτήν,

2:21e **καὶ ὅτι** [**οἴδατε** (ὅτι] πᾶν ψεῦδος ἐκ τῆς ἀληθείας οὐκ **ἔστιν**).

2:22a Τίς **ἐστιν** ὁ ψεύστης

2:22b **εἰ μὴ** ὁ ἀρνούμενος (ὅτι Ἰησοῦς οὐκ **ἔστιν** ὁ Χριστός);

2:22c οὗτός **ἐστιν** ὁ ἀντίχριστος, (ὁ ἀρνούμενος τὸν πατέρα καὶ τὸν υἱόν).

2:23a πᾶς ὁ ἀρνούμενος τὸν υἱὸν οὐδὲ τὸν πατέρα **ἔχει**·

^{2:23b} ὁ ὁμολογῶν τὸν υἱὸν καὶ τὸν πατέρα **ἔχει.**

^{2:24a} (ὑμεῖς <u>ὃ</u> <u>**ἠκούσατε**</u> ἀπ᾽ ἀρχῆς) ἐν ὑμῖν **μενέτω·**

^{2:24b} <u>**ἐὰν**</u> ἐν ὑμῖν **μείνῃ** (<u>ὃ</u> ἀπ᾽ ἀρχῆς ἠκούσατε),

|

^{2:24c} καὶ ὑμεῖς ἐν τῷ υἱῷ καὶ ἐν τῷ πατρὶ **μενεῖτε.**

^{2:25a} καὶ αὕτη **ἐστὶν** ἡ ἐπαγγελία

|

^{2:25b} <u>ἣν</u> αὐτὸς **ἐπηγγείλατο** ἡμῖν, τὴν ζωὴν τὴν αἰώνιον.

^{2:26} Ταῦτα **ἔγραψα** ὑμῖν περὶ τῶν πλανώντων ὑμᾶς.

^{2:27a} <u>καὶ</u> ὑμεῖς τὸ χρῖσμα . . . **μένει** ἐν ὑμῖν,

|

^{2:27b} <u>ὃ</u> **ἐλάβετε** ἀπ᾽ αὐτοῦ

^{2:27c} <u>καὶ</u> οὐ χρείαν **ἔχετε**

|

^{2:27d} <u>ἵνα</u> τις **διδάσκῃ** ὑμᾶς·

^{2:27e} <u>ἀλλ᾽</u> . . . καὶ ἀληθές **ἐστιν**

^{2:27f} <u>καὶ</u> οὐκ **ἔστιν** ψεῦδος,

|

^{2:27fg} <u>ὡς</u> τὸ αὐτοῦ χρῖσμα **διδάσκει** ὑμᾶς περὶ πάντων,

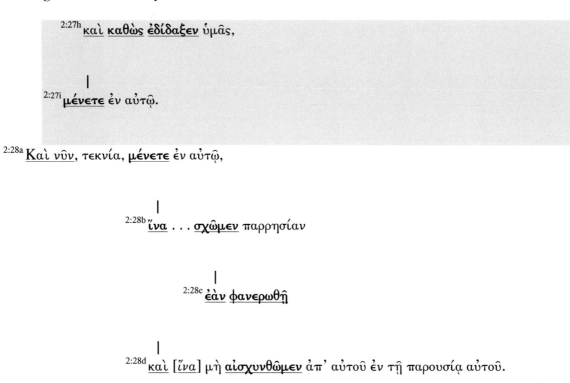

²:²⁷ʰ καὶ **καθὼς ἐδίδαξεν** ὑμᾶς,

²:²⁷ⁱ **μένετε** ἐν αὐτῷ.

²:²⁸ᵃ Καὶ νῦν, τεκνία, **μένετε** ἐν αὐτῷ,

²:²⁸ᵇ **ἵνα** . . . **σχῶμεν** παρρησίαν

²:²⁸ᶜ **ἐὰν φανερωθῇ**

²:²⁸ᵈ **καὶ** [**ἵνα**] μὴ **αἰσχυνθῶμεν** ἀπ᾽ αὐτοῦ ἐν τῇ παρουσίᾳ αὐτοῦ.

²:²⁹ᵃ **ἐὰν εἰδῆτε** (ὅτι δίκαιός **ἐστιν**),

²:²⁹ᵇ **γινώσκετε** (ὅτι καὶ πᾶς ὁ ποιῶν τὴν δικαιοσύνην ἐξ αὐτοῦ **γεγέννηται**).

1 John 3:1–10

Contextual Orientation

Having made an emotive appeal to remain in Jesus (2:18–29), John somewhat sharply (ἴδετε) returns to his theme of love (3:1–10).

John begins with a simple assertion: God gave Jesus that resulted (ἵνα) in followers of Jesus becoming God's children, which in turn becomes the reason (διὰ τοῦτο) why people who do not follow Jesus reject those who do (vv. 1–2). There are, however, benefits of being a child of God: we will one day be like Jesus (αὐτῷ ἐσόμεθα) when he comes (ἐὰν φανερωθῇ), which in turn should affect how followers live in the present (v. 3).

John then draws a contrast between people who practice (ὁ ποιῶν) sin with those who practice righteousness (vv. 4–9). John begins with the incompatibility of a person (πᾶς ὁ) who practices sin and the person's (πᾶς ὁ) fellowship with Jesus (vv. 4–6). John affectionately (τεκνία) warns followers of Jesus not to be deceived about conduct because (ὅτι) a person's (πᾶς ὁ) conduct determines one's paternity (vv. 7–9). Are you God's children or the devil's children? John concludes with a summary statement (ἐν τούτῳ) that also serves as a transitional statement to the next major division of the epistle (v. 10).

Greek Text for Verbal Recognition for 1 John 3:1–10

¹ἴδετε ποταπὴν ἀγάπην δέδωκεν ἡμῖν ὁ πατὴρ ἵνα τέκνα θεοῦ κληθῶμεν· καὶ ἐσμέν. διὰ τοῦτο ὁ κόσμος οὐ γινώσκει ἡμᾶς ὅτι οὐκ ἔγνω αὐτόν. ²Ἀγαπητοί, νῦν τέκνα θεοῦ ἐσμεν, καὶ οὔπω ἐφανερώθη τί ἐσόμεθα. οἴδαμεν ὅτι ἐὰν φανερωθῇ ὅμοιοι αὐτῷ ἐσόμεθα, ὅτι ὀψόμεθα αὐτὸν καθώς ἐστιν. ³καὶ πᾶς ὁ ἔχων τὴν ἐλπίδα ταύτην ἐπ' αὐτῷ ἁγνίζει ἑαυτὸν καθὼς ἐκεῖνος ἁγνός ἐστιν. ⁴Πᾶς ὁ ποιῶν τὴν ἁμαρτίαν καὶ τὴν ἀνομίαν ποιεῖ, καὶ ἡ ἁμαρτία ἐστὶν ἡ ἀνομία. ⁵καὶ οἴδατε ὅτι ἐκεῖνος ἐφανερώθη ἵνα τὰς ἁμαρτίας ἄρῃ, καὶ ἁμαρτία ἐν αὐτῷ οὐκ ἔστιν. ⁶πᾶς ὁ ἐν αὐτῷ μένων οὐχ ἁμαρτάνει· πᾶς ὁ ἁμαρτάνων οὐχ ἑώρακεν αὐτὸν οὐδὲ ἔγνωκεν αὐτόν. ⁷Τεκνία, μηδεὶς πλανάτω ὑμᾶς· ὁ ποιῶν τὴν δικαιοσύνην δίκαιός ἐστιν, καθὼς ἐκεῖνος δίκαιός ἐστιν· ⁸ὁ ποιῶν τὴν ἁμαρτίαν ἐκ τοῦ διαβόλου ἐστίν, ὅτι ἀπ' ἀρχῆς ὁ διάβολος ἁμαρτάνει. εἰς τοῦτο ἐφανερώθη ὁ υἱὸς τοῦ θεοῦ, ἵνα λύσῃ τὰ ἔργα τοῦ διαβόλου. ⁹Πᾶς ὁ γεγεννημένος ἐκ τοῦ θεοῦ ἁμαρτίαν οὐ ποιεῖ, ὅτι σπέρμα αὐτοῦ ἐν αὐτῷ μένει· καὶ οὐ δύναται ἁμαρτάνειν, ὅτι ἐκ τοῦ θεοῦ γεγέννηται. ¹⁰ἐν τούτῳ φανερά ἐστιν τὰ τέκνα τοῦ θεοῦ καὶ τὰ τέκνα τοῦ διαβόλου· πᾶς ὁ μὴ ποιῶν δικαιοσύνην οὐκ ἔστιν ἐκ τοῦ θεοῦ, καὶ ὁ μὴ ἀγαπῶν τὸν ἀδελφὸν αὐτοῦ.

Clausal Outline for Translating 1 John 3:1–10

³:¹ᵃ <u>ἴδετε</u> ποταπὴν ἀγάπην <u>δέδωκεν</u> ἡμῖν ὁ πατὴρ

³:¹ᵇ <u>ἵνα</u> τέκνα θεοῦ <u>κληθῶμεν</u>·

³:¹ᶜ <u>καὶ ἐσμέν</u> [*τέκνα θεοῦ κληθωμεν*].

³:¹ᵈ <u>διὰ τοῦτο</u> ὁ κόσμος οὐ <u>γινώσκει</u> ἡμᾶς

¹ᵉ <u>ὅτι</u> οὐκ <u>ἔγνω</u> αὐτόν.

^{3:2a} Ἀγαπητοί, νῦν τέκνα θεοῦ <u>ἐσμεν</u>,

^{3:2b} καὶ οὔπω <u>ἐφανερώθη</u> τί <u>ἐσόμεθα</u>.

^{3:2c} <u>οἴδαμεν</u> (ὅτι . . . ὅμοιοι αὐτῷ <u>ἐσόμεθα</u>),

      |
^{3:2d} <u>ἐὰν φανερωθῇ</u>

              |
^{3:2e} <u>ὅτι ὀψόμεθα</u> αὐτὸν

                |
^{3:2f} <u>καθώς ἐστιν</u>.

^{3:3a} <u>καὶ</u> πᾶς ὁ ἔχων τὴν ἐλπίδα ταύτην ἐπ᾽ αὐτῷ <u>ἁγνίζει</u> ἑαυτὸν

                |
^{3:3b}<u>καθὼς</u> ἐκεῖνος ἁγνός <u>ἐστιν</u>.

^{3:4a} Πᾶς ὁ ποιῶν τὴν ἁμαρτίαν καὶ τὴν ἀνομίαν <u>ποιεῖ</u>,

^{3:4b} καὶ ἡ ἁμαρτία <u>ἐστὶν</u> ἡ ἀνομία.

^{3:5a} καὶ <u>οἴδατε</u> (ὅτι ἐκεῖνος <u>ἐφανερώθη</u>)

          |
^{3:5b}<u>ἵνα</u> τὰς ἁμαρτίας <u>ἄρῃ</u>,

^{3:5c} καὶ [<u>οἴδατε</u> (<u>ὅτι</u>] ἁμαρτία ἐν αὐτῷ οὐκ <u>ἔστιν</u>).

^{3:6a} πᾶς ὁ ἐν αὐτῷ μένων οὐχ <u>ἁμαρτάνει</u>·

^{3:6b} πᾶς ὁ ἁμαρτάνων οὐχ <u>ἑώρακεν</u> αὐτὸν οὐδὲ <u>ἔγνωκεν</u> αὐτόν.

^{3:7a} Τεκνία, μηδεὶς <u>πλανάτω</u> ὑμᾶς·

^{3:7b} ὁ ποιῶν τὴν δικαιοσύνην δίκαιός <u>ἐστιν</u>,

|
^{3:7b} <u>καθὼς</u> ἐκεῖνος δίκαιός <u>ἐστιν</u>·

^{3:8a} ὁ ποιῶν τὴν ἁμαρτίαν ἐκ τοῦ διαβόλου <u>ἐστίν</u>,

|
^{3:8b} <u>ὅτι</u> ἀπ᾽ ἀρχῆς ὁ διάβολος <u>ἁμαρτάνει</u>.

^{3:8c} <u>εἰς τοῦτο ἐφανερώθη</u> ὁ υἱὸς τοῦ θεοῦ,

|
^{3:8d} <u>ἵνα λύσῃ</u> τὰ ἔργα τοῦ διαβόλου.

^{3:9a} Πᾶς ὁ γεγεννημένος ἐκ τοῦ θεοῦ ἁμαρτίαν οὐ <u>ποιεῖ</u>,

|
^{3:9b} <u>ὅτι</u> σπέρμα αὐτοῦ ἐν αὐτῷ <u>μένει</u>·

^{3:9c} καὶ οὐ <u>δύναται ἁμαρτάνειν</u>,

|
^{3:9d} <u>ὅτι</u> ἐκ τοῦ θεοῦ <u>γεγέννηται</u>.

^{3:10a} <u>ἐν τούτῳ</u> φανερά <u>ἐστιν</u> τὰ τέκνα τοῦ θεοῦ καὶ τὰ τέκνα τοῦ διαβόλου·

^{3:10b} πᾶς ὁ μὴ ποιῶν δικαιοσύνην οὐκ <u>ἔστιν</u> ἐκ τοῦ θεοῦ,

|
3:10c καὶ ὁ μὴ ἀγαπῶν τὸν ἀδελφὸν αὐτοῦ.

1 John 3:11–17

Contextual Orientation

While building (ὅτι) upon the first half of his letter (1:5–3:10), John launches the second half (3:11–5:12) by first underscoring that love and hate are incompatible passions among true followers of Jesus (3:11–18).

As he did in 1:5, John begins with the *gospel* message. Unlike in 1:5 where the *gospel* message underscored (ὅτι) God's ethical characteristic of love, here the *gospel* message is stressed (ἵνα) in this manner: followers of Jesus are to love one another. This expectation of love to be honored among the family of believers (i.e., children of God, v. 11) is immediately contrasted (οὐ καθώς) with Cain's example (i.e., children of the devil, v. 12). In other words, Cain's example is incompatible with God's expectation to love one another. Cain becomes a metaphor for the entire world and representative of the secessionists who have gone out into the world (vv. 13–15; cp. 2:18-19, 4:1).

John then draws two conclusions (καί) for his readers. First, he states that believers will experience strong feelings of abhorrence and acts of hostility from non–believers (v. 13). Second, John reminds his readers that lack of love is evidence of death (vv. 14–15) and the presence of *love is evidence of life* (v 16).

He then draws a contrast between people (πᾶς ὁ) who do not love with those who do. Those who do not love prove that they belong to the sphere of death and future destruction. Furthermore, people who direct strong feelings of abhorrence against followers of Jesus are deemed murderers and their future is bleak (vv. 16–17).

Greek Text for Verbal Recognition for 1 John 3:11–17

¹¹Ὅτι αὕτη ἐστὶν ἡ ἀγγελία ἣν ἠκούσατε ἀπ᾽ ἀρχῆς, ἵνα ἀγαπῶμεν ἀλλήλους· ¹²οὐ καθὼς Κάϊν ἐκ τοῦ πονηροῦ ἦν καὶ ἔσφαξεν τὸν ἀδελφὸν αὐτοῦ· καὶ χάριν τίνος ἔσφαξεν αὐτόν; ὅτι τὰ ἔργα αὐτοῦ πονηρὰ ἦν, τὰ δὲ τοῦ ἀδελφοῦ αὐτοῦ δίκαια.

¹³[καὶ] μὴ θαυμάζετε, ἀδελφοί, εἰ μισεῖ ὑμᾶς ὁ κόσμος. ¹⁴ἡμεῖς οἴδαμεν ὅτι μεταβεβήκαμεν ἐκ τοῦ θανάτου εἰς τὴν ζωήν, ὅτι ἀγαπῶμεν τοὺς ἀδελφούς· ὁ μὴ ἀγαπῶν μένει ἐν τῷ θανάτῳ. ¹⁵πᾶς ὁ μισῶν τὸν ἀδελφὸν αὐτοῦ ἀνθρωποκτόνος ἐστίν, καὶ οἴδατε ὅτι πᾶς ἀνθρωποκτόνος οὐκ ἔχει

ζωὴν αἰώνιον ἐν αὐτῷ μένουσαν. ¹⁶ἐν τούτῳ ἐγνώκαμεν τὴν ἀγάπην, ὅτι ἐκεῖνος ὑπὲρ ἡμῶν τὴν ψυχὴν αὐτοῦ ἔθηκεν· καὶ ἡμεῖς ὀφείλομεν ὑπὲρ τῶν ἀδελφῶν τὰς ψυχὰς θεῖναι. ¹⁷ὃς δ᾽ ἂν ἔχῃ τὸν βίον τοῦ κόσμου καὶ θεωρῇ τὸν ἀδελφὸν αὐτοῦ χρείαν ἔχοντα καὶ κλείσῃ τὰ σπλάγχνα αὐτοῦ ἀπ᾽ αὐτοῦ, πῶς ἡ ἀγάπη τοῦ θεοῦ μένει ἐν αὐτῷ;

Clausal Outline for Translating 1 John 3:11–17

³:¹¹ᵇ <u>ἣν</u> <u>ἠκούσατε</u> ἀπ᾽ ἀρχῆς

|

³:¹¹ᵃ <u>Ὅτι</u> αὕτη <u>ἐστὶν</u> ἡ ἀγγελία . . . , ·

|

³:¹¹ᶜ <u>ἵνα</u> <u>ἀγαπῶμεν</u> ἀλλήλους

|

³:¹²ᵃ οὐ <u>καθὼς</u> Κάϊν ἐκ τοῦ πονηροῦ <u>ἦν</u>

|

³:¹²ᵇ καὶ <u>ἔσφαξεν</u> τὸν ἀδελφὸν αὐτοῦ·

³:¹²ᶜ καὶ χάριν τίνος <u>ἔσφαξεν</u> αὐτόν;

|

³:¹²ᵈ <u>ὅτι</u> τὰ ἔργα αὐτοῦ πονηρὰ <u>ἦν</u>,

³:¹²ᵉ τὰ [ἔργα] δὲ τοῦ ἀδελφοῦ αὐτοῦ δίκαια [<u>ἦν</u>].

³:¹³ᵃ [<u>καὶ</u>] μὴ <u>θαυμάζετε</u>, ἀδελφοί, (<u>εἰ</u> <u>μισεῖ</u> ὑμᾶς ὁ κόσμος).

³:¹⁴ᵃ ἡμεῖς <u>οἴδαμεν</u> (<u>ὅτι</u> <u>μεταβεβήκαμεν</u> ἐκ τοῦ θανάτου εἰς τὴν ζωήν),

|
^{3:14b} ὅτι ἀγαπῶμεν τοὺς ἀδελφούς·

^{3:14c} ὁ μὴ ἀγαπῶν μένει ἐν τῷ θανάτῳ.

^{3:15a} πᾶς ὁ μισῶν τὸν ἀδελφὸν αὐτοῦ ἀνθρωποκτόνος ἐστίν,

^{3:15b} καὶ οἴδατε (ὅτι πᾶς ἀνθρωποκτόνος οὐκ ἔχει ζωὴν αἰώνιον ἐν αὐτῷ μένουσαν).

^{3:16a} ἐν τούτῳ ἐγνώκαμεν τὴν ἀγάπην,

|
^{3:16b} ὅτι ἐκεῖνος ὑπὲρ ἡμῶν τὴν ψυχὴν αὐτοῦ ἔθηκεν·

|
^{3:16c} καὶ [ὅτι] ἡμεῖς ὀφείλομεν ὑπὲρ τῶν ἀδελφῶν τὰς ψυχὰς θεῖναι.

^{3:17a} ὃς δ᾽ ἂν ἔχῃ τὸν βίον τοῦ κόσμου

|
^{3:17b} καὶ [ὃς ἂν] θεωρῇ τὸν ἀδελφὸν αὐτοῦ χρείαν ἔχοντα

|
^{3:17c} καὶ [ὃς ἂν] κλείσῃ τὰ σπλάγχνα αὐτοῦ ἀπ᾽ αὐτοῦ,

|
^{3:17d} πῶς ἡ ἀγάπη τοῦ θεοῦ μένει ἐν αὐτῷ;

1 John 3:18–24

Contextual Orientation

John once again makes an emotive appeal (τεκνία) not to love (μὴ ἀγαπῶμεν) merely in what one says but (ἀλλὰ) in what one does (cf. James 2:14–19). John continues (καί) his thought with what is common knowledge (γνωσόμεθα) for his readers: God knows us better than we know ourselves, despite our lack of confidence (vv. 19–20). John then concludes (Ἀγαπητοί) with some reassurance about a believer's confidence: an untroubled conscience (v. 21), answered prayer requests (v. 22), and the keeping of God's twofold command (vv. 23–24).

Greek Text for Verbal Recognition for 1 John 3:18–24

¹⁸Τεκνία, μὴ ἀγαπῶμεν λόγῳ μηδὲ τῇ γλώσσῃ ἀλλὰ ἐν ἔργῳ καὶ ἀληθείᾳ. ¹⁹[Καὶ] ἐν τούτῳ γνωσόμεθα ὅτι ἐκ τῆς ἀληθείας ἐσμέν, καὶ ἔμπροσθεν αὐτοῦ πείσομεν τὴν καρδίαν ἡμῶν ²⁰ὅτι ἐὰν καταγινώσκῃ ἡμῶν ἡ καρδία, ὅτι μείζων ἐστὶν ὁ θεὸς τῆς καρδίας ἡμῶν καὶ γινώσκει πάντα. ²¹Ἀγαπητοί, ἐὰν ἡ καρδία μὴ καταγινώσκῃ ἡμῶν, παρρησίαν ἔχομεν πρὸς τὸν θεόν, ²²καὶ ὃ ἐὰν αἰτῶμεν λαμβάνομεν ἀπ' αὐτοῦ, ὅτι τὰς ἐντολὰς αὐτοῦ τηροῦμεν καὶ τὰ ἀρεστὰ ἐνώπιον αὐτοῦ ποιοῦμεν. ²³καὶ αὕτη ἐστὶν ἡ ἐντολὴ αὐτοῦ, ἵνα πιστεύσωμεν τῷ ὀνόματι τοῦ υἱοῦ αὐτοῦ Ἰησοῦ Χριστοῦ καὶ ἀγαπῶμεν ἀλλήλους, καθὼς ἔδωκεν ἐντολὴν ἡμῖν. ²⁴καὶ ὁ τηρῶν τὰς ἐντολὰς αὐτοῦ ἐν αὐτῷ μένει καὶ αὐτὸς ἐν αὐτῷ· καὶ ἐν τούτῳ γινώσκομεν ὅτι μένει ἐν ἡμῖν, ἐκ τοῦ πνεύματος οὗ ἡμῖν ἔδωκεν.

Clausal Outline for Translating 1 John 3:18–24

³:¹⁸ᵃΤεκνία, μὴ **ἀγαπῶμεν** λόγῳ μηδὲ τῇ γλώσσῃ

³:¹⁸ᵇ**ἀλλὰ** [ἀγαπῶμεν] ἐν ἔργῳ καὶ ἀληθείᾳ.

³:¹⁹ᵃ[Καὶ] ἐν τούτῳ **γνωσόμεθα** (ὅτι ἐκ τῆς ἀληθείας **ἐσμέν**),

       ³:¹⁹ᵇ(καὶ [ὅτι] ἔμπροσθεν αὐτοῦ **πείσομεν** τὴν καρδίαν ἡμῶν)

          |————————————————————————————|

                              |

                 ³:²⁰ᵃ**ὅτι ἐὰν καταγινώσκῃ** ἡμῶν ἡ καρδία,

3:20b <u>ὅτι</u> μείζων <u>ἐστὶν</u> ὁ θεὸς τῆς καρδίας ἡμῶν

3:20c καὶ [<u>ὅτι</u>] <u>γινώσκει</u> πάντα.

3:21a Ἀγαπητοί, <u>ἐὰν</u> ἡ καρδία μὴ <u>καταγινώσκῃ</u> ἡμῶν,

3:21b παρρησίαν <u>ἔχομεν</u> πρὸς τὸν θεόν,

3:22a καὶ (ὃ <u>ἐὰν</u> <u>αἰτῶμεν</u>) <u>λαμβάνομεν</u> ἀπ᾽ αὐτοῦ,

3:22b <u>ὅτι</u> τὰς ἐντολὰς αὐτοῦ <u>τηροῦμεν</u>

3:22c καὶ [<u>ὅτι</u>] τὰ ἀρεστὰ ἐνώπιον αὐτοῦ <u>ποιοῦμεν</u>.

3:23a καὶ αὕτη <u>ἐστὶν</u> ἡ ἐντολὴ αὐτοῦ,

3:23b <u>ἵνα</u> <u>πιστεύσωμεν</u> τῷ ὀνόματι τοῦ υἱοῦ αὐτοῦ Ἰησοῦ Χριστοῦ

3:23c καὶ [<u>ἵνα</u>] <u>ἀγαπῶμεν</u> ἀλλήλους,

v23d <u>καθὼς</u> <u>ἔδωκεν</u> ἐντολὴν ἡμῖν.

3:24a καὶ ὁ τηρῶν τὰς ἐντολὰς αὐτοῦ ἐν αὐτῷ <u>μένει</u>

3:24b καὶ [<u>μένει</u>] αὐτὸς ἐν αὐτῷ·

³:²⁴ᶜ καὶ ἐν τούτῳ **γινώσκομεν** (ὅτι μένει ἐν ἡμῖν),

³:²⁴ᵈ ἐκ τοῦ πνεύματος (οὗ ἡμῖν ἔδωκεν).

1 John 4:1–6

Contextual Orientation

Having boosted the confidence of these first readers (3:18–24), John turns somewhat abruptly (Ἀγαπητοί) to yet another expectation: distinguish between reliable and misleading "spirits" about Christ (v 1). John makes it clear that teachings about Jesus as a human Messiah distinguish (καί) false teachings, which are against Christ, the Messiah (vv. 2–3).

John's mood now shifts from expectation (4:1–3) to affirmation (τεκνία; vv. 4–6). He first provides a reasoned (ὅτι) contrast between the readers (ἐστε) with people of the world (εἰσίν). Unlike people of the world, followers of Jesus have heavenly origins as God's children and have victory over worldly people because (ὅτι) God's Spirit dwells in them (vv. 4–5a). John then summarizes (διὰ τοῦτο) his point with another "they are" (εἰσίν) – "we are" (ἐσμεν) contrast. While people of the world listens to other people of the world, people who follow Jesus listen to others who follow Jesus (vv. 5b–6b). These contrasts (ἐκ τούτου) are to provide a source of comfort for John's community, which seems to be experiencing disrespect and perhaps contempt.

Greek Text for Verbal Recognition for 1 John 4:1–6

¹Ἀγαπητοί, μὴ παντὶ πνεύματι πιστεύετε, ἀλλὰ δοκιμάζετε τὰ πνεύματα εἰ ἐκ τοῦ θεοῦ ἐστιν, ὅτι πολλοὶ ψευδοπροφῆται ἐξεληλύθασιν εἰς τὸν κόσμον. ²ἐν τούτῳ γινώσκετε τὸ πνεῦμα τοῦ θεοῦ· πᾶν πνεῦμα ὃ ὁμολογεῖ Ἰησοῦν Χριστὸν ἐν σαρκὶ ἐληλυθότα ἐκ τοῦ θεοῦ ἐστιν, ³καὶ πᾶν πνεῦμα ὃ μὴ ὁμολογεῖ τὸν Ἰησοῦν ἐκ τοῦ θεοῦ οὐκ ἔστιν· καὶ τοῦτό ἐστιν τὸ τοῦ ἀντιχρίστου, ὃ ἀκηκόατε ὅτι ἔρχεται, καὶ νῦν ἐν τῷ κόσμῳ ἐστὶν ἤδη.

⁴ὑμεῖς ἐκ τοῦ θεοῦ ἐστε, τεκνία, καὶ νενικήκατε αὐτούς, ὅτι μείζων ἐστὶν ὁ ἐν ὑμῖν ἢ ὁ ἐν τῷ κόσμῳ. ⁵αὐτοὶ ἐκ τοῦ κόσμου εἰσίν· διὰ τοῦτο ἐκ τοῦ κόσμου λαλοῦσιν καὶ ὁ κόσμος αὐτῶν ἀκούει. ⁶ἡμεῖς ἐκ τοῦ θεοῦ ἐσμεν· ὁ γινώσκων τὸν θεὸν ἀκούει ἡμῶν, ὃς οὐκ ἔστιν ἐκ τοῦ θεοῦ οὐκ ἀκούει ἡμῶν. ἐκ τούτου γινώσκομεν τὸ πνεῦμα τῆς ἀληθείας καὶ τὸ πνεῦμα τῆς πλάνης.

Clausal Outline for Translating 1 John 4:1–6

^{4:1a} Ἀγαπητοί, μὴ παντὶ πνεύματι **πιστεύετε**,

^{4:1b} <u>ἀλλὰ</u> <u>δοκιμάζετε</u> τὰ πνεύματα

      |
    ^{4:1c} <u>εἰ</u> ἐκ τοῦ θεοῦ <u>ἐστιν</u>,

      |
    ^{4:1d} <u>ὅτι</u> πολλοὶ ψευδοπροφῆται <u>ἐξεληλύθασιν</u> εἰς τὸν κόσμον.

         ^{4:2a} ἐν τούτῳ **γινώσκετε** τὸ πνεῦμα τοῦ θεοῦ·

         |
^{4:2b} πᾶν πνεῦμα . . . ἐκ τοῦ θεοῦ <u>ἐστιν</u>,

    |
   ^{4:2c} <u>ὃ</u> <u>ὁμολογεῖ</u> Ἰησοῦν Χριστὸν ἐν σαρκὶ <u>ἐληλυθότα</u>,

^{4:3a} <u>καὶ</u> πᾶν πνεῦμα . . . ἐκ τοῦ θεοῦ οὐκ <u>ἔστιν</u>·

   |
  ^{4:3b} <u>ὃ</u> μὴ <u>ὁμολογεῖ</u> τὸν Ἰησοῦν [ἐν σαρκὶ <u>ἐληλυθότα</u>]

^{4:3c} <u>καὶ</u> τοῦτό <u>ἐστιν</u> τὸ [πνεῦμα] τοῦ ἀντιχρίστου,

  |
 ^{4:3d} <u>ὃ</u> <u>ἀκηκόατε</u> (ὅτι ἔρχεται),

  |
 ^{4:3e} <u>καὶ</u> [ὃ] νῦν ἐν τῷ κόσμῳ <u>ἐστὶν</u> ἤδη.

^{4:4a} ὑμεῖς ἐκ τοῦ θεοῦ <u>ἐστε</u>, τεκνία,

^{4:4b} καὶ <u>νενικήκατε</u> αὐτούς,

^{4:4c} <u>ὅτι</u> μείζων <u>ἐστὶν</u> (ὁ ἐν ὑμῖν) ἢ (ὁ ἐν τῷ κόσμῳ).

^{4:5a} αὐτοὶ ἐκ τοῦ κόσμου <u>εἰσίν</u>·

^{4:5b} <u>διὰ τοῦτο</u> ἐκ τοῦ κόσμου <u>λαλοῦσιν</u>

^{4:5c} καὶ ὁ κόσμος αὐτῶν <u>ἀκούει</u>.

^{4:6a} ἡμεῖς ἐκ τοῦ θεοῦ <u>ἐσμεν</u>·

^{4:6b} ὁ γινώσκων τὸν θεὸν <u>ἀκούει</u> ἡμῶν,

^{4:6c} (<u>ὃς</u> οὐκ <u>ἔστιν</u> ἐκ τοῦ θεοῦ) οὐκ <u>ἀκούει</u> ἡμῶν.

^{4:6d} <u>ἐκ τούτου</u> <u>γινώσκομεν</u> τὸ πνεῦμα τῆς ἀληθείας καὶ τὸ πνεῦμα τῆς πλάνης.

1 John 4:7–10

Contextual Orientation

Having affirmed his readers about a correct (*orthodox*) belief concerning true and false teachings (4:1–6), John returns somewhat abruptly (Ἀγαπητοί) to a theme of mutual love (4:7–10). Whereas the first unit (4:1-6) is a test of belief (i.e., Jesus came as a man) and thereby distinguishes between those who belong to God and the world, the second extols mutual love within the community of believers (4:7–10). John seems to be developing his twofold commandment of 3:23 whereby belief in the name of Jesus as well as mutual love are both in keeping with the command already given.

John opens with a reasoned expectation: let us love (ἀγαπῶμεν) because (ὅτι) love is from God. God's love is both the source and thereby the basis for mutual love that identifies whether a person (πᾶς ὁ) has a paternal relationship with God or not (v 7–8). God's love is grounded (ὅτι) in God having sent Jesus with this one intended result (ἵνα), that followers of Jesus might have a permanent relationship with God (v 9). Love is grounded (ὅτι) in God reaching out to mankind first by sending his son as a sacrifice for the sins of the world (v 10).

Greek Text for Verbal Recognition for 1 John 4:7–10

⁷Ἀγαπητοί, ἀγαπῶμεν ἀλλήλους, ὅτι ἡ ἀγάπη ἐκ τοῦ θεοῦ ἐστιν, καὶ πᾶς ὁ ἀγαπῶν ἐκ τοῦ θεοῦ γεγέννηται καὶ γινώσκει τὸν θεόν. ⁸ὁ μὴ ἀγαπῶν οὐκ ἔγνω τὸν θεόν, ὅτι ὁ θεὸς ἀγάπη ἐστίν. ⁹ἐν τούτῳ ἐφανερώθη ἡ ἀγάπη τοῦ θεοῦ ἐν ἡμῖν, ὅτι τὸν υἱὸν αὐτοῦ τὸν μονογενῆ ἀπέσταλκεν ὁ θεὸς εἰς τὸν κόσμον ἵνα ζήσωμεν δι᾽ αὐτοῦ. ¹⁰ἐν τούτῳ ἐστὶν ἡ ἀγάπη, οὐχ ὅτι ἡμεῖς ἠγαπήκαμεν τὸν θεόν, ἀλλ᾽ ὅτι αὐτὸς ἠγάπησεν ἡμᾶς καὶ ἀπέστειλεν τὸν υἱὸν αὐτοῦ ἱλασμὸν περὶ τῶν ἁμαρτιῶν ἡμῶν.

Clausal Outline for Translating 1 John 4:7–10

⁴:⁷ᵃἈγαπητοί, <u>ἀγαπῶμεν</u> ἀλλήλους,

⁴:⁷ᵇ<u>ὅτι</u> ἡ ἀγάπη ἐκ τοῦ θεοῦ <u>ἐστιν</u>,

⁴:⁷ᶜκαὶ πᾶς ὁ ἀγαπῶν ἐκ τοῦ θεοῦ <u>γεγέννηται</u>

⁴:⁷ᵈκαὶ [πᾶς ὁ ἀγαπῶν ἐκ τοῦ θεοῦ] <u>γινώσκει</u> τὸν θεόν.

⁴:⁸ᵃὁ μὴ ἀγαπῶν οὐκ <u>ἔγνω</u> τὸν θεόν,

⁴:⁸ᵇ<u>ὅτι</u> ὁ θεὸς ἀγάπη <u>ἐστίν</u>.

⁴:⁹ᵃ<u>ἐν τούτῳ ἐφανερώθη</u> ἡ ἀγάπη τοῦ θεοῦ ἐν ἡμῖν,

|
$^{4:9b}$ ὅτι τὸν υἱὸν αὐτοῦ τὸν μονογενῆ **ἀπέσταλκεν** ὁ θεὸς εἰς τὸν κόσμον

|
$^{4:9c}$ ἵνα **ζήσωμεν** δι᾽ αὐτοῦ.

$^{4:10a}$ **ἐν τούτῳ ἐστὶν** ἡ ἀγάπη,

|
$^{4:10b}$ οὐχ **ὅτι** ἡμεῖς **ἠγαπήκαμεν** τὸν θεόν,

|
$^{4:10c}$ **ἀλλ᾽ ὅτι** αὐτὸς **ἠγάπησεν** ἡμᾶς

|
$^{4:10d}$ **καὶ [**ὅτι**] ἀπέστειλεν** τὸν υἱὸν αὐτοῦ ἱλασμὸν περὶ τῶν ἁμαρτιῶν ἡμῶν.

1 John 4:11-16c

Contextual Orientation

Moving on from addressing God as the basis for love (4:7–10), John now discusses God's love and the Spirit that "indwells" believers (4:11–16c).[9] The abruptness (ἀγαπητοί) of the transition from v. 12 to v. 13 has become a feature of John's writing style.

Based upon the assumption (εἰ) that God loves us, John underscores a believer's duty (ὀφείλομεν) to love others in the community. Provided (ἐὰν) a community of believers expresses mutual love, those acts of love reflect God's presence and his abiding relationship within the community (v. 12).

---

[9] There is a lack of agreement concerning where this next section begins and where it ends. So we must admit that there are other ways to divide this paragraph. For instance, Painter sees a new paragraph beginning in verse 13 (*1, 2, 3 John*, 227–77; cp. Stott, *The Letters of John*, 167–71), while Smalley sees verses 11-16 together under the rubric "the inspiration of love" (*1, 2, 3 John*, 236). Nevertheless, we agree with Brown that the ἐν τούτῳ in verse 17 cannot begin a new paragraph (*The Epistles of John*, 545-46). Consequently we see 4:7, 11, and 16d as beginning new units thought, each of which begins and ends with a reference to God's love.

John then provides the first of three proofs or tests of God's presence and abiding relationship within a community of believers. The first proof is that God has given (δέδωκεν) them his Spirit. The second proof or test of God's presence and abiding relationship with a community of believers is that they believe (ὃς ἐὰν ὁμολογήσῃ) that Jesus is the Messiah (vv. 14–15). The final proof or test of God's presence and abiding relationship with a community of believers is their having experienced (ἐγνώκαμεν) God's love (v. 16).

Greek Text for Verbal Recognition for 1 John 4:11–16c

¹¹Ἀγαπητοί, εἰ οὕτως ὁ θεὸς ἠγάπησεν ἡμᾶς, καὶ ἡμεῖς ὀφείλομεν ἀλλήλους ἀγαπᾶν. ¹²θεὸν οὐδεὶς πώποτε τεθέαται· ἐὰν ἀγαπῶμεν ἀλλήλους, ὁ θεὸς ἐν ἡμῖν μένει καὶ ἡ ἀγάπη αὐτοῦ τετελειωμένη ἐν ἡμῖν ἐστιν. ¹³Ἐν τούτῳ γινώσκομεν ὅτι ἐν αὐτῷ μένομεν καὶ αὐτὸς ἐν ἡμῖν, ὅτι ἐκ τοῦ πνεύματος αὐτοῦ δέδωκεν ἡμῖν. ¹⁴καὶ ἡμεῖς τεθεάμεθα καὶ μαρτυροῦμεν ὅτι ὁ πατὴρ ἀπέσταλκεν τὸν υἱὸν σωτῆρα τοῦ κόσμου. ¹⁵ὃς ἐὰν ὁμολογήσῃ ὅτι Ἰησοῦς ἐστιν ὁ υἱὸς τοῦ θεοῦ, ὁ θεὸς ἐν αὐτῷ μένει καὶ αὐτὸς ἐν τῷ θεῷ. ¹⁶καὶ ἡμεῖς ἐγνώκαμεν καὶ πεπιστεύκαμεν τὴν ἀγάπην ἣν ἔχει ὁ θεὸς ἐν ἡμῖν.

Clausal Outline for Translating 1 John 4:11–16c

⁴:¹¹ᵃἈγαπητοί, <u>εἰ</u> οὕτως ὁ θεὸς <u>ἠγάπησεν</u> ἡμᾶς,

|

⁴:¹¹ᵇ<u>καὶ</u> ἡμεῖς <u>ὀφείλομεν</u> ἀλλήλους <u>ἀγαπᾶν</u>.

⁴:¹²ᵃθεὸν οὐδεὶς πώποτε <u>τεθέαται</u>·

⁴:¹²ᵇ<u>ἐὰν ἀγαπῶμεν</u> ἀλλήλους,

|

⁴:¹²ᶜὁ θεὸς ἐν ἡμῖν <u>μένει</u>

⁴:¹²ᵈκαὶ ἡ ἀγάπη αὐτοῦ <u>τετελειωμένη</u> ἐν ἡμῖν ἐστιν.

⁴:¹³ᵃ<u>Ἐν τούτῳ γινώσκομεν</u> (ὅτι ἐν αὐτῷ <u>μένομεν</u> καὶ αὐτὸς [<u>μένει</u>] ἐν ἡμῖν)

^{4:13c} <u>ὅτι</u> ἐκ τοῦ πνεύματος αὐτοῦ <u>δέδωκεν</u> ἡμῖν.

^{4:14} <u>καὶ</u> ἡμεῖς <u>τεθεάμεθα</u> καὶ <u>μαρτυροῦμεν</u> (<u>ὅτι</u> ὁ πατὴρ <u>ἀπέσταλκεν</u> τὸν υἱὸν σωτῆρα τοῦ κόσμου).

^{4:15a} <u>ὃς ἐὰν ὁμολογήσῃ</u> (<u>ὅτι</u> Ἰησοῦς <u>ἐστιν</u> ὁ υἱὸς τοῦ θεοῦ),

^{4:15b} ὁ θεὸς ἐν αὐτῷ <u>μένει</u>

^{4:15c} καὶ αὐτὸς [<u>μένει</u>] ἐν τῷ θεῷ.

^{4:16a} <u>καὶ</u> ἡμεῖς <u>ἐγνώκαμεν</u>

^{4:16b} <u>καὶ</u> <u>πεπιστεύκαμεν</u> τὴν ἀγάπην

^{4:16c} <u>ἣν ἔχει</u> ὁ θεὸς ἐν ἡμῖν.

1 John 4:16d–21

Contextual Orientation

Advancing his discussion from a community of believer's duty to love and subsequent proofs of a community's relationship with God (4:11–16c), John advances his theme of love even further with a focus on perfect love (4:16d–21).[10] John returns to an eternal truth: God is (ἐστίν) love and identifies that those who live (μένει) lives of love have a relationship (μένει) with God.

---

[10] There remains a lack of agreement about where to break the verses (see the previous note). Here the challenge is where to end this section. For Brown, the polemical tone against the opponents, which surfaces in verse 20, is sufficient to indicate the start of a new paragraph (*The Epistles of John*, 563 cf. Painter, *1, 2, 3 John*, 277). For Painter, the paragraph begun in verse 16b concludes in verse 21 (*1, 2, 3 John*, 277; Strecker, *The Johannine Letters*, 173). We follow Painter.

John offers a summary (ἐν τούτῳ) of his previous material underscoring perfect love. First God's love is perfected in a community of believers when they imitate it in their own values and behavior, which results (ἵνα) in confidence when they stand before God's judgment. Second, there is (ἔστιν) no fear in love; it is gone (βάλλει) because (ὅτι) fear involves punishment (vv. 17–18).

John returns to a reasoned statement of fact with a contradiction. Followers of Jesus love (ἀγαπῶμεν) because (ὅτι) God loved us first. If they don't, they are liars. For this reason (γὰρ) anyone who refuses to love visible followers of Jesus cannot love an invisible God (vv. 19–21).

Greek Text for Verbal Recognition for 1 John 4:16d–21

¹⁶ᵈ Ὁ θεὸς ἀγάπη ἐστίν, καὶ ὁ μένων ἐν τῇ ἀγάπῃ ἐν τῷ θεῷ μένει καὶ ὁ θεὸς ἐν αὐτῷ μένει. ¹⁷ἐν τούτῳ τετελείωται ἡ ἀγάπη μεθ' ἡμῶν, ἵνα παρρησίαν ἔχωμεν ἐν τῇ ἡμέρᾳ τῆς κρίσεως, ὅτι καθὼς ἐκεῖνός ἐστιν καὶ ἡμεῖς ἐσμεν ἐν τῷ κόσμῳ τούτῳ. ¹⁸φόβος οὐκ ἔστιν ἐν τῇ ἀγάπῃ, ἀλλ' ἡ τελεία ἀγάπη ἔξω βάλλει τὸν φόβον, ὅτι ὁ φόβος κόλασιν ἔχει, ὁ δὲ φοβούμενος οὐ τετελείωται ἐν τῇ ἀγάπῃ. ¹⁹ἡμεῖς ἀγαπῶμεν, ὅτι αὐτὸς πρῶτος ἠγάπησεν ἡμᾶς. ²⁰ἐάν τις εἴπῃ ὅτι Ἀγαπῶ τὸν θεόν, καὶ τὸν ἀδελφὸν αὐτοῦ μισῇ, ψεύστης ἐστίν· ὁ γὰρ μὴ ἀγαπῶν τὸν ἀδελφὸν αὐτοῦ ὃν ἑώρακεν, τὸν θεὸν ὃν οὐχ ἑώρακεν οὐ δύναται ἀγαπᾶν. ²¹καὶ ταύτην τὴν ἐντολὴν ἔχομεν ἀπ' αὐτοῦ, ἵνα ὁ ἀγαπῶν τὸν θεὸν ἀγαπᾷ καὶ τὸν ἀδελφὸν αὐτοῦ.

Clausal Outline Translated for 1 John 4:16d–21

⁴:¹⁶ᵈ Ὁ θεὸς ἀγάπη **ἐστίν**,

⁴:¹⁶ᵉ **καὶ** ὁ μένων ἐν τῇ ἀγάπῃ ἐν τῷ θεῷ **μένει**

⁴:¹⁶ᶠ **καὶ** ὁ θεὸς ἐν αὐτῷ **μένει**.

⁴:¹⁷ᵃ **ἐν τούτῳ τετελείωται** ἡ ἀγάπη μεθ' ἡμῶν,

⁴:¹⁷ᵇ **ἵνα** παρρησίαν **ἔχωμεν** ἐν τῇ ἡμέρᾳ τῆς κρίσεως,

^{4:17c} **ὅτι** . . . καὶ ἡμεῖς **ἐσμεν** ἐν τῷ κόσμῳ τούτῳ.

^{4:17d} **καθὼς** ἐκεῖνός **ἐστιν**

^{4:18a} φόβος οὐκ **ἔστιν** ἐν τῇ ἀγάπῃ,

^{4:18b} **ἀλλ'** ἡ τελεία ἀγάπη ἔξω **βάλλει** τὸν φόβον,

^{4:18c} **ὅτι** ὁ φόβος κόλασιν **ἔχει**,

^{4:18d} ὁ **δὲ** [**ὅτι**] φοβούμενος οὐ **τετελείωται** ἐν τῇ ἀγάπῃ.

^{4:19a} ἡμεῖς **ἀγαπῶμεν**,

^{4:19b} **ὅτι** αὐτὸς πρῶτος **ἠγάπησεν** ἡμᾶς.

^{4:20a} **ἐάν** τις **εἴπῃ** (ὅτι Ἀγαπῶ τὸν θεόν),

^{4:20b} καὶ [**ἐὰν** τις] τὸν ἀδελφὸν αὐτοῦ **μισῇ**,

^{4:20c} ψεύστης **ἐστίν·**

^{4:20d} ὁ **γὰρ** μὴ ἀγαπῶν τὸν ἀδελφὸν αὐτοῦ . . . , τὸν θεὸν . . . οὐ **δύναται** ἀγαπᾶν.

^{4:20e} **ὃν ἑώρακεν**   ^{4:20f} **ὃν** οὐχ **ἑώρακεν**

^{4:21a} <u>καὶ</u> ταύτην τὴν ἐντολὴν <u>ἔχομεν</u> ἀπ' αὐτοῦ,

|

^{4:21b} <u>ἵνα</u> ὁ ἀγαπῶν τὸν θεὸν <u>ἀγαπᾷ</u> καὶ τὸν ἀδελφὸν αὐτοῦ.

1 John 5:1-4

Contextual Orientation

Determining the structural breaks for 1 John 4:7–5:4 is difficult. Further difficulty exists concerning whether 1 John 5:1 begins a new textual unit or not. Whereas Painter suggests that a new section begins at 5:1 because the focus has turned to Christology (p. 289). Brown disagrees, identifying 1 John 4:7-5:4a as one textual unit, whose theme is love and commandments (p. 592). Smalley agrees with Brown that a new section begins with 1 John 4:7 but concludes the section with 5:5, not 5:4a. The difficulty for all commentators and students of 1 John is the author's circular (some would say repetitive) structure. Whatever one's view of the structure of this section, the relationship between rebirth, obedience and Christ is particularly noteworthy.

1 John 4:7–5:4a as a single textual unit with several subunits (4:7-10, 4:11-16a, 4:16b-19, 4:20-5:4a). 1 John 5:1–4 reveals that a person's belief in Jesus identifies his paternal affiliation with God (v. 1a), loves God and other family members (v. 1b), obeys God's commandments (vv. 2-3), and has victory over the evil one (v. 4a).

Clausal Outline for 1 John 5:1–4

^{5:1a} Πᾶς ὁ πιστεύων (<u>ὅτι</u> Ἰησοῦς <u>ἐστιν</u> ὁ Χριστὸς) ἐκ τοῦ θεοῦ <u>γεγέννηται</u>,

^{5:1b} <u>καὶ</u> πᾶς ὁ ἀγαπῶν τὸν γεννήσαντα <u>ἀγαπᾷ</u> [καὶ] τὸν γεγεννημένον ἐξ αὐτοῦ.

^{5:2a} <u>ἐν τούτῳ</u> <u>γινώσκομεν</u> (<u>ὅτι</u> <u>ἀγαπῶμεν</u> τὰ τέκνα τοῦ θεοῦ),

|

^{5:2b} <u>ὅταν</u> τὸν θεὸν <u>ἀγαπῶμεν</u>

|

^{5:2c} <u>καὶ</u> [<u>ὅταν</u>] τὰς ἐντολὰς αὐτοῦ <u>ποιῶμεν</u>.

^{5:3a} αὕτη **γάρ ἐστιν** ἡ ἀγάπη τοῦ θεοῦ,

|

^{5:3b} **ἵνα** τὰς ἐντολὰς αὐτοῦ **τηρῶμεν**·

^{5:3c} **καὶ** αἱ ἐντολαὶ αὐτοῦ βαρεῖαι οὐκ **εἰσίν**,

|

^{5:4a} **ὅτι** πᾶν τὸ γεγεννημένον ἐκ τοῦ θεοῦ **νικᾷ** τὸν κόσμον·

^{5:4b} **καὶ** αὕτη **ἐστὶν** ἡ νίκη ἡ νικήσασα τὸν κόσμον, ἡ πίστις ἡμῶν.

1 John 5:5–12

Contextual Orientation

This is the fifth and final unit of thought for the second half of 1 John 3:11-5:12. Despite the difficulties surrounding where the new textual unit begins (either 1 John 5:4b or 5:5), we have been operating under the assumption that the fifth and final textual unit begins in 5:4b and continues through 5:12.

John begins with faith in Jesus Christ (5:4b-5). What exactly are John's readers to believe about Jesus is testified to by three witnesses: (1) his baptism, which commissioned and empowered Jesus as Messiah, (2) his crucifixion and subsequent resurrection, which provided redemption for those who believe, and (3) the Spirit, who testifies to the accuracy of the community's understanding of Jesus (5:6–8). Thus, the correct understanding of Jesus as the Christ will result in the community's vindication by God and victory over the world. Naturally, this SG begins the first of two subsections for 1 John 5:4b–12.

Verb Recognition for 1 John 5:5–12

⁵τίς [δέ] ἐστιν ὁ νικῶν τὸν κόσμον εἰ μὴ ὁ πιστεύων ὅτι Ἰησοῦς ἐστιν ὁ υἱὸς τοῦ θεοῦ; ⁶Οὗτός ἐστιν ὁ ἐλθὼν δι' ὕδατος καὶ αἵματος, Ἰησοῦς Χριστός· οὐκ ἐν τῷ ὕδατι μόνον ἀλλ' ἐν τῷ ὕδατι καὶ ἐν τῷ αἵματι· καὶ τὸ πνεῦμά ἐστιν τὸ μαρτυροῦν, ὅτι τὸ πνεῦμά ἐστιν ἡ ἀλήθεια. ⁷ὅτι τρεῖς εἰσιν οἱ μαρτυροῦντες, ⁸τὸ πνεῦμα καὶ τὸ ὕδωρ καὶ τὸ αἷμα, καὶ οἱ τρεῖς εἰς τὸ ἕν εἰσιν. ⁹εἰ τὴν μαρτυρίαν τῶν ἀνθρώπων λαμβάνομεν, ἡ μαρτυρία τοῦ θεοῦ μείζων ἐστίν, ὅτι αὕτη ἐστὶν ἡ

μαρτυρία τοῦ θεοῦ, ὅτι μεμαρτύρηκεν περὶ τοῦ υἱοῦ αὐτοῦ. ¹⁰ὁ πιστεύων εἰς τὸν υἱὸν τοῦ θεοῦ ἔχει τὴν μαρτυρίαν ἐν αὑτῷ· ὁ μὴ πιστεύων τῷ θεῷ ψεύστην πεποίηκεν αὐτόν, ὅτι οὐ πεπίστευκεν εἰς τὴν μαρτυρίαν ἣν μεμαρτύρηκεν ὁ θεὸς περὶ τοῦ υἱοῦ αὐτοῦ. ¹¹καὶ αὕτη ἐστὶν ἡ μαρτυρία, ὅτι ζωὴν αἰώνιον ἔδωκεν ἡμῖν ὁ θεός, καὶ αὕτη ἡ ζωὴ ἐν τῷ υἱῷ αὐτοῦ ἐστιν. ¹²ὁ ἔχων τὸν υἱὸν ἔχει τὴν ζωήν· ὁ μὴ ἔχων τὸν υἱὸν τοῦ θεοῦ τὴν ζωὴν οὐκ ἔχει.

Clausal Outline for Translating 1 John 5:5–12

⁵:⁵ᵃτίς [δέ] **ἐστιν** ὁ νικῶν τὸν κόσμον

|
⁵:⁵ᵇ **εἰ μὴ** ὁ πιστεύων (ὅτι Ἰησοῦς **ἐστιν** ὁ υἱὸς τοῦ θεοῦ);

⁵:⁶ᵃ Οὗτός **ἐστιν** ὁ ἐλθὼν δι᾽ ὕδατος καὶ αἵματος, Ἰησοῦς Χριστός·

⁵:⁶ᵇ οὐκ [**ἦλθεν**] ἐν τῷ ὕδατι μόνον

⁵:⁶ᶜ **ἀλλ᾽** [**ἦλθεν**] ἐν τῷ ὕδατι καὶ ἐν τῷ αἵματι·

⁵:⁶ᵈ **καὶ** τὸ πνεῦμά **ἐστιν** τὸ μαρτυροῦν,

|
⁵:⁶ᵉ **ὅτι** τὸ πνεῦμά **ἐστιν** ἡ ἀλήθεια.

⁵:⁷ **ὅτι** τρεῖς **εἰσιν** οἱ μαρτυροῦντες

⁵:⁸ᵃ τὸ πνεῦμα καὶ τὸ ὕδωρ καὶ τὸ αἷμα [**ἐστιν**],

⁵:⁸ᵇ **καὶ** οἱ τρεῖς εἰς τὸ ἕν **εἰσιν**.

⁵:⁹ᵃ **εἰ** τὴν μαρτυρίαν τῶν ἀνθρώπων **λαμβάνομεν**,

^{5:9b} ἡ μαρτυρία τοῦ θεοῦ μείζων **ἐστίν**,

^{5:9c} **ὅτι** αὕτη **ἐστὶν** ἡ μαρτυρία τοῦ θεοῦ,

^{5:9d} **ὅτι** **μεμαρτύρηκεν** περὶ τοῦ υἱοῦ αὐτοῦ.

^{5:10a} ὁ πιστεύων εἰς τὸν υἱὸν τοῦ θεοῦ **ἔχει** τὴν μαρτυρίαν ἐν αὐτῷ·

^{5:10b} ὁ μὴ πιστεύων τῷ θεῷ ψεύστην **πεποίηκεν** αὐτόν,

^{5:10c} **ὅτι** οὐ **πεπίστευκεν** εἰς τὴν μαρτυρίαν

^{5:10d} **ἣν** **μεμαρτύρηκεν** ὁ θεὸς περὶ τοῦ υἱοῦ αὐτοῦ.

^{5:11a} καὶ αὕτη **ἐστὶν** ἡ μαρτυρία,

^{5:11b} **ὅτι** ζωὴν αἰώνιον **ἔδωκεν** ἡμῖν ὁ θεός,

^{5:11c} **καὶ** αὕτη ἡ ζωὴ ἐν τῷ υἱῷ αὐτοῦ **ἐστιν**.

^{5:12a} ὁ ἔχων τὸν υἱὸν **ἔχει** τὴν ζωήν·

^{5:12b} ὁ μὴ ἔχων τὸν υἱὸν τοῦ θεοῦ τὴν ζωὴν οὐκ **ἔχει**.

1 John 5:13-21

Contextual Orientation

As noted above, 1 John can be divided into two major units, 1:5–3:10 and 3:11–5:12 because they have parallel beginnings: "Now this is the gospel" (καὶ ἔστιν αὕτη ἡ ἀγγελία) and "for this is the Gospel" (ὅτι ζωὴν ἔχετε αἰώνιον). Furthermore it suggests that 1 John 1:1–4 is the prologue, and that 1 John 5:13–21 concludes the letter.

Although commentators disagree about whether the final section of 1 John should begin with 5:13 or 5:14, it seems likely that 5:13 begins the final section of 1 John, as shown by an inclusio of similar themes in 5:13 and 5:20 (i.e., Son of God and eternal life). Furthermore, the theme of "knowing" in verse 13 continues throughout the rest of the section, vv. 14-20. Thus 1 John 5:13-21 appears to form a conclusion of sorts to 1 John. Although 5:13-21 is not structured as a logical argument, it revisits some of the main thoughts of the letter (i.e., sin, paternity, the world, the evil one, Jesus as Messiah, eternal life).

First John 5:13–17 is the first of two subsections for the epistle's epilogue. In this first subsection, John introduces the theme of "sin not to death." It is key for understanding John's teaching about sin. John reminds believers that based upon the fact that they have eternal life, They can have confidence when they approach God in prayer (5:13–14), even when it concerns praying for other believers who are living in sin (5:15–17).

First John 5:18–21 is the second subsection for the epistle's epilogue. It has three solemn assertions of knowledge, each introduced with οἴδαμεν in verses 18, 19 and 20. Each statement reflects divine privileges granted true believers, such as being begotten from God (v. 18), belonging to God (v. 19), and knowing the true God (v. 20). Verse 21, then, while admittedly an abrupt ending, serves as the negative counterpart to the three statements in the preceding verses.

Verb Recognition for 1 John 5:13–21

¹³Ταῦτα ἔγραψα ὑμῖν ἵνα εἰδῆτε ὅτι ζωὴν ἔχετε αἰώνιον, τοῖς πιστεύουσιν εἰς τὸ ὄνομα τοῦ υἱοῦ τοῦ θεοῦ. ¹⁴καὶ αὕτη ἐστὶν ἡ παρρησία ἣν ἔχομεν πρὸς αὐτόν, ὅτι ἐάν τι αἰτώμεθα κατὰ τὸ θέλημα αὐτοῦ ἀκούει ἡμῶν. ¹⁵καὶ ἐὰν οἴδαμεν ὅτι ἀκούει ἡμῶν ὃ ἐὰν αἰτώμεθα, οἴδαμεν ὅτι ἔχομεν τὰ αἰτήματα ἃ ᾐτήκαμεν ἀπ' αὐτοῦ. ¹⁶Ἐάν τις ἴδῃ τὸν ἀδελφὸν αὐτοῦ ἁμαρτάνοντα ἁμαρτίαν μὴ πρὸς θάνατον, αἰτήσει, καὶ δώσει αὐτῷ ζωήν, τοῖς ἁμαρτάνουσιν μὴ πρὸς θάνατον. ἔστιν ἁμαρτία πρὸς θάνατον· οὐ περὶ ἐκείνης λέγω ἵνα ἐρωτήσῃ. ¹⁷πᾶσα ἀδικία ἁμαρτία ἐστίν, καὶ ἔστιν ἁμαρτία οὐ πρὸς θάνατον. ¹⁸Οἴδαμεν ὅτι πᾶς ὁ γεγεννημένος ἐκ τοῦ θεοῦ οὐχ ἁμαρτάνει, ἀλλ' ὁ γεννηθεὶς ἐκ τοῦ θεοῦ τηρεῖ αὐτόν, καὶ ὁ πονηρὸς οὐχ ἅπτεται αὐτοῦ. ¹⁹οἴδαμεν ὅτι ἐκ τοῦ θεοῦ ἐσμεν, καὶ ὁ κόσμος ὅλος ἐν τῷ πονηρῷ κεῖται. ²⁰οἴδαμεν δὲ ὅτι ὁ υἱὸς

τοῦ θεοῦ ἥκει, καὶ δέδωκεν ἡμῖν διάνοιαν ἵνα γινώσκομεν τὸν ἀληθινόν· καὶ ἐσμὲν ἐν τῷ ἀληθινῷ, ἐν τῷ υἱῷ αὐτοῦ Ἰησοῦ Χριστῷ. οὗτός ἐστιν ὁ ἀληθινὸς θεὸς καὶ ζωὴ αἰώνιος. [21]Τεκνία, φυλάξατε ἑαυτὰ ἀπὸ τῶν εἰδώλων.

Clausal Outline for Translating 1 John 5:13–21

[5:13a]Ταῦτα **ἔγραψα** ὑμῖν . . . (τοῖς πιστεύουσιν εἰς τὸ ὄνομα τοῦ υἱοῦ τοῦ θεοῦ).

  |
  [5:13b]**ἵνα εἰδῆτε** (ὅτι ζωὴν **ἔχετε** αἰώνιον),

[5:14a]**καὶ** αὕτη **ἐστὶν** ἡ παρρησία

  |
  [5:14b]**ἣν ἔχομεν** πρὸς αὐτόν,

  |
  [5:14c]**ὅτι** . . . **ἀκούει** ἡμῶν.

    |
    [5:14d]**ἐάν** τι **αἰτώμεθα** κατὰ τὸ θέλημα αὐτοῦ

[5:15a]**καὶ ἐὰν οἴδαμεν** (ὅτι **ἀκούει** ἡμῶν)

      |
      [5:15b][**ἀκούει**] (ὃ **ἐὰν αἰτώμεθα**),

  |
  [5:15c]**οἴδαμεν** (ὅτι **ἔχομεν** τὰ αἰτήματα)

      |
      [5:15d]**ἃ ᾐτήκαμεν** ἀπ᾽ αὐτοῦ.

[5:16a]**Ἐάν** τις **ἴδῃ** τὸν ἀδελφὸν αὐτοῦ ἁμαρτάνοντα ἁμαρτίαν μὴ πρὸς θάνατον,

5:16b <u>αἰτήσει</u>,

5:16c καὶ <u>δώσει</u> αὐτῷ ζωήν, (τοῖς ἁμαρτάνουσιν μὴ πρὸς θάνατον),

5:16d <u>ἔστιν</u> ἁμαρτία πρὸς θάνατον·

5:16e οὐ (περὶ ἐκείνης) <u>λέγω</u> (ἵνα <u>ἐρωτήσῃ</u>).

5:17a πᾶσα ἀδικία ἁμαρτία <u>ἐστίν</u>,

5:17b καὶ <u>ἔστιν</u> ἁμαρτία οὐ πρὸς θάνατον.

5:18a <u>Οἴδαμεν</u> (<u>ὅτι</u> πᾶς ὁ γεγεννημένος ἐκ τοῦ θεοῦ οὐχ <u>ἁμαρτάνει</u>,

5:18b <u>ἀλλ'</u> [ὅτι] ὁ γεννηθεὶς ἐκ τοῦ θεοῦ <u>τηρεῖ</u> αὐτόν,

5:18c <u>καὶ</u> [ὅτι] ὁ πονηρὸς οὐχ <u>ἅπτεται</u> αὐτοῦ).

5:19a <u>οἴδαμεν</u> (<u>ὅτι</u> ἐκ τοῦ θεοῦ <u>ἐσμεν</u>,

5:19b <u>καὶ</u> [ὅτι] ὁ κόσμος ὅλος ἐν τῷ πονηρῷ <u>κεῖται</u>).

5:20a <u>οἴδαμεν</u> δὲ (<u>ὅτι</u> ὁ υἱὸς τοῦ θεοῦ <u>ἥκει</u>,

5:20b <u>καὶ</u> [ὅτι] <u>δέδωκεν</u> ἡμῖν διάνοιαν

5:20c <u>ἵνα</u> <u>γινώσκωμεν</u> τὸν ἀληθινόν)·

5:20d καὶ <u>ἐσμὲν</u> ἐν τῷ ἀληθινῷ, ἐν τῷ υἱῷ αὐτοῦ Ἰησοῦ Χριστῷ.

^{5:20e} οὗτός **ἐστιν** ὁ ἀληθινὸς θεὸς καὶ ζωὴ αἰώνιος.

^{5:21} Τεκνία, **φυλάξατε** ἑαυτὰ ἀπὸ τῶν εἰδώλων.

Clausal Outlines Translated and Syntax Explained

"Clausal Outlines Translated and Syntax Explained," re-presents the Greek text with verbs and verbals colored for easy tense recognition. Clausal outlines are re-presented but with an interpretive translation. Finally a detailed syntactical explanation appears for each verb, verbal, and major connecter explaining the interpretive structural outline. While comparing your translation, this section serves to help in further study of 1 John when working with commentaries and other English translations.

1 John 1:1–4

Verb Recognition for 1 John 1:1–4

¹Ὃ **ἦν** ἀπ' ἀρχῆς, ὃ **ἀκηκόαμεν**, ὃ **ἑωράκαμεν** τοῖς ὀφθαλμοῖς ἡμῶν, ὃ **ἐθεασάμεθα** καὶ αἱ χεῖρες ἡμῶν **ἐψηλάφησαν**, περὶ τοῦ λόγου τῆς ζωῆς — ²καὶ ἡ ζωὴ **ἐφανερώθη**, καὶ **ἑωράκαμεν** καὶ **μαρτυροῦμεν** καὶ **ἀπαγγέλλομεν** ὑμῖν τὴν ζωὴν τὴν αἰώνιον ἥτις **ἦν** πρὸς τὸν πατέρα καὶ **ἐφανερώθη** ἡμῖν — ³ὃ **ἑωράκαμεν** καὶ **ἀκηκόαμεν** **ἀπαγγέλλομεν** καὶ ὑμῖν, ἵνα καὶ ὑμεῖς κοινωνίαν **ἔχητε** μεθ' ἡμῶν. καὶ ἡ κοινωνία δὲ ἡ ἡμετέρα μετὰ τοῦ πατρὸς καὶ μετὰ τοῦ υἱοῦ αὐτοῦ Ἰησοῦ Χριστοῦ. ⁴καὶ ταῦτα **γράφομεν** ἡμεῖς ἵνα ἡ χαρὰ ἡμῶν **ᾖ πεπληρωμένη**.

Clausal Outline Translated for 1 John 1:1–4

^{1:1a}Ὃ **ἦν** ἀπ' ἀρχῆς),
^{1:1a}(**That which was** from the beginning)
|
^{1:1b}(ὃ **ἀκηκόαμεν**),
^{1:1b}**which we** have heard)
|
^{1:1c}(ὃ **ἑωράκαμεν** τοῖς ὀφθαλμοῖς ἡμῶν),
^{1:1c}(**which we** have seen with our eyes)

|
^{1:1d} (ὃ ἐθεασάμεθα)
^{1:1d} (**which we** have looked at)

^{1:1e}(καὶ [ὃ] αἱ χεῖρες ἡμῶν ἐψηλάφησαν περὶ τοῦ λόγου τῆς ζωῆς)
^{1:1e} (**and** [*which*] our hands **have touched** about the word, which is life)

^{1:2a} καὶ ἡ ζωὴ ἐφανερώθη,
^{1:2a} for the life **was revealed**

^{1:2b} καὶ ἑωράκαμεν
^{1:2b} and **we have seen**

^{1:2c} καὶ μαρτυροῦμεν
^{1:2c} and **we** *now* **testify**

^{1:2d} καὶ ἀπαγγέλλομεν ὑμῖν τὴν ζωὴν τὴν αἰώνιον
^{1:2d} and **we** *now* **proclaim** to you eteranl life
|
^{1:2e} ἥτις ἦν πρὸς τὸν πατέρα καὶ ἐφανερώθη ἡμῖν —
^{1:2e} **which was** with the Father and **was revealed** to us

^{1:3a} (ὃ ἑωράκαμεν καὶ ἀκηκόαμεν)
^{1:3a} (**that which we have seen** and **heard**)

^{1:3b} ἀπαγγέλλομεν καὶ ὑμῖν,
^{1:3b} and **we** *now* **proclaim** to you also

|
^{1:3c} ἵνα καὶ ὑμεῖς κοινωνίαν ἔχητε μεθ' ἡμῶν.
^{1:3c} **in order that** even **you may have** fellowship with us.

^{1:3d} καὶ ἡ κοινωνία δὲ ἡ ἡμετέρα [ἐστιν] μετὰ τοῦ πατρὸς καὶ μετὰ τοῦ υἱοῦ αὐτοῦ Ἰησοῦ Χριστοῦ.
^{1:3d} And *indeed* our fellowship [*is*] with the Father and with his Son, Jesus, who is the Christ.

^{1:4a} καὶ ταῦτα γράφομεν ἡμεῖς
^{1:4a} Therefore **we are writing** these *things*
|
^{1:4b} ἵνα ἡ χαρὰ ἡμῶν ᾖ πεπληρωμένη.
^{1:4b} **in order that** our joy **may be complete**.

Syntax Explained for 1 John 1:1–4

^{1:1a} ὅ: The Greek word ὅ is a neuter singular nominative from the relative pronoun ὅς, which means, "that which" or "what" (BDAG 725.1bα). Translations vary as to how to render the relative pronoun. Some

translate it "what" (NASB NRSV NET) others "that which" (KJV ASV ESV NIV CNT). **Syntactically,** ὃ introduces a dependent substantival relative clause. The entire relative clause functions as the direct object of "we now proclaim" (ἀπαγγέλλομεν) in verse 3b (cf. Moule, 1984, 34). It is placed in parentheses to show its relationship to *that* verb (ἀπαγγέλλομεν). It parallels four other relative clauses, which are considered "headless," which means they have no grammatical antecedent (Culy 2004, 2). The relative pronoun is in the nominative case and thereby the subject of its verb "was" (ἦν).

ἦν: The Greek word ἦν is a third singular imperfect active indicative from the verb εἰμί that means, "to be" or "to exist" (BDAG 282.1). **Syntactically,** ἦν is the main verb of the first of four dependent relative clauses, "what was from the beginning" (ὃ ἦν ἀπ' ἀρχῆς). This clause serves as part of the compound direct object of the verb "we announce" (ἀπαγγέλλομεν). This relative clause is "headless" and has no apparent antecedent. The contextual antecedent of the pronoun seems to be the person and work of Jesus (see note 1:1a above). The subject of the verb is the relative pronoun "that" (ὃ). **Semantically,** ἦν is a gnomic imperfect: "was" (cf. KJV NASB ESV NIV NLT etc.). John's timeless fact is this: Jesus has existed from the beginning of eternity (cf. John 1:1-14).

Syntactical Nugget: This relative clause is the first of four relative clauses in 1. The question for these relative clauses is this: What or to whom is John referring? The referent could be "the word" in the phrase the "word of life." If this were true, we would expect a masculine pronoun in order to agree with the masculine gender of the "the word," but each of these pronouns is neuter and not masculine. The referent could also be "life" in the phrase "the word of life," but in that case we would expect a feminine pronoun for the same reason. It seems the relative clauses refer to the life and career of Jesus as a whole: his person, words, and deeds (cf. Bateman 2008, 157; Brown 1982, 154-155). John tells his readers that he witnessed the incarnation and ministry of Jesus. Thus Jesus, who was from the beginning, whom our author heard, saw with his own eyes, and even touched, is the one about whom John wants to proclaim.

¹:¹ᵇ ὃ: The Greek word ὃ is a neuter singular accusative from the relative pronoun ὅς that means, "which" (BDAG 725.1bα). **Syntactically,** ὃ introduces a dependent substantival relative clause. The entire relative clause also functions as the direct object of "we now proclaim" (ἀπαγγέλλομεν) in verse 3b (cf. Moule, 1984, 34). It is placed in parentheses to show its relationship to *that* verb (ἀπαγγέλλομεν). It is the second of five relative clauses that are considered "headless," which means it has no grammatical antecedent (Culy 2004, 2). The relative pronoun is in the accusative case and thereby the direct object of its verb "we have heard" (ἀκηκόαμεν).

ἀκηκόαμεν: The Greek word ἀκηκόαμεν is first plural perfect active indicative from the verb ἀκούω that means, "I hear" or "to exercise the faculty of hearing" (BDAG 37.1bα). **Syntactically,** ἀκηκόαμεν is the main verb of this second of four dependent relative clauses, "which we have heard" (ὃ ἀκηκόαμεν). The subject of the verb is an implied "we" embedded in the verb and can be taken as an editorial plural (referring to just John), an inclusive plural (referring to John and his audience), or an exclusive plual (referring to John and a larger group of eyewitnesses). The best option is to take this "we" as an exclusive plural referring to John and a group of eyewitnesses that he represents (Wallace 1996, 394-399; Brown 1982, 158-161; Bateman 2008, 160). **Semantically,** ἀκηκόαμεν is an extensive perfect: "we have heard" (cf. KJV NASB ESV NIV NET etc). The focus is on the completed action upon which John's present testimony is based (Wallace 1996, 577). The point is that John and his associates had personal contact with Jesus and have heard what Jesus said first hand, they now proclaim their experience to others.

^{1:1c} ὅ: The Greek word ὅ is a neuter singular accusative from the relative pronoun ὅς that means, "which" (BDAG 725.1bα). **Syntactically,** ὅ introduces a dependent substantival relative clause. The entire relative clause also functions as the direct object of "we now proclaim" (ἀπαγγέλλομεν) in verse 3b (cf. Moule, 1984, 34). It is placed in parentheses to show its relationship to *that* verb (ἀπαγγέλλομεν). It is the third of five relative clauses that are considered "headless," which means it has no grammatical antecedent (Culy 2004, 2). The relative pronoun is in the accusative case and thereby the direct object of its verb "we have seen" (ἑωράκαμεν).

ἑωράκαμεν: The Greek word ἑωράκαμεν is first plural perfect active indicative from the verb ὁράω that means, "I see" or "I notice" or "to perceive by the eye" (BDAG 719.1b). **Syntactically,** ἑωράκαμεν serves as the governing verb of the third of four dependent relative clauses, "which we have seen with our eyes" (ὅ ἑωράκαμεν τοῖς ὀφθαλμοῖς ἡμῶν). The subject of the verb is an implied "we" and refers back to John and the eyewitnesses to Jesus's ministry. **Semantically,** ἑωράκαμεν is an extensive perfect: "we have heard" (cf. KJV NASB ESV NIV NET etc). The focus is on the completed action upon which John's present testimony is based (Wallace 1996, 577). Once again, the point is that John and his assoicates had personal contact with Jesus but here he emphasizes what they saw Jesus do.

^{1:1d} ὅ: The Greek word ὅ is a neuter singular accusative from the relative pronoun ὅς that means, "which" (BDAG 725.1bα). **Syntactically,** ὅ introduces a dependent substantival relative clause. The entire relative clause also functions as the direct object of "we now proclaim" (ἀπαγγέλλομεν) in verse 3b (cf. Moule, 1984, 34). It is placed in parentheses to show its relationship to *that* verb (ἀπαγγέλλομεν). It is the fourth of five clauses considered "headless," which means it has no grammatical antecedent (Culy 2004, 2). The relative pronoun is in the accusative case and thereby the direct object of its verb "we have looked at" (ἐθεασάμεθα).

ἐθεασάμεθα: The Greek word ἐθεασάμεθα is first plural aorist middle indicative from the verb θεάομαι that means, "I look at" or "I see" or "to have an intent look at something, to take something in with one's eyes" (BDAG 445.1a). **Syntactically,** ἐθεασάμεθα serves as one of the two governing verbs of the fourth of four dependent relative clauses, "which we have looked at" (ὅ ἐθεασάμεθα). The subject of the verb is an implied "we" and refers back to Johnand the group of eyewitnesses to the ministry of Jesus that he represents. **Semantically,** ἐθεασάμεθα is a consummative aorist: "we have looked at" (NASB NRSV NIV NET) or "we have looked upon" (KJV ESV CNT). The stress is on the cessation of an act (Wallace 1996, 559). Once again, John points to the personal contact that he and his associates had at one time with Jesus.

Stylistic Nugget: Each of the verbs in the opening four relative clauses (ἀκηκόαμεν, ἑωράκαμεν, ἐθεασάμεθα), are first person plurals. They all refer to John, the author of this letter, along with a group of eyewitnesses to the earthly ministry of Jesus whereby John's letter is given an air of authority. After having used the perfect tense twice, John now switches to the aorist tense. Why the shift? Contra Brown who believes the shift of tense is merely a stylistic variant (Brown 1982, 296), Porter believes that our author is not just trying to be stylistcally diverse, but that the two aorist tense verbs actually offer supporting information to the perfect tense verbs (Porter 1989, 229-30; cf. Culy 2004, 3). The fact that they looked at him and touched him supports the idea that they were eyewitnesses to the ministry of Jesus. Why does John use two different verbs that mean sight? Commentators propose various shades of meaning between these two verbs. Yet Brown suggests it might be as simple as John having a preferred word for a given tense. He uses ὁράω in the perfect tense and θεάομαι in the aorist (Brown 1982, 162). Yet what must be emphasized is this: John claims to know more than those who appear to be wreaking havoc with the community to whom John is writing because unlike those who are stirring up doubt about Jesus, John knew Jesus personally (Culy 2004, 3).

1:1e [ὅ]: The Greek word [ὅ] is a neuter singular accusative from the relative pronoun ὅς that means, "which" (BDAG 725.1bα). **Syntactically,** [ὅ] introduces an elliptical dependent substantival relative clause. The entire relative clause also functions as the direct object of "we now proclaim" (ἀπαγγέλλομεν) in verse 3b (cf. Moule, 1984, 34). It is placed in parentheses to show its relationship to *that* verb (ἀπαγγέλλομεν). It is the fifth and final relative clause in this group of parallel clauses that is considered "headless," which means it has no grammatical antecedent (Culy 2004, 2). The relative pronoun is in the accusative case and thereby the direct object of its verb "we have touched" (ἐψηλάφησαν).

ἐψηλάφησαν: The Greek word ἐψηλάφησαν is a third plural aorist active indicative from the verb ψηλαφάω that means, "I touch" or "I handle" in quite a literal sense (BDAG 1097.1). **Syntactically,** ἐψηλάφησαν serves as one of the two governing verbs of the fourth of four dependent relative clauses, "which we have looked at and our hands have handled concerning the word of life" (ὃ ἐθεασάμεθα καὶ αἱ χεῖρες ἡμῶν ἐψηλάφησαν περὶ τοῦ λόγου τῆς ζωῆς). The subject of the verb is an implied "we" and refers back to John and the group of eyewitnesses to the ministry of Jesus that he represents. **Semantically,** ἐψηλάφησαν is a consummative aorist: "we have touched" (KJV ASV NASB NRSV NIV). The stress, once again, is on the cessation of the action (Wallace 1996, 559). John underscores the personal contact that John and his associates had at one time with Jesus, his words.

1:2a καί: The Greek word καί is a conjunction that means "for" in this context (BDAG 495.1c). **Syntactically,** καί introduces a conjunctive independent clause "for the life was revealed" (καὶ ἡ ζωὴ ἐφανερώθη), which is providing additional information about the "the life." The entire verse is a parenthical statement and shaded gray in the structural outline. **Semantically,** καί is explanatory: "for" (KJV) and gives us some parenthetical explanation about "the life" (τῆς ζωῆς) (see Culy 2004, 5; Bateman 2008, 162). This "life" is a personification of Jesus, an idea we find often in Johannine thought (John 11:25; 14:6; 1 John 5:20; Rev. 1:18; cf. Brown 1982, 166).

ἐφανερώθη: The Greek word ἐφανερώθη is a third singular aorist passive indicative from the verb φανερόω that means, "I reveal" or "I make known" or "to cause to become visible" (BDAG 1048.1aβ). **Syntactically,** ἐφανερώθη serves as the governing verb of the conjunctive independent clause. The subject of the verb is "the life" (ἡ ζωὴ) which points to the relevance of Jesus's earthly life and ministry (cf. Wallace 1996, 327). **Semantically,** ἐφανερώθη is a consummative aorist: "was revealed" (NRSV NET NLT CNT cf. NIV). The stress again is on the cessation of the action (Wallace 1996, 559). In this opening clause within this parenthetical statement, John draws attention to the personal contact that John and his associates had at one time with Jesus. The idea that Jesus appeared on earth has far reaching implications for us today (cf. 1 Peter 1:20; Heb. 9:26; Brown 1986, 167).

Grammatical Issue: The first four verses of 1 John are one sentence called a period. We find these long sentences or periods throughout the New Testament (i.e., Hebrews 1:1-4, Ephesians 2:1-8, etc.). This particular period is especially difficult to translate because it is interrupted by parenthetical comments (v. 2; cf. Brown 1982, 152). Despite this seemingly parenthetical interruption, however, the point is simple this: John tells his readers that he witnessed the incarnation and ministry of Jesus. Thus Jesus, who was from the beginning, whom our author heard, saw with his own eyes, and even touched, is the one about whom John wants to proclaim.

1:2b καί: The Greek word καί is a conjunction which means "and" (BDAG 494.1b). **Syntactically**, καί introduces the conjunctive independent clause "and we have seen" (καὶ ἑωράκαμεν) that provides additional information about the "life." With one exception (NIV), translations tend to translate καί as "and" (KJV NASB ESV NET NLT). **Semantically**, καί is coordinating conjucntion that links two clauses together. In this clause, John adds further thought about "the life" (or Jesus).

ἑωράκαμεν: The Greek word ἑωράκαμεν is a first plural perfect active indicative from the verb ὁράω that means, "I see" or "I notice" or "to perceive by the eye" (BDAG 719.1b). **Syntactically**, ἑωράκαμεν serves as the governing verb of the conjunctive independent clause. The subject of the verb is an implied "we" and refers back to John and a group of eyewitnesses to the ministry of Jesus that he represents. **Semantically**, ἑωράκαμεν is a extensive perfect: "we have seen" (cf. NASB NRSV NIV NET NLT CNT). Returning to his use of the extensive perfect, the focus is on the completed action upon which his present preaching is based (Wallace 1996, 577). John points to Jesus's time on earth, John and his associates saw him personally.

1:2c καί: The Greek word καί is a conjunction that means "and" (BDAG 494.1b). **Syntactically**, καί introduces an independent conjunctive clause: "and we *now* testify" (καὶ μαρτυροῦμεν). **Semantically,** καί is a coordinating conjunction: "and" (KJV ASV NASB NRSV ESV NET NLT CNT). It provides additional information about John's firsthand experience (Wallace 1996, 671). That inforation is evident with John's next verb.

μαρτυροῦμεν: The Greek word μαρτυροῦμεν is a first plural present active indicative from the verb μαρτυρέω that means, "I declare" or "I bear witness to" or to attest to something based upon personal knowledge (BDAG 618.1b). **Syntactically**, μαρτυροῦμεν serves as the governing verb of the conjunctive independent clause. The assumed subject, "we," refers to John and the group of eyewitnesses he represents. **Semantically**, μαρτυροῦμεν is a progressive present: "*now* we testify" (cf. NLT). It describes something that is in progress (Wallace 1996, 518). John and his associates witnessed the ministry of Jesus firsthand, and they are now in the process of proclaiming Jesus's ministry to others.

1:2d καί: The Greek word καί is a conjunction that means "and" (BDAG 494.1b). **Syntactically**, καί introduces a conjunctive independent clause "And we proclaim to you eternal life" (καὶ ἀπαγγέλλομεν ὑμῖν τὴν ζωὴν τὴν αἰώνιον). Most translations tend to translate καί as "and" (KJV NASB ESV NET NLT etc.). **Semantically**, καί is coordinating conjucntion that links two clauses together. This time, however, John adds a thought about "the life" (or Jesus) as "eternal."

ἀπαγγέλλομεν: The Greek word ἀπαγγέλλομεν is a first plural present active indicative from the verb ἀπαγγέλλω that means, "I proclaim" or to make something known publically (BDAG 95.2). **Syntactically**, ἀπαγγέλλομεν serves as the governing verb of the independent conjunctive clause. The assumed subject, "We," refers to John and the other eyewitnesses whom he represents. **Semantically**, ἀπαγγέλλομεν is a progressive present: "we *now* proclaim" (cf. NASB ESV NIV NLT CNT). John describes his proclamation as something that is in progress (Wallace 1996, 518). The ministry of Jesus that John witnessed is currently being stated publically to others.

1:2e ἥτις: The Greek word ἥτις is a feminine singular nominative from the relative pronoun ὅστις that means, "who" or "one who" (BDAG 730.3). **Syntactically**, ἥτις introduces a compound adjectival relative clause, "*which* was with the father and was revealed to us" (ἥτις ἦν πρὸς τὸν πατέρα καὶ ἐφανερώθη ἡμῖν; cf. KJV ASV NASB ESV NIV CNT). In this situation, ὅτις has taken the place of the simple relative pronoun and occurs quite often in New Testament Greek (BDAG 730.3). The relative clause provides additional information about its antecedent "the life" (τὴν ζωὴν), namely that Jesus (eternal life) was with the father prior to his being revealed on earth.

ἦν: The Greek word ἦν is a third singular imperfect active indicative from the verb εἰμί that means, "to be" or "to exist" (BDAG 282.1). **Syntactically,** ἦν is one of the governing verbs of the compound dependent relative clause "which was with the father and was revealed to us" (ἥτις ἦν πρὸς τὸν πατέρα καὶ ἐφανερώθη ἡμῖν). The subject is the relative pronoun "which" (ἥτις). **Semantically** as it was the case in 1:1a, ἦν is an equative imperfect: "was" (cf. KJV NASB ESV NIV NLT etc.). Whereas John's point in 1:11a was that Jesus existed in eternity (cf. John 1:1-14), here John underscores that before his earthly ministry Jesus was in the presence of the father.

ἐφανερώθη: The Greek word ἐφανερώθη is a third singular aorist passive indicative from the verb φανερόω that means, "I reveal" or "I make known" or "to cause to become visible" (BDAG 1048.1aβ). **Syntactically,** ἐφανερώθη is one of the governing verbs of the compound dependent relative clause "which was with the father and was revealed to us" (ἥτις ἦν πρὸς τὸν πατέρα καὶ ἐφανερώθη ἡμῖν). The subject is the relative pronoun "which" (ἥτις). **Semantically,** ἐφανερώθη is a consummative aorist: "was revealed" (cf. NASB NET NLT CNT). The aorist underscores the cessation of a act: (Wallace 1996, 559). The emphasis on John's past association with Jesus further establishes his authority on the matters he is about to discuss (Culy 2004, 7).

1:3a ὃ: The Greek word ὃ is a neuter singular accusative from the relative pronoun ὅς, which means, "that which" or "what" (BDAG 725.1bα). As it was in 1:1a, translations vary. Some translate it "what" (NASB NRSV NIV NET NLT) others "that which" (KJV ASV ESV CNT). **Syntactically,** ὃ introduces a dependent substantival relative clause with two verbs, "what we have seen and heard" (ὃ ἑωράκαμεν καὶ ἀκηκόαμεν). Like the relative clauses that opens verse 1, this relative clause is also functioning as the direct object of the verb "we proclaim" (ἀπαγγέλλομεν). The relative clause provides the content of what John and his associates proclaim, namely Jesus's earthly ministry. This headless relative clause returns us to the opening group of relative clauses in verse one, but now moves the discussion forward (Culy 2004, 7).

ἑωράκαμεν: The Greek word ἑωράκαμεν is a first plural perfect active indicative from the verb ὁράω that means, "I see" or "I notice" (BDAG 719.1b). **Syntactically,** ἑωράκαμεν serves as one of the governing verbs of the substantivial relative clause "what we have seen and heard" (ὃ ἑωράκαμεν καὶ ἀκηκόαμεν), which serves as the direct object of the verb "we proclaim" (ἀπαγγέλλομεν). The subject of the verb is an implied "we" and refers back to John and his associates. **Semantically,** ἑωράκαμεν is an extensive perfect: "we have seen" (cf. KJV ASV NASB ESV NIV NET CNT). The focus is on the completed action upon which John's present preaching is based (Wallace 1996, 577). Thus it underscores that John *was* an eyewitness of Jesus's ministry, a ministry he *now* announces to others.

ἀκηκόαμεν: The Greek word ἀκηκόαμεν is a first plural perfect active indicative from the verb ἀκούω that means, "I hear" or to have exercised the faculty of hearing (BDAG 37.1bα). **Syntactically,** ἀκηκόαμεν serves as one of the governing verbs of the substantivial relative clause "what we have seen and heard" (ὃ ἑωράκαμεν καὶ ἀκηκόαμεν), which serves as the direct object of the verb "we proclaim" (ἀπαγγέλλομεν). The subject of the verb is an implied "we" and refers back to John and his associates. **Semantically,** ἀκηκόαμεν is a extensive perfect: "we have heard" (cf. KJV ASV NASB ESV NIV NET CNT). The focus, once again, is on the completed action upon which John's preaching is based (Wallace 1996, 577). Thus it too underscores that John *was* an eyewitness of Jesus' ministry, a ministry he *now* announces to others.

^{1:3b} ἀπαγγέλλομεν: The Greek word ἀπαγγέλλομεν is a first plural present active indicative from the verb ἀπαγγέλλω that means, "I proclaim" or to make something known publically (BDAG 95.2). **Syntactically**, ἀπαγγέλλομεν serves as the main verb of the independent clause "what we have seen and heard we proclaim also to you" (ὃ ἑωράκαμεν καὶ ἀκηκόαμεν ἀπαγγέλλομεν καὶ ὑμῖν). The assumed subject, "We," refers to John and the group of eyewitnesses he represents. **Semantically**, ἀπαγγέλλομεν is a progressive present: "we proclaim" (NASB ESV NIV NLT CNT). John restates his proclamation as something that is in progress (Wallace 1996, 518). Jesus *right now* is being proclaimed to those who will listen. Perhaps John is revealing the sequence of how tradition is passed along. Regardless, the ministry of Jesus was originally witnessed by some and is now others are able to participate in that experience through the reception of those traditions (Brown 1982, 170).

καί: The Greek word καί is a conjunction that means "and" (BDAG 494.1b). **Syntactically**, καί introduces a conjunctive independent clause "we now proclaim *also* to you" (ἀπαγγέλλομεν καὶ ὑμῖν). **Semantically**, καί is coordinating conjucntion: "also" (ASV NASB ESV CNT). John stresses a key additional element of his message (Wallace 1996, 671) evident in the next clause.

^{1:3c} ἵνα: The Greek word ἵνα is a conjunction, which means "that" or "in order that" or to denote a purpose or goal (BDAG 475.1aα). **Syntactically**, ἵνα serves to introduce a conjunctive dependent clause, "*in order that* you also may have fellowship with us" (ἵνα καὶ ὑμεῖς κοινωνίαν ἔχητε μεθ᾽ ἡμῶν). This clause is adverbial and modifies the verb "we proclaim" (ἀπαγγέλλομεν). **Semantically**, ἵνα is rendered as a purpose: "in order that" or "that" (KJV; cf. Wallace 1996, 472). The entire conjuctive clause provides John's and the other eyewitnesses' intention for proclaiming Jesus, namely that his readers become partners with them in their relationship with Jesus.

ἔχητε: The Greek word ἔχητε is a second plural present active subjunctive from the verb ἔχω that means, "I have" or to stand in a close relationship with someone (BDAG 420.2a). This verb is also in the subjunctive mood, because it follows a ἵνα. **Syntactically**, ἔχητε serves as the governing verb of the adverbial dependent ἵνα clause. The subject is the emphatic personal pronoun "you" (ὑμεῖς) which refers to John's readers. **Semantically**, ἔχητε is a progressive present: "you may have" (cf. KJV NASB ESV NET etc.). It indicates the relationship John's readers can have with him *right now* through mutual belief in Jesus (Wallace 1996, 518). The fellowship that John describes is not just social interaction, but joint participation in the life and work of God (Culy 2004, 8). John's concern is his mutual fellowship among believers, which he will develop throughout his letter.

^{1:3d} καί: The Greek word καί is a conjunction when used with δέ could be translated "and also" or "but also (BDAG 496.2iγ). **Syntactically**, καί introduces a conjunctive independent clause, "and *indeed* our fellowship is with the Father and His Son, Jesus Christ" (καὶ ἡ κοινωνία δὲ ἡ ἡμετέρα μετὰ τοῦ πατρὸς καὶ μετὰ τοῦ υἱοῦ αὐτοῦ Ἰησοῦ Χριστοῦ). **Semantically**, καί is emphatic: "indeed" (Wallace 1996, 673). It provides affirmation about the fellowship readers have with the author. The translations "indeed" (NET ESV NASB) or "truly" (KJV NRSV) not only indicates that fellowship exists between the reader and John but also with both the father and the son. Take note that this is a conjunctive independent clause not because of καί but because of the next conjunction δέ.

δέ: The Greek word δέ is a conjunction that means "and" (BDAG 213.5b). **Syntactically**, δέ introduces a conjunctive independent clause. It appears in the post-positive position. **Semantically**, δέ is a coordinating connection with an emphatic καί: "and indeed" (NASB ESV NET). It provides more information about a person's fellowship with God the Father and Jesus, who is the Messiah.

[ἐστιν]: The Greek ellipsis ἐστιν is third singular present active indicative from the verb εἰμί that means, "is" or to describe a special connection between the subject and predicate (BDAG 283.2b). **Syntactically**, the elliptical [ἐστιν] serves as the main verb of the conjunctive independent clause (cf. KJV NASB ESV NIV NET etc.). The subject of the verb is "fellowship" (ἡ κοινωνία). **Semantically**, [ἐστιν] is an equative present, whereby John underscores the believer's fellowship as an on-going relationship not just with John and his associates but also with God himself.

1:4a καί: The Greek word καί is a conjunction, which in this context means "therefore" (BDAG 495.1bζ). **Syntactically**, καί introduces a conjunctive independent clause "therefore we write these things" (καὶ ταῦτα γράφομεν ἡμεῖς). John's reference to "we" is an actual "we" (v. 1; see Wallace 1996, 396). **Semantically**, καί is inferential and draws a conclusion from the previous discusion and is translated "therefore" or "thus" (NET). John is drawing a conclusion to his opening statements about his eyewitness pronounments about Jesus ministry.

γράφομεν: The Greek word γράφομεν is a first plural present active indicative from the verb γράφω that means, "I write" or "I compose" as in the composition of a letter (BDAG, 207 2d). **Syntactically**, γράφομεν serves as the main verb of the independent conjunctive clause. The assumed subject "we" refers to John and his other eyewitness associates. The direct object "these things" is probably cataphoric and a reference to the entire letter, making this a purpose statement for the work (Culy 2004, 9). **Semantically**, γράφομεν is a progressive present: "we are writing" (NRSV ESV NET NLT). John points out that he, along with others (ἡμεῖς) are currently writing this letter (Wallace 1996, 518). The pronoun ἡμεῖς is emphatic since technically it is not needed because the pronoun is already embedded in the verb (cf. Wallace 1996, 396). John's desire has compelled him ("therefore") to write this letter. His intention for writing his letter is found in the next ἵνα clause.

1:4b ἵνα: The Greek word ἵνα is a conjunction which means "that" or "in order that" or to denote a purpose or goal (BDAG 475.1aα). **Syntactically**, ἵνα serves to introduce a conjunctive dependent clause, "*in order that* our joy might be completed" (ἵνα ἡ χαρὰ ἡμῶν ᾖ πεπληρωμένη). This clause is adverbial and modifies the verb "we write" (γράφομεν). **Semantically**, ἵνα is classified as purpose: "in order that" or "that" (KJV ASV CNT; cf. Wallace 1996, 472). The entire conjuctive ἵνα clause provides John's intention for writing, which is made clear with the next verb and verbal.

ᾖ πεπληρωμένη: The Greek word πεπληρωμένη is a nominative feminine singular perfect passive participle from the verb πληρόω that means, "to complete" or "to finish" or to bring to completion that which was already begun (BDAG 828.3). The Greek word ᾖ is a third singular present active subjunctive from the verb εἰμί that serves as an auxiliary verb (BDAG 285.11a). **Syntactically**, πεπληρωμένη ᾖ is a perfect periphrastic construction functioning as the main verbal idea of the dependent adverbial ἵνα clause. This two verb construction is "a *round-about* way of saying what could be expressed by a single verb" (Wallace 1996, 647). The subject of the periphrastic construction is "joy" (χαρά). **Semantically**, πεπληρωμένη ᾖ is an intensive perfect: "our joy may be complete" (cf. NRSV ESV NET CNT). The perfect is used to emphasize the results or present state produced by a past action, namely joy (Wallace 1996, 574). John underscores his current joy as it pertains to his reader's shared communion with God.

1 John 1:5–2:2

Verb Recognition for 1 John 1:5–2:2

⁵Καὶ ἔστιν αὕτη ἡ ἀγγελία ἣν ἀκηκόαμεν ἀπ᾽ αὐτοῦ καὶ ἀναγγέλλομεν ὑμῖν, ὅτι ὁ θεὸς φῶς ἐστιν καὶ σκοτία ἐν αὐτῷ οὐκ ἔστιν οὐδεμία.

⁶Ἐὰν εἴπωμεν ὅτι κοινωνίαν ἔχομεν μετ᾽ αὐτοῦ καὶ ἐν τῷ σκότει περιπατῶμεν, ψευδόμεθα καὶ οὐ ποιοῦμεν τὴν ἀλήθειαν· ⁷ἐὰν δὲ ἐν τῷ φωτὶ περιπατῶμεν ὡς αὐτός ἐστιν ἐν τῷ φωτί, κοινωνίαν ἔχομεν μετ᾽ ἀλλήλων καὶ τὸ αἷμα Ἰησοῦ τοῦ υἱοῦ αὐτοῦ καθαρίζει ἡμᾶς ἀπὸ πάσης ἁμαρτίας. ⁸ἐὰν εἴπωμεν ὅτι ἁμαρτίαν οὐκ ἔχομεν, ἑαυτοὺς πλανῶμεν καὶ ἡ ἀλήθεια οὐκ ἔστιν ἐν ἡμῖν. ⁹ἐὰν ὁμολογῶμεν τὰς ἁμαρτίας ἡμῶν, πιστός ἐστιν καὶ δίκαιος ἵνα ἀφῇ ἡμῖν τὰς ἁμαρτίας καὶ καθαρίσῃ ἡμᾶς ἀπὸ πάσης ἀδικίας. ¹⁰ἐὰν εἴπωμεν ὅτι οὐχ ἡμαρτήκαμεν, ψεύστην ποιοῦμεν αὐτὸν καὶ ὁ λόγος αὐτοῦ οὐκ ἔστιν ἐν ἡμῖν.

²:¹Τεκνία μου, ταῦτα γράφω ὑμῖν ἵνα μὴ ἁμάρτητε. καὶ ἐάν τις ἁμάρτῃ, παράκλητον ἔχομεν πρὸς τὸν πατέρα, Ἰησοῦν Χριστὸν δίκαιον· ²καὶ αὐτὸς ἱλασμός ἐστιν περὶ τῶν ἁμαρτιῶν ἡμῶν, οὐ περὶ τῶν ἡμετέρων δὲ μόνον ἀλλὰ καὶ περὶ ὅλου τοῦ κόσμου.

Clausal Outline Translated for 1 John 1:5–2:2

¹:⁵ᵃ <u>Καὶ ἔστιν</u> αὕτη ἡ ἀγγελία
¹:⁵ᵃ <u>Now</u> this **is** the gospel message

              |
          ¹:⁵ᵇ <u>ἣν ἀκηκόαμεν</u> ἀπ᾽ αὐτοῦ
          ¹:⁵ᵇ which we have heard from him

              |
          ¹:⁵ᶜ <u>καὶ [ἣν] ἀναγγέλλομεν</u> ὑμῖν,
          ¹:⁵ᶜ **<u>and</u>** *<u>which</u>* *<u>now</u>* **<u>we proclaim</u>** to you

      |
  ¹:⁵ᵈ <u>ὅτι</u> ὁ θεὸς φῶς <u>ἐστιν</u>
  ¹:⁵ᵈ *namely* **that** God **is** light

      |
  ¹:⁵ᵉ <u>καὶ [ὅτι]</u> σκοτία ἐν αὐτῷ οὐκ <u>ἔστιν</u> οὐδεμία.
  ¹:⁵ᵉ <u>and</u> [*that*] in him there **is** no darkness at all.

    ¹:⁶ᵃ <u>Ἐὰν εἴπωμεν</u> (<u>ὅτι</u> κοινωνίαν <u>ἔχομεν</u> μετ᾽ αὐτοῦ)
    ¹:⁶ᵃ **If <u>we say</u>**, ("<u>We have</u> fellowship with him")

    |
    ¹:⁶ᵇ <u>καὶ [ἐὰν]</u> ἐν τῷ σκότει <u>περιπατῶμεν</u>,
    ¹:⁶ᵇ yet [if] **we** *persist on* **living** in the darkness,

|
^{1:6c} ψευδόμεθα
^{1:6c} __we lie__

^{1:6d} καὶ οὐ __ποιοῦμεν__ τὴν ἀλήθειαν·
^{1:6d} and __we are__ not __practicing__ the truth;

         ^{1:7a} __ἐὰν__ δὲ ἐν τῷ φωτὶ __περιπατῶμεν__
         ^{1:7a} but __if__ we *make it a point to* __live__ in the light

               |
               ^{1:7b} __ὡς__ αὐτός __ἐστιν__ ἐν τῷ φωτί,
               ^{1:7b} __as__ he __is__ in the light,

      |
^{1:7c} κοινωνίαν __ἔχομεν__ μετ᾽ ἀλλήλων
^{1:7c} __we have__ fellowship with one another

^{1:7d} __καὶ__ τὸ αἷμα Ἰησοῦ τοῦ υἱοῦ αὐτοῦ __καθαρίζει__ ἡμᾶς ἀπὸ πάσης ἁμαρτίας.
^{1:7d} __and__ the blood of Jesus, his son, __cleanses__ us from all sins.

       ^{1:8a} __ἐὰν__ __εἴπωμεν__ (ὅτι ἁμαρτίαν οὐκ __ἔχομεν__),
       ^{1:8a} __if__ __we say__, ("We have no sin"),

       |
^{1:8b} ἑαυτοὺς __πλανῶμεν__
^{1:8b} __we deceive__ ourselves

^{1:8c} καὶ ἡ ἀλήθεια οὐκ __ἔστιν__ ἐν ἡμῖν.
^{1:8c} and the truth __is__ not in us.

      ^{1:9a} __ἐὰν__ [ἀλλὰ] __ὁμολογῶμεν__ τὰς ἁμαρτίας ἡμῶν,
      ^{1:9a} [*But*] __if__ __we confess__ our sins,

      |
^{1:9b} πιστός __ἐστιν__ καὶ δίκαιος
^{1:9b} __he is__ faithful and rightous

      |
      ^{1:9c} __ἵνα__ __ἀφῇ__ ἡμῖν τὰς ἁμαρτίας
      ^{1:9c} __to pardon__ our sins

      |
      ^{1:9d} __καὶ__ [*ἵνα*] __καθαρίσῃ__ ἡμᾶς ἀπὸ πάσης ἀδικίας.
      ^{1:9d} __and to declare__ us __purified__ from all unrighteousness.

       ^{1:10a} __ἐὰν__ __εἴπωμεν__ (ὅτι οὐχ __ἡμαρτήκαμεν__),
       ^{1:10a} __If we say__ ("We have not sinned,")

       |
^{1:10b} ψεύστην __ποιοῦμεν__ αὐτὸν
^{1:10b} __we make__ him a liar

¹·¹⁰ᶜ <u>καὶ</u> ὁ λόγος αὐτοῦ οὐκ <u>ἔστιν</u> ἐν ἡμῖν.
¹·¹⁰ᶜ <u>**and**</u> his word <u>**is**</u> not in us.

²·¹ᵃ Τεκνία μου, ταῦτα <u>**γράφω**</u> ὑμῖν
²·¹ᵃ My children, **I** *now* <u>**write**</u> these things to you
                                        |
                        ²·¹ᵇ <u>ἵνα</u> μὴ <u>ἁμάρτητε</u>.
                        ²·¹ᵇ <u>**in order that**</u> <u>**you may**</u> not <u>**sin**</u>.

                ²·¹ᶜ <u>καὶ</u> <u>ἐάν</u> τις [<u>ἐστιν</u>] <u>ἁμάρτῃ</u>,
                ²·¹ᶜ <u>**but**</u> <u>**if**</u> anyone [*does*] sin,
                        |
²·¹ᵈ παράκλητον <u>**ἔχομεν**</u> πρὸς τὸν πατέρα, Ἰησοῦν Χριστὸν δίκαιον·
²·¹ᵈ <u>**we have**</u> an advocate with the Father, Jesus who is the Christ, the righteous one;

²·²ᵃ <u>καὶ</u> αὐτὸς ἱλασμός <u>**ἐστιν**</u> περὶ τῶν ἁμαρτιῶν ἡμῶν,
²·²ᵃ and he himself <u>**is**</u> the atoning sacrifice for our sins,

²·²ᵇ [*καὶ αὐτὸς ἱλασμός* <u>**ἐστιν**</u>] οὐ περὶ τῶν ἡμετέρων δὲ μόνον
²·²ᵇ [*and he is the atoning sacrifice*] not only for our sins,

²·²ᶜ ἀλλὰ [*αὐτὸς ἱλασμός* <u>**ἐστιν**</u>] καὶ περὶ ὅλου τοῦ κόσμου.
²·²ᶜ But also [*he is the atoning sacrifice*] for the whole world.

Syntax Explained for 1 John 1:5–2:2

¹·⁵ᵃ Καί: The Greek word καί is a conjunction that may mean "and" (BDAG 495.1bη) or "now" (BDAG 495.1e). **Syntactically,** καί serves to introduce an independent conjunctive clause: "*now* this is the message" (καὶ ἔστιν αὕτη ἡ ἀγγελία). **Semantically,** καί may be a connective of sentences and rendered "and" (e.g., KJV NASB ESV NIV etc.). Or καί may introduce something new and thereby transitional. In this case, καί is rendered "now" (NET). Thus καί serves to show a slight shift in topic. John is going to move on to discuss the content of the gospel message.

ἔστιν: The Greek word ἔστιν is third singular present active indicative from the verb εἰμί that means, "is" or "to be in close connection with" (BDAG 283.2a). **Syntactically,** ἔστιν serves as the main verb of the conjunctive independent clause. The subject of the verb is the demonstrative pronoun "this one" (αὕτη), due to the grammatical priority of pronouns (Wallace 1996, 42-43). **Semantically,** ἔστιν serves as an equative verb of identity. God is light or God is morally pure.

Syntactical Nugget: The construction "is" (ἔστιν) with "this" (αὕτη) occurs often in 1 John. In this instance, the demonstrative pronoun "this" (αὕτη) is cataphoric and points forward to an epexegetical ὅτι clause "that God is light." It is almost as if John is using these type of constructions to highlight his main points (Brown 1982, 192). If that is true, then John wants his readers to know that they can have fellowship with the Father, the Son, and the followers of Jesus, but only if they walk in the light as God is in the light (Culy 2004, 11).

¹·⁵ᵇ ἥν: The Greek word ἥν is a feminine singular accusative from the relative pronoun ὅς that means, "which" or "that" (BDAG 725.1a). **Syntactically,** ἥν introduces a dependent adjectival compound

relative clause, "which we have heard from him and which we now proclaim to you" (ἣν ἀκηκόαμεν ἀπ᾽ αὐτοῦ καὶ ἀναγγέλλομεν ὑμῖν). The entire relative clause modifies "the message" (ἡ ἀγγελία). **Semantically,** the relative clause is epexegetical: "which" (KJV ASV). The entire clause provides the content of the message, which is clarified in the next verb.

ἀκηκόαμεν: The Greek word ἀκηκόαμεν is a first plural perfect active indicative from the verb ἀκούω that means, "I hear" or to hear something from someone (BDAG 37.1αβ) or denote a body of authoritative teaching (BDAG 38.3d). **Syntactically,** ἀκηκόαμεν serves as one of the governing verbs of the compound relative clause. The subject of the verb is an implied "we" and refers back to John and his other eyewitness assoicates. **Semantically,** ἀκηκόαμεν is a extensive perfect: "we *have* heard" (KJV ASV NASB NRSV ESV NIV NET CNT). It focuses attention on a past action from which a present state emerges (Wallace 1996, 577; Culy 2004, 10). What the eyewitnesses had heard from Jesus himself, John *now* proclaims to others (cf. NLT).

1:5c ἀναγγέλλομεν: The Greek word ἀναγγέλλομεν is a first plural present active indicative from the verb ἀναγγέλλω that means, "I proclaim" or "I announce" or "to provide information" (BDAG 59.2). **Syntactically,** ἀναγγέλλομεν serves as the second governing verb of the relative clause. The assumed subject, "We," refers back to John and his associates. **Semantically,** ἀναγγέλλομεν is a progressive present: "we *now* proclaim" or "we proclaim" (NRSV ESV). It describes that *right now* they are announcing this gospel message to the readers (Wallace 1996, 518).

1:5d ὅτι: The Greek word ὅτι is a conjunction, which means "that" (BDAG 732.2a). **Syntactically,** ὅτι introduces a dependent compound conjunctive clause, "that God is light and in him there is no darkness at all" (ὅτι ὁ θεὸς φῶς ἐστιν καὶ σκοτία ἐν αὐτῷ οὐκ ἔστιν οὐδεμία). **Syntactically,** this ὅτι clause could be functioning in a number of different ways. It could be functioning adverbially giving us the reason for the announcement. We announce what we have seen and heard "*because* God is light." It could also be taken substantivally as the direct of object of the verb giving us the content of the announcement: "God is light'" (NET cf. NIV NLT). Finally, the clause could be functioning substantivally as an epexegetical ὅτι completes the idea of the demonstrative pronoun "this" (αὕτη; *contra* Wallace 1996, 459). The ὅτι + indicative provides the content of the message: "*namely* that God is light" or "that" (KJV ASV NASB NRSV ESV CNT). This is consistent with how John uses ὅτι with the demonstrative pronoun throughout the letter. **Semantically,** ὅτι is epexegetical: "that." The specifics of this ὅτι clause are clarified with the verb.

ἐστιν: The Greek word ἐστιν is third singular present active indicative from the verb εἰμί that means, "is" or "to be in close connection with" (BDAG 282.2a). **Syntactically,** ἐστιν serves as one of the governing verbs of the conjunctive dependent epexegetical ὅτι clause. The subject of the verb is "God" (ὁ θεός). **Semantically,** ἐστιν is a gnomic present that identifies a timeless fact about God. The εἰμί verb equates God with his abiding character. God is light. Thus the content of the message is this: "God is light" or God is ethically pure as symbolized by light.

1:5e ἐστιν: The Greek word ἐστιν is third singular present active indicative from the verb εἰμί that means, "is" or to be in close connection with or with an equative function (BDAG, 283.2a). **Syntactically,** ἐστιν serves as one of the governing verbs of the conjunctive dependent substantival clause functioning in apposition. The subject of the verb is "God" (ὁ θεός). **Semantically,** ἐστιν is a gnomic present presenting a timeless fact about God. There is no ethical impurity or darkness in God's nature.

1:6a Ἐάν: The Greek word ἐάν is a conjunction, which means "if" (BDAG 267.1αβ). Syntactically, ἐάν introduces a dependent conjunctive clause. **Syntactically,** the entire clause functions adverbially: "*if* we say, 'we have fellowship with him,' yet *persist on* living in darkness" (Ἐὰν εἴπωμεν ὅτι κοινωνίαν ἔχομεν μετ' αὐτοῦ καὶ ἐν τῷ σκότει περιπατῶμεν), It modifies two verbs, "we are lying" (ψευδόμεθα) and "we are not practicing" (οὐ ποιοῦμεν). **Semantically**, ἐάν introduces a third class conditional clause: "if" (cf. KJV NASB ESV NIV NET etc.). It offers a hypothetical situation of probability (Wallace 1996, 696). The activity of ἐάν is expressed in the verb.

εἴπωμεν: The Greek word εἴπωμεν is a second plural aorist active subjunctive from the verb λέγω that means, "I speak" or "I say" or "to express oneself orally" (BDAG 588.1). The verb is in the subjunctive mood, because it follows ἐάν. **Syntactically**, εἴπωμεν is one of the governing verbs of the dependent ἐὰν clause. The assumed subject, "we" refers to a hypothetical group of people who claim to have a relationship with a pure God, yet continue in impurity. **Semantically**, εἴπωμεν is a constative aorist: "we say." With one exception (NIV), most translations render εἴπωμεν as "we say" (e.g., KJV NASB ESV NET etc.). It views the action as a whole (Wallace 1996, 557). John speaks of a hypothetical situation whereby a person makes a claim. The specifics of that claim are evident in the ὅτι clause.

ὅτι: The Greek word ὅτι is a conjunction, which means "that" or "for" or as a marker left untranslated (BDAG 732.3). **Syntactically**, ὅτι serves to introduce a dependent conjunctive clause: "*that* we have fellowship with him" (ὅτι κοινωνίαν ἔχομεν μετ' αὐτοῦ). The clause functions substantivally as the direct object of the verb "we say" (εἴπωμεν). The entire clause is placed in parenthesis in order to visualize its contribution to the independent clause. **Semantically**, ὅτι is direct discourse whereby is not translated (ESV NET NIV CNT NLT), but rather quotation marks are employed to underscore the claim (Wallace 1996, 454). That claim is made clear in the rest of the clause.

ἔχομεν: The Greek word ἔχομεν is a first plural present active indicative from the verb ἔχω that means, "I have" or "to stand in a close relationship to some" (BDAG 420.2b). **Syntactically**, ἔχομεν serves as the governing verb of the dependent substantival ὅτι clause. The assumed subject "we" hypothetically refers to any Christian who claims to have a relationship with God yet lives in impurity. **Semantically**, ἔχομεν is a gnomic present: "we have" (cf. KJV NASB ESV NIV NET etc.). It underscores a generic statement that is true at all times (Wallace 1996, 523). John speaks of any person who claims to have "fellowship" (= a relationship) with God.

Stylistic and Theological Nugget: John makes several hypothetical "If we claim . . ." statements (1:6, 8, 10) followed by the three correcting conditional statements introduced by "but if . . ." (1:7, 9; 2:1). Each are mitigated commands politely urging believers to change their behavior (Culy 2004, 14, 16, 18).

1:6b καί: The Greek word καί is a conjunction that means "yet" (BDAG 494.1bε). **Syntactically**, καί introduces a conjunctive dependent clause. **Semantically**, καί is contrastive: "yet" (NASB NIV NET; cf. NLT). It reveals that the hypothetical claims contradict reality. That reality is evident in the rest of the clause.

περιπατῶμεν: The Greek word περιπατῶμεν is a first plural present active subjunctive from the verb περιπατέω that means, "I go about" or "I walk around" or "to go here and there in walking" (BDAG 803.1d). This verb is in the subjunctive mood, because it follows an ἐάν. **Syntactically**, περιπατῶμεν is one of the governing verbs of the dependent ἐάν clause. The assumed subject, "we" refers to a hypothetical group of people who claim to have a relationship with a pure God, yet continue in impurity. **Semantically**, περιπατῶμεν is a customary present: "we *persist on* living" (cf. NLT). It emphasizes the hypothetical pattern of behavior (Wallace 1996, 521). The pattern of behavior contradicts the claim to have a relationship with an ethical God. Lifestyle is not in keeping with their claim.

¹:⁶ᶜ ψευδόμεθα: The Greek word ψευδόμεθα is a first plural present middle indicative from the verb ψεύδομαι that means, "I lie" or "to tell a falsehood" (BDAG 1096.1). This middle verb is probably an example of the true or classical middle where the subject both does and receives the action of the verb (Wallace 1996, 419). **Syntactically,** ψευδόμεθα serves as the main verb of the independent clause. The assumed subject, "we," refers the hypothetical Christian who claims to have a relationship God: "we lie" (ψευδόμεθα) or express a falsehood. **Semantically,** ψευδόμεθα is a gnomic present: "we lie" (cf. KJV NASB ESV NIV NET etc). It underscores a generic statement that is true at all times (Wallace 1996, 523). John makes it clear that any person who says they have "fellowship" (= relationship) with God and yet lives in "darkness" (= morally impure lives) lies.

¹:⁶ᵈ καί: The Greek word καί is a conjunction that means "and" (BDAG 494.1b). **Syntactically,** καί introduces a conjunctive independent clause. **Semantically,** some translations render καί as contrastive ("but" NET NLT; "yet" NIV), but it seems better to recognize the coordinating function of καί ("and" KJV ASV NASB CNT; cf. Culy 2004, 15).

ποιοῦμεν: The Greek word ποιοῦμεν is a first plural present active indicative from the verb ποιέω that means, "I do" or "I practice" or "to carry out an obligation of a moral or social nature" (BDAG 840.3b). **Syntactically,** ποιοῦμεν serves as the main verb of the independent conjunctive clause, "and we are not practicing the truth" (καὶ οὐ ποιοῦμεν τὴν ἀλήθειαν). The assumed subject, "we," refers to the hypothetical Christian who claims to have a relationship with God. **Semantically,** ποιοῦμεν negated with οὐ is a gnomic present: "we are not practicing" (e.g., NASB ESV NET CNT). It underscores a generic statement that is true at all times (Wallace 1996, 523). John makes it clear that any person who says they have "fellowship" (= relationship) with God and yet lives in "darkness" (= morally impure lives) not only lies, but they are also active enemies of the truth (cf. 2:4, 22; 4:1, 20; Brown 1982, 199).

¹:⁷ᵃ ἐάν: The Greek word ἐάν is a conjunction, which means "if" (BDAG 267.1aα). **Syntactically,** ἐάν introduces a dependent conjunctive clause. The entire dependent clause, "but if we live in the light" (ἐάν . . . ἐν τῷ φωτὶ περιπατῶμεν), functions adverbially. It modifies the verb, "have" (ἔχομεν). **Semantically,** ἐάν introduces a third class conditional clause: "if" (cf. KJV NASB ESV NIV NET etc.). It offers a hypothetical situation of probability (Wallace 1996, 696). The activity of ἐάν is expressed in the verb.

δέ: The Greek word δέ is a conjunction, which means "but" or "rather" (BDAG 213.4a). **Syntactically,** δέ is in the post-positive position and introduces the dependent adverbial conditional clause. **Semantically,** δέ is contrastive and introduces a second hypothetical situation or mitigated command (Culy 2004, 16) that is expressed in the next verb.

περιπατῶμεν: The Greek word περιπατῶμεν is a first plural present active subjunctive from the verb περιπατέω that means, "I walk" or "I live" or "to conduct one's life" (BDAG 803.2a). The verb is in the subjunctive mood, because it follows ἐάν. **Syntactically,** περιπατῶμεν is the governing verb of the dependent conjunctive ἐάν clause. The assumed subject, "We," refers to the hypothetical person who habitually lives a lifestyle of purity. **Semantically,** περιπατῶμεν is a gnomic present: "we live" (cf. NLT) or "we walk" (KJV ASV NASB NRSV ESV NIV NET CNT). It underscores a generic statement that is true at all times (Wallace 1996, 523). John speaks of any person who lives in "the light" (= a moral life).

1:7b ὡς: The Greek word ὡς is a conjunction that means "as" (BDAG 1104.3a). **Syntactically,** ὡς identifies the clause as a dependent conjunctive clause: *"as* he is in the light" (ὡς αὐτός ἐστιν ἐν τῷ φωτί; KJV ASV etc.). The entire ὡς clause functions adverbially modifying the verb "we walk" (περιπατῶμεν). **Semantically,** ὡς is a comparative marker for the believer whose character is to evidence moral purity, which is in keeping with God's moral character (cf. 1:5).

ἐστιν: The Greek word ἐστιν is third singular present active indicative from the verb εἰμί that means, "is" or with reference to a condition or circumstance (BDAG 284.3c). **Syntactically,** ἐστιν serves as the main verb of the dependent adverbial clause. The subject of the verb is the emphatic personal pronoun "he" (αὐτός). **Semantically,** ἐστιν serves as an equative verb of identity: "is" (cf. KJV NASB ESV NIV NET etc.). The statement parallels the earlier claim that "God is light," referring to his ethical purity and love for others (Culy 2004, 16).

1:7c ἔχομεν: The Greek word ἔχομεν is a first plural present active indicative from the verb ἔχω that means, "I have" or to stand in a close relationship with someone (BDAG 420.2b). **Syntactically,** ἔχομεν serves as the main verb of the independent clause "we have fellowship with one another" (κοινωνίαν ἔχομεν μετ᾽ ἀλλήλων). The assumed subject, "we," refers to the hypothetical person who walks in moral purity. **Semantically,** ἔχομεν is a gnomic present: "we have" (cf. KJV NASB ESV NIV NET etc.). It underscores a generic statement that is true at all times (Wallace 1996, 523). John speaks of any believer who makes it a point to live a moral life has fellowship with other believers.

1:7d καί: The Greek word καί is a conjunction that means "and" (BDAG 494.1). **Syntactically,** καί introduces a conjunctive independent clause (cf. KJV ASV etc.). **Semantically,** καί is coordinating connective: "and" (cf. KJV NASB ESV NIV NET etc.). It serves to add some addtional thoughts about about fellowship with other believers (Wallace 1996, 671) evident in the next verb.

καθαρίζει: The Greek word καθαρίζει is a third singular present active indicative from the verb καθαρίζω that means, "I make clean" or "I declare clean" or "to purify through ritual cleansing" (BDAG 489.3bα). **Syntactically,** καθαρίζει is the governing verb of the independent καί clause: "and the blood of Jesus, his son, *cleanses us* from all sins" (καὶ τὸ αἷμα Ἰησοῦ τοῦ υἱοῦ αὐτοῦ καθαρίζει ἡμᾶς ἀπὸ πάσης ἁμαρτίας). The subject is "the blood" (τὸ αἷμα). **Semantically,** καθαρίζει is a gnomic present: "cleanses us" (KJV ASV NASB NRSV ESV NET NLT CNT). It underscores a generic statement that is true at all times (Wallace 1996, 523). John makes it clear that any believer who makes it a point to live a moral life is purified from sin.

1:8a ἐάν: The Greek word ἐάν is a conjunction, which means "if" (BDAG 267.1αβ). **Syntactically,** ἐάν introduces a dependent conjunctive clause. The entire dependent clause: *"if* we say, 'we have no sin'" (ἐὰν εἴπωμεν ὅτι ἁμαρτίαν οὐκ ἔχομεν,), functions adverbially. It modifies two verbs, "deceive" (πλανῶμεν) and "is not" (οὐκ ἔστιν). **Semantically,** ἐάν introduces a third class conditional clause: "if" (cf. KJV NASB ESV NIV NET etc.). It offers a hypothetical situation of probability (Wallace 1996, 696). The activity of ἐάν is expressed in the next verb.

εἴπωμεν: The Greek word εἴπωμεν is a first plural aorist active subjunctive from the verb λέγω that means, "I speak" or "I say" (BDAG 588.1). The verb is in the subjunctive mood, because it follows ἐάν. **Syntactically,** εἴπωμεν serves as the main verb of the adverbial dependent clause. The assumed subject, "we" refers to a hypothetical person who claims to have no sin in their life. **Semantically,** εἴπωμεν is a constative aorist: "we say" (KJV ASV NASB NRSV ESV NET CNT) with two exceptions (NIV NLT). It describes an event as a whole (Wallace 1996, 557). John speaks of a hypothetical situation whereby a person makes a claim. The specifics of that claim are evident in the ὅτι clause.

ὅτι: The Greek word ὅτι is a conjunction, which means "that" or "for" or as a marker left untranslated (BDAG 732.3). **Syntactically,** ὅτι serves to introduce a dependent conjunctive clause: "*that* we have no sin" (ὅτι ἁμαρτίαν οὐκ ἔχομεν). This clause functions substantivally as the direct object of the verb "say" (εἴπωμεν). The clause is placed in parenthesis in order to visualize its contribution to the independent clause. **Semantically,** ὅτι is direct discourse whereby it is not translated (ESV NET NIV CNT NLT), but rather quotation marks are used to underscore the claim (Wallace 1996, 454). It highlights the hypothetical statement of a person, which is made clear in the rest of the clause.

ἔχομεν: The Greek word ἔχομεν is a first plural present active indicative from the verb ἔχω that means, "I have" or "to have an opinion about something" (BDAG 421.6). **Syntactically,** ἔχομεν is the governing verb of the dependent conjunctive ὅτι clause. The assumed subject, "we," refers to the hypothetical believer who claims to have no sin. **Semantically,** ἔχομεν is a gnomic present: "we have" (cf. KJV NASB ESV NIV NET etc.). It underscores a generic statement that is true at all times (Wallace 1996, 523). John speaks of any person who boasts: "I don't sin." What John thinks about such a person is clarified with the next verb.

1:8b πλανῶμεν: The Greek word πλανῶμεν is a first plural present active indicative from the verb πλανάω that means, "I deceive" or "I lie" or to stray from a specific way (BDAG 821.1b). **Syntactically,** πλανῶμεν is the governing verb of the independent clause. The assumed subject, "we," refers to the hypothetical believer who claims to have no sin. **Semantically,** πλανῶμεν is a gnomic present: "we deceive" (KJV ASV NRSV ESV NIV CNT). It underscores a generic statement that is true at all times (Wallace 1996, 523). John makes it clear that any person who claims to be without sin is deceived.

1:8c καί: The Greek word καί is a conjunction which means "and" (BDAG 494.1b). **Syntactically,** καί introduces a conjunctive independent clause, "*and* the truth is not in us" (καὶ ἡ ἀλήθεια οὐκ ἔστιν ἐν ἡμῖν). **Semantically,** καί is connective (cf. KJV ASV etc.) and shows that the believer who claims to not have any sin is a liar and does not speak the truth. They have no connection with truth.

ἔστιν: The Greek word ἔστιν is third singular present active indicative from the verb εἰμί that means, "is" or to have a special connection with someone or something (BDAG 283.2b). **Syntactically,** ἔστιν is the main verb of the independent clause. The subject of the verb is "the truth" (ἡ ἀλήθεια). **Semantically,** ἔστιν is a gnomic present: "is" (cf. KJV NASB ESV NIV NET etc). It underscores a generic statement that is true at all times (Wallace 1996, 523). Anyone who claims to be without sin, does not know the truth about themselves.

1:9a ἐάν: The Greek word ἐάν is a conjunction, which means "if" (BDAG 267.1aα). **Syntactically,** ἐάν introduces a dependent conjunctive clause. The entire dependent clause, "*if* we confess our sins" (ἐὰν ὁμολογῶμεν τὰς ἁμαρτίας ἡμῶν), functions adverbially, It modifies the verb, "is" (ἔστιν). **Semantically,** ἐάν introduces a third class conditional clause: "if" (cf. KJV NASB ESV NIV NET etc.). It provides a fourth hypothetical situation (Wallace 1996, 698). The activity of ἐάν is expressed in the next verb.

[ἀλλά]: The Greek word ἀλλά is a conjunction that means "but" (BDAG 44.2). **Syntactically,** [ἀλλά] is elliptical and serves to introduce a conditional thought, "[but] if we confess our sins, he is faithful and righteous to pardon our sins and to declare us purified from all unrighteousness" (ἐὰν ὁμολογῶμεν τὰς ἁμαρτίας ἡμῶν). **Semantically**, [ἀλλά] is contrastive: "but" (NET NLT). It provides a counter claim to the opponents who were claiming that they had not sinned (Wallace 1996, 671). It contrast a person who claims to be of without sin with one who does not.

Stylistic and Theological Nugget: This elliptical ἀλλά is an example of a figure of speech called an anacolution which is the omission of a word. The conjunction is omitted, but a clear contrast is evident from the context (cf. NET NLT). Confession, not denial of sin, is a hallmark of the genuine believer's heart. This focus on wrestling with sin and repentance is a theme that often appears in second temple literature (Daniel 9:20; Prayer of Manasseh; community confessions: Prayer of Azariah; Mark 1:5; James 5:16.

ὁμολογῶμεν: The Greek word ὁμολογῶμεν is a first plural present active subjunctive from the verb ὁμολογέω that means, "I confess" or "I admit" with a focus on an admission of wrong doing (BDAG 708.3c). The verb is in the subjunctive mood, because it follows ἐάν. **Syntactically**, ὁμολογῶμεν is the governing verb of the adverbial dependent ἐὰν clause. The assumed subject, "we" refers to any believer who chooses to confess their sin. **Semantically**, ὁμολογῶμεν is a gnomic present: "we confess" (KJV NASB ESV NIV NET etc.). It underscores a generic statement that is true at all times (Wallace 1996, 523). It seems to be focusing on verbally conceding that a sin has taken place (Culy 2004, 18). John underscores a timeless truth about the person who confesses their sin evident in the next clause.

¹:⁹ᵇ ἐστιν: The Greek word ἐστιν is third singular present active indicative from the verb εἰμί that means, "is" or "to be in close connection with" (BDAG 283.2a). **Syntactically**, ἐστίν is the governing verb of the independent clause: "He *is* faithful and righteous," (πιστός ἐστιν καὶ δίκαιος). The subject of the verb is an implied "he" referring to God who has the prerogative to forgive sins. **Semantically**, ἐστὶν is a gnomic present: "is" (cf. KJV NASB ESV NIV NET etc.). It underscores a generic statement that is true at all times (Wallace 1996, 523). God, by his very nature, is faithful and righteous. Yet that timeless truth about God impacts the person who confesses their sin, which is clearly stated in the next ἵνα clause.

¹:⁹ᶜ ἵνα: The Greek word ἵνα is a conjunction, which means "that" or is weakened altogether and disappears altogether (BDAG 476.2c). **Syntactically**, ἵνα introduce a dependent conjunctive clause, "*to* forgive us our sins and to declare us purified from all unrighteousness" (ἵνα ἀφῇ ἡμῖν τὰς ἁμαρτίας καὶ καθαρίσῃ ἡμᾶς ἀπὸ πάσης ἀδικίας), functions adverbially. It modifies the verb "is" (ἐστιν). **Semantically**, ἵνα introduces a compound result clause: "*resulting in* forgiveness and cleansing" (cf. Wallace 1996, 473). While some translations seem to reflect *result* with "*will* forgive" (NRSV NIV CNT cf. NET) our translation follows (KJV ASV NASB ESV NLT). Regardless of how it is translated, God's faithfulness and justice has results for those who confess their sins: they will be forgiven because of Jesus's death (cp. Culy 2004, 19). This conjunction underscores a conclusion about the nature of God. It is a grounds-conclusion construction.

ἀφῇ: The Greek word ἀφῇ is a third singular aorist active subjunctive from the verb ἀφίημι that means, "I cancel" or "I pardon" in that a person is released from a legal or moral obligation (BDAG 156.2). The verb is in the subjunctive mood, because it follows ἵνα. **Syntactically**, ἀφῇ is the governing verb of the dependent ἵνα clause. The assumed subject, "he" refers to our faithful and just God. **Semantically**, ἀφῇ is a gnomic aorist: "to forgive" (KJV ASV NASB ESV NLT). It presents a timeless fact about God (Wallace 1996, 562). John makes it clear that God "pardons" all those who admit wrongdoing.

1:9d καί: The Greek word καί is a conjunction which means "and" (BDAG 494.1bα). **Syntactically**, καί introduces the second part of the compound dependent clause "and cleanses us from all unrighteousness" (καὶ καθαρίσῃ ἡμᾶς ἀπὸ πάσης ἀδικίας). **Semantically**, καί is a coordinating connective that joins two dependent clauses (cf. KJV ASV etc.). John adds a further thought about the forgiveness of God.

καθαρίσῃ: The Greek word καθαρίσῃ is a third singular aorist active subjunctive from the verb καθαρίζω that means, "I make clean" or "I declare clean" as though through a ritual cleansing (BDAG 488.3b). The verb is in the subjunctive mood, because it follows ἵνα. **Syntactically**, καθαρίσῃ is the second governing verb of the compound adverbial dependent ἵνα clause. This verb is in also in the subjunctive mood because it follows a ἵνα. The assumed subject, "he" refers to our faithful and just God. **Semantically**, καθαρίσῃ is a gnomic aorist: "to declare purified" or "cleanse" (KJV ASV NASB NRSV ESV CNT NLT). It presents timeless fact about God (Wallace 1996, 562). John makes it clear that God declares all those who admit wrongdoing as pure.

1:10a ἐάν: The Greek word ἐάν is a conjunction that means "if" (BDAG 267.1aβ). **Syntactically**, ἐάν identifies the clause as a dependent conjunctive clause. The entire dependent clause, "*if* we say, 'we have not sinned'" (ἐὰν εἴπωμεν ὅτι οὐχ ἡμαρτήκαμεν), functions adverbially. It modifies the verbs "make" (ποιοῦμεν) and "is" (ἔστιν). **Semantically**, ἐάν introduces a third class conditional clause: "if" (cf. KJV NASB ESV NIV NET etc.). It provides a fourth hypothetical situation (Wallace 1996, 698). The activity of ἐάν is expressed in the next verb.

εἴπωμεν: The Greek word εἴπωμεν is a first plural aorist active subjunctive from the verb λέγω that means, "I speak" or "I say" or "to express oneself orally (BDAG 588.1). This verb is in the subjunctive because it follows an ἐάν. **Syntactically**, εἴπωμεν is the governing verb of the adverbial dependent ἐάν clause. The assumed subject, "we" refers to a hypothetical believer that makes the claim that they have never sinned. **Semantically**, εἴπωμεν is a constative aorist: "we say" (KJV ASV NASB NRSV ESV NET CNT) with two exceptions (NIV NLT). It describes an event as a whole (Wallace 1996, 557). John speaks of a hypothetical situation whereby a person makes a claim. The specifics of that claim are evident in the ὅτι clause.

ὅτι: The Greek word ὅτι is a conjunction which generally means "that" or "for" but here in is a mere marker left untranslated (BDAG 732.3). **Syntactically**, ὅτι serves to introduce a dependent conjunctive clause "that we have not sinned" (ὅτι οὐχ ἡμαρτήκαμεν). This clause is functioning substantivally as the direct object of the verb "say" (εἴπωμεν). The clause is placed in parenthesis in order to visualize its contribution to the independent clause. **Semantically**, ὅτι is direct discourse whereby it is not translated (ESV NET NIV NLT), but rather quotation marks are used to underscore the claim (Wallace 1996, 454) It highlights the hypothetical statement of a person, which is made clear in the rest of the clause.

ἡμαρτήκαμεν: The Greek word ἡμαρτήκαμεν is a first plural perfect active indicative from the verb ἁμαρτάνω that means, "I sin" or "I commit a wrong doing" (BDAG 49). **Syntactically**, ἡμαρτήκαμεν serves as the governing verb of the substantival ὅτι clause. It is the direct object of the verb, "we say" (εἴπωμεν). The subject of the verb is an implied "we" and refers to the person who claims to have no sin. **Semantically**, ἡμαρτήκαμεν is a gnomic perfect with an extensive force: "we have no sin" (KJV NASB ESV NIV NET etc.). It reveals a general truth with the focus on the decisive act of verb (Wallace 1996, 580).). John speaks of any person who boasts: "I have no sin." This claim goes further than the one in verse 8. Here it suggests that those who are in Jesus do not sin at all.

^{10b} ποιοῦμεν: The Greek word ποιοῦμεν is a first plural present active indicative from the verb ποιέω that means, "I make" or "I cause" or "I bring about" with a focus on causality (BDAG 840.2h). **Syntactically,** ποιοῦμεν is the main verb of the independent clause: "we make him a liar" (ψεύστην ποιοῦμεν αὐτὸν). The assumed subject, "we," refers any person who claims to have not sinned. "Him" refers to God: "we make God out to be a liar." **Semantically,** ποιοῦμεν is a gnomic present: "we make" (cf. KJV NASB ESV NIV NET etc.). It underscores a generic statement that is true at all times (Wallace 1996, 523). John makes it clear that any person who claims to be sinless makes God out to be a liar.

^{1:10c} καί: The Greek word καί is a conjunction which means "and" (BDAG 494.1b). **Syntactically,** καί introduces a conjunctive independent clause. **Semantically,** καί is a coordinating conjunction: "and" (cf. KJV NASB ESV NIV NET etc.). It joins two independent clauses together (Wallace 1996, 671). So not only is the person a liar, he or she is also without God.

ἔστιν: The Greek word ἔστιν is third singular present active indicative from the verb εἰμί that means, "is" or "to be in close connection with" (BDAG 283.2a). **Syntactically,** ἔστιν serves as the main verb of the independent clause, "and his word is not in him" (καὶ ὁ λόγος αὐτοῦ οὐκ ἔστιν ἐν ἡμῖν). The subject of the verb is "his word" (ὁ λόγος αὐτοῦ). **Semantically,** ἔστιν is a gnomic present: "is" (cf. KJV NASB ESV NIV NET etc.). It presents a timeless fact (Wallace 1996, 562). John makes it clear that any person, who claims to be sinless, has no relationship with God.

^{2:1a} γράφω: The Greek word γράφω is a first singular present active indicative from the verb γράφω that means, "I write" or "I compose" with reference to composing a letter (BDAG, 207 2d). **Syntactically,** γράφω serves as the main verb of the independent clause "my children, I *now* write these things to you" (Τεκνία μου, ταῦτα γράφω ὑμῖν). The assumed subject, "I," refers to John. **Semantically,** γράφω is a progressive present: "I *right now* write" or "I am writing" (NASB NRSV ESV NET NLT). It reveals an event occurring *right now* (Wallace 1996, 518). John gives emphasis to his current writing of the letter.

^{2:1b} ἵνα: The Greek word ἵνα is a conjunction, which means "that" or "in order that" or to denote a purpose or goal (BDAG 475.1aα). **Syntactically,** ἵνα introduces a dependent conjunctive clause: "*in order that you may* not sin" (ἵνα μὴ ἁμάρτητε). This clause is functioning adverbially, modifying the verb "I am writing" (γράφω). **Semantically,** ἵνα introduces a purpose clause: "in order that" or "that" (KJV). Many translations, however, appear to render ἵνα as result (NASB NRSV ESV NIV NET NLT CNT). It indicates intention (cf. Wallace 1996, 472). John's intention is evident in the next verb.

ἁμάρτητε: The Greek word ἀπολέσητε is a second plural aorist active subjunctive from the verb ἁμαρτάνω that means, "I sin" or "I 'transgress' against divinity," or "to commit a wrong" (BDAG 49.a). It is in the subjunctive because it follows a ἵνα. **Syntactically,** ἀπολέσητε is the governing verb of the adverbial dependent ἵνα clause. The assumed subject, "you" refers to the community to whom John is writing. **Semantically,** ἀπολέσητε is a constative aorist: "may not sin" (ASV NASB NRSV ESV NET CNT). It describes sinning as an event as a whole (Wallace 1996, 557). John does not want his readers to sin period. This clause, just like the ἐάν clauses from chapter one, serves as a mitigated command. John gently commands the readers not to sin.

^{2:1c} καί: The Greek word καί is a conjunction which means "and" or "but" (BDAG 496.2c). **Syntactically,** καί introduces the dependent conjunction clause: "*but* if anyone does sin" (καὶ ἐάν τις ἁμάρτῃ). The entire dependent clause is adverbial modifying "we have" (ἔχομεν). **Semantically,** καί is contrastive: "but" (NRSV ESV NIV NET CNT NLT). John denotes a contrast to the previous ἵνα clause

ἐάν: The Greek word ἐάν is a conjunction, which means "if" (BDAG 267.1αβ). **Syntactically**, the conjunction ἐάν identifies the clause as a dependent clause. The entire dependent clause, "if anyone does sin (ἐάν τις ἁμάρτῃ) is functioning adverbially. It modifies the verb, "we have" (ἔχομεν). **Semantically**, ἐάν introduces a third class conditional clause of probability: "if" (cf. KJV NASB ESV NIV NET etc). The condition is uncertain of fulfillment but still likely (Wallace 1996, 696). The uncertain condition is expressed in the next verb.

ἁμάρτῃ: The Greek word ἁμάρτῃ is a third singular aorist active subjunctive from the verb ἁμαρτάνω that means, "I sin" or "I 'transgress' against divinity," or "to commit a wrong" (BDAG 49.a). **Syntactically**, ἁμάρτῃ serves as the governing verb of the dependent adverbial clause. The verb is in the subjunctive because ἐάν takes the subjunctive. The subject of the verb is the pronoun τις and refers to any believer who might fall into sin. The generic understanding of any person. **Semantically**, ἁμάρτῃ is a gnomic aorist: "sin" (cf. KJV NASB ESV NIV NET etc). It speaks of a timeless truth with no specifics (Wallace 1996, 562). John underscores a generic event that happens in every believer's life, they sin. But John does not leave the reader hanging. The resolution is found in the next clause.

2:1d ἔχομεν: The Greek word ἔχομεν is a first plural present active indicative from the verb ἔχω that means, "I have" or "to have something at one's disposal" (BDAG 420.1c). **Syntactically**, ἔχομεν is the main verb of the independent clause: "*we have* an advocate with the Father, Jesus, the Christ, the righteous one" (παράκλητον ἔχομεν πρὸς τὸν πατέρα, Ἰησοῦν Χριστὸν δίκαιον). The assumed subject, "we," refers to John, his associates, and his readers. They have at their disposal an advocate. This advocate is Jesus who is with "the" (τόν) Father. The article is an article of *par excellence* (Wallace 1996, 223). **Semantically**, ἔχομεν is a gnomic present: "we have" (cf. KJV NASB ESV NIV NET etc.). It underscores a generic statement that is true at all times (Wallace 1996, 523). John speaks of any believer who sins. They have an advocate who intercedes for them. His name is Jesus who is both the Messiah and the one who is right with God.

2:2a καί: The Greek word καί is a conjunction which means "and" (BDAG 494.1b). **Syntactically**, καί introduces a conjunctive independent clause: "and he himself is the atoning sacrifice for our sins" (καὶ αὐτὸς ἱλασμός ἐστιν περὶ τῶν ἁμαρτιῶν ἡμῶν). **Semantically**, καί is coordinating connective: "and" (KJV ASV NASB NRSV NET CNT). It adds further information about the person and work of Jesus on behalf of the believer. That additional information is found in the rest of the clause.

ἐστιν: The Greek word ἐστιν is third singular present active indicative from the verb εἰμί that means, "is" or "to be in close connection with" (BDAG 283.2a). **Syntactically**, ἐστιν serves as the main verb of the independent clause. The subject of the verb is the emphatic pronoun "he" (αὐτὸς). **Semantically**, ἐστιν is an equative present: "is" (cf. KJV NASB ESV NIV NET etc.). It underscores a generic statement that is true at all times (Wallace 1996, 523). John speaks of any believer who sins. They have an advocate who intercedes for them because of his atoning sacrifice (Culy 2004, 23).

δέ: The Greek word δέ is a conjunction that means "but" or "rather" (BDAG 44.1a). **Syntactically**, δέ introduces an independent clause with an ellipsis: "and (he is the atoning sacrifice) not only for our sins" ([ἱλασμός ἐστιν] οὐ περὶ τῶν ἡμετέρων δὲ μόνον). **Semantically**, δέ is loosely connective and gives us some more information about the atoning work of Jesus. His sacrifice was not only for believers.

2:2c ἀλλὰ καί: The Greek word ἀλλά is a conjunction that means "but" (BDAG 45.2). The Greek word καί is an conjunction, which means "also" (BDAG 495.1f). **Syntactically**, ἀλλὰ καὶ introduces a independent conjunctive clause with an ellipsis, "*but also* (he is the atoning sacrifice) for the whole world" (ἀλλὰ [ἰλασμός ἐστιν] καὶ περὶ ὅλου τοῦ κόσμου). **Semantically**, ἀλλὰ καὶ is coordinating contrastive with an adjunctive conjunction: "but also" (cf. KJV NASB ESV NIV NET etc.). Contrary (ἀλλά) to believing that Jesus is the atoning sacrifice for the sins of only believers, he is also (καί) for the atoning sacrifice the sins of the entire world.

1 John 2:3–11

Verb Recognition for 1 John 2:3–11

³Καὶ ἐν τούτῳ γινώσκομεν ὅτι ἐγνώκαμεν αὐτόν, ἐὰν τὰς ἐντολὰς αὐτοῦ τηρῶμεν. ⁴ὁ λέγων ὅτι Ἔγνωκα αὐτόν, καὶ τὰς ἐντολὰς αὐτοῦ μὴ τηρῶν, ψεύστης ἐστίν, καὶ ἐν τούτῳ ἡ ἀλήθεια οὐκ ἔστιν· ⁵ὃς δ' ἂν τηρῇ αὐτοῦ τὸν λόγον, ἀληθῶς ἐν τούτῳ ἡ ἀγάπη τοῦ θεοῦ τετελείωται. ἐν τούτῳ γινώσκομεν ὅτι ἐν αὐτῷ ἐσμεν· ⁶ὁ λέγων ἐν αὐτῷ μένειν ὀφείλει καθὼς ἐκεῖνος περιεπάτησεν καὶ αὐτὸς περιπατεῖν.

⁷Ἀγαπητοί, οὐκ ἐντολὴν καινὴν γράφω ὑμῖν, ἀλλ' ἐντολὴν παλαιὰν ἣν εἴχετε ἀπ' ἀρχῆς· ἡ ἐντολὴ ἡ παλαιά ἐστιν ὁ λόγος ὃν ἠκούσατε. ⁸πάλιν ἐντολὴν καινὴν γράφω ὑμῖν, ὅ ἐστιν ἀληθὲς ἐν αὐτῷ καὶ ἐν ὑμῖν, ὅτι ἡ σκοτία παράγεται καὶ τὸ φῶς τὸ ἀληθινὸν ἤδη φαίνει. ⁹ὁ λέγων ἐν τῷ φωτὶ εἶναι καὶ τὸν ἀδελφὸν αὐτοῦ μισῶν ἐν τῇ σκοτίᾳ ἐστὶν ἕως ἄρτι. ¹⁰ὁ ἀγαπῶν τὸν ἀδελφὸν αὐτοῦ ἐν τῷ φωτὶ μένει, καὶ σκάνδαλον ἐν αὐτῷ οὐκ ἔστιν· ¹¹ὁ δὲ μισῶν τὸν ἀδελφὸν αὐτοῦ ἐν τῇ σκοτίᾳ ἐστὶν καὶ ἐν τῇ σκοτίᾳ περιπατεῖ, καὶ οὐκ οἶδεν ποῦ ὑπάγει, ὅτι ἡ σκοτία ἐτύφλωσεν τοὺς ὀφθαλμοὺς αὐτοῦ.

Clausal Outline Translated for 1 John 2:3–11

²:³ᵃ **Καὶ** ἐν τούτῳ **γινώσκομεν** (ὅτι **ἐγνώκαμεν** αὐτόν),
²:³ᵃ *Now* by this **we know** (that *we have known* him),

> ²:³ᵇ **ἐὰν** τὰς ἐντολὰς αὐτοῦ **τηρῶμεν.**
> ²:³ᵇ **If we** *persist in* **keeping** his commandments.

²:⁴ᵃ ὁ λέγων (ὅτι Ἔγνωκα αὐτόν), καὶ τὰς ἐντολὰς αὐτοῦ μὴ τηρῶν, ψεύστης ἐστίν,
²:⁴ᵃ The one who says ("I know him"), but who does not *persist in* keeping his commands, **is** a liar,

²:⁴ᵇ καὶ ἐν τούτῳ ἡ ἀλήθεια οὐκ ἔστιν·
²:⁴ᵇ and the truth **is** not in this person

²:⁵ᵃ ὃς δ' ἂν <u>τηρῇ</u> αὐτοῦ τὸν λόγον,
²:⁵ᵃ **But whoever *persists in* keeping** his word,

²:⁵ᵇ ἀληθῶς ἐν τούτῳ ἡ ἀγάπη τοῦ θεοῦ <u>τετελείωται</u>.
²:⁵ᵇ truly, in this person, our love for God **has been perfected**.

²:⁵ᶜ ἐν τούτῳ <u>γινώσκομεν</u> (ὅτι ἐν αὐτῷ <u>ἐσμεν</u>)·
²:⁵ᶜ By this, <u>**we know**</u> (<u>that</u> <u>we are</u> in him);

²:⁶ᵃ ὁ λέγων ἐν αὐτῷ μένειν <u>ὀφείλει</u> . . . καὶ αὐτὸς <u>περιπατεῖν</u>.
²:⁶ᵃ The one who says that he abides in him **must** . . . also himself *persist in* **living**.

²:⁶ᵇ <u>καθὼς</u> ἐκεῖνος <u>περιεπάτησεν</u>
²:⁶ᵇ <u>**just as**</u> that one [= Jesus] <u>**lived**</u>.

²:⁷ᵃ Ἀγαπητοί, οὐκ ἐντολὴν καινὴν <u>γράφω</u> ὑμῖν,
²:⁷ᵃ Beloved, **I write** no new command to you,

²:⁷ᵇ <u>ἀλλ'</u> ἐντολὴν παλαιὰν [*γράφω*]
²:⁷ᵇ <u>**but**</u> [*I now write*] an old command

²:⁷ᶜ <u>ἣν</u> <u>εἴχετε</u> ἀπ' ἀρχῆς·
²:⁷ᶜ <u>**which**</u> <u>**you have had**</u> *as an obligation* from the beginning;

²:⁷ᵈ ἡ ἐντολὴ ἡ παλαιά <u>ἐστιν</u> ὁ λόγος
²:⁷ᵈ The old command **is** the word

²:⁷ᵉ <u>ὃν</u> <u>ἠκούσατε</u>.
²:⁷ᵉ <u>**which**</u> <u>**you have heard**</u>.

²:⁸ᵇ <u>ὅ</u> <u>ἐστιν</u> ἀληθὲς ἐν αὐτῷ καὶ ἐν ὑμῖν,
²:⁸ᵇ <u>**which**</u> <u>**is**</u> true in him [Jesus] and in you.

²:⁸ᵃ <u>πάλιν</u> ἐντολὴν καινὴν <u>γράφω</u> ὑμῖν,
²:⁸ᵃ <u>On the other hand</u>, <u>**I *now* write**</u> to you a new command,

²:⁸ᶜ <u>ὅτι</u> ἡ σκοτία <u>παράγεται</u>
²:⁸ᶜ <u>**because**</u> the darkness **is passing away** *right now*

²:⁸ᵈ <u>καὶ [ὅτι]</u> τὸ φῶς τὸ ἀληθινὸν ἤδη <u>φαίνει</u>.
²:⁸ᵈ <u>and [*because*]</u> true light **is *already* shining**.

²:⁹ ὁ λέγων ἐν τῷ φωτὶ εἶναι καὶ τὸν ἀδελφὸν αὐτοῦ μισῶν ἐν τῇ σκοτίᾳ <u>ἐστὶν</u> ἕως ἄρτι.
²:⁹ The one who claims to be in the light and yet *persists* in hating his brother *and sister* **is** still in the darkness until now.

²:¹⁰ᵃ ὁ ἀγαπῶν τὸν ἀδελφὸν αὐτοῦ ἐν τῷ φωτὶ **μένει**,
²:¹⁰ᵃ [*In contrast to*] the one who *persists* in loving his brother *and sister* **abides** in the light,

²:¹⁰ᵇ καὶ σκάνδαλον ἐν αὐτῷ οὐκ **ἔστιν·**
²:¹⁰ᵇ and in that person [him], **there is** no cause for stumbling.

²:¹¹ᵃ ὁ δὲ μισῶν τὸν ἀδελφὸν αὐτοῦ ἐν τῇ σκοτίᾳ **ἐστὶν**
²:¹¹ᵃ **But** the one who *persists* in hating his brother *and sister* **is** in the darkness

²:¹¹ᵇ καὶ ἐν τῇ σκοτίᾳ **περιπατεῖ**
²:¹¹ᵇ and *so* **he** *is* **walking** in the darkness

²:¹¹ᶜ καὶ οὐκ **οἶδεν** ποῦ ὑπάγει,
²:¹¹ᶜ and **he does** not **know** where he is going,

²:¹¹ᵈ ὅτι ἡ σκοτία **ἐτύφλωσεν** τοὺς ὀφθαλμοὺς αὐτοῦ.
²:¹¹ᵈ **because** the darkness **has blinded** his eyes.

Syntax Explained for 1 John 2:3–11

²:³ᵃ Καί: The Greek word καί is a conjunction which can mean "and" or "now" in this context (BDAG, 495). **Syntactically**, καί introduces an independent conjunctive clause, "*Now* by this we know that we have we have known him," (καὶ ἐν τούτῳ γινώσκομεν ὅτι ἐγνώκαμεν αὐτόν). **Semantically**, καί can either be a simple connective or transitional. If this καί ("and") is a simple connective it would add an additional thought to the discussion on the nature of sin (KJV ASV ESV NLT; Culy 2004, 24). It seems more likely though that this καί is transitional (NRSV NET). John moves the discussion from God being light (1:5) and his three claims (1:6, 8, 10) and counter-claims (1:7, 9; 2:1). John now addresses how to know believers have fellowship with God.

ἐν τούτῳ: The Greek word ἐν is a preposition that means "by" (BDAG 328.5b). The Greek word τούτῳ is declined as a dative singular neuter from the demonstrative pronoun τοῦτο, which means "this one" (BDAG 741.1bβ). **Syntactically**, ἐν τούτῳ is a prepositional phrase that is part of an independent conjunctive clause, unlike other occurrences in 1 John (2:4, 5 [twice], 3:10, 16, 19, 24; 4:2, 9, 10, 13, 17; 5:2). **Semantically**, ἐν τούτῳ expresses means: "by this" (NASB ESV NET CNT). The clause can either be anaphoric, pointing back to the preceding discussion, or cataphoric, pointing forward. Usually the prepositional phrase is cataphoric, if it is followed by a subordinating conjunction that is epexegetical to the demonstrative, "this" (τούτῳ; cf. Brown 1982, 217). In this case, the clause is cataphoric and explained in the subsequent ἐάν clause.

γινώσκομεν: The Greek word γινώσκομεν is a first plural present active indicative from the verb γινώσκω that means, "I know" or "I know about" or "I arrive at a knowledge of someone" (BDAG 200.1c). **Syntactically**, γινώσκομεν is the main verb of the conjunctive independent clause. The subject of the verb is an implied "we" and refers to anyone who desires to have a relationship with God. **Semantically**, γινώσκομεν is a gnomic present: "we know" (ASV NASB ESV NET CNT NLT). It identifies something that is true at any time (Wallace 1996, 523). The content of what John's readers know is found in the next ὅτι clause.

ὅτι: The Greek word ὅτι is a conjunction, which means "that" or to identify content after a verb of mental perception (BDAG 731.1c). **Syntactically,** ὅτι introduces a substantival dependent conjunctive clause: "*that* we have known him" (ὅτι ἐγνώκαμεν αὐτόν). The entire ὅτι clause functions as the direct object of the verb: "we know" (γινώσκομεν). The clause is placed in parenthesis in order to visualize its contribution to the independent clause. **Semantically,** ὅτι is an indirect discourse: "that" (cf. KJV NASB ESV NIV NET etc.). The entire ὅτι clause provides the content of the verb "we know" (γινώσκομεν; Wallace 1996, 456). Yet the specifics of that knowledge are found in the next verb.

ἐγνώκαμεν: The Greek word ἐγνώκαμεν is a first plural perfect active indicative from the verb γινώσκω that means, "I know" or "I know about" or "I arrive at a knowledge of someone" (BDAG, 200 1c). **Syntactically,** ἐγνώκαμεν serves as the governing verb of the substantival dependent ὅτι clause. The subject of the verb is an implied "we" embedded in the verb and refers to anyone who desires to have a relationship with God. **Semantically,** ἐγνώκαμεν is a gnomic perfect with extensive force: "we have come to know" (NASB EVS NIV *contra* the intensive rendering "we know": KJV ASV NRSV NLT CNT). Its gnomic force provides something that is envisioned as true on many occasions while focusing on the completed action of the past (Wallace 1996, 580). John identifies a timeless truth for a believer's confidence concerning their relationship with God, which is clarified in the next ἐάν clause.

2:3b ἐάν: The Greek word ἐάν is a conjunction, which means "if" (BDAG 267.1aα). **Syntactically,** ἐάν identifies the clause as a dependent conjunctive clause. The entire dependent clause, "if we *persist in* keeping his commands" (ἐὰν τὰς ἐντολὰς αὐτοῦ τηρῶμεν), functions adjectivally (epexegetically). It modifies the demonstrative pronoun, "by this" (ἐν τούτῳ). **Semantically,** ἐάν introduces a third class conditional clause: "if" (cf. KJV NASB ESV NIV NET etc.). The condition is uncertain of fulfillment but still likely (Wallace 1996, 696). This clause also serves as another mitigated command. John politely urges those who believe to not abuse God's grace, but to seek to keep God's commands, especially the command to love others (Culy 2004, 25).

τηρῶμεν: The Greek word τηρῶμεν is a first plural present active subjunctive from the verb τηρέω that means, "I keep," "I observe," or "to persist in obedience" (BDAG 1002.3). It is a subjunctive because it follows an ἐάν. **Syntactically,** τηρῶμεν serves as the governing verb of the dependent ἐάν clause that provides the content of the demonstrative pronoun, "this" (τούτῳ). The assumed subject "we" refers to any believer who desires to have a relationship with God. **Semantically,** τηρῶμεν is a gnomic present with a customary present force: "we *persist in* keeping" or "we keep" (KJV ASV NASB ESV NIV NET CNT). It identifies something that is true at any time (Wallace 1996, 523). Followers of Jesus who obey God's commands (= of loving others) can be assured of their relationship with God.

2:4a λέγων: The Greek word λέγων is a nominative masculine singular present active participle from the verb λέγω, which means, "I maintain," "I declare," or "I proclaim as teaching" (BDAG 590.2e). **Syntactically,** λέγων is a substantival participle functioning as part of the compound subject of the compound verbs, "is" (ἐστίν) and "is" (ἐστίν). **Semantically,** λέγων is a gnomic present: "the one who says" (NASB NET) or "whoever says" (NRSV ESV). It introduces a generic person's statement that is true at any time (Wallace 1996, 615). John directs attention to people who make a claim, which is specified in the next ὅτι clause.

ὅτι: The Greek word ὅτι is a conjunction, which means "that" (BDAG 732.3). **Syntactically,** ὅτι serves to introduce a dependent substantival ὅτι clause "I know him" (ὅτι Ἔγνωκα αὐτόν) functions as the direct object of the substantival participle of speech, "saying" (λέγων). The entire clause is placed in parenthesis in order to visualize its contribution to the independent clause. **Semantically**, ὅτι is classified as direct discourse, giving us the content of a hypothetical claim and is typically not translated. Instead, quotation marks appear (cf. NASB NRSV ESV NIV NET NLT CNT). Any person who claims to have a relationship with God, yet does not keep his commands is a liar.

Ἔγνωκα: The Greek word ἔγνωκα is a first singular perfect active indicative from the verb γινώσκω that means, "I know," "I know about," or "I arrive at a knowledge of someone" (BDAG 200.1c). **Syntactically**, ἔγνωκα is the governing verb of a dependent ὅτι clause that functions as the direct object of the substantival participle of speech "saying" (λέγων). It serves as part of the compound subject of the compound verbs "is" (ἐστίν) and "is" (ἐστίν). The subject of the verb is an implied "I" embedded in the verb and refers to any hypoethical individual who claims to have a relationship with God. **Semantically**, ἔγνωκα is a gnomic perfect with extensive force: "we have come to know" (NASB NRSV NET). Its gnomic force provides something that is envisioned as true on many occasions while focusing on the completed action of the past (Wallace 1996, 580). John is providing a timeless truth about anyone who says they have a relationship with God. That relationship is defined in the next verbal.

τηρῶν: The Greek word τηρῶν is a nominative masculine singular present active participle from the verb τηρέω, which means, "I keep," "I observe," "I fulfill," "I pay attention to, esp. of law and teaching. The idea is "I persist in obedience" (BDAG 1002.3). **Syntactically**, τηρῶν is a substantival participle functioning as part of the compound subject of the compound verbs, "is" (ἐστίν) and "is" (ἐστίν). **Semantically**, τηρῶν is a gnomic present with a customary present force: "we *persist in* keeping" or "we keep" (NASB ESV NET CNT; cf. KJV ASV). It presents a generic statement to describe something that is true any time (Wallace 1996, 521, 615). So someone who claims to have a relationship with God, yet refuses to keep his commands is problematic. That problem is made clear with the next verb.

Grammatical Nugget: The participles "keeping" (τηρῶν) and "saying" (λέγων) are substantival. They share an article "the" (ὁ) and are connected by καί: "and" (KJV ASV NASB).

ὁ <u>λέγων</u> (ὅτι Ἔγνωκα αὐτόν), <u>καὶ</u> τὰς ἐντολὰς αὐτοῦ μὴ <u>τηρῶν</u>

According to the Granville Sharp Rule this means that these two substantives (λέγων and τηρῶν) should be read together with a high level of unity, having the same referrant. Some translations render καί as "yet" or "but" (NRSV ESV NIV NET CNT CNT), but the Granville Sharp Rule argues that this is not the case here. Instead, both participles should be taken substantivally and should retain a high level of unity (Wallace 1996, 275).

ἐστίν: The Greek word ἐστίν is third singular present active indicative from the verb εἰμί that means, "is" or "to be in close connection with" (BDAG 283.2a). **Syntactically**, ἐστίν serves as one of the main verbs of a compound independent clause. The subject of the verb is the compound participial clauses "the one who says that I know him and who does not *persist in* keeping his commands" (ὁ λέγων ὅτι Ἔγνωκα αὐτόν, καὶ τὰς ἐντολὰς αὐτοῦ μὴ τηρῶν). **Semantically**, ἐστίν is a gnomic present with equative force: "is" (cf. KJV NASB ESV NIV NET etc.). It underscores a generic statement that is true at all times (Wallace 1996, 523). Any person who claims to have a relationship with God yet refuses to keep God's commands is equated with being a liar.

2:4b καί: The Greek word καί is a conjunction which means "and" (BDAG 494.1b). **Syntactically,** καί introduces an independent conjunctive clause: "*and* the truth is not in this person" (καὶ ἐν τούτῳ ἡ ἀλήθεια οὐκ ἔστιν). **Semantically,** καί is coordinating connective: "and" (BDAG 494.1b). It adds to John's discussion about the person who claims to have a relationship with God. The prepositional phrase "in this *person*" (ἐν τούτῳ) is anaphoric pointing back to the hypothetical person who claims to have a relationship with God and yet refuses to keep his commands. The details about John's additional thought is found in the rest of the clause.

ἐστίν: The Greek word ἐστιν is third singular present active indicative from the verb εἰμί that means, "I am" or "I exist" (BDAG 282d.1). **Syntactically,** ἐστίν is one of the main verbs of a compound independent clause. The subject of the verb is the compound participial clauses: "the one who says that I know him and who does not *persist in* keeping his commands" (ὁ λέγων ὅτι Ἔγνωκα αὐτόν, καὶ τὰς ἐντολὰς αὐτοῦ μὴ τηρῶν). **Semantically,** ἐστίν is a gnomic present: "is" (cf. KJV NASB ESV NIV NET etc.). It underscores a generic statement that is true at all times (Wallace 1996, 523). A person who claims to have a relationship with God but does not follow his commands, that such a person does not possess the truth. For a similar construction refer back to 1 John 1:6, "we lie and do not practice the truth."

2:5a δ': The Greek word δέ is a conjunction, which means "but" and marks a contrast (BDAG 213.4a). **Syntactically,** δέ is in the post-positive position and introduces a dependent indefinite relative clause: "*But* whoever *persists in* keeping his words" (ὃς δ' ἂν τηρῇ αὐτοῦ τὸν λόγον). **Semantically,** δέ is contrastive: "but" (KJV NASB ESV NIV NET etc.). It counters false claims (Wallace 1996, 671). The one who knows God is the one who desires to keep his commands, especially the command to love other believers.

ὅς...ἂν: The Greek word ὅς is a nominative masculine singular from the relative pronoun ὅς which means, "who" (BDAG 727.1jα). The Greek particle ἂν is untranslateable and serves to make a definite relative clause indefinite (BAGD 57.1b; cf. Wallace 1996, 343). **Syntactically,** ὅς...ἂν introduces a dependent indefinite relative clause: "whoever" (NASB NRSV ESV NET NCT). It functions adjectivally modifying the demonstrative pronoun "this" (τούτῳ). It clarifies the demonstrative pronoun "this" (τούτῳ). For other instances of the indefinite relative clause in 1 John, see 3:17, 22; 4:15; 5:15; cf. 3 John 5.

τηρῇ: The Greek word τηρῇ is a third singular present active subjunctive from the verb τηρέω that means, "I keep," "I observe," "I fulfill," "I pay attention to, esp. of law and teaching. The idea is "I persist in obedience" (BDAG 1002.3). This verb is in the subjunctive mood because it follows an ἂν. **Syntactically,** τηρῇ is the governing verb of the dependent indefinite relative clause. The subject is the indefinite relative construction: "whoever." **Semantically,** τηρῇ is a gnomic present: "*persists* in keeping" or "keeps" (NASB ESV CNT; cf. KJV ASV). It introduces something that is true all the time (Wallace 1996, 523). The details of that timeless truth are revealed in the next clause.

2:5b τετελείωται: The Greek word τετελείωται is a third singular perfect passive indicative from the verb τελειόω that means, "I make perfect" or "I finish" (BDAG 996.2dβ). **Syntactically,** τετελείωται is the main verb of the independent clause: "truly in this person our love for God *is perfected*" (ἀληθῶς ἐν τούτῳ ἡ ἀγάπη τοῦ θεοῦ τετελείωται). The subject of the verb is "the love of God" (ἡ ἀγάπη τοῦ θεοῦ). **Semantically,** τετελείωται is is a gnomic perfect with extensive force: "has been perfected" (ASV NASB NET; cf. NRSV). Its gnomic force provides something that is envisioned as true on many occasions while focusing on the completed action of the past (Wallace 1996, 580). Wallace, however, considers τετελείωται as a futuristic perfect: "will be perfected" (Wallace 1996, 581). Regardless of the translation, when anyone keeps the word of God, their love for God is perfected.

²:⁵ᶜ ἐν τούτῳ : The Greek word ἐν is a preposition that means "by" (BDAG 328.5b). The Greek word τούτῳ is declined as a dative singular neuter from the demonstrative pronoun τοῦτο, which means "this one" (BDAG 741.1bβ). **Syntactically,** ἐν τούτῳ introduces an independent prepositional clause: "*by this* we know that we are in him" (ἐν τούτῳ γινώσκομεν ὅτι ἐν αὐτῷ ἐσμεν). The construction, "by this" (ἐν τούτῳ) is common in 1 John (2:3, 4, 5 [twice], 3:10, 16, 19, 24; 4:2, 9, 10, 13, 17; 5:2). **Semantically,** ἐν τούτῳ expresses means: "by this" (NASB ESV NET CNT). The clause can either be anaphoric, pointing back to the preceding discussion, or cataphoric, pointing forward. This one is anaphoric. It summarizes the author's rebuttal (Culy 2004, 29). The content of John's summary is evident in the next verb.

γινώσκομεν: The Greek word γινώσκομεν is a first plural present active indicative from the verb γινώσκω that means, "I know" or "I know about" or "I arrive at a knowledge of someone" (BDAG 200.1c). **Syntactically,** γινώσκομεν is the main verb of the independent prepositional clause: "by this *we know* that we are in him" (ἐν τούτῳ γινώσκομεν ὅτι ἐν αὐτῷ ἐσμεν). The assumed subject, "we," refers to any believer who keeps the word of God. **Semantically,** γινώσκομεν is a customary present: "we know" (ASV NASB NIV NET NLT CNT). It speaks of a pattern of behavior (Wallace 1996, 521). A believer who persists in obeying God's command can rest assured of something or knows something, which is made known in the next ὅτι clause.

ὅτι: The Greek word ὅτι is a conjunction, which means "that" (BDAG 731.1c). **Syntactically,** ὅτι introduces a dependent conjunctive clause: "*that* we are in him" (ὅτι ἐν αὐτῷ ἐσμεν). It functions substantivally as the direct object of the verb "we know" (γινώσκομεν). The clause is placed in parenthesis in order to visualize its contribution to the independent clause. **Semantically,** ὅτι is a indirect discourse: "that" (KJV ASV NASB ESV NET CNT). It reveals John's thoughts (Wallace 1996, 456). Those thoughts are evident in the rest of the clause.

ἐσμεν: The Greek word ἐσμεν is first plural present active indicative from the verb εἰμί that means, "be" or I exist in a close relationship with someone (BDAG 283.3b). **Syntactically,** ἐσμεν is the governing verb of the dependent substantival ὅτι clause. The clause functions as the direct object of the verb "we know" (γινώσκομεν). The subject of the verb is an implied "we" embedded in the verb and refers to any believer who desires to keep the words of God. **Semantically,** ἐσμεν is a gnomic present: "we are" (cf. KJV NASB ESV NIV NET etc.). It introduces something that is true all the time (Wallace 1996, 523). Followers of Jesus know they have a relationship with God, when they persist in keeping God's commands.

²:⁶ᵃ λέγων: The Greek word λέγων is a nominative masculine singular present active participle from the verb λέγω, which means, "I say," "I give expression to" or "to express oneself orally" (BDAG 588.1aγ). **Syntactically,** λέγων is a substantival participle that functions as the subject of the verb "ought" (ὀφείλει). **Semantically,** λέγων has a gnomic force: "the one who says" (NASB NET) or "whoever says" (NRSV ESV NIV). It presents a generic statement to describe something that is true any time (Wallace 1996, 523, 615). John directs attention to people who make a claim, which is specified in the next verb.

μένειν: The Greek word μένειν is a present active infinitive from the verb μένω that means, "I remain" or "I remain," "I continue," "I abide," or of someone who does not leave a certain realm or sphere (BDAG 631.1aβ). **Syntactically,** μένειν is the direct object of the participle of communication: "the one who says" (λέγων). Since μένειν is not a structural marker, it is not underlined. **Semantically**, μένειν is an infinitive of indirect discourse: "that he abides" (KJV ASV NASB NRSV ESV), "walk" (NIV CNT), or "live" (NLT). It provides the content of the verbal of speech or completes the verbal of communication (Wallace 1996, 603). John draws attention to the person who lives a certain way maintains a relationship with God.

ὀφείλει: The Greek word ὀφείλει is a third singular present active indicative from the verb ὀφείλω that means, "I am obligated" or to be under obligation to meet certain social and moral expectation (BDAG 743.2αβ). **Syntactically**, ὀφείλει is the main verb of the independent clause: "the one who says that he abides in him *ought* also himself to persist in living" (ὁ λέγων ἐν αὐτῷ μένειν ὀφείλει . . . καὶ αὐτὸς περιπατεῖν.). The subject is the participial phrase, "the one who says that he abides in him" (ὁ λέγων ἐν αὐτῷ μένειν). It underscores an obligation of any person who claims to have a relationship with God. **Semantically**, ὀφείλει is a gnomic present: "we must" (NIV) or "we are obligated" or "we ought" (cf. KJV NASB ESV NET etc). It is a generic statement to describe something that is true any time (Wallace 1996, 523). John underscores a believers ongoing obligation. That obligation is revealed in the infinitive (περιπατεῖν).

περιπατεῖν: The Greek word περιπατεῖν is a present active infinitive from the verb περιπατέω that means, "I walk" or "I live" or to conduct one's life as a habit of conduct (BDAG 803.2αγ). **Syntactically**, περιπατεῖν is part of the main verb and underlined as a major structural marker. The pronoun, "he" (αὐτός) is not the subject of this infinitive, instead "he" (αὐτός) is resumptive and points back to the subject of "ought" (ὀφείλει; Culy 2004, 30). **Semantically**, περιπατεῖν is a complementary infinitive: "to walk" (cf. KJV NASB ESV NIV NET etc). The infinitive completes the thought of the verb "ought" (ὀφείλει; cf. Wallace 1996, 598). The believer who claims to have a relationship with God is obligated to conduct one's life in a certain manner, which is made clear in the καθώς clause.

2:6b καθώς: The Greek word καθώς is a conjunction, which means "just as" or "even as" (BDAG, 493 2). **Syntactically**, καθώς introduces a dependent conjunctive clause. The entire dependent clause, "*just as* that one lived" (καθὼς ἐκεῖνος περιεπάτησεν), functions adverbially modifying the verb "I ought . . . to persist in living" (ὀφείλει . . . περιπατεῖν). The clause is placed under περιπατεῖν to so subordination. **Semantically**, καθώς is comparative: "just as" (NRSV NET CNT), "as" (NASB NIV NLT), or "even as" (KJV ASV). It describes the way in which a beleiver who claims to have a relationship with God should live. They should live as "that one" (ἐκεῖνος), which is a technical term for Jesus (Brown 1982, 261; cf. Culy 2004, 30). The one who claims to have a relationship with God should conduct their lives in a manner similar to that of Jesus.

περιεπάτησεν: The Greek word περιεπάτησεν is a third singular aorist active indicative from the verb περιπατέω that means, "I walk" or "I live" or to conduct one's life as a habit of conduct (BDAG, 803 2αγ). **Syntactically**, περιεπάτησεν is the governing verb of the dependent adverbial clause. The subject of the verb is the emphatic demonstrative pronoun "that one" (ἐκεῖνος) and refers to Jesus himself. **Semantically**, περιεπάτησεν is a constative aorist: "he lived" or "he walked (KJV ASV NASB NRSV ESV NET CNT). It describes Jesus's manner of living as a whole (Wallace 1996, 557). Anyone who claims to have a relationship with God should live like Jesus did.

2:7a γράφω: The Greek word γράφω is a first singular present active indicative from the verb γράφω that means, "I write" or "I compose" with reference to composing a letter (BDAG, 207 2d). **Syntactically**, γράφω is the main verb of the independent clause: "Beloved, I am writing no new command to you" (Ἀγαπητοί, οὐκ ἐντολὴν καινὴν γράφω ὑμῖν). The assumed subject "I" refers to the author.

Semantically, γράφω is a progressive present negated with οὐκ: "I am writing no new command" (NRSV ESV CNT) or "I am not writing a new command" (NRSV NIV NET NLT) or "I write no new command" (KJV). It describes something that is occurring right now (Wallace 1996, 518). John points out that what he is writing is not new.

2:7b ἀλλ': The Greek word ἀλλά is a conjunction, which means "but" or "rather" after a previous negative statement (BDAG 44.1a). **Syntactically**, ἀλλά identifies the clause as a conjunctive independent clause, "*but* I now write an old command" (ἀλλ' ἐντολὴν παλαιὰν). **Semantically**, ἀλλά is contrastive: "but" (cf. KJV NASB ESV NIV NET etc.) or "rather" (NLT). John is about to counter what his readers may think with an elliptical clause.

[γράφω]: The elliptical Greek word γράφω is first singular present active indicative from the verb γράφω that means, "I write" or "I compose" with reference to composing a letter (BDAG 207.2d). **Syntactically**, γράφω is the main verb of the independent contrastive clause. The subject of the verb is the assumed "I" which is embedded in the verb and refers to the author. **Semantically**, γράφω is a progressive present: "I *now* write." It tells what John is currently doing (Wallace 1996, 518). John underscores that the command John is currently writing about is an old command.

2:7c ἣν: The Greek word ἣν is accusative singular feminine from the relative pronoun ὅς which means, "which" or "that" (BDAG 725.1a). **Syntactically**, ἣν introduces an adjectival relative clause: "which you have had *as an obligation* from the beginning" (ἣν εἴχετε ἀπ' ἀρχῆς). The entire clause modifies the noun "command" (ἐντολὴν) This relative pronoun is in the accusative case because it serves as the direct object of the verb "we have had" (εἴχετε). Whether the relative pronoun is translated "that" (NASB ESV CNT) or "which" (KJV ASV NASB NIV NET), the entire clause underscores a command they have had from the beginning. It provides further information about the command.

εἴχετε: The Greek word εἴχετε is a second plural imperfect active indicative from the verb ἔχω that means, "I have" or to experience something in the sense of an obligation (BDAG 421.7aδ). **Syntactically**, εἴχετε is the governing verb of the dependent adjectival relative clause. The assumed subject, "you" refers to the readers/hearers. **Semantically**, εἴχετε is a pluperfective imperfect: "you have had *as an obligation*" (cf. NASB NRSV NIV NET NLT; Wallace 1996, 549). In essence it is a command given previous to the writing of this short letter, it has been in their possession since that time, and they have been obligated to keep that command.

2:7d ἐστιν: The Greek word ἐστιν is third singular present active indicative from the verb εἰμί that means, "is" and has an equative function of identifying something with something (BDAG 283.2). **Syntactically**, ἐστιν is the main verb of the independent clause "the old command is the word" (ἡ ἐντολὴ ἡ παλαιά ἐστιν ὁ λόγος). The subject of the verb is the noun "command" (ἡ ἐντολὴ). **Semantically**, ἐστιν is an equative present: "is" (cf. KJV NASB ESV NIV NET etc.). It equates the old command with the word.

2:7e ὃν: The Greek word ὃν is an accusative singular masculine from the relative pronoun ὅς which means, "who, which, that" (BDAG 725.a). **Syntactically**, ὃν introduces an adjectival relative clause, "which you have heard" (ὃν ἠκούσατε), modifying the noun "word" (ὁ λόγος). The entire relative clause provides further information about the "word," which is found in its verb.

ἠκούσατε: The Greek word ἠκούσατε is a second plural aorist active indicative from the verb ἀκούω that means, "I hear" or to hear something from someone (BDAG 37.1aβ) or denote a body of authoritative teaching (BDAG 38, 3d). **Syntactically**, ἠκούσατε is the governing verb of the relative clause. The subject of the verb is an implied "you" embedded in the verb, which refers to the readers/hearers of the letter. **Semantically**, ἠκούσατε is a consummative aorist: "you have heard" (KJV NASB NRSV ESV NIV NET CNT). It describes a conclusion or cessation of an act as a whole (Wallace 1996, 559). John describes the "word" as a body of authoritative teachings that has been in the possession of his readers since they first came into the faith.

2:8a γράφω: The Greek word γράφω is a first singular present active indicative from the verb γράφω that means, "I write" or "I compose" with reference to composing a letter (BDAG 207.2d). **Syntactically**, γράφω is the main verb of an independent clause "on the other hand I am *now* writing to you a new command" (πάλιν ἐντολὴν καινὴν γράφω ὑμῖν). The assumed subject "I" refers to the author. The adverb "again" (πάλιν) sets up a contrast. In this context πάλιν should be translated as "on the other hand" (BDAG 753, 4; cf. NASB NET), contrasting the old command that was received from Jesus has a new application in their lives today, because they are living in a new era where hatred is losing and love is winning (Culy 2004, 32). **Semantically**, γράφω is a progressive present: "I *now* write" or "I am writing" (NASB NRSV ESV NIV NLT CNT). It tells what John is currently doing (Wallace 1996, 518). John is *right now* writing a letter.

2:8b ὅ: The Greek word ὅ is a nominative singular neuter from the relative pronoun ὅς which means, "who, which, that" (BDAG 727.1gβ). **Syntactically**, ὅ introduces a dependent relative clause: "*which* is true in him and in you" (ὅ ἐστιν ἀληθὲς ἐν αὐτῷ καὶ ἐν ὑμῖν). In order to follow the Greek word order and our interpretation, the clause is placed above the independent clause in the structural outline. The clause is difficult to interpret. (1) It seems natural to classify it as adjectival describing the new command, but it does not agree with the noun "command" (ἐντολὴν) in gender. (2) It could be functioning substantivally in apposition to the entirety of the previous clause. In that case the new command would equal that which is true. (3) It could be functioning substantivally modifying the subsequent clause "because the darkness is passing away and the true light is already shining" (ὅτι ἡ σκοτία παράγεται καὶ τὸ φῶς τὸ ἀληθινὸν ἤδη φαίνει), telling us that this further statement is true. The best option seems to be to take it (4) as an adjectival relative clause referring to the whole discussion that precedes. The specifics of the command are made know in the rest of the clause.

ἐστιν: The Greek word ἐστιν is third singular present active indicative from the verb εἰμί means "is" or "to show how something is to be understood" (BDAG 282.2c). **Syntactically**, ἐστιν is the governing verb of the dependent relative clause. The subject of the verb is the relative pronoun "which" (ὅ). **Semantically**, ἐστιν is an equative present: "is" (cf. KJV NASB ESV NIV NET etc.). Through the relative clause, ἐστιν equates the command his readers have heard with Jesus. The command to love others is not new in time. It is true in both the life of Jesus and in the life of John's readers.

2:8c ὅτι: The Greek word ὅτι is a conjunction, which means "because" (BDAG 732.4a). **Syntactically**, ὅτι introduces dependent conjunctive clause: "*because* the darkness is passing away" (ὅτι ἡ σκοτία παράγεται). The decision about the adjectival relative clause referring to the whole discussion that precedes affects the interpretation of this ὅτι clause. This clause, then, is not providing the content of "new command" (ἐντολὴν καινὴν) but rather it functions adverbially. And while it could modify the verb "is" (ἐστὶν) and translated "which is true because the darkness is passing away" providing the reason why the command is true. The ὅτι clause is modifying the verb "write" (γράφω). **Semantically**, ὅτι is causal: "because" (cf. KJV NASB ESV NIV NET etc.). It provides the reason why John is writing to them (Wallace 1996, 460). That reason is rather ground breaking and expounded in the clause's verb.

παράγεται: The Greek word παράγεται is a third singular present passive indicative from the verb παράγω that means, "I pass away" or going out of existence (BDAG 761.4b). **Syntactically**, παράγεται is one governing verbs of the ὅτι clause. The subject is "the darkness" (ἡ σκοτία). **Semantically**, παράγεται is a progressive present: "is passing" (ASV NASB NRSV ESV NIV NET CNT) or "is disappearing" (NLT). It tells what is happening right now (Wallace 1996, 518). The first reason John is wrting it to identify a change that is happening in the reader's situation. As God's kingdom advances, the darkness *right now* is going out of existence. The culmination of the ages has been set in motion, and in light of that fact, the readers should love one another (Culy 2004, 34-35).

2:8d [ὅτι]: The Greek word ὅτι is a conjunction that means "because" (BDAG 732.4a). **Syntactically**, [ὅτι] is an ellipsis and serves to introduce the second part of the dependent clause: "and [*because*] the light is already shining" (καὶ [ὅτι] τὸ φῶς τὸ ἀληθινὸν ἤδη φαίνει). It too modifies the verb "write" (γράφω). **Semantically**, ὅτι is causal: "because." It provides the second reason why John is currently writing to them about the love command, which is evident in the next verb.

φαίνει: The Greek word φαίνει is a third singular present active indicative from the verb φαίνω that means, "I shine" or "to shine" or "to produce light" (BDAG 1046.1a). **Syntactically**, φαίνει is one of the compound governing verbs of the dependent conjunctive. The subject of the verb is "the light" (τὸ φῶς). **Semantically**, φαίνει is a progressive present: "is already shinning" (cf. NASB ESV NIV NET etc.) or "is shining *now*" (KJV). It tells what is happening right now (Wallace 1996, 518). It points out that *right now* (KJV) the kingdom of God is advancing. The second reason John writes is because the true light is already shining.

2:9 λέγων: The Greek word λέγων is a nominative masculine singular present active participle from the verb λέγω, which means, "I say" or "I give expression to" or "to express oneself orally" (BDAG 588.1αγ). **Syntactically**, λέγων is a substantival participle functioning as part of the compound subject of the verb "is" (ἐστίν). **Semantically**, λέγων has a gnomic force: "the one who says" (NASB NET) or "whoever says" (NRSV ESV). It presents a generic statement to describe something that is true any time (Wallace 1996, 523, 615). John draws attention to people who make a claim that is specified in the next verb.

εἶναι: The Greek word εἶναι is a present active infinitive from the verb εἰμί that means, "I live in accordance with" (BDAG 284.3c). **Syntactically**, εἶναι is the direct object of the participle of communication, "the one who says" (λέγων). Since εἶναι is not a structural marker, it is not underlined. **Semantically**, εἶναι is an infinitive of indirect discourse: "anyone who claims *to be*" (NIV) or "the one who says *he is*" (NASB NET cf. CNT) or "whoever says *he is*" (NRSV ESV). It is providing the content of the verbal of speech or completing the verbal of communication (Wallace 1996, 603). The claim is that they live in accordance with the light (= God) or that they have a relationship with God.

μισῶν: The Greek word μισῶν is a nominative masculine singular present active participle from the verb μισέω, which means, "I hate" or "I detest" or "to have a strong aversion to" (BDAG 652.1a). **Syntactically**, μισῶν is a substantival participle functioning as part of the compound subject of the verb "is" (ἐστίν). And though it is possible to interpret the participle with an adverbial temporal sense "while hating" (NRSV), most translations render the participle as substantival (e.g., KJV NASB ESV NIV NET). **Semantically**, μισῶν has a gnomic force: "the one who *persists* in hating." John provides another timeless reality (Wallace 1996, 523, 615). The person who has a continual strong aversion for another believer cannot have a relationship with a loving and pure God.

ἐστίν: The Greek word ἐστιν is third singular present middle (active) indicative from the verb εἰμί that means, "is" and has an equative function of identifying something with something else (BDAG 283.2). **Syntactically**, ἐστίν is the main verb of the independent clause: "the one who claims to be in the light 'and yet' (καί; BDAG 495.1bη) persists in hating his brother and sister *is* still in the darkness until now (ὁ λέγων ἐν τῷ φωτὶ εἶναι καὶ τὸν ἀδελφὸν αὐτοῦ μισῶν ἐν τῇ σκοτίᾳ ἐστὶν ἕως ἄρτι). The subject of the verb is compound phrase "the one who claims to be in the light and yet persists in hating his brother and sister" (ὁ λέγων ἐν τῷ φωτὶ εἶναι καὶ τὸν ἀδελφὸν αὐτοῦ μισῶν). **Semantically**, ἐστίν is equative with gnomic force: "is" (cf. KJV NASB ESV NIV NET etc.). John is elucidating the timeless truth (Wallace 1996, 523) that anyone who claims to have a relationship with God will not hate other believers, but instead love them.

2:10a ἀγαπῶν: The Greek word ἀγαπῶν is a nominative masculine singular present active participle from the verb ἀγαπάω that means, "I love" or to have a warm regard for and interest in another person (BDAG 5.1aα). **Syntactically**, ἀγαπῶν is a participle functioning substantivally as the subject of the verb "remains" (μένει). **Semantically**, ἀγαπῶν has a gnomic force: "the one who loves" (NASB NET) or "whoever loves" (NRSV ESV NIV). John provides another timeless reality (Wallace 1996, 523, 615). The person who makes it a practice to love fellow believers abides in the light or has a relationship with God.

μένει: The Greek word μένει is a third singular present active indicative from the verb μένω that means, "I remain" or "I stay" or "to remain in a certain realm or sphere" (BDAG 630.1aβ). **Syntactically**, μένει is the main verb of the independent clause "the one who loves his brother and sister remains in the light" (ὁ ἀγαπῶν τὸν ἀδελφὸν αὐτοῦ ἐν τῷ φωτὶ μένει). The subject is the participial phrase "the one who loves his brother and sister" (ἀγαπῶν τὸν ἀδελφὸν αὐτοῦ). **Semantically**, μένει is a gnomic present with a customary present force: "abides" (KJV ASV NASB ESV CNT) or "lives" (NRSV NIV cf. NLT). John provides another timeless reality (Wallace 1996, 523, 615). The person who *persists* in loving other Christians lives in the light like God does.

2:10b καί: The Greek word καί is a conjunction which in this context means "and" (BDAG 494.1b). **Syntactically**, καί introduces a independent conjunctive clause "and in him there is no stumbling block" (καὶ σκάνδαλον ἐν αὐτῷ οὐκ ἔστιν). **Semantically**, καί is coordinating connective: "and" (cf. KJV NASB ESV NIV NET etc.). It provides additional information about the believer who loves his brother and sister (Wallace 1996, 671). Such a believer is not a stumbling block .

Lexical Nugget: What is a stumbling block? This is the only time that this noun is used in Johannine literature. It normally refers to an obstacle that causes someone to trip. In John 6:61, the cognate verb is used to talk about Jesus' teaching being the cause for someone to stumble or trip. The idea here seems to be that a believer who loves his fellow Christians will not give another a cause to fall away from the faith (Bateman 2008, 235).

ἔστιν: The Greek word ἔστιν is third singular present active indicative from the verb εἰμί that means, "there is" or "to show how something is to be understood" (BDAG, 283.2ca). **Syntactically**, ἔστιν is the main verb of the independent conjunctive clause. The subject of the verb is an implied "there" embedded in the third person singular verb. **Semantically**, ἔστιν is a gnomic present: "is" (cf. KJV NASB ESV NIV NET etc.). It presents another timeless truth (Wallace 1996, 523). Anyone who loves his fellow believer will not become a stumbling block to that believer's faith.

2:11a δέ: The Greek word δέ is a conjunction, which means "but" (BDAG 213.4). **Syntactically**, δέ is in the post-positive position that introduces an independent conjunctive clause "*but* the one who persists in hating his brother and sister is in the darkness" (ὁ δὲ μισῶν τὸν ἀδελφὸν αὐτοῦ ἐν τῇ σκοτίᾳ ἐστὶν). **Semantically**, δέ is a marker of contrast: "but" (e.g., KJV NASB ESV NIV NET etc.). It gives an opposing truth to the idea that the believer who loves has a relationship with God. The counter truth is that the one who hates his fellow believers does not have a relationship with God. He is in the darkness, not the light.

μισῶν: The Greek word μισῶν is a nominative masculine singular present active participle from the verb μισέω, which means, "I hate" or "I detest" or "to have a strong aversion to" (BDAG 652.1a). **Syntactically**, μισῶν is a substantival participle functioning as the subject of the verb "is" (ἐστὶν). **Semantically**, μισῶν is a gnomic present with a customary present force: "the one who hates" (NASB NET cf. CNT) or "whoever hates" (NRSV ESV NIV). It presents a generic statement to describe something that is true any time (Wallace 1996, 521, 615). Thus the person who *persists* in hating other believers cannot possibly have a relationship with a loving and pure God.

ἐστιν: The Greek word ἐστιν is third singular present active indicative from the verb εἰμί that means, "I am" or describes a special connection between subject and predicate (BDAG 282.2b). **Syntactically**, ἐστιν is the main verb of the independent clause: "but the one who persists in hating his brother and sister *is* in the darkness" (ὁ δὲ μισῶν τὸν ἀδελφὸν αὐτοῦ ἐν τῇ σκοτίᾳ ἐστὶν). The subject of the verb is the substantival participial phrase "the one who hates his brother and sister" (ὁ … μισῶν τὸν ἀδελφὸν αὐτοῦ). **Semantically**, ἐστιν is a gnomic present: "is" (cf. KJV NASB ESV NIV NET etc.). It presents another timeless truth (Wallace 1996, 523). Anyone who hates his brother and sister cannot have a relationship with God.

2:11b καί: The Greek word καί is a conjunction which in this context means "and so" (BDAG 494.1c). **Syntactically**, καί introduces a conjunctive independent clause "*and so* he is walking in the darkness" (καὶ ἐν τῇ σκοτίᾳ περιπατεῖ). **Semantically**, καί is an inferential connective: "and so" (cf. NLT). It provides a conclusion about the believer who hates his brother and sister. Such a believer is described with the next verb.

περιπατεῖ: The Greek word περιπατεῖ is a third singular present active indicative from the verb περιπατέω that means, "I walk" or "I live" or to go about here or there in imagery or non-literal sense (BDAG 803.1d). **Syntactically**, περιπατεῖ serves as the main verb of the independent conjunctive clause. The assumed subject "he/she" refers to any believer who hates other Christians. **Semantically**, περιπατεῖ is a gnomic present with customary present force: "he is walking" or "walks" (cf. KJV NASB ESV NIV NET etc.). It presents a generic statement to describe something that is true any time (Wallace 1996, 521, 615). Any professing believer who persists in hating other Christians *lives* in darkness. Even though the verb is intended to convey the idea of lifestyle, it should be translated here as "walking" since it is part of an extended metaphor describing the one who hates his fellow believers (Culy 2004, 37).

2:11c καί: The Greek word καί is a conjunction which means "and" (BDAG 494.1b). **Syntactically**, καί introduces a conjunctive independent clause, "and he does not know where he is going" (καὶ οὐκ οἶδεν ποῦ ὑπάγει). **Semantically**, καί is a coordinating connective: "and" (KJV ASV NASB NRSV ESV NET CNT). It shows that John is adding a further thought about the believer who hates his brother and sister evident with the next verb.

οἶδεν: The Greek word οἶδεν is a third singular perfect active indicative from the verb οἶδα that means, "I know" or "I understand" or "I recognize" or "to grasp the meaning of something" (BDAG 694.4). **Syntactically**, οἶδεν is the governing verb of the independent conjunctive clause: "and he does not know where he is going" (καὶ οὐκ οἶδεν ποῦ ὑπάγει). The assumed subject, "he," refers to any believer who hates his fellow Christians. **Semantically**, the negated οἶδεν is a perfect with present force: "does not know" (οὐκ οἶδεν; e.g., KJV NASB ESV NIV NET). Some verbs, like οἶδα, almost exclusively appear in the perfect tense without the perfect's aspectual significance (Wallace 1996, 579-580). Believers who hate other believers fail to grasp their lives of darkness.

ποῦ: The Greek word ποῦ is a conjunction, which means "where" and is an interrogative reference with an implication of movement (BDAG 858.2b). **Syntactically**, ποῦ introduces a dependent substantival clause, "*where* he is going" (ποῦ ὑπάγει). It is the direct object of the verb "know" (οἶδεν). **Semantically**, ποῦ has an adverbial force and funtions locatively, describing the fact that the believer who is in the darkness has no idea in what direction he is heading (Wallace 1996, 676).

ὑπάγει: The Greek word ὑπάγει is a third singular present active indicative from the verb ὑπάγω that means, "I go" or to be moving in a certain direction (BDAG 1028.2b). **Syntactically**, ὑπάγει is the governing verb of the dependent substantival locative clause: "where he is going" (ποῦ ὑπάγει). The assumed subject "he" refers to any believer who hates his fellow Christians. **Semantically**, ὑπάγει is a gnomic present with the force of a customary present: "he is going" (cf. KJV NASB ESV NIV NET etc.). It presents a generic statement to describe something that is true any time (Wallace 1996, 521, 615). Anyone who claims to have a relationship with God yet hates his fellow Christians is not headed in the right direction, *namely* they are not going to the Father as Jesus went to the Father (cf. John 7:33; 16:5).

2:11d ὅτι: The Greek word ὅτι is a conjunction, which means "because" (BDAG, 732.4a). **Syntactically**, ὅτι introduces an adverbial dependent clause: "*because* the darkness has blinded his eyes" (ὅτι ἡ σκοτία ἐτύφλωσεν τοὺς ὀφθαλμοὺς αὐτοῦ), modifying the verb "know" (οἶδεν). **Semantically**, ὅτι is a marker of causality: "because" (e.g., KJV NASB ES NIV NET etc.). It provides the reason why the believer who hates other Christians does not know where he is going. The reason is clearly evident in the clause's verb.

ἐτύφλωσεν: The Greek word ἐτύφλωσεν is a third singular aorist active indicative from the verb τυφλόω that means, "I am blind" or "to deprive of sight" (BDAG 1021). **Syntactically**, ἐτύφλωσεν serves as the governing verb of the adverbial dependent clause. The subject of the verb is "the darkness" (ἡ σκοτία). **Semantically**, ἐτύφλωσεν is a constative aorist: "has blinded" (KJV ASV ESV NIV NET CNT). It states an event as a whole (Wallace 1996, 557). Believers who hate other believers are blinded by their own immorality. This is a figurative usage of the word "blindness" that draws attention to those people whose hatred has led them to be spiritually blind.

1 John 2:12–17

Verb Recognition for 1 John 2:12–17

¹²Γράφω ὑμῖν, τεκνία, ὅτι ἀφέωνται ὑμῖν αἱ ἁμαρτίαι διὰ τὸ ὄνομα αὐτοῦ. ¹³γράφω ὑμῖν, πατέρες, ὅτι ἐγνώκατε τὸν ἀπ' ἀρχῆς. γράφω ὑμῖν, νεανίσκοι, ὅτι νενικήκατε τὸν πονηρόν. ¹⁴ἔγραψα ὑμῖν, παιδία, ὅτι ἐγνώκατε τὸν πατέρα. ἔγραψα ὑμῖν, πατέρες, ὅτι ἐγνώκατε τὸν ἀπ'

ἀρχῆς. ἔγραψα ὑμῖν, νεανίσκοι, ὅτι ἰσχυροί ἐστε καὶ ὁ λόγος τοῦ θεοῦ ἐν ὑμῖν μένει καὶ νενικήκατε τὸν πονηρόν.

¹⁵Μὴ ἀγαπᾶτε τὸν κόσμον μηδὲ τὰ ἐν τῷ κόσμῳ. ἐάν τις ἀγαπᾷ τὸν κόσμον, οὐκ ἔστιν ἡ ἀγάπη τοῦ πατρὸς ἐν αὐτῷ· ¹⁶ὅτι πᾶν τὸ ἐν τῷ κόσμῳ, ἡ ἐπιθυμία τῆς σαρκὸς καὶ ἡ ἐπιθυμία τῶν ὀφθαλμῶν καὶ ἡ ἀλαζονεία τοῦ βίου, οὐκ ἔστιν ἐκ τοῦ πατρὸς ἀλλὰ ἐκ τοῦ κόσμου ἐστίν. ¹⁷καὶ ὁ κόσμος παράγεται καὶ ἡ ἐπιθυμία αὐτοῦ, ὁ δὲ ποιῶν τὸ θέλημα τοῦ θεοῦ μένει εἰς τὸν αἰῶνα.

Clausal Outline Translated for 1 John 2:12–17

²:¹² **Γράφω** ὑμῖν, τεκνία, (ὅτι ἀφέωνται ὑμῖν αἱ ἁμαρτίαι διὰ τὸ ὄνομα αὐτοῦ).
²:¹² **I** *now* **write** to you, children, (that for your benefit your sins have been pardoned because of
Jesus name).

²:¹³ᵃ **γράφω** ὑμῖν, πατέρες, (ὅτι ἐγνώκατε τὸν ἀπ᾽ ἀρχῆς).
²:¹³ᵃ **I** *now* **write** to you, fathers, (that you have known him who is from the beginning).

²:¹³ᵇ **γράφω** ὑμῖν, νεανίσκοι, (ὅτι νενικήκατε τὸν πονηρόν).
²:¹³ᵇ **I** *now* **write** to you, young people, (that you have overcome the evil one).

²:¹⁴ᵃ **ἔγραψα** ὑμῖν, παιδία, (ὅτι ἐγνώκατε τὸν πατέρα).
²:¹⁴ᵇ **I have written** to you, children, (that you have known the Father).

²:¹⁴ᵇ **ἔγραψα** ὑμῖν, πατέρες, (ὅτι ἐγνώκατε τὸν [πατέρα] ἀπ᾽ ἀρχῆς).
²:¹⁴ᵇ **I have written** to you, fathers, (that you have known the [*Father*] from the beginning).

²:¹⁴ᶜ **ἔγραψα** ὑμῖν, νεανίσκοι, (ὅτι ἰσχυροί ἐστε
²:¹⁴ᶜ **I have written** to you, young people, (that you are strong,

|

²:¹⁴ᵈ καὶ [ὅτι] ὁ λόγος τοῦ θεοῦ ἐν ὑμῖν μένει
²:¹⁴ᵈ and [*that*] the Word of God abides in you

|

²:¹⁴ᵉ καὶ [ὅτι] νενικήκατε τὸν πονηρόν).
ᵛ¹⁴ᵉ and [*that*] you have conquered the Evil One).

²:¹⁵ᵃ Μὴ **ἀγαπᾶτε** τὸν κόσμον μηδὲ τὰ ἐν τῷ κόσμῳ.
²:¹⁵ᵃ Do not **love** the world nor the things in the world.

²:¹⁵ᵇ **ἐάν** τις **ἀγαπᾷ** τὸν κόσμον,
²:¹⁵ᵇ **If** anyone *persists in* **loving** the world,

|

²:¹⁵ᶜ οὐκ **ἔστιν** ἡ ἀγάπη τοῦ πατρὸς ἐν αὐτῷ·
²:¹⁵ᶜ the love of the Father **is** not in him;

^{2:16a} ὅτι πᾶν τὸ ἐν τῷ κόσμῳ, . . . οὐκ ἔστιν ἐκ τοῦ πατρὸς

^{2:16a} **For** *this reason* all that is in the world . . . **is** not from the Father

> ἡ ἐπιθυμία τῆς σαρκὸς
> the flesh that desires

> καὶ ἡ ἐπιθυμία τῶν ὀφθαλμῶν
> and the eyes that desire

> καὶ ἡ ἀλαζονεία τοῦ βίου,
> and the boastful pride about one's life

^{2:16b} ἀλλὰ ἐκ τοῦ κόσμου ἐστίν.

^{2:16b} but **they are** from the world.

^{2:17a} καὶ ὁ κόσμος παράγεται καὶ ἡ ἐπιθυμία αὐτοῦ,

^{2:17a} And the world **is passing away**, and also its lusts;

^{2:17b} ὁ δὲ ποιῶν τὸ θέλημα τοῦ θεοῦ μένει εἰς τὸν αἰῶνα.

^{2:17b} but the one who does the will of God **remains** forever.

Syntax Explained for 1 John 2:12–17

^{2:12} Γράφω: The Greek word γράφω is a first singular present active indicative from the verb γράφω that means, "I write" or "I compose" with reference to composing a letter (BDAG 207.2d). **Syntactically**, γράφω serves as the main verb of the independent clause: "*I now write* to you, children" (γράφω ὑμῖν, τεκνία). The assumed subject "I" refers to the author. **Semantically**, γράφω is a progressive present: "I now write" or "I write" (KJV ASV NIV CNT) or "I am writing (KJV ASV NIV NLT CNT). It tells what John is currently doing (Wallace 1996, 518). John is *right now* writing a letter.

ὅτι: The Greek word ὅτι is a conjunction, which means "that" (BDAG 731.1a). **Syntactically**, ὅτι introduces a dependent conjunctive clause: "*that* for your benefit your sins have been pardoned because of Jesus's name" (ὅτι ἀφέωνται ὑμῖν αἱ ἁμαρτίαι διὰ τὸ ὄνομα αὐτοῦ). The ὅτι clauses may be substantival serving as the direct object of the verb, "I am writing" (γράφω). It is placed in parenthesis in order to visualize its contribution to the independent clause. **Semantically**, ὅτι is an indirect discourse: "that" (NET). It signals the content of what John is writing (Wallace 1996, 45).

Structural Nugget: Verse 12–14 has six parallel constructions. Each begins with some form of the verb "I write" (γράφω or ἔγραψα) after which follows a dependent ὅτι clause. The ὅτι clauses could be classified in one of two ways. On the one hand, they may all be adverbial, modifying the verb, "I write" (γράφω), giving us the reason why he is writing that particular truth (for the viewpoint that these clauses should be taken causally: "because" (KJV ASV NASB ESV NIV NLT CNT; cf. Culy 2004, 29). On the other hand the ὅτι clauses may be substantival serving as the direct object of the verb, "I am writing" (γράφω). In normal usage when a verb of communication is used followed by a ὅτι clause, the clause that follows functions as the direct object, explicating the content of the communication (BDAG 731.1a).

ἀφέωνται: The Greek word ἀφέωνται is a third singular perfect passive indicative from the verb ἀφίημι that means, "I forgive" or "I cancel" or "I pardon" or to release someone from legal or moral obligation (BDAG 156.2). **Syntactically**, ἀφέωνται is the governing verb of the substantival dependent ὅτι clause. The subject is the plural noun, "*your* sins" (αἱ ἁμαρτίαι). **Semantically**, ἀφέωνται is an extensive perfect: "have been forgiven" (NASB NIV NET NLT). John's emphasis is on the completed act of forgiveness in past time rather than the present results (Wallace 1996, 577). John underscores that believers live in a state of forgiveness "because (διά + accusative) of his name."

2:13a γράφω: The Greek word γράφω is a first singular present active indicative from the verb γράφω that means, "I write" or "I compose" with reference to composing a letter (BDAG 207.2d). **Syntactically**, γράφω is the main verb of the independent clause: "*I now write* to you, fathers" (γράφω ὑμῖν, πατέρες,). The assumed subject "I" refers to the author. **Semantically**, γράφω is a progressive present: "I now write" or "I write" (KJV ASV NIV CNT) or "I am writing (KJV ASV NIV NLT CNT). It tells what John is currently doing (Wallace 1996, 518). John is *right now* writing a letter.

ὅτι: The Greek word ὅτι is a conjunction, which means "that" (BDAG 731.1a). **Syntactically**, ὅτι introduces a dependent clause: "*that* you have known him who is from the beginning" (ὅτι ἐγνώκατε τὸν ἀπ᾽ ἀρχῆς). The clause is substantival and functions as the direct object of the verb, "I am now writing" (γράφω). It is placed in parenthesis in order to visualize its contribution to the independent clause. **Semantically**, ὅτι is an indirect discourse: "that" (NET). It signals the content of what John is writing (Wallace 1996, 45).

ἐγνώκατε: The Greek word ἐγνώκατε is a second plural perfect active indicative from the verb γινώσκω that means, "I know" or "I come to know" or to have come to the knowledge of some person (BDAG 200.6aβ). **Syntactically**, ἐγνώκατε is the governing verb of the substantival dependent ὅτι clause. The subject of the verb is an implied "you (plural)" embedded in the verb and refers to the community. **Semantically**, ἐγνώκατε is an extensive perfect: "you have known" (KJV NASB NIV NET CNT) John's emphasis is on the completed act of knowing someone in past time rather than the present results (Wallace 1996, 577). John's point is that this community has had and continues to have a personal knowledge of Jesus.

Synatactical Nugget: The construction "the one who is from the beginning" (τὸν ἀπ᾽ ἀρχῆς) has an article (τόν) preceding a prepositional phrase. In this case the article functions as a nominalizer, turning the prepositional phrase into a substantive, which in this case serves as the direct object of the verb "you have known" (ἐγνώκατε) (Culy 2004, 40; cf. Wallace 1996, 231-236). This language is a reference to Jesus and links back to the previous description of him in the prologue of the book (1 John 1:1–4).

2:13b γράφω: The Greek word γράφω is a first singular present active indicative from the verb γράφω that means, "I write" or "I compose" with reference to composing a letter (BDAG 207.2d). **Syntactically**, γράφω is the main verb of the independent clause: "*I now write* to you, young people" (γράφω ὑμῖν, νεανίσκοι). The assumed subject "I" refers to the author. **Semantically**, γράφω is a progressive present: "I now write" or "I write" (KJV ASV NIV CNT) or "I am writing (KJV ASV NIV NLT CNT). It tells what John is currently doing (Wallace 1996, 518). John is *right now* writing a letter.

ὅτι: The Greek word ὅτι is a conjunction, which means "that" (BDAG 731.1a). **Syntactically**, ὅτι introduces a dependent clause: "*that* you have overcome the evil one" (ὅτι νενικήκατε τὸν πονηρόν). The clause is substantival and is functioning as the direct object of the verb, "I am writing" (γράφω). It is placed in parenthesis in order to visualize its contribution to the independent clause.

Semantically, ὅτι is an indirect discourse: "that" (NET). It signals the content of what John is writing (Wallace 1996, 45).

νενικήκατε: The Greek word νενικήκατε is a second plural perfect active indicative from the verb νικάω that means, "I overcome" or "I vanquish" or "to overcome someone" (BDAG 673.2a). **Syntactically**, νενικήκατε is the governing verb of the substantival dependent ὅτι clause. The subject of the verb is an implied "you (plural)" embedded in the verb and refers to the young believers among the intended recipients. **Semantically**, νενικήκατε is an extensive perfect: "you have overcome" (KJV ASV NASB ESV NIV CNT). John's emphasis is on the completed act of victory (Wallace 1996, 577). The "evil one" (τὸν πονηρόν) occurs five times in the letter (2:13, 14; 3:12; 5:18, 19), and is a reference to Satan. John assures the believer in 1 John 5:18-19 that while the evil one rules the world and motivates the antichrists (Brown 1982, 304), he still cannot harm the believer.

2:14a ἔγραψα: The Greek word ἔγραψα is a first singular aorist active indicative from the verb γράφω that means, "I write" or "I compose" with reference to composing a letter (BDAG 207.2d). **Syntactically**, ἔγραψα is the main verb of the independent clause: "*I have written* to you, children" (ἔγραψα ὑμῖν, παιδία). The assumed subject "I" refers to the author. **Semantically**, ἔγραψα is an epistolary aorist: "I have written" (KJV ASV NASB NET NLT). John underscores what he has just written (Wallace 1996, 563). John has just written to the "children" or "new believers"

ὅτι: The Greek word ὅτι is a conjunction, which means "that" (BDAG 731.1a). **Syntactically**, ὅτι serves to introduce a dependent conjunctive clause "that you have known the father" (ὅτι ἐγνώκατε τὸν πατέρα). The clause is substantival and is functioning as the direct object of the verb, "I have written" (ἔγραψα). It is placed in parenthesis in order to visualize its contribution to the independent clause. **Semantically**, ὅτι is an indirect discourse: "that" (NET). It signals the content of what John is writing (Wallace 1996, 45).

ἐγνώκατε: The Greek word ἐγνώκατε is a second plural perfect active indicative from the verb γινώσκω that means, "I come to know" or to have come to the knowledge of some person (BDAG 200.6aβ). **Syntactically**, ἐγνώκατε is the governing verb of the substantival dependent ὅτι clause. The subject of the verb is an implied "you (plural)" embedded in the verb and refers to the children among the intended recipients. **Semantically**, ἐγνώκατε is an extensive perfect: "you have known" (NET NLT; cf. CNT NRSV) John's emphasis is on the completed act of knowing someone in past time rather than the present results (Wallace 1996, 577). John's point is that members of this community whether interpreted as literal "children" or "children in the faith" (NLT) have had and continue to have a personal knowledge of God.

2:14b ἔγραψα: The Greek word ἔγραψα is a first singular aorist active indicative from the verb γράφω that means, "I write" or "I compose" with reference to composing a letter (BDAG 207.2d). **Syntactically**, ἔγραψα is the main verb of the independent clause "I have written to you, fathers" (ἔγραψα ὑμῖν, πατέρες). The assumed subject "I" refers to the author. **Semantically**, ἔγραψα is an epistolary aorist: "I have written" (KJV ASV NASB NET NLT). John underscores what he has just written (Wallace 1996, 563). John has just written to the "fathers" or "mature believers."

ὅτι: The Greek word ὅτι is a conjunction, which means "that" (BDAG 731.1a). **Syntactically**, ὅτι serves to introduce a dependent conjunctive clause "that you have known the one who is from the beginning" (ὅτι ἐγνώκατε τὸν ἀπ' ἀρχῆς). The clause is substantival and is functioning as the direct object of the verb, "I have written" (ἔγραψα). It is placed in parenthesis in order to visualize its contribution to the independent clause. See the complete discussion about the six parallel ὅτι clauses under 12:12. **Semantically**, ὅτι is an indirect discourse: "that" (NET). It signals the content of what John is writing (Wallace 1996, 45).

ἐγνώκατε: The Greek word ἐγνώκατε is a second plural perfect active indicative from the verb γινώσκω that means, "I come to know" or to have come to the knowledge of some person (BDAG 200.6αβ). **Syntactically**, ἐγνώκατε is the governing verb of the substantival dependent ὅτι clause. The subject of the verb is an implied "you (plural)" embedded in the verb and refers to the fathers among the intended recipients. **Semantically**, ἐγνώκατε is an extensive perfect: "you have known" (KJV NIV NET CNT). John's emphasis is on the completed act of knowing someone in past time rather than the present results (Wallace 1996, 577). John's point is that members of this community whether interpreted as literal "fathers" or "mature" (NLT) has had and continues to have a personal knowledge of God.

2:14c ἔγραψα: The Greek word ἔγραψα is a first singular aorist active indicative from the verb γράφω that means, "I write" or "I compose" with reference to composing a letter (BDAG 207.2d). **Syntactically**, ἔγραψα is the main verb of the independent clause "*I have written to you, young people*" (ἔγραψα ὑμῖν, νεανίσκοι). The assumed subject "I" refers to the author. **Semantically**, ἔγραψα is an epistolary aorist: "I have written" (KJV ASV NASB NET NLT; cf. Wallace 1996, 563). John has just written to the "young people" or "young believers" among his recipients about how they are strong, how the word of God lives in them, and how they have victory over the evil one.

ὅτι: The Greek word ὅτι is a conjunction, which means "that" (BDAG 731.1a). **Syntactically**, ὅτι introduces a dependent conjunctive clause: "*that you are strong and the word of God abides in you and you have conquered the evil one*" (ὅτι ἰσχυροί ἐστε καὶ ὁ λόγος τοῦ θεοῦ ἐν ὑμῖν μένει καὶ νενικήκατε τὸν πονηρόν). The ὅτι clause is substantival and is functioning as the direct object of the verb, "I have written" (ἔγραψα). It is placed in parenthesis in order to visualize its contribution to the independent clause. **Semantically**, ὅτι is an indirect discourse: "that" (NET). It signals the content of what John is writing (Wallace 1996, 45).

ἐστε: The Greek word ἐστε is second plural present active indicative from the verb εἰμί that means, "is" or describes a special connection between subject and predicate (BDAG 282.2b). **Syntactically**, ἐστε serves as the governing verb of the first part of the compound substantival dependent ὅτι clause, "you are strong" (ἰσχυροί ἐστε). The subject of the verb is an implied "you (plural)" referring to the recipients of the letter, specifically the younger believers. **Semantically**, ἐστε is an equative present. It equates John's young believers with stregth because of their relationship with God.

2:14d καί: The Greek word καί is a conjunction which in this context means "and" (BDAG 494.1bα). **Syntactically**, καί introduces a dependent conjunctive clause: "and [that] God's word abides in you" (καὶ [ὅτι] ὁ λόγος τοῦ θεοῦ ἐν ὑμῖν μένει). It is the second part of the compound ὅτι clause. **Semantically**, καί is connective and gives us additional information about these young believers. Not only are they strong, but they are strong because God's word lives in them.

[ὅτι]: The Greek word ὅτι is a conjunction, which means "that" (BDAG 731.1a). **Syntactically**, [ὅτι] is an ellipsis and serves to introduce the second part of the compound dependent clause: "and [*that*] the word of God abides in you" (καὶ [ὅτι] ὁ λόγος τοῦ θεοῦ ἐν ὑμῖν μένει). The compound clause is substantival and functions as part of a compound direct object of the verb, "I have written" (ἔγραψα). **Semantically**, ὅτι is indirect discourse: "that." It signals the content of what John is writing (Wallace 1996, 45).

μένει: The Greek word μένει is a third singular present active indicative from the verb μένω that means, "I remain," "I continue," "I abide" or of someone does not leave a certain realm or sphere (BDAG 631.1aβ). **Syntactically**, μένει is the governing verb of the second part of the compound substantival dependent ὅτι clause: "and God's word abides in you" (καὶ ὁ λόγος τοῦ θεοῦ ἐν ὑμῖν μένει). The subject is the phrase, "the word of God" (ὁ λόγος τοῦ θεοῦ). **Semantically**, μένει is a customary present: "abides" (KJV ASV NASB NRSV ESV CNT) or "lives" (NIV NLT). John gives emphasis to the word of God that lives continually in the young believers.

2:14e καί: The Greek word καί is a conjunction which in this context means "and" (BDAG 494.1bα). **Syntactically**, καί introduces a dependent conjunctive clause: "and you have overcome the evil one" (καὶ νενικήκατε τὸν πονηρόν). It is the third part of the compound ὅτι clause. **Semantically**, καί is connective and gives us additional information about young believers. Not only are they strong because God's word lives in them, but they also can have assurance that they have victory over the devil because of the work of Jesus.

[ὅτι]: The Greek word ὅτι is a conjunction, which means "that" (BDAG 731.1a). **Syntactically**, [ὅτι] is an ellipsis and serves to introduce the third part of the compound dependent clause: "and [*that*] you have conquered the Evil One" (καὶ [ὅτι] νενικήκατε τὸν πονηρόν). The compound clause is substantival and also functions as part of the compound direct object of the verb, "I have written" (ἔγραψα). **Semantically**, ὅτι is indirect discourse: "that." It signals the content of what John is writing (Wallace 1996, 45).

νενικήκατε: The Greek word νενικήκατε is a second plural perfect active indicative from the verb νικάω that means, "I overcome" or "I vanquish" or "to overcome someone" (BDAG 673.2a). **Syntactically**, νενικήκατε is the governing verb of the third part of the substantival dependent [ὅτι] clause. The subject of the verb is an implied "you (plural)" embedded in the verb and refers to the young people among the intended recipients. **Semantically**, νενικήκατε is an extensive perfect: "you have overcome" (KJV ASV NASB ESV NIV CNT). John's emphasis is on the completed act of victory (Wallace 1996, 577). John underscores how Jesus overcame the evil one and now these young believers currently live in victory as long as they remain in orthodox teaching.

2:15a ἀγαπᾶτε: The Greek word ἀγαπᾶτε is second plural present active imperative from the verb ἀγαπάω that means, "I love" or to have a high esteem for or satisfaction with something (BDAG 5.2b). **Syntactically**, ἀγαπᾶτε is the main verb of the compound independent clause: "do not *love* the world nor the things in the world" (Μὴ ἀγαπᾶτε τὸν κόσμον μηδὲ τὰ ἐν τῷ κόσμῳ). The subject of the imperative is an implied "you (plural)" and refers to the readers of John's letter. **Semantically**, the negated μὴ ἀγαπᾶτε is an imperative of prohibition that forbids an action: "do not love" (Wallace 1996, 487; cf. NASB ESV NIV NET CNT). John forbids his readers to hold the world or its sinful trappings in high esteem.

Syntactical Nugget: While a traditional understanding of the present imperative + μη was to command the cessation of an act that was already ongoing (cf. Wallace 1996, 724), tradition may not fit this context. The context suggests John's confidence in their salvation and Christian life in verses 12–14. He does it again in verses 20-21. It seems likely that John is laying out a general principle for Christian living, "Do not love the world" (Bateman 2008, 259). We also encounter another article + prepositional phrase construction, "*the things* of the world" (τὰ ἐν τῷ κόσμῳ). In this case the article is a nominalizer and turns the whole phrase into a substantive, which serves as part of the compound direct object of the imperative "do not love" (μὴ ἀγαπᾶτε) (Wallace 1996, 231-236).

²ː¹⁵ᵇ ἐάν: The Greek word ἐάν is a conjunction, which means "if" (BDAG 267.1aα). **Syntactically**, the conjunction identifies the clause as a dependent clause. The entire dependent clause, "if anyone loves the world" (ἐάν τις ἀγαπᾷ τὸν κόσμον), functions adverbially. It modifies the verb, "is" (ἔστιν). **Semantically**, ἐάν introduces a third class conditional clause of probability: "if" (cf. KJV NASB ESV NIV NET etc). The condition is uncertain of fulfillment but still likely (Wallace 1996, 696). What that uncertain condition is is determined in the next verb.

ἀγαπᾷ: The Greek word ἀγαπᾷ is third singular present active subjunctive from the verb ἀγαπάω that means, "I love" or to have a high esteem for or satisfaction with something (BDAG 5.2b). The verb is in the subjunctive because ἐάν takes the subjunctive. **Syntactically**, ἀγαπᾷ is the governing verb of the dependent adverbial clause. The subject is the impersonal pronoun "anyone" (τις) and refers to anyone who loves the world and its trappings. **Semantically**, ἀγαπᾷ is a gnomic present with a customary present force: *"persists in* loving" or "loves" (cf. NASB ESV NIV NET). It underscores a timeless truth about people (Wallace 1996, 523). John emphasizes a point about anyone who has an infatuation with the immorality and hatred of the world. That point is driven home in the next clause.

²ː¹⁵ᶜ ἔστιν: The Greek word ἔστιν is third singular present active indicative from the verb εἰμί that means, "is" or describes a special connection between subject and predicate (BDAG 282.2b). **Syntactically**, ἔστιν is the main verb of the independent clause: "the love of the father is not in him" (οὐκ ἔστιν ἡ ἀγάπη τοῦ πατρὸς ἐν αὐτῷ). The subject of the verb is the phrase "the love of the father" (ἡ ἀγάπη τοῦ πατρὸς). **Semantically**, ἔστιν is a gnomic present: "is" (cf. KJV NASB ESV NIV NET etc.). It underscores a timeless truth about God (Wallace 1996, 523). The person infatuated with the immorality and hatred of the world does not have a relationship with God.

²ː¹⁶ᵃ ὅτι: The Greek word ὅτι is a conjunction, which means "for" or "for this reason" (BDAG 733.4). **Syntactically**, ὅτι introduces an independent conjunctive clause, "*For this reason* all that is in the world, the flesh that desires, the eyes that desire, and the boastful pride about one's life, is not from the father" (ὅτι πᾶν τὸ ἐν τῷ κόσμῳ, ἡ ἐπιθυμία τῆς σαρκὸς καὶ ἡ ἐπιθυμία τῶν ὀφθαλμῶν καὶ ἡ ἀλαζονεία τοῦ βίου, οὐκ ἔστιν ἐκ τοῦ πατρὸς). The ὅτι clause, though adverbial of cause, appears to have a loose connection with the previous independent clause. **Semantically**, ὅτι is an explanatory conjunction, giving us some clarification about what "the world" is: "for" (cf. KJV NASB ESV NIV etc.) or "because" (NET). We find another article + prepositional phrase here "which is in the world" (τὸ ἐν τῷ κόσμῳ). The article in this instance serves as an adjectivizer, which changes the phrase into a adjectival modifier, clarifying the substantival adjective "all" (πᾶν) (Culy 2004, 44).

ἔστιν: The Greek word ἔστιν is third singular present active indicative from the verb εἰμί that means, "is" or describes a special connection between subject and predicate (BDAG 282.2b). **Syntactically**, ἔστιν is the governing verb of the independent clause. The subject is the phrase, "all that is in the world" (πᾶν τὸ ἐν τῷ κόσμῳ). It further describes the flesh that desires, the eyes that desire, and the boastful pride about one's life. **Semantically**, ἔστιν is a gnomic present: "is" (cf. KJV NASB ESV NIV NET etc.). It underscores a timeless truth about the self-centeredness of the world (Wallace 1996, 523). It is not from God.

²ː¹⁶ᵇ ἀλλά: The Greek word ἀλλά is a conjunction, which means "but" after a previous negative statement (BDAG 44.1a). **Syntactically**, ἀλλά identifies the clause as a independent conjunctive clause: "*But all that is in the world* is from the world" (ἀλλὰ ἐκ τοῦ κόσμου ἐστίν). **Semantically**, ἀλλά is contrastive: "but" (KJV ESV NIV NET etc.). John emphasizes that the lust of the flesh, the lust of the eyes, and the boastful pride of life are not from God, but from the self-centered world system.

ἐστιν: The Greek word ἐστιν is third singular present active indicative from the verb εἰμί that means, "is" or describes a special connection between subject and predicate (BDAG 282.2b). **Syntactically**, ἐστιν is the main verb of the independent clause. The subject of the verb is an implied "all that is in the world." It refers back to the phrase earlier in the verse that describes the flesh that desires, the eyes that desire, and the boastful pride about one's life. **Semantically**, ἐστιν is a gnomic present: "is" (cf. KJV NASB ESV NIV NET etc.). It underscores a timeless truth about self-centeredness (Wallace 1996, 523). It is not from God but instead it is from the world and its values.

2:17a   καί: The Greek word καί is a conjunction which in this context means "and" (BDAG 494.1ba). **Syntactically**, καί introduces an independent conjunctive clause "and the world is passing away, also its lusts" (καὶ ὁ κόσμος παράγεται καὶ ἡ ἐπιθυμία αὐτοῦ). **Semantically**, καί is a coordinating connective: "and" (KJV ASN NRSV NET EST NLT). John adds a further thougt about the nature of the world system evident in the next verb.

παράγεται: The Greek word παράγεται is a third singular present passive indicative from the verb παράγω that means, "I pass away" or "I disappear" or "to go out of existence" (BDAG, 761.4b). **Syntactically**, παράγεται is the main verb of the independent clause. The subject is "the world" (ὁ κόσμος) and refers to the selfish lusts of the world system. **Semantically**, παράγεται is a progressive present: "is passing away" (NASB ESV NET CNT cf. NLT) or "are passing" (NRSV). John underscores the *right now* reality that the world system is going out of existence (Wallace 1996, 518).

2:17b   δέ: The Greek word δέ is a conjunction, which means "but" or "rather" (BDAG 213.4). **Syntactically**, δέ is in the post-positive position and introduces the independent conjunctive clause: "*but* the one who does the will of God remains forever" (ὁ δὲ ποιῶν τὸ θέλημα τοῦ θεοῦ μένει εἰς τὸν αἰῶνα). **Semantically**, δέ is a marker of contrast: "but" (cf. KJV NASB ESV NIV NET etc.).

μένει: The Greek word μένει is a third singular present active indicative from the verb μένω that means, "I remain," "I continue," "I abide" or of someone does not leave a certain realm or sphere (BDAG 631.1aβ). **Syntactically**, μένει is the main verb of the independent clause. It is the subject of the phrase, "the one who does the will of God" (ὁ . . . ποιῶν τὸ θέλημα τοῦ θεοῦ). **Semantically**, μένει is a customary present: "abides" (KJV ASV ESV CNT) or "lives" (NASB NRSV NIV NLT). John points out that while the world and its lusts are currently passing away, the one who does God's will is never going to pass away.

1 John 2:18–29

Verb Recognition for 1 John 2:18–29

[18]Παιδία, ἐσχάτη ὥρα ἐστίν, καὶ καθὼς ἠκούσατε ὅτι ἀντίχριστος ἔρχεται, καὶ νῦν ἀντίχριστοι πολλοὶ γεγόνασιν· ὅθεν γινώσκομεν ὅτι ἐσχάτη ὥρα ἐστίν. [19]ἐξ ἡμῶν ἐξῆλθαν, ἀλλ᾽ οὐκ ἦσαν ἐξ ἡμῶν· εἰ γὰρ ἐξ ἡμῶν ἦσαν, μεμενήκεισαν ἂν μεθ᾽ ἡμῶν· ἀλλ᾽ ἵνα φανερωθῶσιν ὅτι οὐκ εἰσὶν πάντες ἐξ ἡμῶν. [20]καὶ ὑμεῖς χρῖσμα ἔχετε ἀπὸ τοῦ ἁγίου, καὶ οἴδατε πάντες. [21]οὐκ ἔγραψα ὑμῖν ὅτι οὐκ οἴδατε τὴν ἀλήθειαν, ἀλλ᾽ ὅτι οἴδατε αὐτήν, καὶ ὅτι πᾶν ψεῦδος ἐκ τῆς ἀληθείας οὐκ ἔστιν.

²²Τίς ἐστιν ὁ ψεύστης εἰ μὴ ὁ ἀρνούμενος ὅτι Ἰησοῦς οὐκ ἔστιν ὁ Χριστός; οὗτός ἐστιν ὁ ἀντίχριστος, ὁ ἀρνούμενος τὸν πατέρα καὶ τὸν υἱόν. ²³πᾶς ὁ ἀρνούμενος τὸν υἱὸν οὐδὲ τὸν πατέρα ἔχει· ὁ ὁμολογῶν τὸν υἱὸν καὶ τὸν πατέρα ἔχει. ²⁴ὑμεῖς ὃ ἠκούσατε ἀπ' ἀρχῆς ἐν ὑμῖν μενέτω· ἐὰν ἐν ὑμῖν μείνῃ ὃ ἀπ' ἀρχῆς ἠκούσατε, καὶ ὑμεῖς ἐν τῷ υἱῷ καὶ ἐν τῷ πατρὶ μενεῖτε. ²⁵καὶ αὕτη ἐστὶν ἡ ἐπαγγελία ἣν αὐτὸς ἐπηγγείλατο ἡμῖν, τὴν ζωὴν τὴν αἰώνιον. ²

²⁶Ταῦτα ἔγραψα ὑμῖν περὶ τῶν πλανώντων ὑμᾶς. ²⁷καὶ ὑμεῖς τὸ χρῖσμα ὃ ἐλάβετε ἀπ' αὐτοῦ μένει ἐν ὑμῖν, καὶ οὐ χρείαν ἔχετε ἵνα τις διδάσκῃ ὑμᾶς· ἀλλ' ὡς τὸ αὐτοῦ χρῖσμα διδάσκει ὑμᾶς περὶ πάντων, καὶ ἀληθές ἐστιν καὶ οὐκ ἔστιν ψεῦδος, καὶ καθὼς ἐδίδαξεν ὑμᾶς, μένετε ἐν αὐτῷ.

²⁸Καὶ νῦν, τεκνία, μένετε ἐν αὐτῷ, ἵνα ἐὰν φανερωθῇ σχῶμεν παρρησίαν καὶ μὴ αἰσχυνθῶμεν ἀπ' αὐτοῦ ἐν τῇ παρουσίᾳ αὐτοῦ. ²⁹ἐὰν εἰδῆτε ὅτι δίκαιός ἐστιν, γινώσκετε ὅτι καὶ πᾶς ὁ ποιῶν τὴν δικαιοσύνην ἐξ αὐτοῦ γεγέννηται.

Clausal Outline Translated for 1 John 2:18–29

^{2:18a}Παιδία, ἐσχάτη ὥρα ἐστίν,
^{2:18a}Children, **it is** the last hour,

> ^{2:18b}καὶ καθὼς ἠκούσατε (ὅτι ἀντίχριστος ἔρχεται),
> ^{2:18b}and **as you heard** (that the antichirst is coming),
> |

^{2:18c}καὶ νῦν ἀντίχριστοι πολλοὶ γεγόνασιν·
^{2:18c}even now many antichrists **have appeared**;
> |

> ^{2:18d}ὅθεν γινώσκομεν (ὅτι ἐσχάτη ὥρα ἐστίν).
> ^{2:18d}whereby **we** *now* **know** (that it is the last hour).

^{2:19a}ἐξ ἡμῶν ἐξῆλθαν,
^{2:19a}**They went out** from us,

^{2:19b}ἀλλ' οὐκ ἦσαν ἐξ ἡμῶν·
^{2:19b}but **they were** not of us;

> ^{2:19c}εἰ γὰρ ἐξ ἡμῶν ἦσαν,
> ^{2:19c}for *you see* **if they had been** of us,
> |

^{2:19d}μεμενήκεισαν ἂν μεθ' ἡμῶν·
^{2:19d}**they would have remained** with us;

^{2:19e} ἀλλ' [ἐξῆλθαν]
^{2:19e} **but** [*they did go out*],

       |

     ^{2:19f} ἵνα **φανερωθῶσιν** (ὅτι οὐκ εἰσὶν πάντες ἐξ ἡμῶν).
     ^{2:19f} so that **it would be shown** (that they all <u>are</u> not of us).

^{2:20a} <u>καὶ</u> ὑμεῖς χρῖσμα **ἔχετε** ἀπὸ τοῦ ἁγίου,
^{2:20a} **But you have** an anointing from the Holy One,

^{2:20b} καὶ <u>οἴδατε</u> πάντα.
^{2:20b} and **you know** all *things*.

^{2:21a} οὐκ **ἔγραψα** ὑμῖν
^{2:21a} **I have** not **written** to you

     |

     ^{2:21b} **ὅτι** οὐκ <u>**οἴδατε**</u> τὴν ἀλήθειαν,
     ^{2:21b} **because you** do not **know** the truth,

^{2:21c} ἀλλ' [ἔγραψα ὑμῖν]
^{2:21c} **but** *rather* [*I have written*] to you

     |

     ^{2:21d} **ὅτι** <u>**οἴδατε**</u> αὐτήν,
     ^{2:21d} **because you know** it,

     |

     ^{2:21e} καὶ **ὅτι** [οἴδατε (ὅτι] πᾶν ψεῦδος ἐκ τῆς ἀληθείας οὐκ **ἔστιν**).
     ^{2:21e} <u>and</u> **because** [*you know* (*that*] no lie **is** of the truth).

^{2:22a} Τίς <u>**ἐστιν**</u> ὁ ψεύστης
^{2:22a} Who **is** the liar

     |

     ^{2:22b} <u>εἰ μὴ</u> ὁ ἀρνούμενος (<u>ὅτι</u> Ἰησοῦς οὐκ <u>**ἔστιν**</u> ὁ Χριστός);
     ^{2:22b} <u>except</u> the one who *persists* in denying (<u>that</u> Jesus **is** the Christ);

^{2:22c} οὗτός <u>**ἐστιν**</u> ὁ ἀντίχριστος, (ὁ ἀρνούμενος τὸν πατέρα καὶ τὸν υἱόν).
^{2:22c} This **is** the antichrist, (*namely* the one who *persists* in denying the Father and the Son).

^{2:23a} πᾶς ὁ ἀρνούμενος τὸν υἱὸν οὐδὲ τὸν πατέρα **ἔχει**·
^{2:23a} Whoever *persists* in denying the Son does not **have** the Father;

^{2:23b} ὁ ὁμολογῶν τὸν υἱὸν καὶ τὸν πατέρα **ἔχει**.
^{2:23b} the one who *persists* in their confession of the Son **has** the Father also.

^{2:24a} (ὑμεῖς <u>ὃ</u> **ἠκούσατε** ἀπ' ἀρχῆς) ἐν ὑμῖν **μενέτω**·
^{2:24a} **Let** (**what you** yourselves **have heard** from the beginning) **remain** in you;

            ^{2:24b} <u>**ἐὰν**</u> ἐν ὑμῖν **μείνῃ** (<u>ὃ</u> ἀπ' ἀρχῆς <u>ἠκούσατε</u>),
            ^{2:24b} **if** (<u>what</u> <u>you</u> have heard from the beginning) **remains** in you,

|

2:24c καὶ ὑμεῖς ἐν τῷ υἱῷ καὶ ἐν τῷ πατρὶ **μενεῖτε**.
2:24c **you** also **will remain** in the Son and in the Father.

2:25a καὶ αὕτη **ἐστὶν** ἡ ἐπαγγελία
2:25a Now this **is** the promise

       |

2:25b **ἣν** αὐτὸς **ἐπηγγείλατο** ἡμῖν, τὴν ζωὴν τὴν αἰώνιον.
2:25b **which he** (= God) himself **made** to us: eternal life.

2:26 Ταῦτα **ἔγραψα** ὑμῖν περὶ τῶν πλανώντων ὑμᾶς.
2:26 **I have written** these *things* to you concerning those who *persist in their attempt* to mislead you.

2:27a καὶ ὑμεῖς τὸ χρῖσμα . . . **μένει** ἐν ὑμῖν,
2:27a Now as for you, the anointing . . . **remains** *continually* in you.

       |

2:27b **ὃ ἐλάβετε** ἀπ' αὐτοῦ
2:27b **that you have received** from him

2:27c καὶ οὐ χρείαν **ἔχετε**
2:27c And **you have** no need

       |

2:27d **ἵνα** τις **διδάσκῃ** ὑμᾶς·
2:27d **that** anyone **teach** you;

2:27e **ἀλλ'** . . . καὶ ἀληθές **ἐστιν**
2:27e **but** . . . now it (i.e., anointing) **is** true

2:27f **καὶ** οὐκ **ἔστιν** ψεῦδος,
2:27f **and it is** not a lie,

       |

2:27fg **ὡς** τὸ αὐτοῦ χρῖσμα **διδάσκει** ὑμᾶς περὶ πάντων,
2:27g **as** his anointing *continually* **teaches** you about all things,

2:27h **καὶ καθὼς ἐδίδαξεν** ὑμᾶς,
2:27h and **just as** he *has* **taught** you,

       |

2:27i **μένετε** ἐν αὐτῷ.
2:27i *make it a practice to* **remain** in him.

2:28a Καὶ **νῦν**, τεκνία, **μένετε** ἐν αὐτῷ,
2:28a **Even now**, children, *make it a practice to* **remain** in him,

       |

2:28b **ἵνα** . . . **σχῶμεν** παρρησίαν
2:28b **so that** . . . **we may have** confidence

       |

2:28c **ἐὰν φανερωθῇ**
2:28c **when he appears**

|
²:²⁸ᵈ <u>καὶ</u> [<u>ἵνα</u>] μὴ <u>αἰσχυνθῶμεν</u> ἀπ᾽ αὐτοῦ ἐν τῇ παρουσίᾳ αὐτοῦ.
²:²⁸ᵈ and [*so that*] **we may** not **shrink away** from him at his coming.

²:²⁹ᵃ <u>ἐὰν</u> <u>εἰδῆτε</u> (ὅτι δίκαιός ἐστιν),
²:²⁹ᵃ **If** you **know** (that he is righteous),

|
²:²⁹ᵇ <u>γινώσκετε</u> (ὅτι καὶ πᾶς ὁ ποιῶν τὴν δικαιοσύνην ἐξ αὐτοῦ <u>γεγέννηται</u>).
²:²⁹ᵇ **You** also know (<u>that</u> everyone who practices righteousness <u>has been fathered</u> by him).

Syntax Explained for 1 John 2:18–29

²:¹⁸ᵃ ἐστίν: The Greek word ἐστίν is third singular present active indicative from the verb εἰμί that means, "it is" (BDAG 286.11d). **Syntactically**, ἐστίν is the main verb of the independent clause: "Children, *it is* the last hour," (Παιδία, ἐσχάτη ὥρα ἐστίν). The subject of the verb is an implied "it," referring to the time at hand. **Semantically**, ἐστίν is an equative present: ἔστιν serves as an equative verb of identity. The last hour is now.

Grammatical Nugget: The phrase "the last hour," (ἐσχάτη ὥρα ἐστίν) is a good example of Colwell's Rule which states, "Definite predicate nouns which precede the verb usually lack the article . . . A predicate nominative which precedes the verb cannot be translated an an indefinite or a qualitative noun solely because of the absence of the article; if the context suggests that the predicate is definite, it should be translated as a definite noun" (Wallace 1996, 257). While it might be tempting to translate the phrase indefinitely as "a last hour," Colwell's Rule suggests that while there is no definite article, the idea is still definite: "this is *the* last hour" (cf. KJV NASB ESV NIV NET etc.).

²:¹⁸ᵇ καὶ καθώς: The Greek word καί is a conjunction that means "and" (BDAG 496.2i). The Greek word καθώς is an adverbial conjunction, which means "just as" or "as" (BDAG 493.1). **Syntactically**, καὶ καθώς functions adverbially introducing a dependent conjunctive clause: "*and as* you have heard that the antichrist is coming" (καὶ καθὼς ἠκούσατε ὅτι ἀντίχριστος ἔρχεται). It modifies the verb, "appeared" (γεγόνασιν). Together, καὶ καθώς **semantically** is compartive: "and as" (KJV ASV NRSV ESV NIV CNT). John is about to underscore a comparison about the appearance of false teachers (antichrists).

ἠκούσατε: The Greek word ἠκούσατε is second plural aorist active indicative from the verb ἀκούω that means, "I hear" or "to receive news or information about something" (BDAG, 38 3). **Syntactically**, ἠκούσατε is the main verb of the dependent καὶ καθώς clause. The subject of the verb is an implied "you" and refers back to the the readers/hearers of the letter. **Semantically**, ἠκούσατε is a constative aorist: "you heard" (ASV NASB NET). It views the event as a whole (Wallace 1996, 557). John refers to information the community recieved about an Antichrist.

ὅτι: The Greek word ὅτι is a conjunction, which means "that" (BDAG 731d.1b). **Syntactically**, ὅτι introduces a dependent conjunctive clause: "*that* the Antichrist is coming" (ὅτι ἀντίχριστος ἔρχεται). The clause is placed in parenthesis in order to visualize its contribution to the dependent καθώς clause. The clause is substantival and is functioning as the direct object of the verb, "you have heard" (ἠκούσατε). **Semantically**, ὅτι is indirect discourse: "that" (cf. KJV NASB ESV NET). It reveals the content of what was heard (Wallace 1996, 456-58). More specifically, John disloses what believers were taught, which is clarified in the rest of the clause.

ἔρχεται: The Greek word ἔρχεται is a third singular present middle indicative from the verb ἔρχμομαι that means, "I come" or to make an appearance before the public (BDAG 394.1bβ). **Syntactically**, ἔρχεται is the governing verb of the dependent conjunctive ὅτι clause. The subject is "the Antichrist" (ἀντίχριστος). **Semantically**, ἔρχεται is a futuristic present: "shall come" (KJV) or "is coming" (NASB NRSV ESV NIV NET NLT CNT). "The present tense describes an event *begun* in present time but completed in the future" (Wallace 1996, 537). John's readers have heard that antichrist will come in the future.

2:18c καὶ νῦν: The Greek word καί is a coordinating conjunction which means "and" (BDAG 496.2i). The Greek word νῦν is an adverb that means "now" (BDAG 681.1aα). **Syntactically**, καὶ νῦν introduces a independent conjunctive clause: "even now many antichrists have appeared" (καὶ νῦν ἀντίχριστοι πολλοὶ γεγόνασιν). **Semantically**, καὶ νῦν is a temporal marker with the focus on the present moment: "and now" (BDAG 681.1; cf. NLT). While maintaining the present force, καὶ νῦν is ascensive: "even now" (KJV ASV NASB NIV) or "so now" (NRSV ESV NET). John adds an addition point about false teachers (antichrists) (Wallace 1996, 670-671).

γεγόνασιν: The Greek word γεγόνασιν is a third plural perfect active indicative from the verb γίνομαι that means, "I come" or "I appear" or "to be present at a given time" (BDAG 199.8). **Syntactically**, γεγόνασιν is the main verb of the independent clause. The subject is the phrase "many antichrists" (ἀντίχριστοι πολλοί). **Semantically**, γεγόνασιν is an extensive perfect: "have come" (NRSB NIV CNT) or "have appeared" (NASB NLT). John's focus is on the completed act of knowing someone in past time rather than the present results: "is coming" (ESV NET; cf. Wallace 1996, 577). So not only is an Antichrist coming in the future, he's here even now via the false teachers who have infiltrated the community.

2:18d ὅθεν: The Greek word ὅθεν is an adverbial conjunction that means "from which" (BDAG 692.1b). **Syntactically**, ὅθεν introduces a dependent conjunctive clause. It is an adverbial conjunction clause: "*from which* we now know that it is the last hour" (ὅθεν γινώσκομεν ὅτι ἐσχάτη ὥρα ἐστίν), is functioning adverbially, modifying the verb, "have come" (γεγόνασιν). **Semantically**, ὅθεν is an inferential conjunction: "whereby" (KJV ASV; cf. ESV) or "from this" (NASB NRSV NET NLT), or "by this" (CNT). It provides a deduction about the false teachers (Wallace 1996, 673; BDAG 692.1b) clearly evident in the rest of the clause.

γινώσκομεν: The Greek word γινώσκομεν is a first plural present active indicative from the verb γινώσκω that means, "I know" or to come to know about something (BDAG, 200.1c). **Syntactically**, γινώσκομεν is the governing verb of the dependent ὅθεν clause. The subject of the verb is an implied "we" embedded in the verb and refers to both John and the readers. **Semantically**, γινώσκομεν is a progressive present: "we *now* know" or "we know" (cf. KJV NASB ESV NIV NET etc.). It underscores something that is known *right now* (Wallace 1996, 518). The content of what is known is evident in the ὅτι clause.

ὅτι: The Greek word ὅτι is a conjunction, which means "that" after verbs of perception (BDAG 731.1c). **Syntactically**, ὅτι introduces a dependent conjunctive clause: "*that* it is the last hour" (ὅτι ἐσχάτη ὥρα ἐστίν). The clause is substantival and is functioning as the direct object of the verb, "we know" (γινώσκομεν). The entire ὅτι clause is placed in parenthesis in order to visualize its contribution to the independent clause. **Semantically**, ὅτι is indirect discourse: "that" (KJV ASV NASB NRSV ESV NET CNT NLT). It provides the content what believers can now know (Wallace 1996, 456), which is clear in the rest of the ὅτι clause.

ἐστίν: The Greek word ἐστίν is third singular present active indicative from the verb εἰμί that means, "it is" (BDAG 286.11d). **Syntactically**, ἐστίν is the governing verb of the dependent ὅτι clause. The subject of the verb is an implied "it" and refers to the time period that the readers currently find themselves in. **Semantically**, ἐστίν is an equative present: "it is" (cf. KJV NASB ESV NIV NET etc.). It equates the current time period with the last hour. The verse ends the way it began with the phrase "it is the last hour" (ἐσχάτη ὥρα ἐστίν). This rhetorical device is called an inclusion or framing and it serves to heighten and stress the theme of the verse.

2:19a ἐξῆλθαν: The Greek word ἐξῆλθαν is a third plural aorist active indicative from the verb ἐξέρχμομαι that means, "I depart" or "I leave" or "to discontinue an association" (BDAG 348.4). **Syntactically**, ἐξῆλθαν is the main verb of the independent clause: *"they went out* from us" (ἐξ ἡμῶν ἐξῆλθαν). The subject of the verb is an implied "they" and refers to the false teachers or "antichrists" who had recently left their ranks. **Semantically**, ἐξῆλθαν is a constative aorist: "they went out" (cf. KJV NASB ESV NIV NET etc.) or "they *left*" (NLT). John states an historical fact (Wallace 1996, 557). False teachers left their community of faith. The prepositional phrase, "from us" (ἐξ ἡμῶν), has an emphatic position at the beginning of the verse that makes their leaving even more prominent (Culy 2004, 48).

2:19b ἀλλ': The Greek word ἀλλά is a conjunction that means "but" or "yet" (BDAG 44.2). **Syntactically**, ἀλλά identifies the clause as a independent conjunctive clause: *"But* they were not of us" (ἀλλ' οὐκ ἦσαν ἐξ ἡμῶν). **Semantically**, ἀλλά is contrastive: "but" (cf. KJV NASB ESV NIV NET etc.). John provides the other side of the issue (BDAG 44.2). Even though a group of people was at one time part of their congregation, they never really belonged (cf. Brown 1984, 174). Just because they were at their gatherings, did not mean that they were really part of them.

ἦσαν: The Greek word ἦσαν is third plural imperfect active indicative from the verb εἰμί that means, "is" or "to be in close connection with" (BDAG 283.2a). **Syntactically**, ἦσαν is the main verb of the independent clause. The subject of the verb is an implied "they" and refers back to the false teachers or the "antichrists" who had recently left the church. **Semantically**, ἦσαν is an ingressive imperfect: "were" (KJV ASV NASB ESV CNT) or "did not really belong" (NRSV NIV NET). It that stresses the beginning of a past action (not part of the community) that was confirmed after they left (Wallace 1996, 545-56). This clause serves as an identity marker for these secessionists. They were not really part of the church to begin with (Culy 2004, 49).

2:19c εἰ γάρ: The Greek word εἰ is a conjunction, which means "if" (BDAG 278.6e). The second conjunction, γάρ is in the post-positive position and means "for" or "you see" (BDAG 189.2). **Syntactically**, εἰ and γάρ introduce a dependent conjunctive clause: *"for if* they were of us" (εἰ γὰρ ἐξ ἡμῶν ἦσαν). The clause functions adverbially as the protasis of a conditional clause. It modifies the verb, "they would have remembered" (μεμενήκεισαν). **Semantically**, εἰ γάρ introduces a second-class conditional clause: "for *you see* if" (cp. KJV ASV NASB NRSV ESV NIV CNT). Another possibility is "because if" (NET; cf. BDAG 189.1b). It assumes an untruth is given for the sake of an argument as a clarification or explanation for leaving (Wallace 1996, 694-696). That assumed untruth is evident in the rest of the clause.

ἦσαν: The Greek word ἦσαν is third plural imperfect active indicative from the verb εἰμί that means, "is" or "to be in close connection with" (BDAG 283.2c). **Syntactically**, ἦσαν is the main verb of the independent clause. The subject of the verb is an implied "they" and refers back to the false teachers or the "antichrists" who had recently left the orthodox behind. **Semantically**, ἦσαν appears to be a pluperfective imperfect: "they had been" (KJV ASV NASB NRSV ESV CNT) or "they had belonged" (NIV NET; cf. Wallace 1996, 549). This clause is the first part of John's thought. "If it were true that antichrists were part of the church" is completed with the next clause.

2:19d μεμενήκεισαν: The Greek word μεμενήκεισαν is a third plural pluperfect active indicative from the verb μένω that means, "I remain" or "I stay" or to remain in fellowship with someone (BDAG, 631.1b). **Syntactically**, μεμενήκεισαν is the main verb of the independent clause that serves as the apodosis of the second-class condition. The subject is an implied "they" embedded in the verb and refers to the antichrists. **Semantically**, μεμενήκεισαν is an intensive pluperfect: "would have remained" (NASB NRSV ESV NET) or "would have continued" (KJV ASV ESV CNT) or "would have stayed" (NLT). John focuses on the results (Wallace 1996, 583). Had the antichrists been part of the community, they never would have left.

Semantical Nugget: The pluperfect is not very common in the New Testament, only occurring eighty-six times of those at least sixteen times in John's Gospel. It is slightly different than the perfect tense. While the perfect tense describes an action that was completed in the past but has effects into the present, the pluperfect describes an action that was completed in the past and that had ongoing effects, but those effects do not necessarily reach into the present (Wallace 1996, 583). John argues that true believers never would have left to follow a false teaching. The very fact that a group of people left the community proves they were never true believers.

2:19e ἀλλ': The Greek word ἀλλά is a conjunction that means "but" or "yet" (BDAG 44.2). **Syntactically**, ἀλλά identifies the clause as a independent conjunctive clause: "*But* they did go out" (ἀλλ'[ἐξῆλθαν]). The elliptical verb ἐξῆλθαν is implied from the context. This combination of ἀλλά + ἵνα appears many times in the Gospel of John and almost always includes an elliptical verb (John 1:8, 31; 3:17; 9:3; 11:52; 12:9, 47; 13:18: 14:31; 15:25: 17:15). **Semantically**, ἀλλά is contrastive: "but" (cf. KJV NASB ESV NIV NET etc.). John provides the other side of the issue (BDAG 44.2).

2:19f ἵνα: The Greek word ἵνα is a conjunction, which means "that" (BDAG 476.2f). **Syntactically**, ἵνα introduces a dependent conjunctive clause: "*so that* it would be shown that they are all not of us" (ἵνα φανερωθῶσιν ὅτι οὐκ εἰσὶν πάντες ἐξ ἡμῶν). The entire ἵνα clause is adverbial. It modifies the elliptical verb "they went out" ([ἐξῆλθαν]). **Semantically**, the entire ἵνα clause appears to have the force of a result infinitive: "that" (KJV ASV NRSV ESV NIV CNT) or "so that" (NRSV). The emphasis is on the *outcome* of their leaving. It showed that they were never part of the church.

φανερωθῶσιν: The Greek word φανερωθῶσιν is a third plural aorist passive subjunctive from the verb φανερόω that means, "I disclose" or "I show" or "I make known" or "to cause to become known (BDAG 1048.2bβ). The verb is in the subjunctive mood because it is part of a ἵνα clause. **Syntactically**, φανερωθῶσιν is the governing verb of the dependent adverbial result clause. The assumed subject "they" refers to the secessionists who have left the community to follow after false teachings. **Semantically**, φανερωθῶσιν is a constative aorist: "it would be known" (NASB) or "it would be shown" (BDAG 1048.2bβ). Perhaps the best rendering is "it proved" (NLT) or "they made it plain" (NRSV). John states an historical fact (Wallace 1996, 557), which is articulated in the next ὅτι clause.

ὅτι: The Greek word ὅτι is a conjunction, which means "that" after verbs of perception (BDAG 731.1c). **Syntactically**, ὅτι serves to introduce a dependent conjunctive clause: "*that* they are not all of us" (ὅτι οὐκ εἰσὶν πάντες ἐξ ἡμῶν). The clause functions substantivally as the direct object of the verb, "it might be shown" (φανερωθῶσιν). The clause is placed in parenthesis in order to visualize its contribution to the dependent ἵνα clause. **Semantically**, ὅτι is indirect discourse: "that" (cf. KJV NASB ESV NIV NET etc.). The ὅτι provides the content of what has been shown.

εἰσίν: The Greek word εἰσίν is third plural present active indicative from the verb εἰμί that means, "I am" as a way of denoting a close relationship with someone (BDAG 285.10) or to have a close connection with (BDAG 283.2a). **Syntactically**, εἰσίν is the main verb of the dependent ὅτι clause. The subject of the verb is an implied "they" referring to secessionists. **Semantically**, εἰσίν negated with οὐκ is equative: "are not" (ASV NASB ESV) or "were not" (KJV CNT). John says the false teachers are not part of the community, simply based on their decision to leave it.

2:20a καί: The Greek word καί is a conjunction that means "but" (BDAG 495.2a). **Syntactically**, καί introduces a independent conjunctive clause: "*but* you have an anointing from the holy one" (καὶ ὑμεῖς χρῖσμα ἔχετε ἀπὸ τοῦ ἁγίου). **Semantically**, καί is contrastive: "but" (KJV NASB NRSV ESV NIV CNT NLT). It gives contrastive information about John's readers. Unlike those who left the community, John's readers have a special anointing from God which gives them assurance that they are "of us." This contrast is highlighted even more by the presence of the emphatic personal pronoun "you" (ὑμεῖς).

ἔχετε: The Greek word ἔχετε is a second plural present active indicative from the verb ἔχω that means, "I have" or to have something within oneself (BDAG 420.1d). **Syntactically**, ἔχετε is the main verb of the independent conjunctive clause. The assumed subject "you" refers to the readers of the letter. **Semantically**, ἔχετε is a customary present: "you have" (cf. KJV NASB ESV NIV NET etc.). It points out that the readers have the continual presence of God in their life through this special anointing from the holy one (Wallace 1996, 521).

2:20b καί: The Greek word καί is a conjunction which means "and" (BDAG 494.2ba). **Syntactically**, καί introduces an independent conjunctive clause: "*and* you know all things" (καὶ οἴδατε πάντες). **Semantically**, καί coorinating connective: "and" (cf. KJV NASB NIV ESV NET etc.). John's conjunctive clauses provide additional information about his readers.

οἴδατε: The Greek word οἴδατε is a second plural perfect active indicative from the verb οἶδα that means, "I know" or to know about something (BDAG 693.1b). **Syntactically**, οἴδατε is the governing verb of the independent conjunctive clause. The assumed subject "you" refers to the believer who has received an anointing from God. **Semantically**, οἴδατε is a perfect with present force: "you know all *things*" (KJV ASV). John underscores that all believers have an anointing from God, which enables them to know all things. Some verbs, like οἶδα, almost exclusively appear in the perfect tense without the perfect's aspectual significance (Wallace 1996, 579-580).

2:21a ἔγραψα: The Greek word ἔγραψα is a first singular aorist active indicative from the verb γράφω that means, "I write" or "I compose" some literary composition like a letter (BDAG, 207d 2d). **Syntactically**, ἔγραψα is the main verb of the independent clause "I have not written to you" (οὐκ ἔγραψα ὑμῖν). The assumed subject "I" refers to the author. **Semantically**, ἔγραψα is a epistolary aorist: "I have not written" (KJV ASV NASB NET; cf. 2:14a, 14b, 14c). John's stress is on what he has just written in *this* letter and the reader's full awareness of the truth. However, it is possible that John refers to another letter written earlier (Wallace 1996, 563).

2:21b ὅτι: The Greek word ὅτι is a conjunction which means "because" or "since" (BDAG 732.4b). **Syntactically**, ὅτι introduces a dependent conjunctive clause: "*because* you do not know the truth" (ὅτι οὐκ οἴδατε τὴν ἀλήθειαν). The clause is functioning adverbially. It modifies the verb, "I have written" (ἔγραψα). **Semantically**, ὅτι is causal: "because" (KJV ASV NASB NRSV ESV NIV CNT NLT). It provides the reason why John is currently writing (Wallace 1996, 460). John provides a reason why he is not writing to them, which clarified in the next verb.

Syntactical Nugget: Verse 21 has three ὅτι clauses, which are translated several ways. One rendering is to translate all three clauses as causal. It gives three different reasons why John is writing, "I did not write because . . . because . . . because" (ASV NASB ESV NIV CNT NLT). A second rendering is to classify all three clauses as indirect discourse. It gives a summary content about what John is writing about, "I did not write that . . . but that . . . and that" (NET; Brown 1982, 350). Finally, the first two clauses are causal, giving reasons why John is writing and then the third ὅτι clause as indirect discourse (KJV NRSV). The latter view has two additional options. The third ὅτι clause could be the direct object of the verb "I have written" (I did not write because . . . but because . . . and that) or as the direct object of an elliptical "you know" (I did not write because . . . but because you know it and [you know] that). The presence of the καί seems to rule out the last option. The καί seems to connect the third ὅτι clause with the second ὅτι clause. The option of classifying all three as indirect discourse all serving as the direct object of "I have written" (ἔγραψα) seems to make little sense as well. Why would John be writing them to assure them of something of which they are already assured? See Culy 2004, 53-54. The best option is a mixed view whereby all three ὅτι clauses are causal. They provide three reasons why John is writing. The third ὅτι clause has an elliptical indirect discourse "you know that." (and [you know] that no lie comes from the truth). See 2:21d and 2:21e.

οἴδατε: The Greek word οἴδατε is a second plural perfect active indicative from the verb οἶδα that means, "I know" or to have information about something (BDAG 693.1b). **Syntactically**, οἴδατε serves as the governing verb of the dependent conjunctive clause. The assumed subject "you" refers to the readers of the letter. **Semantically**, οἴδατε is a perfect with present force negated with οὐκ: "you do not know" (cf. KJV NASB ESV NIV NET etc.). Verbs like οἶδα appear regularly in the perfect tense without the perfect's aspectual significance (Wallace 1996, 579-580). It underscores the reason why John is not writing. It is not because they are unaware of the truth, but because they know it.

2:21c ἀλλ᾽: The Greek word ἀλλά is a conjunction that means "but" or "but rather" (BDAG 44.1a). **Syntactically**, ἀλλά identifies the clause as an independent conjunctive clause: "*But rather* [I am writing] (ἀλλ᾽[ἔγραψα]). **Semantically**, ἀλλά is contrastive statement: "but rather" or "but" (cf. KJV NASB ESV NIV NET etc.). Because it follows a previous negative statement, John underscores that believers are not unaware of the truth *instead* they know it.

[ἔγραψα] This elliptical Greek word ἔγραψα is a first singular aorist active indicative from the verb γράφω that means, "I write" or "I compose" some literary composition like a letter (BDAG, 207d 2d). The elliptical verb [ἔγραψα] is implied from the context. **Syntactically**, [ἔγραψα] is the main verb of the independent clause: "I have not written to you" (οὐκ ἔγραψα ὑμῖν). The assumed subject "I" refers to the author. **Semantically**, ἔγραψα is a consummative aorist: "I have not written" (KJV ASV NASB NET). John's stress is on what he has just written in *this* letter (Wallace 1996, 559).

2:21d ὅτι: The Greek word ὅτι is a conjunction which means "because" or "since" (BDAG 732.4b). **Syntactically**, ὅτι introduces a dependent conjunctive clause: "*because* you know it" (ὅτι οἴδατε αὐτήν). This ὅτι clause functions adverbially. It modifies the elliptical verb, "I have written" ([ἔγραψα]). **Semantically**, ὅτι is causal: "because" (ASV NASB ESV NIV CNT NLT). It provides the second reason why John is writing (Wallace 1996, 460). See "Syntactical Nugget" after 2:21b ὅτι.

οἴδατε: The Greek word οἴδατε is a second plural perfect active indicative from the verb οἶδα that means, "I know" or to have information about something (BDAG 693.1b). **Syntactically**, οἴδατε serves as the governing verb of the dependent conjunctive clause. The assumed subject "you" refers to the readers of the letter. **Semantically**, οἴδατε is a perfect with present force: "they know" (cf. KJV NASB ESV NIV NET etc.). The verb οἶδα appears regularly in the perfect tense with present force (Wallace 1996, 579-580). John is writing because they know the truth.

2:21e καί: The Greek word καί is a conjunction which means "and" (BDAG 494.1b). **Syntactically**, καί introduces a dependent conjunctive clause: "*and* because [you know (that] no lie is of the truth" (καὶ ὅτι [οἴδατε ὅτι] πᾶν ψεῦδος ἐκ τῆς ἀληθείας οὐκ ἔστιν). **Semantically**, καί is a coordinating connecter: "and" (cf. KJV NASB ESV NIV NET etc.). The clause provides additional information about the readers.

ὅτι: The Greek word ὅτι is a conjunction which means "because" or "since" (BDAG 732.4b). **Syntactically**, ὅτι introduces a dependent conjunctive clause: "*because* [you know (that] no lie is of the truth)" (ὅτι [οἴδατε ὅτι] πᾶν ψεῦδος ἐκ τῆς ἀληθείας οὐκ ἔστιν). This ὅτι clause functions adverbially. It modifies the elliptical verb, "I have written" ([ἔγραψα]). **Semantically**, ὅτι is causal: "because" (ASV NASB ESV NIV CNT NLT). It provides the third reason why John is writing.

ἔστιν: The Greek word ἔστιν is third singular present active indicative from the verb εἰμί that means, "is" or to describe a special connection between the subject and predicate (BDAG 283.2b). **Syntactically**, ἔστιν is the governing verb of the dependent substantival clause. The elliptical phrase, "you know that" (οἴδατε ὅτι), is implied from the context. The subject of the verb is the phrase "every lie" (πᾶν ψεῦδος). **Semantically**, ἔστιν is a gnomic present: "is" (cf. KJV ASB NASB ESV NET CNT). It describes a general principle about a lie and a truth (Wallace 1996, 523). There is no connection between a lie and the truth.

2:22a ἔστιν: The Greek word ἔστιν is third singular present active indicative from the verb εἰμί that means, "is" or to show how something is to be understood (BDAG 283.2c). **Syntactically**, ἔστιν is the main verb of the independent clause: "Who is the liar" (Τίς ἐστιν ὁ ψεύστης). The subject of the verb is the interrogative pronoun, "who" (τίς) due to the priority of pronouns (Wallace 1996, 43). **Semantically**, ἔστιν is a gnomic present: "is" (cf. KJV NASB ESV NIV NET etc.). It asks a generaic question for identifying a liar (Wallace 1996, 523).

2:22b εἰ μή: The Greek word εἰ is an adverbial conjunction, which typically means "if" (BDAG 277). The Greek word μή is an adverb, which typically means "not" (BDAG 644). However, the construction εἰ + μή is a subcategory of the conditional conjuction that expresses a contrast or an exception, "but" or "except" (BDAG 278.6iα; 644.1aα). **Syntactically**, εἰ μή introduces a dependent conjunctive clause. **Semantically**, εἰ μή points out a negative exception: "except" or "but" (KJV ASV NASB ESV NET CNT). It introduces John's answer to his interrogative statemtent. If anyone is a liar, it is the one who denies that Jesus is the Messiah.

ἀρνούμενος: The Greek word ἀρνούμενος is a nominative masculine singular present middle participle from the verb ἀρνέομαι that means, "I deny" or to state that something is not true (BDAG, 732.2). **Syntactically**, ἀρνούμενος is a substantival participle. It functions as the subject of the elliptical verb "is" ([ἐστὶν]). **Semantically**, ἀρνούμενος is a gnomic present with customary force: "persists in denying" or "denies" (cf. KJV NASB ESV NIV NET etc.). It identifies a timeless fact for those who practice a pattern of behavior (Wallace 1996, 521, 615). John underscores the one who continually denies that Jesus is the Christ. What is universally true about that person is clarified in the next ὅτι clause.

ὅτι: The Greek word ὅτι is a conjunction, which means "that" (BDAG 732.1a). **Syntactically**, ὅτι introduces a dependent conjunctive clause: "*that* Jesus is not *the* Christ" (ὅτι Ἰησοῦς οὐκ ἔστιν ὁ Χριστός). This ὅτι clause functions substantivally as the direct object of the participle, "the one who denies" (ὁ ἀρνούμενος). It is placed in parenthesis in order to visualize its contribution to the independent clause. The article "the" (ὁ) before "Christ" (Χριστός) is par excellence that identifies Jesus as a Messiah who is in a class by himself (Wallace 1996, 223). There has never been nor will there ever be another Messiah like Jesus. **Semantically**, ὅτι is indirect discourse: "that" (cf. KJV NASB ESV NIV NET etc.). John provides the explicit content of what the liars are denying (Wallace 1996, 456-58). They will not admit that Jesus is the Messiah.

ἔστιν: The Greek word ἔστιν is third singular present active indicative from the verb εἰμί that means, "is" or to describe a special connection between the subject and predicate (BDAG 283.2cα). **Syntactically**, ἔστιν is the governing verb of the dependent ὅτι clause. In spite of the fact that Messiah is articular and Jesus is anarthrous, the subject of the verb is "Jesus" (Ἰησοῦς) due to word order (Wallace 1996, 44). Proper nouns are generally the subject (Culy 2004, 55). **Semantically**, ἔστιν is an equative present: "is" (cf. KJV NASB ESV NIV NET etc.). John links Jesus to his rightful title. Jesus is the Christ (= Messiah).

2:22c ἔστιν: The Greek word ἔστιν is third singular present active indicative from the verb εἰμί that means, "is" or to describe a special connection between the subject and predicate (BDAG 283.2cα). **Syntactically**, ἔστιν is the main verb of the independent clause: "this *is* the antichrist, the one who persists in denying the Father and the Son" (οὗτός ἐστιν ὁ ἀντίχριστος, ὁ ἀρνούμενος τὸν πατέρα καὶ τὸν υἱόν). The subject of the verb is the demonstrative pronoun "this one" (οὗτός) due to the priority of pronouns over articular nouns (Wallace 1996, 44). **Semantically**, ἔστιν is an equative present: "is" (cf. KJV NASB ESV NIV NET etc.). John links the one who denies the Messiahship of Jesus to be against Christ (= the antichrist).

ἀρνούμενος: The Greek word ἀρνούμενος is a nominative masculine singular present middle participle from the verb ἀρνέομαι the means, "I deny" or to disclaim association with a person (BDAG, 732.3c). **Syntactically**, ἀρνούμενος could either be an adjectival participle describing an attribute of one of these "antichrists" or a substantival participle functioning appositionally, further naming one of these "antichrists." Either way the participle gives us further information about these antichrists. **Semantically**, ἀρνούμενος is a gnomic present with customary force: "the one who persists in denying" or "denies" (cf. KJV NASB ESV NIV NET etc.). It identifies a timeless fact for those who practice a pattern of behavior (Wallace 1996, 521, 615). John underscores the identity of *anyone* who continually denies that Jesus is God's Messiah. That person is against Christ (= the antichrist).

2:23a ἀρνούμενος: The Greek word ἀρνούμενος is a nominative masculine singular present middle participle from the verb ἀρνέομαι, which means, "I deny" or to disclaim association with a person (BDAG, 732.3b). **Syntactically**, ἀρνούμενος is adjectival and modifies the substantival adjective "everyone" (πᾶς). **Semantically**, ἀρνούμενος is a gnomic present with customary force: "the one who persists in denying" or "denies" (cf. KJV NASB ESV NIV NET etc.). It identifies a timeless fact for those who practice a pattern of behavior (Wallace 1996, 521, 615). John underscores a timeless truth about the person who continually repudiates or disowns Jesus as Messiah, which revealed in the next verb.

ἔχει: The Greek word ἔχει is a third singular present active indicative from the verb ἔχω that means, "I have" or to stand in a close relationship with someone (BDAG 420.2b). **Syntactically**, ἔχει is the main verb of the independent clause: "whoever persists in denying the Son does not have the Father (πᾶς ὁ ἀρνούμενος τὸν υἱὸν οὐδὲ τὸν πατέρα ἔχει). The subject is the phrase "everyone who denies the son" (πᾶς ὁ ἀρνούμενος τὸν υἱόν). **Semantically**, ἔχει is a gnomic present negated with οὐδὲ: "does not have" (KJV ASV NET; NLT). John underscores a timeless fact (Wallace 1996, 523). The one who persists in their denial of Jesus as Messiah cannot have a relationship with God.

2:23b ὁμολογῶν: The Greek word ὁμολογῶν is a nominative masculine singular present active participle from the verb ὁμολογέω, which means, "I confess" or to profess an allegiance to someone publically (BDAG 708.4b). **Syntactically**, ὁμολογῶν functions substantivally as the subject of the verb, "has" (ἔχει). **Semantically**, ὁμολογῶν is a gnomic present with customary present: "the one who *persists* in their confession." It identifies a timeless fact for those who practice a pattern of behavior (Wallace 1996, 521, 615). John underscores that the person who continually confesses that Jesus is Messiah, which revealed in the next verb.

ἔχει: The Greek word ἔχει is a third singular present active indicative from the verb ἔχω that means, "I have" or to stand in a close relationship with someone (BDAG 420.2b). **Syntactically**, ἔχει is the main verb of the independent clause: "whoever persists in their confession of the Son also has the Father" (ὁ ὁμολογῶν τὸν υἱὸν καὶ τὸν πατέρα ἔχει). The subject is the phrase "whoever confesses the son" (ὁ ὁμολογῶν τὸν υἱόν). **Semantically**, ἔχει is a gnomic present: "has" (cf. KJV NASB ESV NIV NET etc.). John underscores a timeless fact (Wallace 1996, 523). The one who *persists* in their confession of Jesus as Messiah has a relationship with God.

2:24a ὃ: The Greek word ὃ is a neuter accusative singular from the relative pronoun ὅς, which means, "that which" or "what" (BDAG 725.1bα). **Syntactically**, ὃ introduces a dependent relative clause: "*what* you yourselves have heard from the beginning" (ὑμεῖς ὃ ἠκούσατε ἀπ' ἀρχῆς). The relative clause functions substantivally: "what you yourselves have heard" (NRSV ESV NIV ET NLT). It is the subject of the third person imperative "let . . . remain" (μενέτω): It is placed in parentheses to visualize it's contribution to the independent clause.

ἠκούσατε: The Greek word ἠκούσατε is a second plural aorist active indicative from the verb ἀκούω that means, "I hear" or to hear something from someone (BDAG 37.1aβ) or denote a body of authoritative teaching (BDAG 38.3d). **Syntactically**, ἠκούσατε is the governing verb of the dependent relative clause. The subject of the verb within the relative clause is the emphatic pronoun "you" (ὑμεῖς) which refers to the readers/hearers of the letter. **Semantically**, ἠκούσατε is a consummative aorist: "have heard" (KJV NIV NET). It describes a conclusion or cessation of an act as a whole (Wallace 1996, 559). John wants his readers to persist in their teaching about Jesus that they have had since the beginning of their faith journey (cf. 2:7).

μενέτω: The Greek word μενέτω is a third singular present active imperative from the verb μένω that means, "I remain" or of someone who does not leave a relationship (BDAG 631.1aβ). **Syntactically**, μενέτω is the main verb of the independent clause: "Let *it* remain in you" (ἐν ὑμῖν μενέτω). The subject is "what you yourselves have heard from the beginning" (ὑμεῖς ὃ ἠκούσατε ἀπ' ἀρχῆς). **Semantically**, μενέτω is an imperative of command: "let . . . remain" or "let . . . abide" (KJV ASV NASB NRSV ESV CNT). It assumes an *on-going process*: "let *the teaching continually* remain in you" (Wallace 1996, 485). John expects his readers to persist in the teaching about Jesus, which they have had since the beginning of their Christian faith.

^{2:24b} ἐάν: The Greek word ἐάν is a conjunction, which means "if" (BDAG 267.1aβ). **Syntactically**, the conjunction ἐάν identifies the clause as a dependent conjunctive clause. The entire dependent clause: "if what you have heard from the beginning remains in you" (ἐὰν ἐν ὑμῖν μείνῃ ὃ ἀπ' ἀρχῆς ἠκούσατε). It functions adverbially. It modifies the verb, "you remain" (μενεῖτε). **Semantically**, ἐάν introduces a third class conditional clause of probability: "if" (cf. KJV NASB ESV NIV NET etc). The condition is uncertain of fulfillment but still likely (Wallace 1996, 696). John speaks of a probability for his readers that is clarified with the next verb.

μείνῃ: The Greek word μείνῃ is a third singular aorist active subjunctive from the verb μένω that means, "I remain" or "I abide" or "I continue" or of "someone who does not leave" (BDAG 631.1aβ). The verb is in the subjunctive because it is part of an ἐὰν clause. **Syntactically**, μείνῃ is the governing verb of the dependent adverbial conditional ἐάν clause. The subject is the substantival relative clause: "what you have heard from the beginning" (ὃ ἀπ' ἀρχῆς ἠκούσατε). **Semantically**, μείνῃ is a constative aorist: "remains" (KJV ESV NIV NET NLT). It views their belief as whole or in a summary fashion (Wallace 1996, 257). The probability for John's readers is that if they remain in the correct teaching about Jesus, they will have an abiding relationship with God (Culy 2004, 57).

ὃ: The Greek word ὃ is a neuter singular accusative from the relative pronoun pronoun ὅς, which means, "that which" or "what" (BDAG 725.1bα). **Syntactically**, ὃ introduces a dependent relative clause: "*what* you have heard from the beginning" (ὃ ἀπ' ἀρχῆς ἠκούσατε). The entire clause functions as the subject of the verb "remain" (μείνῃ). The relative clause is placed in parenthesis in order to visualize its substantival contribution to the dependent ἐάν clause. John reminds his readers about the message they heard about Jesus when they first came to the faith.

ἠκούσατε: The Greek word ἠκούσατε is a second plural aorist active indicative from the verb ἀκούω that means, "I hear" or to hear something from someone (BDAG 37.1aβ) or denote a body of authoritative teaching (BDAG, 38 3d). **Syntactically**, ἠκούσατε is the governing verb of the dependent headless relative clause. The subject of the verb is an implied "you" embedded in the verb, which refers to the readers of the letter. **Semantically**, ἠκούσατε is a consummative aorist: "have heard" (KJV). It describes a conclusion or cessation of an act (Wallace 1996, 559). John once again describes a body of authoritative teachings that has been in their possession since they first came into the faith (cf. 2:7).

^{2:24c} καί: The Greek word καί is a conjunction that means "also" and is not intended to coordinate or connect clauses (BDAG 44.2a). **Syntactically**, καί is part of the independent clause. It *does not* introduce an independent conjunctive clause. **Semantically**, καί is adjunctive: "also" (KJV ASV NASB NIV NET; cf. "too," ESV; Wallace 1996, 671). It underscores the abiding relationship that a believer has with God provided they persist in the teachings about Jesus that they accepted when they first got saved.

μενεῖτε: The Greek word μενεῖτε is a second plural future active indicative from the verb μένω that means, "I remain" or "I abide" or "I continue" or of "someone who does not leave" (BDAG 631.1aβ). The future tense formative "σ" has dropped out because the stem of μένω ends in a liquid consonant (cf. Mounce 2009, 171; Wenham 2003, 104-05). **Syntactically**, μενεῖτε is the main verb of the independent clause: "You also *will remain* in the Son and in the Father" (καὶ ὑμεῖς ἐν τῷ υἱῷ καὶ ἐν τῷ πατρὶ μενεῖτε). The subject is the emphatic personal pronoun, "you" (ὑμεῖς). **Semantically**, μενεῖτε is a predictive future: "you will remain" (KJV NET NLT). It speaks of something that will take place (Wallace 1996, 568). John underscores that when his readers remain in the correct teaching about Jesus, they will have an abiding relationship with God.

²·²⁵ᵃ καί: The Greek word καί is a conjunction that may mean "and" (BDAG 495.1bη) or "now" (BDAG 495.1e). **Syntactically**, καί introduces an independent conjunctive clause: *"now* this is the promise" (καὶ αὕτη ἐστὶν ἡ ἐπαγγελία). **Semantically**, καί may be a connective of sentences and rendered "and" (e.g., KJV NASB ESV NIV etc.) or it may introduce something new and thereby transitional. In this case, καί is rendered "now" (NET) as it is in 1:5. John begins a new section about a continual relationship believers can have with God.

ἐστίν: The Greek word ἐστιν is third singular present active indicative from the verb εἰμί that means, "is" or to show how something is to be understood (BDAG 283.2cα). **Syntactically**, ἐστίν is the governing verb of the independent clause. The subject of the verb is the demonstrative pronoun "this" (αὕτη) because pronouns have priority over articular nouns (Wallace 1996, 41-42). The construction (demonstrative pronouns + εἰμί) occurs often in 1 John as John's way to highlight main ideas (Brown 1982, 192). It points foward to the relative clause. **Semantically** ἐστίν is an equative present: "is" (cf. KJV NASB ESV NIV NET etc.). The construction equates what God has promised with what is found in the next relative clause.

²·²⁵ᵇ ἥν: The Greek word ἥν is an accusative singular feminine from the relative pronoun ὅς that means, "which" or "that" (BDAG 726.2dδ). **Syntactically**, ἥν introduces an adjectival relative clause: *"which* he himself made to us, eternal life" (ἥν αὐτὸς ἐπηγγείλατο ἡμῖν, τὴν ζωὴν τὴν αἰώνιον). The entire clause modifies the demonstrative pronoun "this" (αὕτη). The relative pronoun ἥν is accusative because it functions as the direct object of the verb, "he promised" (ἐπηγγείλατο). **Semantically**, the relative clause is epexegetical and rendered "that" (JKV ESV NET). It provides the content of the promise. God himself has promised the abiding believer eternal life.

ἐπηγγείλατο: The Greek word ἐπηγγείλατο is third singular aorist middle indicative from the verb ἐπαγγέλλομαι that means, "I promise" (BDAG 356.1b). **Syntactically**, ἐπηγγείλατο is the governing verb of the dependent relative clause. The subject is the emphatic personal pronoun, "he himself" and refers to God. **Semantically**, ἐπηγγείλατο is a constative aorist: "he made" or "he promised" (KJV NASB NIV NLT CNT). It describes the action as a whole (Wallace 1996, 557). John underscores God's promise of eternal life to his readers who remains in the truth about Jesus. The phrase "eternal life" (τὴν ζωὴν τὴν αἰώνιον) functions in apposition to the relative pronoun "which" (ἥν) identifying the content of the promise which is eternal life.

²·²⁶ᵃ ἔγραψα: The Greek word ἔγραψα is a first singular aorist active indicative from the verb γράφω that means, "I write" or to correspond with someone in writing (BDAG 207.2c). **Syntactically**, ἔγραψα is the main verb of the independent clause: "I have written these things to you concerning those who persist in their attempts to mislead you" (Ταῦτα ἔγραψα ὑμῖν περὶ τῶν πλανώντων ὑμᾶς). The assumed subject "I" refers to the author. **Semantically**, ἔγραψα is an epistolary aorist: "I have written" (KJV ASV NASB NET CNT; cf. 2:14a, 14b, 14c, 21a, 21c). John underscores what he has just written (Wallace 1996, 563) as a warning about those who are trying to lead them astray.

πλανώντων: The Greek word πλανώντων is a nominative masculine singular present active participle from the verb πλανάω, which means, "I deceive" or "I mislead" or to cause someone to go astray (BDAG 821.1a). **Syntactically**, πλανώντων is a substantival participle functioning as the object of the preposition, "about" (περὶ). **Semantically**, πλανώντων is a customary present: "those who *persist in their attempts* to mislead" (or "deceive," cf. NASB ESV NET CNT). It describes a pattern of behavior (Wallace 1996, 521). John points out that there are those who are continually trying to deceive and lead them to believe false teachings about the nature of Jesus.

$^{2:27a}$ καὶ ὑμεῖς: The Greek word καί is a conjunction that means "but" (BDAG 495.1bη) or "now" (BDAG 495.1e). **Syntactically**, καί serves to introduce an independent conjunctive clause: "*now as for you* the anointing that you have received from him remains continually in you" (καὶ ὑμεῖς τὸ χρῖσμα ὃ ἐλάβετε ἀπ' αὐτοῦ μένει ἐν ὑμῖν). **Semantically**, this construction (καί + the pendent nominative ὑμεῖς) is transitional: "now as for you" (NET; *contra* "but" KJV ESV NLT CNT). It serves to move the discusion in a slightly different direction. Many translations, however, translate καὶ ὑμεῖς "as for you" (ASV NASB NRSV NIV; see Wallace 1996, 51). It seems John turns his attention away from the deceivers and back to believers. The nature of John's turn of attention is evident in the next verb.

μένει: The Greek word μένει is a third singular present active indicative from the verb μένω that means, "I remain" or "I abide" or "I continue" or of "someone who does not leave" (BDAG 631.1aβ). **Syntactically**, μένει is the main verb of the independent clause. The subject is the noun, "the anointing" (τὸ χρῖσμα). **Semantically**, μένει is a customary present: "remains *continually*" (cf. NIV) or "lives *continually*" (NLT; cf. Wallace 1996, 521). John emphasizes that true believers are equipped with the constant presence of the Spirit.

$^{2:27b}$ ὅ: The Greek word ὅ is a neuter singular accusative from the relative pronoun ὅς that means, "which" or "that" (BDAG 725.1a). **Syntactically**, ὅ introduces an adjectival relative clause, "*that* you have received from him" (ὃ ἐλάβετε ἀπ' αὐτοῦ). The antecedent of this relative pronoun is the noun, "the anointing" (τὸ χρῖσμα). This relative clause provides additional information about the anointing, namely that its origin is from God. Whether translated "which" (KJV ASV NASB CNT) or "that" (NRSV ESV NET), John highlights something about the anointing, which is revealed in the next verb.

ἐλάβετε: The Greek word ἐλάβετε is a second plural aorist active indicative from the verb λαμβάνω that means, "I receive" or to be a receiver (BDAG, 584.10c). **Syntactically**, ἐλάβετε is the governing verb of the relative clause. The assumed subject, "you" refers to the readers. **Semantically**, ἐλάβετε is a consummative aorist: "you have received" (KJV NLT CNT). It emphasizes what believers have already received (Wallace 1996, 559). John tells his readers that the Spirit they have received (2:18) remains in them.

$^{2:27c}$ καί: The Greek word καί is a conjunction which means "and" (BDAG 494.1ba). **Syntactically**, καί introduces an independent clause: "*and* you have no need" (καὶ οὐ χρείαν ἔχετε). **Semantically**, καί is coordinating connective: "and" (cf. KJV NASB ESV NIV NET etc.). It gives us some additional information about the presence of the Spirit in the life of the believer.

ἔχετε: The Greek word ἔχετε is a second plural present active indicative from the verb ἔχω that means, "I have" or to have a need of something from someone (BDAG 421.7aδ). **Syntactically**, ἔχετε serves as the main verb of the independent clause. The subject is the implied "you" embedded in the verb and refers to the orthodox readers of the letter. **Semantically**, ἔχετε is a customary present negated with οὐ: "you have no" (NASB ESV NET). It speaks of a pattern of behavior (Wallace 1996, 521). John underscores that in addition to having the Holy Spirit, his readers have no needs. What they have no need of is revealed in the next clause.

$^{2:27d}$ ἵνα: The Greek word ἵνα is a conjunction, which means "that" (BDAG 476.2ca). **Syntactically**, ἵνα introduces a dependent conjunctive clause: "*that* anyone teach you" (ἵνα τις διδάσκῃ ὑμᾶς). **Semantically**, ἵνα is an epexegetical "that" (KJV ASV ESV CNT) explaining how it is that believers have no need for a teacher, they have God's Spirit (Culy 2004, 60), even though Wallace lists this ἵνα as an example of a result ἵνα (1996, 473) functioning as an adverb modifying the verb, "have" (ἔχετε). If result, the believer's anointing from God results in having no need for a teacher: "so you have no need" (NRSV NLT). It seems better, however, to see this as an adjectival clause, describing the nature or content of the "need" (χρείαν).

διδάσκῃ: The Greek word διδάσκῃ is a third singular present active subjunctive from the verb διδάσκω that means, "I teach" or "to provide instruction in a formal or informal setting" (BDAG 241.2d). The verb is in the subjunctive mood because it is part of a ἵνα clause. **Syntactically**, διδάσκῃ is the governing verb of the dependent ἵνα clause. It modifies the noun, "need" (χρείαν). The subject is the pronoun "anyone" (τις). **Semantically**, διδάσκῃ is a customary present: "teach" (KJV ASV ESV CNT). John's highlights that his readers who have a Spirit anointing from God do not also need an instructor to aid them in distinguishing truth from error.

EXCURSUS

The syntax for the clauses 27e to 27h is very difficult. There are at least three options from which to choose. First there is the one presented in the structural outline (cf. NET). But there are two other options worthy of discussion. Five clauses are disputed here: 1. "but as his anointing teaches you about all things" (ἀλλ' ὡς τὸ αὐτοῦ χρῖσμα διδάσκει ὑμᾶς περὶ πάντων); 2. "and is true" (καὶ ἀληθές ἐστιν); 3. "and is no lie" (καὶ οὐκ ἔστιν ψεῦδος); 4. "and even as it taught you" (καὶ καθὼς ἐδίδαξεν ὑμᾶς); and 5. "but . . . remain in him" (ἀλλ' . . . μένετε ἐν αὐτῷ). Moving beyond the option in the structural outline, a second option is to see one independent thought with two adverbial comparisons dependent on it, along with one parenthetical comment (seemingly NASB NRSV). John wants his readers in this case to remain in the truth about Jesus (5), just as his anointing is currently teaching them about all things (1) and as it has indeed already taught them (3). The parenthetical comment (gray shading) would be describing this anointing: it is true (2) and is not a lie (3).

^{27e} ὡς τὸ αὐτοῦ χρῖσμα **διδάσκει** ὑμᾶς περὶ πάντων,
^{27e} **as** his anointing **teaches** you about all things,

^{27f} καὶ ἀληθές **ἐστιν**
^{27ef} and it is true

^{27fg} καὶ οὐκ **ἔστιν** ψεῦδος,
^{27g} and **it is** not a lie,

^{27h} καὶ **καθὼς ἐδίδαξεν** ὑμᾶς,
^{27h} and **just as he has taught** you,

^{27i} ἀλλ' . . . **μένετε** ἐν αὐτῷ.
^{27i} **but** . . . **remain** in him.

A third option is to see one independent thought with three adverbial comparisons dependent on it. In this case John wants his readers to remain in the truth about Jesus (5), just as God's anointing is currently teaching them about all things (1), just as that anointing is true (2) and not a lie (3), and just as it has already taught them (4).

^{27e} ἀλλ' . . . **μένετε** ἐν αὐτῷ.
^{27e} **but** . . . **remain** in him.

$$^{27f} \text{ } \underline{\dot{\omega}\varsigma} \text{ τὸ αὐτοῦ χρῖσμα } \textbf{διδάσκει} \text{ ὑμᾶς περὶ πάντων,}$$

^{27f} **as** his anointing **teaches** you about all things,

|

$$^{27g} \text{ καὶ } [\underline{\dot{\omega}\varsigma}] \text{ ἀληθές } \underline{\textbf{ἐστιν}} \text{ } ^{27fg}\underline{\text{καὶ}} \text{ οὐκ } \underline{\textbf{ἔστιν}} \text{ ψεῦδος,}$$

^{27g}and it is true ^{27g}and **it is** not a lie,

|

$$^{27h} \underline{\text{καὶ}} \text{ } \underline{\textbf{καθὼς}} \text{ } \underline{\textbf{ἐδίδαξεν}} \text{ ὑμᾶς,}$$

^{27h} and **just as** **he has taught** you,

Now let us we resume the option introduced in the structural outline above, which sees two independent thoughts, each with its own adverbial comparison (NET). In this instance, John would first tell them that the anointing, which teaches them all things (1) is true (2) and is no lie (3). Then he tells them to remain in Jesus and the correct teaching about him (5), just as it was taught to them (4). See also Bateman 2008, 308-309.

2:27e ἀλλ᾽: The Greek word ἀλλά is a conjunction that means "but" (BDAG 45.3). **Syntactically**, ἀλλά identifies the clause as an independent conjunctive clause: "*But . . . now it is true and is no lie*" (ἀλλ᾽ . . . καὶ ἀληθές ἐστιν καὶ οὐκ ἔστιν ψεῦδος). The conjunction "but" (ἀλλά) before this independent clause indicates that the preceding statement in 2:27c-d is a settled matter (BDAG 45.3). **Semantically**, ἀλλά is contrastive "but" (cf. KJV NASB ESV NIV NET etc.). It emphasizes that they do not need someone other than their anointing to help them distinguish between truth and error.

καί: The Greek word καί is typically a conjunction that means "and" (BDAG 494.1b). **Syntactically**, some translations appear to indicate that καί introduces an independent clause, "and it is true" (KJV ASV NASB NRSV ESV) or merely "is true" (NET NLT: cf. "is real," NIV). Yet it seems that while the conjunction ἀλλά introduces a contrastive independent clause, καί draws us back to the anointing of 27a (cf. NET). **Semantically**, καί is resumptive and need not be translated (NET NLT). It is, however, translated in the outline above as "now." John desires for the readers to know more about their anointing. (For a similar construction, cf. 1 John 2:18; John 6:5; Bateman 2008, 309).

ἐστιν: The Greek word ἐστιν is third singular present active indicative from the verb εἰμί that means, "is" or to show how something is to be understood (BDAG 283.2cα). **Syntactically**, ἐστιν is the main verb of the independent clause. The subject of the verb is an implied "it," referring to the anointing which was given to them by God. **Semantically**, ἐστιν is equative: "is" (cf. KJV NASB ESV NIV NET etc.). John equates their anointing (1 John 2:18) with truth.

2:27f καί: The Greek word καί is a conjunction that means "and" (BDAG, 494.1b). **Syntactically**, καί introduces an independent clause: "*and is no lie*" (καὶ οὐκ ἔστιν ψεῦδος). **Semantically**, καί is a coordinating conjunction that connects two independent clauses: "but ... now it is true" with "and it is not a lie." The connective provides additional information about the Spirit's anointing.

ἐστιν: The Greek word ἐστιν is third singular present active indicative from the verb εἰμί that means, "is" or to show how something is to be understood (BDAG 283.2cα). **Syntactically**, ἐστιν is the main verb of the independent καί clause. The subject of the verb is an implied "it" referring to the anointing which was given to them by God. **Semantically**, ἐστιν is equative with a negating οὐκ: "is not" (cf. KJV NASB ESV NIV NET etc.). John adds (καί) another equative about their annointing (1 John 2:18), it is not a lie.

2:27g ὡς: The Greek word ὡς is a conjunction that means "as" or to mark a specific function (BDAG 1104.3a). **Syntactically**, ὡς introduces a dependent clause: *"as his anointing continually teaches you about all things"* (ὡς τὸ αὐτοῦ χρῖσμα διδάσκει ὑμᾶς περὶ πάντων). The entire dependent clause functions adverbially. It modifies the two verbs "is" (ἐστιν) and "is" (ἐστιν). **Semantically**, ὡς is comparative: "as" (cf. KJV NASB ESV NIV NET etc.). John underscores a comparison evident with the next veb.

διδάσκει: The Greek word διδάσκει is a third singular present active indicative from the verb διδάσκω that means, "I teach" or "to provide instruction in a formal or informal setting" (BDAG 241.2d). **Syntactically**, διδάσκει is the governing verb of the dependent adverbial clause. It modifies the two verbs, "is" (ἐστιν) and "is" (ἐστιν). The subject is the implied "it" embedded in the verb and refers to the anointing that they have received from God. **Semantically**, διδάσκει is a customary present: *"continually* teaches" (cf. KJV NASB ESV NIV NET etc.). It reveals a pattern of behavior (Wallace 1996, 521). John personifies the anointing to be a teacher. John's emphasizes that the Spirit continually teaches them.

2:27h καί: The Greek word καί is a conjunction that means "and" (BDAG 494.1bι). **Syntactically**, καί introduces a dependent conjunctive clause: *"and just as he has taught you"* (καὶ καθὼς ἐδίδαξεν ὑμᾶς). **Semantically**, καί appears to introduce a parenthetical idea: *"and just as* he has taught" (cf. ESV NIV NLT) and the entire clause appears in a gray box. John is building upon the simple truth.

καθώς: The Greek word καθώς is a conjunction that means "just as" (BDAG 493.1). **Syntactically**, καθώς is part of the dependent καί clause. The entire dependent clause: *"just as he has taught you"* (καθὼς ἐδίδαξεν ὑμᾶς) functions adverbially modifying the verb "remain" (μένετε). **Semantically**, καθώς is comparative: "just as" (NSB NRSV ESV NIV NET CNT NLT) or "even as" (KJV ASV). John introduces a comparison with the preceding clause about the Spirit's continual teaching.

ἐδίδαξεν: The Greek word ἐδίδαξεν is a third singular aorist active indicative from the verb διδάσκω that means, "I teach" or "to provide instruction in a formal or informal setting" (BDAG 241.2d). **Syntactically**, ἐδίδαξεν is the governing verb of the dependent adverbial clause. The subject is the implied "it" embedded in the verb and refers to the anointing that believers have received from God. **Semantically**, ἐδίδαξεν is a consummative aorist: "he has taught" (cf. KJV NASB ESV NIV NET ect.). It emphasizes the cessation of an act (Wallace 1996, 559). John compares the Spirit's current teaching (2:27g) with what the Spirit has taught in the past. There is a consistency in the Spirit's teaching.

2:27i μένετε: The Greek word is a second person plural present active imperative from the verb μένω that means, "I remain" or of someone who does not leave a certain realm (BDAG 631.2aβ). **Syntactically**, μένετε is the main verb of the independent asyndeton clause: *"make it a practice to remain in him"* (μένετε ἐν αὐτῷ). **Semantically,** is an imperative of command: "make it a practice to remain" or "remain" (NET NLT) or "abide" (KJV ASV NASB NRSV ESV CNT). The command is an ongoing process (Wallace 1996, 485).

2:28a Καὶ νῦν: The Greek word καί is a conjunction that means "and" (BDAG, 496.2iγ). The Greek word νῦν is an adverb that means "now" as it pertains to a certain situation (BDAG 681.2a). **Syntactically**, καὶ νῦν introduces a independent conjunctive clause: *"Even now, children, make it a practice to remain in him"* (καὶ νῦν, τεκνία, μένετε ἐν αὐτῷ). **Semantically**, καὶ νῦν is ascensive: "even now" (or "and now" KJV ESV NIV NET etc.). It summarizes the preceding discusion by adding a point of focus (Wallace 1996, 670-671). While some tranlsations consider it as introducing a new section

(NRSV NIV NET NLT), it seems John is closing out a section of his teaching here by giving the readers a proper application. A similar use of καὶ νῦν occurs in 2:18 as a conclusion of the ethical discussion of 2:12–17. Here in verse 28, John concludes his doctrinal discussion (2:18-27). The answer to both discussions is to abide in Jesus and the correct teaching about his nature (Culy 2004, 62).

μένετε: The Greek word μένετε is a second plural present active imperative from the verb μένω that means, "I remain" or of someone who does not leave a certain realm (BDAG 631.2aβ). **Syntactically**, μένετε is the main verb of the independent clause. The subject is the implied "you" embedded in the verb and refers to the readers. **Semantically**, μένετε is an imperative of command: "*make it a practice to* remain." It assumes an on-going process (Wallace 1996, 485). John exhorts his readers to continually maintain their relationship with Jesus.

2:28b ἵνα: The Greek word ἵνα is a conjunction, which means "that" or "so that" (BDAG 475.1a/3). **Syntactically**, ἵνα introduces a dependent conjunctive clause: "*so that* when he appears, we may have confidence and so that we may not shrink away from him at his coming" (ἵνα ἐὰν φανερωθῇ σχῶμεν παρρησίαν καὶ μὴ αἰσχυνθῶμεν ἀπ' αὐτοῦ ἐν τῇ παρουσίᾳ αὐτοῦ). The entire dependent clause functions adverbially. It modifies the verb "remain" (μένετε). **Semantically**, ἵνα is either result (BDAG 475.3) or purpose-result (Wallace 1996, 473-474): "so that" (NET; perhaps NASB NRSV ESV NLT CNT). John presents the first purpose-result for those who remain in Jesus: the inner sense of confidence when Jesus returns.

σχῶμεν: The Greek word σχῶμεν is a first plural aorist active subjunctive from the verb ἔχω that means, "I have" or to experience an inner condition (BDAG 421.7aβ). The verb is in the subjunctive mood because it is part of a ἵνα clause. **Syntactically**, σχῶμεν is the governing verb of the first part of the dependent ἵνα clause. The subject is an implied "we" embedded in the verb and refers to John and his readers. John adds himself into this admonition by using the first person plural, giving the reader the impression that "we are all in this together" (Culy 2004, 63). **Semantically**, σχῶμεν is a constative aorist: "we may have" (cf. KJV NASB ESV NIV NET etc). John views the possessing of an inner condition of "confidence" (παρρησίαν) or "courage" (NLT) as a whole (Wallace 1996, 557). The result of remaining in Jesus is confidence.

2:28c ἐάν: The Greek word ἐάν is a conjunction that means "when" or marks the prospect of an action in the future (BDAG 268.2). **Syntactically**, the conjunction ἐάν identifies the clause as a dependent clause. The entire dependent clause, "when he appears" (ἐὰν φανερωθῇ) functions adverbially. It modifies the verb, "we might have" (σχῶμεν). **Semantically**, ἐάν is a temporal conjunction with a meaning similar to the adverb ὅταν (see ἐάν in 12:32, 14:3). There is certainty about the believer who remains in Jesus: he or she will be able to stand before him with confidence.

φανερωθῇ: The Greek word φανερωθῇ is third singular aorist passive subjunctive from the verb φανερόω that means, "I appear" or "to cause someone to become visible" (BDAG 1048.1aβ). The verb is in the subjunctive mood because it is part of a ἐάν clause. **Syntactically**, φανερωθῇ is the governing verb of the dependent ἐάν clause. The verb is in the subjunctive because it is part of an ἐάν clause. The subject of the verb is an implied "he" embedded in the verb that refers to Jesus. **Semantically**, φανερωθῇ is a constative aorist: "he appears" (NASB ESV NIV NET CNT) or more pointedly, "he returns" (NLT). It points to a future event as a whole (Wallace 1996, 557). John underscores the certainty of the coming of Jesus and his reader's confidence when Jesus returns.

2:28d καί: The Greek word καί is a conjunction which means "and" (BDAG 494.1b). **Syntactically**, καί introduces a dependent conjunctive clause: "*and* so that we may not shrink away him at his coming" (καὶ [ἵνα] μὴ αἰσχυνθῶμεν ἀπ᾽ αὐτοῦ ἐν τῇ παρουσίᾳ αὐτοῦ). **Syntactically**, καὶ introduces the second part of a compound dependent ἵνα clause. **Semantically**, καί adds additional purpose—result of remaining in the correct teaching about Jesus. Not only will remaining in Jesus result in confidence when Jesus appears, but it will also result in those believers not being put to eschatological shame by him as well.

[ἵνα]: The Greek word ἵνα is a conjunction, which means "that" or "so that" (BDAG 475.1a/3). **Syntactically**, [ἵνα] is elliptical and introduces the second dependent clause, "and [so that] we may not shrink away from him at his coming" ([ἵνα] καὶ μὴ αἰσχυνθῶμεν ἀπ᾽ αὐτοῦ ἐν τῇ παρουσίᾳ αὐτοῦ). The clause functions adverbially modifying the verb "remain" (μένετε). **Semantically**, [ἵνα] is classified as either result (BDAG 475.3) or purpose-result (Wallace 1996, 473-474): "so that" (NET; perhaps NASB NRSV ESV NLT CNT). John presents his second purpose-result.

αἰσχυνθῶμεν: The Greek word αἰσχυνθῶμεν is a first plural aorist passive subjunctive from the verb αἰσχύνω that means, "I shame" or to experience shame or be disgraced before someone (BDAG 30.2). The verb is in the subjunctive mood because it is part of a ἵνα clause. **Syntactically**, αἰσχυνθῶμεν is the governing verb of the elliptical dependent adverbial ἵνα clause. The assumed subject, "we" embedded in the verb refers to John and the readers of his letter. **Semantically**, μὴ αἰσχυνθῶμεν is a constative aorist: "not ashamed" (KJV ASV CNT) or "to be put to shame" (NRSV). It points to a future event as a whole (Wallace 1996, 557). John underscores the necessity for believers to cultivate a persistent relationship with Jesus so to avoid disgrace. This sense of shame before a God who judges is common elsewhere (see Isa. 1:24, 29; Rev. 6:15-17).

2:29a ἐάν: The Greek word ἐάν is a conjunction, which means "if" or "to denote what is expected to occur under certain circumstances" (BDAG 267.1aα; see the semantics of οἶδα below). **Syntactically**, ἐάν identifies the clause as a dependent conjunctive clause. The entire clause: "*if* you know that he is righteous" (ἐὰν εἰδῆτε ὅτι δίκαιός ἐστιν) functions adverbially. It modifies the verb, "you know" (γινώσκετε). **Semantically**, ἐάν introduces a third class conditional clause presenting us with a likely condition (Wallace 1996, 696). John speaks of a probability for his readers that is clarified with the next verb.

εἰδῆτε: The Greek word εἰδῆτε is a second plural perfect active subjunctive from the verb οἶδα that means, "I know" or to have information about someone (BDAG 693.1e). The verb is in the subjunctive mood because it is part of a ἐάν clause. **Syntactically**, εἰδῆτε is the governing verb of the dependent conjunctive ἐὰν clause. It is functioning adverbially. It modifies the verb, "you know" (γινώσκετε). The assumed subject "you" refers to the recipients of the letter. **Semantically**, εἰδῆτε is a perfect with present force: "you know" (cf. KJV NASB ESV NIV NET etc). It shows that if a believer knows that God is righteous, that they should also know that others who are righteous are his children.

ὅτι: The Greek word ὅτι is a conjunction which means "that" or to identify content after a verb of mental perception (BDAG 731.1c). **Syntactically**, ὅτι introduces a dependent conjunctive clause: "*that* he is righteous" (ὅτι δίκαιός ἐστιν). The entire clause is substantival. It functions as the direct object of the verb "you know" (εἰδῆτε). The clause is placed in parenthesis in order to visualize its contribution to the dependent clause. **Semantically**, ὅτι is an indirect discourse: "that" (KJV NASB ESV NIV NET etc.). John discloses the content of the believer's knowledge found in the rest of the clause.

ἐστιν: The Greek word ἐστιν is third singular present active indicative from the verb εἰμί that means, "is" or to be in close connection with someone or in statements of identity (BDAG 283.2a). **Syntactically**, ἐστιν is the governing verb of the dependent direct object clause. The subject of the verb is an implied "he." **Semantically**, ἐστιν is an equative present. It equates God or Jesus with the righteous one.

Interpretive Nugget: The implied subject of "is" (ἐστιν) is problematic. On the one hand, "he" could refer to God, the Father. God the Father is the pronoun at the end of the verse: "has been fathered by him" (ἐξ αὐτοῦ γεγέννηται). In the phrase, "has been fathered by him," αὐτος refers to God, the Father because elsewhere in 1 John, it always refers to him (cf. 3:9; 4:7; 5:1, 4, 18). Furthermore it is the Father who is called "the righteous one" (δίκαιός) in 1 John 1:9. On the other hand, "he" could be Jesus. The antecedent is the "righteous one" in 2:1 refers to Jesus. Furthermore, Jesus's return has been the recent focus of discussion in 2:28. Perhaps there is some purposeful Trinitarian ambiguity and thereby may not be a case of either/or, but a case of both/and (Culy 2004, 65).

2:29b γινώσκετε: The Greek word γινώσκετε is a second plural present active indicative from the verb γινώσκω that means, "I know" or to have come to the knowledge of a person (BDAG 200.6c). **Syntactically**, γινώσκετε is the main verb of the independent clause: *"you* also *know* that everyone who practices righteousness has been fathered by him" (γινώσκετε ὅτι καὶ πᾶς ὁ ποιῶν τὴν δικαιοσύνην ἐξ αὐτοῦ γεγέννηται). The assumed subject "you" refers to the recipients of the letter. While this verb could be an imperative instead of an indicative, knowledge is rarely commanded in Johannine literature. Knowledge is more of a result of one's status as a believer (Bateman 2008, 315; Brown 1982, 382-383). **Semantically**, γινώσκετε is a customary present: "you know" (KJV NASB ESV NIV NET). It speaks of a pattern of knowledge (Wallace 1996, 527). John's readers possess the knowledge that God is righteous, and they should also possess the knowledge that those who are righteous are his progeny.

ὅτι: The Greek word ὅτι is a conjunction, which means "that" or to identify content after a verb of mental perception (BDAG 731.1c). **Syntactically**, ὅτι introduces a dependent conjunctive clause: *"that* everyone who practices righteousness has been fathered by him" (ὅτι καὶ πᾶς ὁ ποιῶν τὴν δικαιοσύνην ἐξ αὐτοῦ γεγέννηται). The entire clause is functioning substantivally as the direct object of the verb "you know" (γινώσκετε). The entire ὅτι clause is placed in parenthesis in order to visualize its contribution to the independent clause. **Semantically**, ὅτι is indirect discourse: "that" (KJV ASV NASB ESV NIV NET CNT). It provides the content of what the one who knows that God is righteous should also know (Wallace 1996, 454). John's readers should understand that anyone else who is righteous is that way because they are children of God himself.

γεγέννηται: The Greek word γεγέννηται is a third singular perfect passive indicative from the verb γεννάω that means, "I become the parent of" or "to exercise the role of a parental figure" (BDAG 193.1b). **Syntactically**, γεγέννηται is the governing verb of the dependent substantival direct object clause. The subject is "everyone" (πᾶς) and the adjectival participial phrase that modifies it, "who practices righteousness" (ὁ ποιῶν τὴν δικαιοσύνην). **Semantically**, γεγέννηται is both gnomic and extensive perfect: "has been fathered" (NET) or "has been born" (NRSV ESV NIV). It is gnomic because of the generic subject (πᾶς) while extensive in that the focus is on the decisive relationship between the God and the believer (Wallace 1996, 580). This generic or proverbial force may also be rendered intensive: "is born" (KJV NASB CNT; cf. ASV) with an emphasis on the results of the present condition of the believer. Regardless of where one places the emphasis of the perfect, John's point is simply this: believers have been fathered by God in the past and that past event has continuing results in the present (cf. 3:9; 4:7; 5:1, 4, 18). The focus is upon those who practice righteousness: they have had an on-going relationship with God.

1 John 3:1–10

Verb Recognition for 1 John 3:1–10

¹ἴδετε ποταπὴν ἀγάπην δέδωκεν ἡμῖν ὁ πατὴρ ἵνα τέκνα θεοῦ κληθῶμεν· καὶ ἐσμέν. διὰ τοῦτο ὁ κόσμος οὐ γινώσκει ἡμᾶς ὅτι οὐκ ἔγνω αὐτόν. ²Ἀγαπητοί, νῦν τέκνα θεοῦ ἐσμεν, καὶ οὔπω ἐφανερώθη τί ἐσόμεθα. οἴδαμεν ὅτι ἐὰν φανερωθῇ ὅμοιοι αὐτῷ ἐσόμεθα, ὅτι ὀψόμεθα αὐτὸν καθώς ἐστιν. ³καὶ πᾶς ὁ ἔχων τὴν ἐλπίδα ταύτην ἐπ᾽ αὐτῷ ἁγνίζει ἑαυτὸν καθὼς ἐκεῖνος ἁγνός ἐστιν. ⁴Πᾶς ὁ ποιῶν τὴν ἁμαρτίαν καὶ τὴν ἀνομίαν ποιεῖ, καὶ ἡ ἁμαρτία ἐστὶν ἡ ἀνομία. ⁵καὶ οἴδατε ὅτι ἐκεῖνος ἐφανερώθη ἵνα τὰς ἁμαρτίας ἄρῃ, καὶ ἁμαρτία ἐν αὐτῷ οὐκ ἔστιν. ⁶πᾶς ὁ ἐν αὐτῷ μένων οὐχ ἁμαρτάνει· πᾶς ὁ ἁμαρτάνων οὐχ ἑώρακεν αὐτὸν οὐδὲ ἔγνωκεν αὐτόν. ⁷Τεκνία, μηδεὶς πλανάτω ὑμᾶς· ὁ ποιῶν τὴν δικαιοσύνην δίκαιός ἐστιν, καθὼς ἐκεῖνος δίκαιός ἐστιν· ⁸ὁ ποιῶν τὴν ἁμαρτίαν ἐκ τοῦ διαβόλου ἐστίν, ὅτι ἀπ᾽ ἀρχῆς ὁ διάβολος ἁμαρτάνει. εἰς τοῦτο ἐφανερώθη ὁ υἱὸς τοῦ θεοῦ, ἵνα λύσῃ τὰ ἔργα τοῦ διαβόλου. ⁹Πᾶς ὁ γεγεννημένος ἐκ τοῦ θεοῦ ἁμαρτίαν οὐ ποιεῖ, ὅτι σπέρμα αὐτοῦ ἐν αὐτῷ μένει· καὶ οὐ δύναται ἁμαρτάνειν, ὅτι ἐκ τοῦ θεοῦ γεγέννηται. ¹⁰ἐν τούτῳ φανερά ἐστιν τὰ τέκνα τοῦ θεοῦ καὶ τὰ τέκνα τοῦ διαβόλου· πᾶς ὁ μὴ ποιῶν δικαιοσύνην οὐκ ἔστιν ἐκ τοῦ θεοῦ, καὶ ὁ μὴ ἀγαπῶν τὸν ἀδελφὸν αὐτοῦ.

Clausal Outline Translated for 1 John 3:1–10

³:¹ᵃἴδετε ποταπὴν ἀγάπην δέδωκεν ἡμῖν ὁ πατὴρ
³:¹ᵃ**Consider** what sort of love the Father **has granted** to us

      |

      ³:¹ᵇἵνα τέκνα θεοῦ κληθῶμεν·
      ³:¹ᵇ**that we should be called** children of God;

³:¹ᶜκαὶ ἐσμέν [τέκνα θεοῦ κληθωμεν].
³:¹ᶜ*indeed* **we** *really* **are** [*called children of God*].

³:¹ᵈδιὰ τοῦτο ὁ κόσμος οὐ γινώσκει ἡμᾶς
³:¹ᵈ**For this reason**, the world does not **know** us,

   |

   ¹ᵉὅτι οὐκ ἔγνω αὐτόν.
   ¹ᵉ**that** it (= the world) did not **know** him.

³:²ᵃ Ἀγαπητοί, νῦν τέκνα θεοῦ **ἐσμεν**,
³:²ᵃ Beloved, **we are** God's children,

³:²ᵇ καὶ οὔπω **ἐφανερώθη** τί **ἐσόμεθα**.
³:²ᵇ and what **we will be** whenever (*he comes*) has not been revealed.

³:²ᶜ **οἴδαμεν** (ὅτι . . . ὅμοιοι αὐτῷ **ἐσόμεθα**),
³:²ᶜ **We know** (that . . . we will be like him [=Jesus]).

    ³:²ᵈ **ἐὰν φανερωθῇ**
    ³:²ᵈ **when he appears**

        ³:²ᵉ **ὅτι ὀψόμεθα** αὐτὸν
        ³:²ᵉ **because we will see** him (= Jesus)

            ³:²ᶠ **καθώς ἐστιν**.
            ³:²ᶠ **as he is**.

³:³ᵃ καὶ πᾶς ὁ ἔχων τὴν ἐλπίδα ταύτην ἐπ' αὐτῷ **ἁγνίζει** ἑαυτὸν
³:³ᵃ And *so* everyone who has this hope in him **purifies** himself

        ³:³ᵇ **καθὼς** ἐκεῖνος ἁγνός **ἐστιν**.
        ³:³ᵇ **even as** he (=Jesus) **is** pure.

³:⁴ᵃ Πᾶς ὁ ποιῶν τὴν ἁμαρτίαν καὶ τὴν ἀνομίαν **ποιεῖ**,
³:⁴ᵃ Everyone who practices sin also **practices** lawlessness,

³:⁴ᵇ καὶ ἡ ἁμαρτία **ἐστὶν** ἡ ἀνομία.
³:⁴ᵇ *indeed* sin **is** lawlessness.

³:⁵ᵃ καὶ **οἴδατε** (ὅτι ἐκεῖνος **ἐφανερώθη**)
³:⁵ᵃ And **you know** (that he [= Jesus] appeared)

    ³:⁵ᵇ **ἵνα** τὰς ἁμαρτίας **ἄρῃ**,
    ³:⁵ᵇ **in order to take away** sin

³:⁵ᶜ καὶ [**οἴδατε** (ὅτι] ἁμαρτία ἐν αὐτῷ οὐκ **ἔστιν**).
³:⁵ᶜ And [*you know* (*that*] in him (= Jesus) **there is** no sin).

³:⁶ᵃ πᾶς ὁ ἐν αὐτῷ μένων οὐχ **ἁμαρτάνει**·
³:⁶ᵃ Everyone who abides in him (= Jesus) does not *persist in* **sin**;

³:⁶ᵇ πᾶς ὁ ἁμαρτάνων οὐχ **ἑώρακεν** αὐτὸν οὐδὲ **ἔγνωκεν** αὐτόν.
³:⁶ᵇ everyone who *makes it a practice* to sin **has** neither **seen** him nor **known** him.

³:⁷ᵃ Τεκνία, μηδεὶς **πλανάτω** ὑμᾶς·
³:⁷ᵃ Children, **let** no one **mislead** you;

^{3:7b} ὁ ποιῶν τὴν δικαιοσύνην δίκαιός **ἐστιν**,
^{3:7b} the one who makes it a practice to be righteous **is** righteous,

> ^{3:7b}**καθὼς** ἐκεῖνος δίκαιός **ἐστιν**·
> ^{3:7b}**even as** that one (= Jesus) **is** righteous;

^{3:8a} ὁ ποιῶν τὴν ἁμαρτίαν ἐκ τοῦ διαβόλου **ἐστίν**,
^{3:8a} The one who practices sin **comes from** the devil,

> ^{3:8b}**ὅτι** ἀπ᾽ ἀρχῆς ὁ διάβολος **ἁμαρτάνει**.
> ^{3:8b}**because** the devil *persists in* **sinning** from the beginning.

^{3:8c}**εἰς τοῦτο ἐφανερώθη** ὁ υἱὸς τοῦ θεοῦ,
^{3:8c}**For this purpose** the Son of God **appeared**,

> ^{3:8d}**ἵνα λύσῃ** τὰ ἔργα τοῦ διαβόλου.
> ^{3:8d}*namely* **that he might destroy** the works of the devil.

^{3:9a}Πᾶς ὁ γεγεννημένος ἐκ τοῦ θεοῦ ἁμαρτίαν οὐ **ποιεῖ**,
^{3:9a}Everyone who has been fathered by God **does** not **practice** sin,

> ^{3:9b}**ὅτι** σπέρμα αὐτοῦ ἐν αὐτῷ **μένει**·
> ^{3:9b}**because** God's seed **remains** in him;

^{3:9c}καὶ οὐ **δύναται ἁμαρτάνειν**,
^{3:9c}and **he is** not **able to sin**,

> ^{3:9d}**ὅτι** ἐκ τοῦ θεοῦ **γεγέννηται**.
> ^{3:9d}**because he has been fathered** by God.

^{3:10a}ἐν τούτῳ φανερά **ἐστιν** τὰ τέκνα τοῦ θεοῦ καὶ τὰ τέκνα τοῦ διαβόλου·
^{3:10a} By this the children of God and the children of the devil **are** made clear;

^{3:10b}πᾶς ὁ μὴ ποιῶν δικαιοσύνην οὐκ **ἔστιν** ἐκ τοῦ θεοῦ,
^{3:10b}everyone who does not practice righteousness **is** not of God

> ^{3:10c}**καὶ** ὁ μὴ ἀγαπῶν τὸν ἀδελφὸν αὐτοῦ.
> ^{3:10c}that *is* the one who persists in not loving his brother *and sister*.

Syntax Explained for 1 John 3:1–10

^{3:1a}ἴδετε: The Greek word ἴδετε is a second plural aorist active imperative from the verb ὁράω that means, "I see" or "to be mentally or spiritually perceptive" or "consider" (BDAG 720.4b). **Syntactically**, ἴδετε serves as the governing verb of the independent clause: *consider* what sort of love (which) the father has granted to us" (ἴδετε ποταπὴν ἀγάπην δέδωκεν ἡμῖν ὁ πατὴρ). The subject of the imperative is an implied "you" and refers to the readers of the letter. In this case the imperative clearly marks off

the beginning of a new section and a new train of thought, stressing the great exclamation about God's love that follows. **Semantically**, ἴδετε is an imperative of command: "behold" (KJV ASV) or "see" (NASB NRSV ESV NET NLT CNT) or "consider." It underscores the action as whole (Wallace 1996, 485). John urges his readers to focus attention upon or to marvel at this great spiritual truth: God has lavished his love on them.

δέδωκεν: The Greek word δέδωκεν is a third singular perfect active indicative from the verb δίδωμι that means, "I give" or "to grant by formal action" general of God (BDAG 242.13). **Syntactically**, δέδωκεν is the main verb of the independent clause. The subject of the verb is God "the father" (ὁ πατὴρ). The noun that is funcitoning as the direct object, love (ἀγάπην), is qualfied by the interrogative adjective "what sort of" (ποταπὴν). This interrogative is used to express both the quantity (how much) and quality (how great the) of the love being described (Brown 1982, 387). We also learn that this love comes from the Father. **Semantically**, δέδωκεν is an extensive perfect: "has given" (NRSV ESV NET CNT) or "has bestowed" (KJV ASV) or "has granted." It emphasizes the completed action (Wallace 1996, 577). John highlights the love the Father has granted his readers in the past that continues to reap benefits in the present.

3:1b ἵνα: The Greek word ἵνα is a conjunction that means "that" (BDAG 476.2e). **Syntactically**, ἵνα introduces a dependent conjunctive clause: "*that* we should be called children of God" (ἵνα τέκνα θεοῦ κληθῶμεν). The entire ἵνα clause is adjectival, modifying "what sort of love" (ποταπὴν ἀγάπην; Culy 2004, 66). **Semantically**, the ἵνα clause is an epexegetical conjunction: "that" (KJV ASV NASB ESV NLT CNT). It provides the content of the "sort of love" given to believers (Wallace 1996, 456), which is defined in the next verb.

κληθῶμεν: The Greek word κληθῶμεν is a first plural aorist passive subjunctive from the verb καλέω that means, "I call" or "to identify by name" (BDAG 503.1d). The verb is in the subjunctive mood because it is part of a ἵνα clause. **Syntactically**, κληθῶμεν is the governing verb of the adverbial dependent clause. The subject of the verb is an implied "we" embedded in the verb and refers to anyone on whom God has lavished his love through Jesus. **Semantically**, κληθῶμεν is a constative aorist: "should be called" (KJV ASV NRSV ESV NIV NET CNT). John provides an overall description of the identity believers have when they receive God's love (Wallace 1996, 557). John's readers are now God's children. The love indicates parentage that is from God. The word "child" is being used figuratively and describes the relationship of the believer to God the Father though faith in Jesus (see 2:29; 3:9, 4:7; 5:1, 4, and 18; also in the Gospel of John 1:12 and esp. 11:52).

3:1c καί: The Greek word καί is a conjunction which means "and so" or "indeed" or "to introduce a result that comes from what precedes" (BDAG 495.1bζ). **Syntactically**, καί introduces an independent clause, "*and so* we *really* are" (καὶ ἐσμέν). **Semantically**, καί is emphatic: "*and so*" with "*really*" (BDAG 495.1bζ; Wallace 1996, 673). Other transaltions add "and *such*" (ASV NASB ESV CNT) or "and *indeed*" (NET) to underscore the author's emphasis. We merely translate as "indeed" since John repeats a similar usage in verse 4b (cf. NET). Here John gives emphasis to a simple fact clarified in the next verb.

ἐσμέν: The Greek word ἐσμέν is first plural present active indicative from the verb εἰμί that means, "is" or to be in close connection with someone (BDAG 283.2a). **Syntactically**, ἐσμέν is the main verb of the independent clause. The subject of the verb is an implied "we" referring to John and to the readers of his letter who have faith in Jesus. **Semantically**, ἐσμέν is an equative present: "we are" (cf. KJV NASB ESV NIV NET etc.). John affirms the special father/child relationship with God. The elliptical direct object "children of God" [τέκνα θεοῦ κληθῶμεν] is implied from the previous clause (Bateman 2008, 321). John's emphasis is that followers of Jesus are God's children.

3:1d διὰ τοῦτο: The Greek word διά is a preposition, which means "for this reason" (BDAG 223.B2a). The Greek word τοῦτο is declined as an accusative singular neuter from the demonstrative pronoun τοῦτο, which means "this one" (BDAG 741.1bα). **Syntactically**, διὰ τοῦτο is a prepositional phrase introducing an independent clause: "*For this reason*, the world does not know us" (διὰ τοῦτο ὁ κόσμος οὐ γινώσκει ἡμᾶς). This particular construction occurs frequently in the New Testament and is a very important structural marker in 1 John (3:1; 4:5). **Semantically**, διὰ τοῦτο can be anaphoric pointing back to the preceding discussion or cataphoric pointing forward. This construction points forward (cataphoric) to the ὅτι clause (contra an anaphoric construction in Strecker 1996, 87). Thus the ὅτι clause is epexegetical to the demonstrative pronoun and provides its content (Culy 2004, 67). The content is specified with the next verb.

γινώσκει: The Greek word γινώσκει is a third singular present active indicative from the verb γινώσκω that means, "I know" or "to arrive at a knowledge of someone" (BDAG 199.1b). **Syntactically**, γινώσκει is the main verb of the independent clause. The subject of the verb is "the world" (ὁ κόσμος). **Semantically**, οὐ γινώσκει ἡμᾶς is a customary present: "did not know us" (cf. KJV NASB ESV NIV NET). It describes a pattern of behavior (Wallace 1996, 521). John underscores the content of his reasoning about the world's lack of respect and misunderstanding of Jesus followers, the world system has never understood or respected God either.

3:1e ὅτι: The Greek word ὅτι is a conjunction, which means "that" after a preceding demonstrative pronoun (BDAG, 732.2a). **Syntactically**, ὅτι introduces the dependent adjectival clause: "*that* it did not know him" (ὅτι οὐκ ἔγνω αὐτόν). It modifies the demonstrative pronoun, "this" (τοῦτο). **Semantically**, ὅτι is classified as epexegetical to τοῦτο and therefore rendered "that" (ESV NIV CNT; *contra* an adverbial rendering of "because" in KJV ASV NASB NRSV NET NLT; cf. BDAG 732.4a). Thus the entire ὅτι clause provides the content of the demonstrative pronoun "this" (τοῦτο). That content is evident in the next verb.

ἔγνω: The Greek word ἔγνω is a third singular aorist active indicative from the verb γινώσκω that means, "I know" or "to arrive at a knowledge of someone" or to make an acquaintance with someone (BDAG 1991b). **Syntactically**, ἔγνω is the governing verb of the dependent adjectival clause. The subject of the verb is an implied "it" embedded in the verb and refers to the world system that does not understand God or his children. **Semantically**, ἔγνω is a constative aorist: "know" (cf. KJV NASB ESV NIV NET etc.). It summarizes knowledge as a whole (Wallace 1996, 557). John speaks of the world's inability or unwillingness of the world to understand God.

3:2a ἐσμεν: The Greek word ἐσμεν is first plural present active indicative from the verb εἰμί that means, "is" or "to be in close connection with" (BDAG 283.2a). **Syntactically**, ἐσμεν is the main verb of the independent clause, "Beloved, now *we are* God's children" (Ἀγαπητοί, νῦν τέκνα θεοῦ ἐσμεν). The subject of the verb is an implied "we," referring to both John and recipients of the letter who have put their faith in Jesus. **Semantically**, ἐσμεν is an equative present. John identifies or equates his readers with being God's children. The temporal adverb "now" (νῦν) adds emphasis to the statement that his readers are currently God's children, and sets up a contrast with the future indicatives (ἐσόμεθα) which are in the next clauses.

3:2b καί: The Greek word καί is a conjunction which means "and" (BDAG 494.1bγ). **Syntactically**, καί introduces an independent conjunctive clause: "*and* what we will be has not yet been revealed" (καὶ οὔπω ἐφανερώθη τί ἐσόμεθα). **Semantically**, καί is a coordinating connective that occurs with an expression of time (BDAG 494.1bγ). It introduces additional information about the reader's identity with Jesus, which is evident in rest of the clause.

ἐφανερώθη: The Greek word ἐφανερώθη is a third singular aorist passive indicative from the verb φανερόω that means, "I reveal" or to cause to become visible publicly (BDAG 1048.1b). **Syntactically**, ἐφανερώθη is the main verb of the conjunctive independent clause. The subject of the verb is the entire interrogative clause "what we will be" (τί ἐσόμεθα) that refers to the mystery of the new nature of believers when Jesus returns. **Semantically**, ἐφανερώθη is a constative aorist negated with οὔπω: "has not yet been revealed" (passive, NET CNT) or "has not yet appeared" (NRSV ESV). It focuses on an event as a whole (Wallace 1996, 557). While this mysterious resurrection life has not yet been revealed completely, readers know that they are children of God. The future, however, remains clouded in mystery.

ἐσόμεθα: The Greek word ἐσόμεθα is first plural future (middle) indicative from the verb εἰμί that means, "is" or "to be in close connection with someone" (BDAG 283.2a). **Syntactically**, ἐσόμεθα is the governing verb of the dependent conjunctive clause: "what *we will be*" (τί ἐσόμεθα). It functions as the subject of the verb, "has been revealed" (ἐφανερώθη). The subject of the verb is an implied "we" referring to both John and the readers of the letter. **Semantically**, ἐσόμεθα is a predictive future: "will be" (cf. KJV NASB ESV NIV NET etc.; Wallace 1996, 568). John tells his readers that their future identity at the return of Jesus has not yet been fully disclosed. John does not leave his readers hanging. The next clause helps clear-up this mystery.

3:2c οἴδαμεν: The Greek word οἴδαμεν is a first plural perfect active indicative from the verb οἶδα that means, "I know" or to have information about something (BDAG 692.1e). **Syntactically**, οἴδαμεν is the main verb of the independent asyndeton clause. The assumed subject "we" refers to John and the readers of the letter. **Semantically**, οἴδαμεν is a perfect with present force: "we know" (cf. KJV NASB ESV NIV NET etc.). Verbs like οἶδα, almost always appear in the perfect tense without the perfect's aspectual significance (Wallace 1996, 579-580). John underscores the mystery that surrounds the believer's identity when Jesus returns, they do know something about the mystery, which becomes evident in the next ὅτι clause.

ὅτι: The Greek word ὅτι is a conjunction, which means "that" (BDAG 731.1c). **Syntactically**, ὅτι introduces a dependent conjunctive clause: "*that* when he appears, we will be like him" (ὅτι ἐὰν φανερωθῇ ὅμοιοι αὐτῷ ἐσόμεθα). It functions as the direct object of the verb "we know" (οἴδαμεν). The clause is placed in parenthesis in order to visualize its contribution to the independent clause. **Semantically**, ὅτι is an indirect discourse following a verb of perception: "that" (cf. KJV NASB ESV NIV NET etc.). John provides the content of information known.

ἐσόμεθα: The Greek word ἐσόμεθα is first plural future (middle) indicative from the verb εἰμί that means "is" or "to be in close connection with someone" (BDAG 283.2a). **Syntactically**, ἐσόμεθα is the governing verb of the dependent substantival clause. The subject of the verb is an implied "we" referring to John and the readers of his letter. **Semantically**, ἐσόμεθα is a predictive future: "will be" (cf. KJV NASB ESV NIV NET etc.; Wallace 1996, 568). John describes the believer's future identity when Jesus returns, namely that they will be "like him" (ὅμοιοι αὐτῷ). The pronoun "him" is once again problematic. Does "him" refer to the Father or Jesus? It seems in this case, it refers to Jesus due to his second appearing (contra BDAG 706.a). They know that even though they do not have all the facts, they do understand this much: they will be like Jesus someday. That timeframe is clarified in the next ἐὰν clause.

^{3:2d} ἐάν: The Greek word ἐάν is a conjunction, which means "when" or to underscore action in a point of time (BDAG 268.2). **Syntactically**, ἐάν identifies the clause as a dependent conjunctive clause. The entire dependent clause: "*when* he appears" (ἐὰν φανερωθῇ) functions adverbially. It modifies the verb, "we will be" (ἐσόμεθα). **Semantically**, ἐάν is a temporal conjunction: "when" (NASB NRSV ESV NIV CNT NLT). It introduces a third class condition (Wallace 1996, 696). In this instance, like the usage in 1 John 2:28, the meaning approaches that of the adverb ὅταν (cf. John 12:32, 14:3). The idea here is not that Jesus' coming might or might not happen, but that when it happens, the believer can be assured that he will be like him (= Jesus).

φανερωθῇ: The Greek word ἐφανερώθη is a third singular aorist passive indicative from the verb φανερόω that means, "I appear" or to cause to become visible publicaly (BDAG 1048.1aβ). The verb is in the subjunctive mood because it is part of an ἐάν clause. **Syntactically**, ἐφανερώθη is the governing verb of the dependent adverbial clause. The subject of the verb is an implied "he" embedded in the verb and refers to Jesus. It is possible that the subject of this verb could be an implied "what we will be" (τί ἐσόμεθα), carried over from the previous instance of this verb in 3:1 (Brown 1982, 393-394). It seems unlikely because there are pronouns in the following phrases that seem to point to Jesus. Also, this verb is further explained by the following verb "we will see" (ὀψόμεθα). The fact that the object of this subsequent verb is Jesus is because of his return that is the subject of discussion (Culy 2004, 69). **Semantically**, ἐφανερώθη is a constative aorist: "he appears" (KJV NASB ESV NIV NLT CNT). It describes an event as a whole (Wallace 1996, 557). John speaks of what happens when Jesus returns.

^{3:2e} ὅτι: The Greek word ὅτι is a conjunction that means "because" (BDAG 732.4a). **Syntactically**, ὅτι introduces a dependent conjunctive clause: "*because* we will see him" (ὅτι ὀψόμεθα αὐτὸν). The entire ὅτι clause is adverbial. It modifies the verb, "we will be" (ἐσόμεθα). **Semantically**, ὅτι is causal: "because" (NASB ESV NET). John gives his readers the reason why they know that they will be like Jesus when he returns. It is because they will see Jesus first hand and have a face-to-face encounter with him.

ὀψόμεθα: The Greek word ὀψόμεθα is a first plural future middle indicative from the verb ὁράω that means, "I see" or to perceive someone by eye or to notice someone (BDAG 719.A1c). **Syntactically**, ὀψόμεθα serves as the governing verb of the dependent adverbial clause. The subject of the verb is an implied "we" and refers back to John and the readers of his letter. **Semantically**, ὀψόμεθα is a predictive future: "we will see" (KJV NASB ESV NIV NET etc.). It emphasizes something yet to occur (Wallace 1996, 568). John emphasizes that his readers will one day have a face-to-face encounter with Jesus when he returns.

^{3:2f} καθώς: The Greek word καθώς is a conjunction that means "just as" or "as" (BDAG 493.1). **Syntactically**, καθώς introduces a conjunctive dependent clause. The entire dependent clause, "*as* he is" (καθὼς ἐστιν) functions adverbially. It modifies the verb "we will see" (ὀψόμεθα). **Semantically**, καθώς is comparative: "as" (KJV NRSV ESV NIV NLT CNT) or "just as" (NASB NET). John makes a comparison about the way his readers will see Jesus when he returns.

ἐστιν: The Greek word ἐστιν is third singular present active indicative from the verb εἰμί that means, "is" or to be in close connection with something (BDAG 283.2a). **Syntactically**, ἐστίν is the main verb of the dependent adverbial clause. The subject of the verb is an implied "he" which refers to Jesus. **Semantically**, ἐστίν is an equative verb that serves to identify something about Jesus when he returns. John's readers will see Jesus in his resurrected body (Acts 1:3, 11).

^{3:3a} καί: The Greek word καί is a conjunction which means "and so" or "to introduce a result that comes from what precedes" (BDAG 495b 1bζ). **Syntactically**, καί introduces a conjunctive independent clause: "*and* everyone who has this hope in him purifies himself" (καὶ πᾶς ὁ ἔχων τὴν ἐλπίδα ταύτην ἐπ' αὐτῷ ἁγνίζει ἑαυτὸν). **Semantically**, καί is a coordinating connective: "and" (cf. KJV NASB ESV NIV NET etc.). It introduces additional information about the reader's identity when Jesus returns evident in the rest of the clause.

ἔχων: The Greek word ἔχων is a nominative masculine singular present active participle from the verb ἔχω that means, "I have" or to experience an emotion or inner possession (BDAG 421.7αβ). **Syntactically**, ἔχων is an adjectival participle modifying the adjective "each" (πᾶς). The entire phrase, "everyone who has this hope" (πᾶς ὁ ἔχων τὴν ἐλπίδα ταύτην) functions as the subject of the verb "purifies" (ἁγνίζει). **Semantically**, ἔχων is a gnomic present: "everyone" (ASV NASB ESV NIV NET CNT). The participle is being used in generic utterances (Wallace 1996, 615). John describes a timeless fact about people in general, which is clarified in the next verb.

ἁγνίζει: The Greek word ἁγνίζει is a third singular present active indicative from the verb ἁγνίζω that means, "I purify" or "to cause to be morally pure" (BDAG 12.2). **Syntactically**, ἁγνίζει is the main verb of the independent conjunctive clause. The subject is the entire phrase "everyone who has this hope in him" (πᾶς ὁ ἔχων τὴν ἐλπίδα ταύτην ἐπ' αὐτῷ). It refers to any person who believes in Jesus and is looking forward to transformation at his return. **Semantically**, ἁγνίζει is a gnomic present: "purifies" (cf. KJV NASB ESV NIV NET etc.). The verb is part of the generic statement that was introduced with the generic participle (Wallace 1996, 523–24). John underscores a timeless truth about possessing hope for a future transformation that affects the present desire to live an ethical lifestyle in the here and now (cf. Brown 1982, 398).

^{3:3b} καθώς: The Greek word καθώς is a conjunction, which means "just as" or "as" or "even as" (BDAG 493.1). **Syntactically**, καθώς introduces a dependent conjunctive clause. The entire dependent καθώς clause, "*even as* he is pure" (καθὼς ἐκεῖνος ἁγνός ἐστιν) functions adverbially. It modifies the verb "purifies" (ἁγνίζει). **Semantically**, καθώς is comparative: "even as" (KJV ASV) or "just as" (NASB NRSV NIV NLT CNT). John is making a comparison between Jesus and his readers, which is revealed in the rest of the καθώς clause.

ἐστιν: The Greek word ἐστιν is third singular present active indicative from the verb εἰμί that means, "is" or "to be in close connection with" (BDAG 283.2a). **Syntactically**, ἐστίν is the governing verb of the dependent adverbial clause. The subject of the verb is the emphatic demonstrative pronoun "that one" (ἐκεῖνος) and refers to Jesus. **Semantically**, ἐστίν is an equative present: "he is" (cf. KJV NASB ESV NIV NET etc.). John states a generic truth that compares and equates his readers with the purity of Jesus's character.

^{3:4a} ποιῶν: The Greek word ποιῶν is a nominative masculine singular present active participle from the verb ποιέω that means, "I practice" or "I do" or "I commit" or to refuse to carry out an obligation of a moral or social nature (BDAG 840.3c). **Syntactically**, ποιῶν is the first in a series of adjectival participles in this discussion on sin. The entire participial phrase "everyone who *practices* sin" (ὁ ποιῶν τὴν ἁμαρτίαν) modifies the adjective "each" (πᾶς). It is in contrast to the "the one who practices righteousness" (πᾶς ὁ ποιῶν τὴν δικαιοσύνην) from 2:29 (Brown 1986, 398). John contrasts the one who is righteous and has been fathered by God with the one who habitually sins. **Semantically**, ποιῶν is a gnomic present: "everyone who practices" (ποιῶν; NASB ESV NET) or "commits" (KJV NRSV CNT). John presents a timeless maxim about people (Wallace 1996, 523). Generally, people who live a lifestyle of sin have a problem. That problem is disclosed in the next verb.

ποιεῖ: The Greek word ποιεῖ is a third singular present active indicative from the verb ποιέω that means, "I practice" or "I do" or "I commit" or to refuse to carry out an obligation of a moral or social nature (BDAG 840.3c). **Syntactically**, ποιεῖ is the main verb of the independent asyndeton clause: "everyone who practices sin also practices lawlessness" (πᾶς ὁ ποιῶν τὴν ἁμαρτίαν καὶ τὴν ἀνομίαν ποιεῖ). The subject of ποιεῖ is the entire participial phrase, "everyone who practices sin" (πᾶς ὁ ποιῶν τὴν ἁμαρτίαν). The καὶ here is functioning adjunctively and should be translated as "also" (Wallace 1996, 671). **Semantically**, ποιεῖ is a gnomic present: "everyone who practices" (NASB ESV NET). John describes another timeless fact about people who live a lifestyle of sin: they also practice lawlessness.

3:4b καί: The Greek word καί is a conjunction which means "and so" or "to introduce a result that comes from what precedes" (BDAG 495.1bζ). **Syntactically**, καί introduces an independent conjunctive clause: "*and so* sin *really* is lawlessness" (καὶ ἡ ἁμαρτία ἐστὶν ἡ ἀνομία). **Semantically**, some translations interpret καί as explanatory – "for" (KJV NLT), or a coordinating connective – "and" (ASV NASB), "also" (ESV), but the best choice is an emphatic conjunction – "indeed" (NET), "in fact" (NIV) or "and so" along with "really." John links the gnomic truth about anyone who practices sins with another gnomic truth evident in the rset of the clause.

ἐστίν: The Greek word ἐστίν is third singular present active indicative from the verb εἰμί that means, "is" or "to be in close connection with" (BDAG 283.2a). **Syntactically**, ἐστίν is the main verb of the independent conjunctive clause. The subject of the verb is the noun "sin" (ἡ ἁμαρτία). **Semantically**, ἐστίν is an equative present: "is" (cf. KJV NASB ESV NIV NET etc.). John equates sin with lawlessness. John's timeless fact is that sin is the same as lawlessness.

Theological Nugget: What is this sin in 1 John? It is a refusal to love others. John revealed in 2:9-11 that there was a group of people who were ignoring the love command issued by Jesus in John 13:34-35, a point restated in 1 John 3:23. Therefore, John says refusing to love is both sin and a an indication of lawlessness (Bateman 2008, 336).

3:5a καί: The Greek word καί is a conjunction which means "and" (BDAG 494.1bγ). **Syntactically**, καί introduces a conjunctive independent clause: "*and* you know that Jesus appeared" (καὶ οἴδατε ὅτι ἐκεῖνος ἐφανερώθη). **Semantically**, καί is coordinating connective: "and" (KJV ASV NET NLT CNT; *contra* "but" NIV). John is about to link gnomic information about sin with the first coming of Jesus.

οἴδατε: The Greek word οἴδατε is a second plural perfect active indicative from the verb οἶδα that means, "I know" or to have information about something (BDAG 692.1e). **Syntactically**, οἴδατε is the main verb of the independent conjunctive clause. The assumed subject "you" refers to the readers of the letter. **Semantically**, οἴδατε is a perfect with present force: "you know" (cf. KJV NASB ESV NIV NET etc). This verb appears in the perfect tense without the perfect's aspectual significance (Wallace 1996, 579-580). John's readers are aware that Jesus came, which is spelled out in the next ὅτι clause.

ὅτι: The Greek word ὅτι is a conjunction, which means "that" (BDAG 731.1c). **Syntactically**, ὅτι introduces a dependent conjunctive clause: "*that* he was manifested" (ὅτι ἐκεῖνος ἐφανερώθη). The entire clause functions as the direct object of the verb "you know" (οἴδατε). The clause is placed in parenthesis in order to visualize its contribution to the independent clause. The emphatic demonstrative pronoun "that one" (ἐκεῖνος = Jesus) functions as the subject. **Semantically**, ὅτι is an indirect discourse following a verb of perception: "that" (cf. KJV NASB ESV NIV NET etc.). John provides the content of information known to his readers about Jesus.

ἐφανερώθη: The Greek word ἐφανερώθη is a third singular aorist passive indicative from the verb φανερόω that means, "I reveal" or "I appear" or to cause to become visible publicaly (BDAG 1048.1aβ). **Syntactically**, ἐφανερώθη is the governing verb of the dependent ὅτι clause. The demonstrative pronoun "that one" (ἐκεῖνος) functions as the subject. In fact this particular demonstrative seems to refer to Jesus in the Johannine epistles. **Semantically**, ἐφανερώθη is a constative aorist: "he appeared" (NASB NIV NET CNT) or "came" (NLT). John underscores the first coming of Jesus as a whole (Wallace 1996, 557). It is the event John mentioned in 1:1–4 in order to reinforce his humanity. Jesus's intention for coming is disclosed in the next clause.

3:5b   ἵνα: The Greek word ἵνα is a conjunction that means "in order that" or "to denote purpose, aim or goal" (BDAG 475.1aε). **Syntactically**, ἵνα introduces a dependent conjunctive clause: "*in order* to take away sin" (ἵνα τὰς ἁμαρτίας ἄρῃ). Syntactically, the ἵνα clause is adverbial. It modifies the verb "he appeared" (ἐφανερώθη). **Semantically**, ἵνα is a purpose conjunction: "in order that" (NASB ESV). John provides the intention for Jesus's coming (Wallace 1996, 472). The intention is evident in the clause's verb.

ἄρῃ: The Greek word ἄρῃ is a third singular aorist active subjunctive from the verb αἴρω that means, "I take away" or "I remove" (BDAG 29.3). The verb is in the subjunctive mood because it is part of an ἵνα clause. **Syntactically**, ἄρῃ is the governing verb of the dependent adverbial ἵνα clause. The subject of the verb is an implied "he" and refers to Jesus. **Semantically**, ἄρῃ is a constative aorist: "take away" (cf. KJV NASB ESV NIV NET etc.). John describes Jesus's once for all sacrifice as an event as a whole (Wallace 1996, 557). The intention for Jesus's coming into the world was to take away sins. Jesus removed the sins of the world (2:2), he is the redeemer (1:29), he cleanses sin (1:7), and he provides atonement for sins (2:2; 4:10).

3:5e   καί: The Greek word καί is a conjunction which means "and" or (BDAG 494.1ba). **Syntactically**, καί introduces a independent conjunctive clause, "and [*you know* (*that*] there is no sin in him" (καὶ [ὅτι] ἁμαρτία ἐν αὐτῷ οὐκ ἔστιν). **Semantically**, καί is a coordinating connective: καί as "and" (KJV ASV NASB NRSV ESV NIV NET NLT CNT). It joins what John's readers know in the independent clause of verse 5a,b about Jesus's first coming with additonal knowledge about Jesus.

[οἴδατε (ὅτι]: The Greek word οἴδατε is a second person plural perfect active indicative from the verb οἶδα that means, "I know" or to have information about something (BDAG 692.1e). **Syntactically**, elliptical [οἴδατε] is the main verb of the independent conjunctive clause. The assumed subject "you" refers to the readers of the letter. **Semantically**, οἴδατε is a perfect with present force: "you know." This verb appears in the perfect tense without the perfect's aspectual significance (Wallace 1996, 579-580). John's readers are aware about Jesus, which is spelled out in the elliptical [.... (ὅτι] clause. The clause is placed in parenthesis in order to visualize its contribution to the independent clause. It seems best to imply an elliptical ὅτι to make this clause parallel to the first.

ἔστιν: The Greek word ἔστιν is third singular present active indicative from the verb εἰμί that means, "is" or "to be in close connection with" (BDAG 283.2a). **Syntactically**, ἔστιν is the governing verb of the dependent conjunctive clause introduced by an elliptical ὅτι. The subject of the verb is "there" embedded in the verb. **Semantically**, the negated (οὐκ) ἔστιν is an gnomic present: "there is no" (cf. KJV NASB ESV NIV NET etc.). John presents a timeless fact about Jesus. He is sinless.

3:6a   μένων: The Greek word μένων is a nominative masculine singular present active participle from the verb μένω that means, "I remain" or "I abide" or "I continue" or of "someone who does not leave" (BDAG 631.1aβ). **Syntactically**, μένων functions as an adjectival participle that modifies the adjective "every" (πᾶς). The entire participial phrase "everyone who abides in him" (ὁ ἐν αὐτῷ μένων) serves as the subject of the verb "sin" (ἁμαρτάνει). **Semantically**, μένων is a gnomic present: "everyone who remains" or "resides" (NET) or "abides" (KJV ASV NASB NRSV ESV CNT) or "lives" (NIV; cf. NLT). John presents a timeless truth that is almost always true about any follower of Jesus. That gnomic truth is disclosed in the next verb (Wallace 1996, 523, 615 *contra* 524–25).

ἁμαρτάνει: The Greek word ἁμαρτάνει is a third singular present active indicative from the verb ἁμαρτάνω that means, "I sin" or "to commit a wrong" (BDAG 49.a). **Syntactically**, ἁμαρτάνει is the main verb of the independent asyndeton clause. The subject of the verb ἁμαρτάνει is the entire participial clause, "everyone who abides in him does not persist in sin" (πᾶς ὁ ἐν αὐτῷ μένων οὐχ ἁμαρτάνει). The rather lengthy subject refers to those who have an abiding relationship with Jesus. **Semantically**, the negated (οὐχ) ἁμαρτάνει is a gnomic present: "does not *persist* in sin." John once again speaks of a general or timeless fact (Wallace 1996, 523). Any follower of Jesus who continues to maintain correct teaching about Jesus's humanity and messiahship will not want to live a life of habitual sin.

3:6b ἁμαρτάνων: The Greek word ἁμαρτάνων is a nominative masculine singular present active participle from the verb ἁμαρτάνω that means, "I sin" or to commit a wrong against God or God's commands (BDAG 49.a). **Syntactically**, ἁμαρτάνων is an adjectival participle. The entire participial phrase "everyone one who sins" (ὁ ἁμαρτάνων) modifies the adjective "every" (Πᾶς). The entire contruction functions as the subject of the compound verbs, "has seen" (ἑώρακεν) and "has known" (ἔγνωκεν). **Semantically**, ἁμαρτάνων is a gnomic present: "who makes it a practice to sin." John once again presents a timeless fact (Wallace 1996, 523, 615 *contra* 524–25). John is making a generic statement about anyone who lives a lifestyle of sin.

ἑώρακεν: The Greek word ἑωράκαμεν is a third singular perfect active indicative from the verb ὁράω that means, "I see" or "to be mentally or spiritually perceptive" (BDAG, 720.4b). **Syntactically**, ἑωράκαμεν is the first main verb in the compound independent asyndeton clause, "everyone who sins *has* neither *seen* him nor knows him" (πᾶς ὁ ἁμαρτάνων οὐχ ἑώρακεν αὐτὸν οὐδὲ ἔγνωκεν αὐτόν). The subject of the verb is the phrase "everyone who sins" (πᾶς ὁ ἁμαρτάνων). **Semantically**, the negated οὐχ ἑωράκαμεν is rendered as a gnomic perfect with an extensive perfect force: "has neither seen" (KJV ASV NET; cf. "either seen" NASB NRSV ESV NIV). John's focus is on a generic subject where a decisive act of judgment has been carried out (Wallace 1996, 580). John focuses on the fact that anyone who lives a life of habitual sin has not seen God.

ἔγνωκεν: The Greek word ἔγνωκεν is a third singular perfect active indicative from the verb γινώσκω that means, "I know" or to arrive at a personal knowledge of someone (BDAG 199.1b). **Syntactically**, ἔγνωκεν serves as the second main verb in the compound independent asyndeton clause, "everyone who sins has neither seen him nor *known* him" (πᾶς ὁ ἁμαρτάνων οὐχ ἑώρακεν αὐτὸν οὐδὲ ἔγνωκεν αὐτόν). The subject of the verb is the phrase "everyone who sins" (πᾶς ὁ ἁμαρτάνων). Like "has seen" (ἑωράκαμεν), "has known" (ἔγνωκεν) is **semantically** an extensive perfect (JKV NRSV ESV ESV NIV NET CNT). John's focus is on a generic subject where a decisive act of judgment has been carried out (Wallace 1996, 580). John focuses on the fact that anyone who lives a life of habitual sin has not known God.

3:7a πλανάτω: The Greek word πλανάτω is a third singular present active imperative from the verb πλανάω that means, "I deceive" or "I mislead" or to cause someone to stray from a specific way via misleading or deceiving (BDAG 821.1b). **Syntactically**, πλανάτω is the main verb of the independent asyndeton clause "Children, *let* no one *deceive* you" (Τεκνία, μηδεὶς πλανάτω ὑμᾶς). The subject is the indefinite pronoun "no one" (μηδεὶς). **Semantically**, πλανάτω is an imperative of prohibition that forbids an action: "do not be mislead" (Wallace 1996, 487; cf. "deceive" KJV NASB NRSV ESV NET NLT CNT; "lead astray" ASV NIV). The force of the present imperative is to "command an action as an ongoing process" (Wallace, 1996, 485). The present tense imperative + μηδεὶς intensifies John's expectation. John forbids believers to succumb to false teaching about Jesus as Messiah and his command to love (Brown 1982, 429).

Translational Nugget: Although third person imperatives are difficult to translate because English only has second person imperatives, the most common ways to translate a third person imperative are "let no one deceive you" or "let no third party deceive you." As in 2:15a ἀγαπᾶτε, the present imperative should not be pressed to assume that John is urging his readers to stop something that they were already doing, as if the entire congregation were already deceived.

3:7b ποιῶν: The Greek word ποιῶν is a nominative masculine singular present active participle from the verb ποιέω that means, "I do" or "I practice" or "to carry out an obligation of a moral or social nature" (BDAG 8403b). **Syntactically**, ποιῶν is the subject of the verb "is" (ἐστιν). **Semantically**, ποιῶν is a gnomic present with a customary force: "the one who makes it a practice" (cf. NASB NET). John again shares generic utterance (Wallace 1996, 521, 523). John describes anyone who makes it a habit to live a righteous lifestyle is clarified with the next verb.

ἐστιν: The Greek word ἐστιν is third singular present active indicative from the verb εἰμί that means "is" or "to be in close connection with" (BDAG 283.2a). **Syntactically**, ἐστιν is the main verb of the independent asyndeton clause. The subject of the verb is the participial phrase "the one who practices righteousness" (ὁ ποιῶν τὴν δικαιοσύνην). **Semantically**, ἐστιν is an equative gnomic present: "is." John presents a timeless fact (Wallace 1996, 524). Anyone who lives righteously is equated with being a righteous person.

3:7c καθώς: The Greek word καθώς is a conjunction, which means "just as" or "even as" (BDAG 493.1). **Syntactically**, καθώς introduces a dependent conjunctive clause. The entire dependent clause, "just as he is righteous" (καθὼς ἐκεῖνος δίκαιός ἐστιν), is functioning adverbially modifying the verb "is" (ἐστιν). Semantically, καθώς is comparative: "even as" (KJV ASV NLT) or "just as" (NASB NRSV NIV NET CNT). John makes a comparison about the person who is righteous; they are like Jesus.

ἐστιν: The Greek word ἐστιν is third singular present active indicative from the verb εἰμί that means, "is" or "to be in close connection with" (BDAG 283.2a). **Syntactically**, ἐστιν is the governing verb of the dependent adverbial clause. The subject of the verb is the demonstrative pronoun "that one" (ἐκεῖνος) which is a reference to Jesus. **Semantically**, ἐστιν is an equative gnomic present: "he is" (cf. KJV NASB ESV NIV NET etc.). John presents a timeless fact (Wallace 1996, 524). Jesus is righteous. John underscores time and again that Jesus's life was characterised by righteousness. This is the third time that Jesus has been called righteous (cf. 2:1 and 2:29).

3:8a ποιῶν: The Greek word ποιῶν is a nominative masculine singular present active participle from the verb ποιέω that means, "I practice" or "I do" or "I commit" or to refuse to carry out an obligation of a moral or social nature (BDAG 840.3b). **Syntactically**, ποιῶν functions substantivally. The entire participial phrase "The one who practices sin" (ὁ ποιῶν τὴν ἁμαρτίαν) is the subject of the verb ἐστίν. It is set in contrast to the "the one who practices righteousness" (πᾶς ὁ ποιῶν τὴν δικαιοσύνην). The one who practices righteousness is contrasted with the one who practices sin. **Semantically**, ποιῶν is a gnomic present with a cusomary force: "the one who makes it a practice" (cf. NASB NET John again shares a generic utterance (Wallace 1996, 521, 523). While the one finds their exemplar in

Jesus, the other finds their exemplar in the deceiver. In very black and white terms, John leaves no room for middle ground. Behavior determines whether a person is a child of God or a child of the Devil.

ἐστιν: The Greek word ἐστιν is third singular present active indicative from the verb εἰμί that means, "I come from" or "to have a point of derivation or origin" (BDAG 285.8). **Syntactically**, ἐστιν serves as the main verb of the independent asyndeton clause. The subject of the verb is the participial phrase "the one who practices sin" (ὁ ποιῶν τὴν ἁμαρτίαν). **Semantically**, ἐστιν is an equative gnomic present intended to describe a point of origin: "he comes from" (or "is of" KJV ASV NASB ESV NIV NET CNT). Anyone who persists in sin is of the Devil.

3:8b ὅτι: The Greek word ὅτι is a conjunction which means "because" or "for" (BDAG 732.4a). **Syntactically**, ὅτι introduces a dependent conjunctive clause: "*because* the Devil persists in sinning from the beginning" (ὅτι ἀπ᾿ ἀρχῆς ὁ διάβολος ἁμαρτάνει). The clause is adverbial modifying the verb "is" (ἐστιν). **Semantically**, ὅτι is causal: "because" (NET) or "for" (JKV ASV NASB NRSV ESV). John is about to provide the reason for linking habitual sinners with the devil and is evident in the rest of the clause.

ἁμαρτάνει: The Greek word ἁμαρτάνει is a third singular present active indicative from the verb ἁμαρτάνω that means, "I sin" or to commit a wrong against God or God's commands (BDAG 49.a). **Syntactically**, ἁμαρτάνει is the governing verb of the adverbial dependent clause. The subject of the verb is the proper noun "the Devil" (ὁ διάβολος). The Devil is a hostile spirit that stands against God and his work (Culy 2004, 76). **Semantically**, ἁμαρτάνει is a customary present: *persists in* sinning" (cf. KJV ASV), It speaks of a pattern of behavior (Wallace 1996, 521). But translations typically render the verb "has been sinning" (NRSV ESV NIV NET NLT) or "has sinned" (CNT). Regardless, the reason for linking habitual sinners with the devil is because the devil has a record of sinning since the beginning of creation (Job 1; Gen. 3).

3:8c εἰς τοῦτο: The Greek word εἰς is a preposition that means "for this reason" or "for this purpose" (BDAG 290.4f). The Greek word τοῦτο is an accusative singular neuter from the demonstrative pronoun τοῦτο. **Syntactically**, εἰς τοῦτο is a prepositional phrase introducing an independent prepositional clause: "*For this purpose*, the Son of God appeared" (εἰς τοῦτο ἐφανερώθη ὁ υἱὸς τοῦ θεοῦ). This kind of prepositional construction occurs frequently in the New Testament and is a very important structural marker. **Semantically**, εἰς τοῦτο expresses a statement of purpose (BDAG 741.1b) and often translated: "for this purpose" (KJV NET). John speaks of the intention for Jesus's coming.

ἐφανερώθη: The Greek word ἐφανερώθη is a third singular aorist passive indicative from the verb φανερόω that means, "I reveal" or "I appear" or to cause to become visible publically (BDAG 1048.1aβ). **Syntactically**, ἐφανερώθη is the main verb of the independent clause introduced by a prepositional phrase. The subject of the verb is the phrase "the Son of God" (ὁ υἱὸς τοῦ θεοῦ). **Semantically**, ἐφανερώθη is a constative aorist: "he appeared" (NASB ESV NIV CNT). While the prepositional phrase could be anaphoric, pointing back to the preceding discussion, the ἵνα clause makes it catophorical. John refers to the historical fact of Jesus's first advent as a whole (Wallace 1996, 557). The purpose behind the coming of Jesus appears in the ἵνα clause.

3:8d ἵνα: The Greek word ἵνα is a conjunction, which means "that" (BDAG 476.1e). **Syntactically**, ἵνα serves to introduce a conjunctive dependent clause: "*that* he might destroy the works of the devil" (ἵνα λύσῃ τὰ ἔργα τοῦ διαβόλου). **Syntactically**, the ἵνα clause is substantival. It clarifies the demonstrative pronoun "this" (τοῦτο). **Semantically**, ἵνα is appositional: "*namely* that" (KJV ASV). It provides the content of the demonstrative (*contra* Wallace 1996, 472; cf, 475). Since the prepositional phrase "For this purpose" (εἰς τοῦτο) is telic in nature, this clause underscores one of John's purposes for Jesus coming into the world. That purpose is described with the next verb

λύσῃ: The Greek word λύσῃ is a third singular aorist active subjunctive from the verb λύω that means, "I destroy" or "I bring an end to" or "to do away with" (BDAG 607.4). The verb is in the subjunctive mood because it is part of an ἵνα clause. **Syntactically**, λύσῃ is the governing verb of the ἵνα clause. The subject of the verb is an implied "he" embedded in the verb and refers to Jesus, who is the Son of God (=Messiah). **Semantically**, λύσῃ is a constative aorist: "he might destroy" (cf. KJV ASV) or "to destroy" (NASB NRSV ESV NET NLT). John describes an event as a whole (Wallace 1996, 557). John provides an overal picture about Jesus's activities: he abolished the Devil's work.

3:9a γεγεννημένος: The Greek word γεγεννημένος is a nominative masculine singular perfect passive participle from the verb γεννάω that means, "I become the parent of" or "to exercise the role of a parental figure" (BDAG 193.1b). **Syntactically**, γεγεννημένος functions adjectivally. It modifies the substantival adjective "each" (πᾶς). The entire participial phrase "Everyone who is born of God" (πᾶς ὁ γεγεννημένος ἐκ τοῦ θεοῦ) is the subject of the verb ποιεῖ. John continues to contrast the behavior of those who have been fathered by God and those who belong to the Devil. **Semantically**, γεγέννηται is both a gnomic and extensive perfect: "has been fathered" (NET) or "has been born" (NRSV cf. NLT). It is gnomic because of the generic subject (πᾶς) while extensive in that the focus is on the decisive relationship between God and the believer (Wallace 1996, 580). This generic or proverbial force may also be rendered as intensive: "is born" (KJV ASV NASB NIV; cf. ESV CNT) with an emphasis on the results of the present condition of the believer. Regardless of where one places the emphasis of the perfect, John's point is simply this: believers have been fathered by God in the past and that past event has continuing results in the present (cf. 2:29; 4:7; 5:1, 4, 18). The focus is upon those who practice righteousness: they have had an on-going relationship with God.

ποιεῖ: The Greek word ποιεῖ is a third singular present active indicative from the verb ποιέω that means, "I practice" or "I do" or "I commit" or to refuse to carry out an obligation of a moral or social nature (BDAG 840.3c). **Syntactically**, ποιεῖ is as the main verb of the independent clause "everyone who is Fathered by of God does not practice sin" (πᾶς ὁ γεγεννημένος ἐκ τοῦ θεοῦ ἁμαρτίαν οὐ ποιεῖ). **Semantically**, the negated (οὐ) ποιεῖ is a gnomic present: "does not practice" (e.g. NASB ESV NLT CNT). John provides another timeless truth (Wallace 1996, 523). Anyone who is fathered by God has entered into a life-changing relationship with him, and it changes the way that person lives. He or she does not make it a practice to sin. John's reasoning is clearly stated in the next clause.

3:9b ὅτι: The Greek word ὅτι is a conjunction which means "because" or "for" (BDAG 732.4a). **Syntactically**, ὅτι introduces a dependent conjunctive clause: "*because* God's seed remains in him" (ὅτι σπέρμα αὐτοῦ ἐν αὐτῷ μένει). The clause is adverbial modifying the verb "does" (ποιεῖ). **Semantically**, ὅτι is causal: "because" (e.g. KJV NASB ESV NIV NET etc.). John provides the reason why the child of God will not sin (Wallace 1996, 460), which John discloses with the next verb.

μένει: The Greek word μένει is a third singular present active indicative from the verb μένω that means, "I remain," "I continue," "I abide" or of someone does not leave a certain realm or sphere (BDAG 631.1aβ). **Syntactically**, μένει is the governing verb of the dependent adverbial clause. The subject is the noun, "seed" (σπέρμα). **Semantically**, μένει is a customary present: "*continually* remains" (e.g. KJV NIV). It provides a pattern of behavior (Wallace 1996, 527). The reason (ὅτι) a child of God will not sin is because God's seed remains in them.

^{3:9c} καί: The Greek word καί is a conjunction which means "and" (BDAG 494.1bα). **Syntactically**, καί introduces an independent conjunctive clause: "*and* he is not able to persist in sin" (καὶ οὐ δύναται ἁμαρτάνειν). **Semantically**, καί is a coordinating connective of two independent clauses: "and" (KJV ASV NASB ESV NET CNT). John provides additional information about the one who is fathered by God. Culy suggests that while this clause is clearly a logical connective, that it has the force of a result clause and is closely related to the idea that God's seed remains in us (Culy 2004, 78). This seems be indicated in NLT with a translation of καί as "so"

δύναται: The Greek word δύναται is a third singular present middle/passive indicative from the verb δύναμαι that means, "I am able" or "to be capable of something" or to have the capacity for something (BDAG, 262.c). **Syntactically**, δύναται serves as the main verb of the conjunctive independent καί clause. The subject of the verb is an implied "he" embedded in the verb and refers to the one who is fathered by God. **Semantically**, the negated (οὐ) δύναται is a gnomic present: he is *not* able" (NET) or "he cannot (KJV ASV NASB ESV CNT). It speaks of a general truth about anyone (*contra* Wallace 1996, 524). Yet the verb demands a complementary verbal to clarify John's point, which is discussed next.

ἁμαρτάνειν: The Greek word ἁμαρτάνειν is a present active infinitive from the verb ἁμαρτάνω that means, "I sin" or "to commit a wrong" (BDAG 49.a). **Syntactically**, ἁμαρτάνειν is part of the *negated* main verb of the independent καί clause: "he is *not* able to sin" (οὐ δύναται ἁμαρτάνειν). **Semantically**, ἁμαρτάνειν is a complementary infinitive that completes the thought of the negated finite verb: "he is not able" (οὐ δύναται). It clarifies that the one who is fathered by God is incapable of habitual sin (Wallace 1996, 599). Any person (see πᾶς in 3:9b) who has this special father/child relationship with God through belief in Jesus cannot *persist* in sin.

^{3:9d} ὅτι: The Greek word ὅτι is a conjunction which means "because" or "for" (BDAG 732.4a). **Syntactically**, ὅτι serves to introduce a dependent conjunctive clause: "*because* he is born of God" (ὅτι ἐκ τοῦ θεοῦ γεγέννηται). The clause is adverbial. It modifies the verb "is able" (δύναται). **Semantically**, ὅτι is causal: "because" (e.g. KJV NASB ESV NIV NET etc.). John provides the reason why believers are not able to sin (Wallace 1996, 460), which John discloses with the next clause.

Structural Nugget: Here we chiastically come back around to where we started. The one who is fathered by God (A) does not sin (B), because God's seed remains in him (C). In fact, he is not able to sin (B'), because he is fathered by God (A').

γεγέννηται: The Greek word γεγέννηται is a third singular perfect passive indicative from the verb γεννάω that means, "I become the parent of" or "to exercise the role of a parental figure" (BDAG 193.1b). **Syntactically**, γεγέννηται is the governing verb of the dependent adverbial clause. The subject is an implied "he" embedded in the verb and refers to the believer. **Semantically**, γεγέννηται is both gnomic and extensive perfect: "has been fathered" (NET) or "has been born" (ESV CNT NIV cf. NRSV). It is gnomic because of the generic subject (πᾶς) mentioned in 3:9a while extensive in that the focus is on the decisive relationship between God and the believer (Wallace 1996, 580). Others translate the perfect as an intensive perfect: "is born" (KJV NASB CNT; cf. ASV NLT) with an emphasis on the results of the present condition of the believer. Regardless of where one places the emphasis of the perfect, John's point is simply this: believers have been fathered by God in the past and that past event has continuing results in the present (cf. 2:29; 4:7; 5:1, 4, 18). Regardless, the person who has been born of God enters into a state where they do not habitually sin and hate, but rather are characterized instead by God's spiritual DNA.

^{3:10a} ἐν τούτῳ: The Greek word ἐν is a preposition, which means "by" (BDAG 328.5b). The Greek word τούτῳ is declined as a dative singular neuter from the demonstrative pronoun τοῦτο, which means "this one" (BDAG 741.1bβ). **Syntactically**, ἐν τούτῳ is a prepositional phrase introducing an independent prepositional clause "*By this* the children of God and the children of the Devil are made clear" (ἐν τούτῳ φανερά ἐστιν τὰ τέκνα τοῦ θεοῦ καὶ τὰ τέκνα τοῦ διαβόλου). The construction, "by this" (ἐν τούτῳ) appears often in 1 John (2:3, 4, 5, 3:16, 19, 24; 4:2, 9, 10, 13, 17; 5:2). **Semantically**, ἐν τούτῳ means: "by this" (NASB ESV NET CNT). The clause can either be anaphoric, pointing back to the preceding discussion, or cataphoric, pointing forward. The phrase points forward. After a lengthy discussion of how to tell the difference between someone fathered by God and someone who is not, John clarifies how to tell the difference, a person's lifestyle. The one whose life is characterized by hate and impurity cannot possibly have God's seed in him.

ἐστιν: The Greek word ἐστιν is third singular present active indicative from the verb εἰμί that means, "is" or "to describe a special connection with" (BDAG 283.2b). **Syntactically**, ἐστιν is the main verb of the independent clause. The subjects of the verb are the compound neuter plural nouns "children" (τέκνα) and "children" (τέκνα). In New Testament Greek plural neuter nouns take a singular verb. **Semantically**, ἐστιν is an equative present: "are" (cf. KJV NASB ESV NIV NET etc.). It equates people as either children of God or children of the Devil. A person's parentage is *evident* (φανερά) in their lifestyle.

^{3:10b} ποιῶν: The Greek word ποιῶν is a nominative masculine singular present active participle from the verb ποιέω that means, "I practice" or "I do" or "I commit" or to refuse to carry out an obligation of a moral or social nature (BDAG 840.3b). **Syntactically**, ποιῶν functions adjectivally. It modifies the substantival adjective "each" (πᾶς). The entire participial phrase "Everyone *who* does not *practice* righteousness" (πᾶς ὁ μὴ ποιῶν δικαιοσύνην) is the subject of the verb, "is" (ἐστίν). **Semantically**, ποιῶν is a gnomic present expressing a timeless maxim about anyone "who does not practice" (NASB NET) moral or socially accepted behavior (Wallace 1996, 523). Once again, John's point is very black and white, there is no middle ground. Either your behavior exhibits that you are a child of God or a child of the Devil.

ἔστιν: The Greek word ἔστιν is third singular present active indicative from the verb εἰμί that means, "is" or "to describe a special connection with" (BDAG 283.2b). **Syntactically**, ἔστιν is the main verb of the independent clause. The subject of the verb is the participial phrase "everyone who does not practice righteousness" (πᾶς ὁ μὴ ποιῶν δικαιοσύνην). **Semantically**, ἔστιν is a gnomic present that identifies who is not a child of God. John states a timeless maxim. Anyone who practices unrighteousness does not have a relationship with God.

^{3:10c} καί: The Greek word καί is a conjunction that means "and" (BDAG 494.1b). **Syntactically**, καί introduces an independent conjunctive clause: "*that is* the one who persists in not loving his brother and sister" (καὶ ὁ μὴ ἀγαπῶν τὸν ἀδελφὸν αὐτοῦ). The entire clause functions adjectivally. **Semantically**, καί is explanatory conjunction: "that is" (Wallace 1996, 673). The clause, then, would further define the unrighteous person already described: "Everyone who does not practice righteousness, *that is*, the one who does not love his brother and sister is not from God."

Syntactical Nugget: The Greek conjunction καί can be interpreted in a number of ways. (1) It could be a coordinating conjunction giving us additional information. In that case we would imply another verb and prepositional phrase and set this clause as parallel to the one previous, "Everyone who does not practice righteousness is not from God, and everyone who does not love his brother [is not from God]" (cf. Culy 2004, 79). (2) It could be a correlative conjunction expressing contrary relationships whereby καί is rendered "neither" (KJV ASV) or "nor" (NASB NRSV ESV NIV CNT). (3) It could be an explanatory conjunction, "that is" (Wallace 1996, 673). The clause, then, would further define the unrighteous person already described, "Everyone who does not practice righteousness, *that is*, the one who does not love his brother is not from God." Yet one last option does not differ from an epexegetical rendering (NET, BDF 1961, 202 § 394) or an appositional rendering (Smalley 1984; 177, 181). Either the explanatory, epexegetical, or appositional options convey the same idea. John equates unrighteous behavior with a refusal to love throughout the letter. The one who practices unrighteousness is the one who does not love.

ἀγαπῶν: The Greek word ἀγαπῶν is a nominative masculine singular present active participle from the verb ἀγαπάω that means, "I love" or to have a warm regard for and interest in another person (BDAG 5.1aα). **Syntactically**, ἀγαπῶν functions substantivally. The entire participial phrase "The one who persists in not loving his brother" (ὁ μὴ ἀγαπῶν τὸν ἀδελφὸν αὐτοῦ) is epexegetical. It provides further information about the one who is not from God. **Semantically**, ἀγαπῶν is a gnomic present with a customary present force: "the one who *persists* in not loving." It speaks of a generic person's pattern of behavior (Wallace 1996, 527, 615). Anyone who practices a lifestyle of habitual sin (= not loving) cannot possibly be fathered by God.

1 John 3:11–17

Verb Recognition for 1 John 3:11–17

¹¹Ὅτι αὕτη ἐστὶν ἡ ἀγγελία ἣν ἠκούσατε ἀπ' ἀρχῆς, ἵνα ἀγαπῶμεν ἀλλήλους· ¹²οὐ καθὼς Κάϊν ἐκ τοῦ πονηροῦ ἦν καὶ ἔσφαξεν τὸν ἀδελφὸν αὐτοῦ· καὶ χάριν τίνος ἔσφαξεν αὐτόν; ὅτι τὰ ἔργα αὐτοῦ πονηρὰ ἦν, τὰ δὲ τοῦ ἀδελφοῦ αὐτοῦ δίκαια.

¹³[καὶ] μὴ θαυμάζετε, ἀδελφοί, εἰ μισεῖ ὑμᾶς ὁ κόσμος. ¹⁴ἡμεῖς οἴδαμεν ὅτι μεταβεβήκαμεν ἐκ τοῦ θανάτου εἰς τὴν ζωήν, ὅτι ἀγαπῶμεν τοὺς ἀδελφούς· ὁ μὴ ἀγαπῶν μένει ἐν τῷ θανάτῳ. ¹⁵πᾶς ὁ μισῶν τὸν ἀδελφὸν αὐτοῦ ἀνθρωποκτόνος ἐστίν, καὶ οἴδατε ὅτι πᾶς ἀνθρωποκτόνος οὐκ ἔχει ζωὴν αἰώνιον ἐν αὐτῷ μένουσαν. ¹⁶ἐν τούτῳ ἐγνώκαμεν τὴν ἀγάπην, ὅτι ἐκεῖνος ὑπὲρ ἡμῶν τὴν ψυχὴν αὐτοῦ ἔθηκεν· καὶ ἡμεῖς ὀφείλομεν ὑπὲρ τῶν ἀδελφῶν τὰς ψυχὰς θεῖναι. ¹⁷ὃς δ' ἂν ἔχῃ τὸν βίον τοῦ κόσμου καὶ θεωρῇ τὸν ἀδελφὸν αὐτοῦ χρείαν ἔχοντα καὶ κλείσῃ τὰ σπλάγχνα αὐτοῦ ἀπ' αὐτοῦ, πῶς ἡ ἀγάπη τοῦ θεοῦ μένει ἐν αὐτῷ;

Clausal Outline Translated for 1 John 3:11–17

3:11b ἣν ἠκούσατε ἀπ᾽ ἀρχῆς
3:11b **that you heard** from the beginning
|
3:11a Ὅτι αὕτη ἐστὶν ἡ ἀγγελία . . . , ·
3:11a **For** this **is** the *gospel* message . . .
|
3:11c ἵνα ἀγαπῶμεν ἀλλήλους
3:11c *namely* **that we should love** one another;
|
3:12a οὐ **καθὼς** Κάϊν ἐκ τοῦ πονηροῦ **ἦν**
3:12a not **as** Cain *who* **was** of the evil one
|
3:12b καὶ **ἔσφαξεν** τὸν ἀδελφὸν αὐτοῦ·
3:12b and *who brutally* **murdered** his brother (= Abel);

3:12c καὶ χάριν τίνος **ἔσφαξεν** αὐτόν;
3:12c and why did **he** *brutally* **murder** him (= Abel)?
|
3:12d **ὅτι** τὰ ἔργα αὐτοῦ πονηρὰ **ἦν**,
3:12d **because** his deeds **were** evil,

3:12e τὰ [ἔργα] δὲ τοῦ ἀδελφοῦ αὐτοῦ δίκαια [**ἦν**].
3:12e but his brother's [*deeds* **were**] righteous.

3:13a [καὶ] μὴ **θαυμάζετε**, ἀδελφοί, (**εἰ μισεῖ** ὑμᾶς ὁ κόσμος).
3:13a And *so*, **do** not **be surprised**, brothers *and sisters*, (that the world hates you).

3:14a ἡμεῖς **οἴδαμεν** (**ὅτι μεταβεβήκαμεν** ἐκ τοῦ θανάτου εἰς τὴν ζωήν),
v14a **We know** (that we have passed out of death into life).
|
3:14b **ὅτι ἀγαπῶμεν** τοὺς ἀδελφούς·
3:14b **because we** *persistantly* **love** our brothers *and sisters*.

3:14c ὁ μὴ ἀγαπῶν **μένει** ἐν τῷ θανάτῳ.
3:14c The one who does not *persist in* love **abides** in death.

3:15a πᾶς ὁ μισῶν τὸν ἀδελφὸν αὐτοῦ ἀνθρωποκτόνος **ἐστίν**,
3:15a Everyone who *persists in hating* his brother *and sister* **is** a murderer,

3:15b καὶ **οἴδατε** (ὅτι πᾶς ἀνθρωποκτόνος οὐκ **ἔχει** ζωὴν αἰώνιον ἐν αὐτῷ μένουσαν).
3:15b and **you know** (that no murderer possesses eternal life abiding in him *or her*).

^{3:16a} ἐν τούτῳ **ἐγνώκαμεν** τὴν ἀγάπην,
^{3:16a} By this **we know** love,

|
^{3:16b} **ὅτι** ἐκεῖνος ὑπὲρ ἡμῶν τὴν ψυχὴν αὐτοῦ **ἔθηκεν·**
^{3:16b} **that** that one (= Jesus) **gave up** his life for us;

|
^{3:16c} καὶ [**ὅτι**] ἡμεῖς **ὀφείλομεν** ὑπὲρ τῶν ἀδελφῶν τὰς ψυχὰς **θεῖναι.**
^{3:16c} and [*that*] **we are obligated to give up** our lives for our brothers *and sisters*.

> ^{3:17a} **ὃς** δ᾽ ἂν **ἔχῃ** τὸν βίον τοῦ κόσμου
> ^{3:17a} but **whoever possesses** the resources of the world
>
> |
> ^{3:17b} καὶ [**ὃς ἂν**] θεωρῇ τὸν ἀδελφὸν αὐτοῦ χρείαν **ἔχοντα**
> ^{3:17b} and [*whoever*] **percieves** his brother *and sister* pocessessing a need
>
> |
> ^{3:17c} καὶ [**ὃς ἂν**] **κλείσῃ** τὰ σπλάγχνα αὐτοῦ ἀπ᾽ αὐτοῦ,
> ^{3:17c} and [*whoever*] **shuts off** his heart against him or her,

|
^{3:17d} πῶς ἡ ἀγάπη τοῦ θεοῦ **μένει** ἐν αὐτῷ;
^{3:17d} How does the love of God **remain** in him or her?

Syntax Explained for 1 John 3:11–17

^{3:11a} Ὅτι: The Greek word ὅτι is a conjunction that means "for" (BDAG 732.4b). **Syntactically**, ὅτι introduces the independent conjunctive clause: "*For* this is the gospel message" (Ὅτι αὕτη ἐστὶν ἡ ἀγγελία). While there remains a connection with the previous clause, the subordination is so loose that the translation "for" is best and thereby presented as an independent clause. **Semantically**, ὅτι is explanatory or inferential: "for" (KJV ASV NASB NRSV ESV NET CNT). John introduces a new section that builds on the previous one. He moves from how our parentage relates to our behavior to examine the life of love expected by God.

Structural Nugget: Brown points out that John now moves into the second main section of his letter (the first section also beginning with a similar structure in 1 John 1:5; cf. Brown 1982, 440). Culy disagrees and understands this clause to be functioning adverbially, giving us the reason why we can discover someone's parentage by the way we treat one another. He then insists that the main break in structure occurs in verse 13 rather than here in verse 11 (Culy 2004, 80).

ἐστίν: The Greek word ἐστιν is third singular present active indicative from the verb εἰμί that means, "is" or "to be in close connection with" (BDAG 283.2a). **Syntactically**, ἐστίν is the main verb of the conjunctive independent clause. The subject of the verb is the demonstrative pronoun "this one" (αὕτη), due to the grammatical priority of pronouns (Wallace 1996, 42-43). **Semantically**, ἐστίν is a gnomic. John is about to provide the content of a timeless message (Wallace 1996, 523). The demonstrative pronoun "this one" (αὕτη) points forward to an epexegetical ἵνα clause. It is almost as if John is using these type of constructions to highlight his main points (Brown 1982, 192). But first there is a relative clause.

^{3:11b} ἦν: The Greek word ἦν is accusative singular feminine from the relative pronoun ὅς that means, "that" (BDAG 715.1a). **Syntactically**, ἦν introduces an adjectival relative clause, "*that* you heard from the beginning" (ἣν ἠκούσατε ἀπ᾽ ἀρχῆς). It modifies the noun "message" (ἀγγελία). The relative pronoun is in the accusative case because it is the direct object of the verb "you heard" (ἠκούσατε). The relative clause provides further information about the message revealed in the next verb.

ἠκούσατε: The Greek word ἠκούσατε is a second plural aorist active indicative from the verb ἀκούω that means, "I hear" or "to have exercised the faculty of hearing" (BDAG 37.1a). **Syntactically**, ἠκούσατε is the governing verb of the relative clause. The subject of the verb is an implied "you" embedded in the verb and refers to the recipients of the letter. **Semantically**, ἠκούσατε is a constative aorist: "you heard" (KJV ASV NIV CNT). John merely speaks of the event as a whole (Wallace 1995, 557). John's readers have heard this message in the past and they are hearing it again. It is not a new message. Believers are to love others.

^{3:11c} ἵνα: The Greek word ἵνα is a conjunction, which means "that" (BDAG 476.2e). **Syntactically**, ἵνα introduces a conjunctive dependent clause: "*namely that* we should love one another" (ἵνα ἀγαπῶμεν ἀλλήλους). The entire ἵνα clause is substantival. It clarifies the demonstrative pronoun "this" (αὕτη). **Semantically**, ἵνα is an appositional conjunction: "*namely* that" (KJV ASV NASB ESV NLT CNT). It clarifies the demonstrative pronoun "this" (αὕτη). It is almost idiomatic within Johannine literature (Wallace 1996, 475). John's clarification is evident in the next verb.

ἀγαπῶμεν: The Greek word ἀγαπῶμεν is a first plural present subjunctive indicative from the verb ἀγαπάω that means, "I love" or "to have a warm regard for and interest in another" person (BDAG 5.1aα). The verb is in the subjunctive mood because it is part of an ἵνα clause. **Syntactically**, ἀγαπῶμεν is the governing verb of the conjunctive dependent clause. The subject of the verb is an implied "we" and refers to John and the readers of his letter. **Semantically**, ἀγαπῶμεν is a customary present: "we should love" (e.g., KJV NASB ESV NIV NET etc.). John speaks of a pattern of behavior (Wallace 1996, 527). The message the readers have heard since their conversion is that they *are to persist in loving others.*

Syntactical Nugget: John's "message" (ἀγγελία) to love one another parallels 1 John 1:5. There the "message" (ἀγγελία) speaks of God as light. The subsequent discussion is then on how his followers should live ethical lives in the light. Here in this parallel construction the content of the gospel is that believers are to love each other. Therefore, the gospel's ethical implications are that followers of Jesus are to imitate a God who is light and love by living ethically and justly (cp. 3:23b ἵνα).

^{3:12a} καθώς: The Greek word καθώς is a conjunction that means, "just as" or "as" (BDAG 493.1). **Syntactically**, καθώς introduces a dependent conjunctive clause. The entire καθώς clause, "not *as* Cain" (οὐ καθὼς Κάϊν) functions adverbially. It modifies the verb "we love" (ἀγαπῶμεν). It is best to imply an elliptical verb and direct object from the previous clause to make the best sense of the author's flow of thought, "not as Cain [loved his brother]" (Culy 2004, 81). **Semantically**, καθώς is comparative: "as" (KJV ASV NASB). Here opposites are compared. Believers who are expected to love are compared with Cain.

ἦν: The Greek word ἦν is a third singular imperfect active indicative from the verb εἰμί that means, "is" or "to have a point of derivation or origin" (BDAG 285.8). **Syntactically**, ἦν is the main verb of this conjunctive dependent clause "[Cain] was from the evil one" (ἐκ τοῦ πονηροῦ ἦν). The subject is an implied "he" embedded in the verb, which refers to Cain. **Semantically**, ἦν is an equative imperfect: *"who* was" (KJV NASB NRSV ESV NET CNT). In this comparative, John shows Cain's close derivation or origin with the evil one or the Devil.

^{3:12b} καί: The Greek word καί is a conjunction that means "and" (BDAG 4941ba). **Syntactically**, καί introduces a dependent conjunctive clause: *"and* who brutally butchered his brother" (καὶ ἔσφαξεν τὸν ἀδελφὸν αὐτοῦ). **Semantically**, καί is coordinating connective that some additional information about Cain: "and" (e.g., KJV NASB ESV NIV NET etc.).

ἔσφαξεν: The Greek word ἔσφαξεν is a third singular aorist active indicative from the verb σφάξω that means, "I butcher" or "I murder" (BDAG 979). **Syntactically**, ἔσφαξεν is the main verb of the conjunctive dependent clause, "and *who brutally butchered* his brother" (καὶ ἔσφαξεν τὸν ἀδελβὸν αὐτοῦ). The subject of the verb is an implied "he" embedded in the verb and refers to Cain. **Semantically**, ἔσφαξεν is an constative aorist: *"who brutally butchered"* ("murdered," cf. NRSV ESV NIV NET CNT). It describes Cain's action as a whole (Wallace 1996, 557). John provides a heightened sense of what Cain did with his word for murder (σφάξω). It implies that Cain's murder of his brother Abel was exceptionally brutal and violent.

^{3:12c} καί: The Greek word καί is a conjunction which means "and" (BDAG 4941ba). **Syntactically**, καί introduces an interrogative independent clause: *"and* for why did he brutally murder him (= Abel)" (καὶ χάριν τίνος ἔσφαξεν αὐτόν). The prepositional phrase "χάριν τίνος" appears rarely in the New Testament but is rendered "for the sake of what" or "for what reason" (BDAG 1078.b and 1007.1aβ; cf. Culy 2004, 81) and introduces a question. **Semantically**, καί is a coordinating connective: "and" (cf. KJV NASB ESV NIV NET etc.). It introduces a clause with some additional information about Cain evident in the next verb.

ἔσφαξεν: The Greek word ἔσφαξεν is a third singular aorist active indicative from the verb σφάξω that means, "I butcher" or "I murder" (BDAG 979). **Syntactically**, ἔσφαξεν is the governing verb of the interrogative independent clause. The assumed subject "he" refers to Cain. **Semantically**, ἔσφαξεν is an constative aorist: "he butchered" ("murder," NRSV ESV NIV CNT). John provides an overall picture of Cain's murder of his brother Abel as a whole with emphasis on the historical fact (Wallace 1996, 557). In questioning Cain's motivation, John underscores the motivation for Cain's murder of his brother Abel with the subsequent ὅτι clause.

^{3:12d} ὅτι: The Greek word ὅτι is a conjunction that means "because" or "for" (BDAG 732.4a). **Syntactically**, ὅτι introduces a dependent conjunctive clause: *"because* his deeds were evil, but his brothers were righteous" (ὅτι τὰ ἔργα αὐτοῦ πονηρὰ ἦν, τὰ δὲ τοῦ ἀδελφοῦ αὐτοῦ δίκαια). The entire ὅτι clause functions adverbially, modifying the verb, "murdered" (ἔσφαξεν). **Semantically**, ὅτι is causal (cf. KJV NASB ESV NIV NET etc.). It provides the reason why Cain murdered his brother (Wallace 1996, 460) and evident in the rest of the clause.

ἦν: The Greek word ἦν is a third singular imperfect active indicative from the verb εἰμί that means, "is" or to describe a special connection with someone (BDAG 284.2b). **Syntactically**, ἦν is the governing verbs of the dependent adverbial clause. The subject is the nominal phrase "his works" (τὰ ἔργα αὐτοῦ). **Semantically**, ἦν is an equative imperfect: "were" (cf. KJV NASB ESV NIV NET etc.). Here John has a plural subject with a verb in the singular to describe Cain's collective works as a whole (Wallace 1996, 400). It identifies All of Cain's deeds are evil and is one reason why he *brutally* butchering or *brutally* murdered his brother.

^{3:12e} τὰ [ἔργα] δέ . . . [ἦν]: The Greek word δέ is a coordinating conjunction that means "but" or to mark a contrast (BDAG 213.4a). **Syntactically**, δέ is in the post-positive position. It introduces the second part of the dependent adverbial clause: "*But* the [deeds] of his brother [were] righteous" (τὰ [ἔργα] δὲ τοῦ ἀδελφοῦ αὐτοῦ δίκαια [ἦν]). To make sense of this clause, an elliptical "deeds" [ἔργα] is supplied along with an elliptical "were" [ἦν] implied from the first part of the compound sentence. **Semantically**, δέ is contrastive: "but" (NET; contra "and," e.g., KJV ESV NIV etc.). John contrasts Abel's deeds with Cain's. While Cain practiced evil, his borther practiced righteousness. This difference made Cain envious which provided him with his second motivation for butcher his own brother.

^{3:13a} [καί]: The Greek word καί is an elliptical conjunction which means "and so" or "indeed" or "to introduce a result that comes from what precedes" (BDAG 495.1bζ). **Syntactically**, καί introduces an independent clause: "[*And so*] do not be surprised, brothers and sisters" ([καὶ] μὴ θαυμάζετε, ἀδελφοί). **Semantically**, καί is inferential and draws a conclusion: "And so" or "so" (NLT CNT) or "therefore" (NET). Many translations do not recognize the textual variant [καί] and leave it untranslated (KJV ASV NASB NRSV ESV NIV). Regardless, John is about to draw a conclusion evident in the next verb.

θαυμάζετε: The Greek word θαυμάζετε is a second plural present active imperative from the verb θαυμάζω that means, "I am surprised" or to be disturbed by something (BDAG 444.1aγ). **Syntactically**, θαυμάζετε is the main verb of the independent clause. The assumed subject, "you" refers to the readers/hearers. **Semantically**, θαυμάζετε is a customary present: "surprised" (NASB ESV NIV NET NLT). It speaks of a pattern of behavior (Wallace 1996, 521). John draws a conclusion for his readers. He tells then not to be disturbed or don't bc surprise, a surprised evident in the direct object.

εἰ: The Greek word εἰ is a conjunction, which means "that" (BDAG 278.2). **Syntactically**, εἰ identifies the clause as a dependent conjunctive clause. The entire dependent clause, "that the world hates you" (εἰ μισεῖ ὑμᾶς ὁ κόσμος), functions substantivally. It is the direct object of the verb (Smalley 1984, 187). It is a content marker for the verb "surprised" (θαυμάζετε). It is possible to interpret εἰ adverbially: "if" (KJV ASV NASB NIV NET NLT CNT) and thereby function as the protasis of a conditional clause modifying "marvel" (θαυμάζετε). **Semantically**, εἰ introduces the content: "that" (NRSV ESV). Thus believers who find themselves as an object of the world's hate should not be surprised. The wicked have felt this way about the righteous ever since Cain and Abel. John tells the readers that they shouldn't be surprised when the world hates them.

μισεῖ: The Greek word μισεῖ is a third singular present active indicative from the verb μισέω that means "I hate" or "I detest" or "to have a strong aversion to" (BDAG 652.1a). **Syntactically**, μισεῖ is the governing verb of the dependent substantival clause. The subject of the verb is the noun "the world" (κόσμος). **Semantically**, μισεῖ is a customary present: "hates" (cf. KJV NASB ESV NIV NET etc.). It speaks of a pattern of behavior (Wallace 1996, 521). The world's system is persistent in its opposition to believers. Therefore believers should not be surprised when it hates them as well (John 15:18; 17:14; cf. Brown 1982, 445).

^{3:14a} οἴδαμεν: The Greek word οἴδαμεν is a first plural perfect active indicative from the verb οἶδα that means, "I know" or to have information about something (BDAG 693.1e). **Syntactically**, οἴδαμεν is the governing verb of the independent asyndeton clause: "and *we know* that we have passed from death into life" (ἡμεῖς οἴδαμεν ὅτι μεταβεβήκαμεν ἐκ τοῦ θανάτου εἰς τὴν ζωήν). The subject is the emphatic pronoun "we" (ἡμεῖς), referring to both John and his readers. Since the pronoun is already

assumed in the verbal ending, its presence here is emphatic (Wallace 1996, 321). John contrasts the murderous behavior of Cain and the world system that Cain represents with that of those who love others as a result of their relationship with Jesus. **Semantically**, οἴδαμεν is a perfect with present force. Some verbs, like οἶδα, almost exclusively appear in the perfect tense without the perfect's aspectual significance (Wallace 1996, 579). What exactly John's readers know appears in the ὅτι clause.

ὅτι: The Greek word ὅτι is a conjunction, which means "that" (BDAG 732.3). **Syntactically**, ὅτι introduces a dependent clause: "*that* we have passed from death into life" (ὅτι μεταβεβήκαμεν ἐκ τοῦ θανάτου εἰς τὴν ζωήν). The clause is substantival. It functions as the direct object of the verb of perception "we know" (οἴδαμεν). The clause is placed in parenthesis in order to visualize its contribution to the independent clause. **Semantically**, ὅτι is a indirect discourse: "that" (cf. KJV NASB ESV NIV NET etc.). It provides the content of what believers know (Wallace 1996, 454) evident in the next verb.

μεταβεβήκαμεν: The Greek word μεταβεβήκαμεν is a first plural perfect active indicative from the verb μεταβαίνω that means, "I pass over" or "I move" or to change from one condition to another (BDAG, 638.2a). **Syntactically**, μεταβεβήκαμεν is the governing verb of the dependent substantival clause. The assumed subject "we" refers to John and his readers. **Semantically**, μεταβεβήκαμεν is an extensive perfect: "we have passed" (KJV ASV NASB NRSV ESV NIV CNT). John's focus is on the past event of conversion which clearly affects present behavior (Wallace 1996, 577). Believers can know that they have truly passed from death to eternal life, because their behavior of love reflects the change. The change in status from death to life for the believer parallels the common Johannine theme of changing from darkness to light (John 3:19-21; 8:12; 12:35, 46; 1 John 2:9-11). Those who place their faith in Jesus no longer find themselves in darkness, death, and hatred, but have crossed over to light, life, and love (Bateman 2008, 373). Believers who love their fellow Christians have changed their status from death to life.

3:14b ὅτι: The Greek word ὅτι is a conjunction that means "because" or "for" (BDAG 732.4a). **Syntactically**, ὅτι introduces a dependent conjunctive clause: "*because* we love our brothers and sister" (ὅτι ἀγαπῶμεν τοὺς ἀδελφούς). The clause is adverbial. It modifies the verb "we know" (οἴδαμεν). **Semantically**, ὅτι is causal: "because" (cf., KJV NASB ESV NIV NET etc.). John provides the reason why his readers know that they have changed from death to life. That reason is found in the rest of the clause.

ἀγαπῶμεν: The Greek word ἀγαπῶμεν is a first plural present active indicative from the verb ἀγαπάω that means, "I love" or to have a warm regard for and interest in another person (BDAG 5.1aα). **Syntactically**, ἀγαπῶμεν is the governing verb of the dependent adverbial clause. **Semantically**, ἀγαπῶμεν is a customary present: "we *persistently* love" (or "we love"; e.g., KJV NASB ESV NIV NET etc.). John's point is that the believer makes it a habit to love his brothers and sisters (Wallace 1996, 521). The article before the definite plural direct object of this verb "the brothers" (τοὺς ἀδελφούς) could be just an individualizing article "the brothers," but morely likely from context we should translate it like a possessive pronoun, "your brothers" (Wallace 1996, 215-216). In this way it is clear that where this love is shown most clearly is in how believers treat their fellow Christians.

3:14c ἀγαπῶν: The Greek word ἀγαπῶν is a nominative masculine singular present active participle from the verb ἀγαπάω that means, "I love" or to have a warm regard for and interest in another person (BDAG 5.1aα). **Syntactically**, ἀγαπῶν is a participle functioning substantivally as the subject of the verb "remains" (μένει). **Semantically**, the negated (μὴ) ἀγαπῶν is a gnomic present with the force of a customary present: "the one who does not *persist* in love" or "the one who does not love" (NET) or "whoever does not love" (NASB ESV), or "anyone who does not love" (NIV CNT NLT). John identifies a timeless fact about any person (Wallace 1996, 523, 615). Anyone who withholds love from others has not crossed over into eternal life, but remains in death.

μένει: The Greek word μένει is a third singular present active indicative from the verb μένω that means, "I remain," "I continue," "I abide" or of someone does not leave a certain realm or sphere (BDAG 631.1aβ). **Syntactically**, μένει is the main verb of the independent asyndeton clause. The subject is the participial phrase, "the one who does not love" (ὁ μὴ ἀγαπῶν). It refers to any believer who does not give of himself for his fellow Christians. **Semantically**, μένει is a gnomic present: "abides" (KJV ASV NASB NRSV ESV CNT) or "remains" (NIV NET). It identifies a timeless fact (Wallace 1996, 523). It demonstrates that the one who refuses to love other believers "is still dead" (NLT). Death here is *not* physical death or the termination one's life, but a type of spiritual death which encompassess condemnation and destruction (John 8:21-24). This future is not a cause of worry for those who love fellow believers.

3:15a μισῶν: The Greek word μισῶν is a nominative masculine singular present active participle from the verb μισέω that means "I hate" " or "I detest" or "to have a strong aversion to" (BDAG 652.1a). **Syntactically**, μισῶν is an adjectival participle modifying the adjective "every" (πᾶς). The entire participial clause is functioning as the subject of the verb, "is" (ἐστὶν), due to the grammatical priority of weightier phrases (Culy 2004, 85). **Semantically**, μισῶν is a gnomic present with the force of a customary present: "everyone who persists in hating" (cf. NASB ESV NET) or "anyone who hates" (NIV CNT NLT). John identifies a timeless fact about any hateful person (Wallace 1996, 523, 615). In the rest of the clause he equates them with murderers.

ἐστιν: The Greek word ἐστιν is third singular present active indicative from the verb εἰμί that means, "is" or "to be in close connection with" (BDAG 282.2a). **Syntactically**, ἐστιν is the main verb of the independent asyneton adverbial clause. The subject of the verb is the participial phrase. **Semantically**, ἐστιν is a gnomic present: "is" (cf., KJV NASB ESV NIV NET etc.). It presents a timeless fact about those who hate other people (Wallace 1996, 523). Actions of hate are tantamount to murder. This is most likely hyperbole following the teachings of Jesus on anger and hate in the sermon on the Mount (Matt. 5:21-22; see also John 8:44 where the Devil is also called a murderer).

3:15b καί: The Greek word καί is a conjunction which means "and" (BDAG 494.1ba). **Syntactically**, καί introduces an independent conjunctive clause: "and you know that no murderer possesses eternal life abiding in him" (καὶ οἴδατε ὅτι πᾶς ἀνθρωποκτόνος οὐκ ἔχει ζωὴν αἰώνιον ἐν αὐτῷ μένουσαν). **Semantically**, καί is connective providing additional information about hateful murderers evident in the next verb and its direct object.

οἴδατε: The Greek word οἴδατε is a second plural perfect active indicative from the verb οἶδα that means, "I know" or to have information about something (BDAG 693.1e). **Syntactically**, οἴδατε is the main verb of the independent conjunctive clause. The assumed subject "you" refers to the orthodox readers of the letter. **Semantically**, οἴδαμεν is a perfect with present force: "we know" (cf., KJV NASB ESV NIV NET etc.). Some verbs, like οἶδα, almost exclusively appear in the perfect tense without the perfect's aspectual significance (Wallace 1996, 579). What John's readers know appears in the ὅτι clause.

ὅτι: The Greek word ὅτι is a conjunction, which means "that" after verbs of perception (BDAG 731.1c). **Syntactically**, ὅτι introduces the dependent conjunctive clause: "*that* no murderer possesses eternal life abiding in him or her" (ὅτι πᾶς ἀνθρωποκτόνος οὐκ ἔχει ζωὴν αἰώνιον ἐν αὐτῷ μένουσαν). It functions substantivally as the direct object of the verb of perception, "you know" (οἴδατε). The clause is placed in parenthesis in order to visualize its contribution to the independent clause. **Semantically**, ὅτι is an indirect discourse: "that" (cf., KJV NASB ESV NIV NET etc.). It provides the content of what John's readers know (Wallace 1996, 454). John's readers are aware about those people who claim to be believers yet continue to live in hatred of their brothers and sisters. What they know is found in the next verb.

ἔχει: The Greek word ἔχει is a third singular present active indicative from the verb ἔχω that means, "I have" or "I possess" (BDAG 420.1a). **Syntactically**, ἔχει is the governing verb of the dependent substatival clause. The subject is the nominal phrase "every murderer" (πᾶς ἀνθρωποκτόνος). It refers to anyone who habitually hates other believers. **Semantically**, ἔχει is a gnomic present: "possesses" (*contra* "has" ; NASB ESV NIV NET CNT). The verb points to a timeless fact (Wallace 1996, 523) about the believer who hates his brothers or sisters and is thereby a murderer and has an eternal problem.

μένουσαν: The Greek word μένουσαν is an accusative singular feminine present active participle from the verb μένω that means, "I remain," "I continue," "I abide" or "of someone who does not leave a certain realm or sphere" (BDAG 631.1aβ). **Syntactically**, μένουσαν is an adjectival participle modifying the noun "life" (ζωὴν). We could also classify this participle as a double accusative or an object complement (we know that every murderer does not have eternal life *to be* dwelling in him). It seems more likely, however, to be adjectival, because of the grammatical agreement with the noun (Bateman 2008, 378). **Semantically**, μένουσαν is a customary present: "abiding" (KJV ASV NASB NRSV ESV CNT), "residing" (NET) or just "in him" (NIV NLT). It reveals an ongoing state (Wallace 1996, 521). This statement suggests that the ones who hates their fellow believers cut themselves off from both the present and future eschatological privilege of eternal life. This idea is in direct contast to the ones who love their fellow believers and so have passed over from spiritual death to spiritual life (Culy 2004, 85-86; cf. Brown 1982, 447).

3:16a ἐν τούτῳ: The Greek word ἐν is a preposition that means "by" (BDAG 328.5b). The Greek word τούτῳ is declined as a dative singular neuter from the demonstrative pronoun τοῦτο, which means "this one" (BDAG 741.1bβ). **Syntactically**, ἐν τούτῳ is a prepositional phrase introducing an independent prepositional clause "*By this* we know love" (ἐν τούτῳ ἐγνώκαμεν τὴν ἀγάπην). The construction, "by this" (ἐν τούτῳ) is common in 1 John (2:3, 4, 5 [twice]; 3:10, 16, 19, 24; 4:2, 9, 10, 13, 17; 5:2). **Semantically**, ἐν τούτῳ can either be anaphoric or cataphoric. Here it is cataphoric because of the epexegetical ὅτι clause. The ὅτι clause below will provide the content of the demonstrative pronoun.

ἐγνώκαμεν: The Greek word ἐγνώκαμεν is a first plural perfect active indicative from the verb γινώσκω that means, "I know" or "to have come to know" something (BDAG 200.6aα). **Syntactically**, ἐγνώκαμεν is the main verb of the independent clause. The subject of the verb is an implied "we" embedded in the verb and refers to the readers who live in love for other believers. **Semantically**, ἐγνώκαμεν is an intensive perfect: "we know" (NASB NRSV ESV CNT). It focuses attention on the present state that results from a completed event (Wallace 1996, 574). Those who believe have heard about the example of the self-giving life of Jesus and they truly know what love is all about.

3:16b ὅτι: The Greek word ὅτι is a conjunction, which means "that" (BDAG 732.2a). **Syntactically**, ὅτι serves to introduce the dependent adjectival clause: "*that* that one gave up his life for us" (ὅτι ἐκεῖνος ὑπὲρ ἡμῶν τὴν ψυχὴν αὐτοῦ ἔθηκεν). It modifies the demonstrative pronoun, "this" (τοῦτο).

Semantically, ὅτι is epexegetical: "that" (ASV NASB ESV NET CNT). The ὅτι clause explains or clarifies the demonstrative (Wallace 1996, 459). The other demonstrative pronoun, "that one" (ἐκεῖνος), refers to Jesus in 1 John. Therefore, believers know what love is by looking to the self-giving example of Jesus.

ἔθηκεν: The Greek word ἔθηκεν is a third singular aorist active indicative from the verb τίθημι that means, "I take off" or "I give up" or "I remove" (BDAG 1003.1bβ). **Syntactically**, ἔθηκεν is the governing verb of the dependent adjectival clause. The subject of ἔθηκεν is the demonstrative pronoun "that one" (ἐκεῖνος) and refers to Jesus. **Semantically**, ἔθηκεν is a constative aorist: "he laid down" (KJV ASV NASB NRSV ESV NIV NET CNT) or "he gave up" (NLT). It explains the event of Jesus' death as a whole (Wallace 1996, 557). The phrase "give up his life" (τὴν (ψυχὴν αὐτοῦ ἔθηκεν) is an idiom referring "to die voluntarily" or "to surrender" (LN 23.113; cf. Culy 2004, 87). It is used euphemstically as a kind way of expressing that Jesus died. Jesus (ἐκεῖνος) showed the ultimate form of love when he died voluntarily for others.

3:16c   καί: The Greek word καί is a conjunction that means "and" (BDAG 494.1b). **Syntactically**, καί introduces a conjunctive independent clause: "*and* [that] we ought to give up our lives for our brothers and sister" (καὶ ἡμεῖς ὀφείλομεν ὑπὲρ τῶν ἀδελφῶν τὰς ψυχὰς θεῖναι). The article before "lives" (τὰς ψυχὰς) should be translated with the possessive pronoun "our" (Wallace 1996, 215). **Semantically**, καί is a coordinating conjunction joining two dependent clauses together: "and" (KJV ASV NASB NRSV ESV NIV CNT), though some (NLT NET) render καί as though it introduces a result from what Jesus did (cf. BDAG 495.1bζ). Since Jesus showed what love is by giving up his personal interests and life for his followers, then his followers should follow his example, which is evident in the next two words.

ὀφείλομεν: The Greek word ὀφείλομεν is a first plural present active indicative from the verb ὀφείλω that means, "I am obligated" or to be under obligation to meet certain social and moral expectations (BDAG 743.2aβ). **Syntactically,** ὀφείλομεν is the main verb of the independent conjunctive clause. The subject is the emphatic personal pronoun "we" (ἡμεῖς). It refers to the readers of the letter. The pronoun does not need to be expressed, but its presence heightens the fact that believers should imitate the sacrifice of Jesus. **Semantically**, ὀφείλομεν is a customary present: "we must" or "we are obligated" or "we ought" (cf. KJV NASB ESV NIV NET etc). While the word "we must" indicates the believer's obligation, the customary present indicates an ongoing action (Wallace 1996, 521). John underscores a believer's ongoing obligation. That obligation is revealed by the infinitive (θεῖναι).

θεῖναι: The Greek word θεῖναι is an aorist active infinitive from the verb τίθημι that means, "I take off" or "I give up" or "I remove" (BDAG 1003.1bβ). **Syntactically**, θεῖναι is part of the main verb of the clause, "we ought" (ὀφείλομεν). **Semantically**, θεῖναι is a complementary infinitive: "we ought to give up" (NLT) though most render the verb "to lay down" (cf. KJV NASB ESV NIV NET etc.). The infinitive completes the thought of the verb "ought" (ὀφείλομεν; cf. Wallace 1996, 598, 664). The one who believes in Jesus ought to live for others because Jesus gave of himself for them.

3:17a   δ': The Greek word δέ is a conjunction, which means "but" (BDAG 213.4a). **Syntactically**, δέ is in the post-positive position and introduces a dependent indefinite relative clause ὃς ἂν: "*But* whoever pocesses resources of the world and sees his brother and sister in need and closes his heart against him" (ὃς δ᾽ ἂν ἔχῃ τὸν βίον τοῦ κόσμου). It modifies the personal pronoun "him" (αὐτῷ). **Semantically**, δέ has adversative force: "but" (KJV ASV NASB ESV NET CNT) though some translations do not translate δέ (NRSV NIV NLT). John esentially questions how God's love can reside in a confessing follower of Jesus who has the resources to show compassion and yet does not love his brother and sister.

ὅς . . . ἄν: The Greek ὅς is a masculine singular nominative from the relative pronoun ὅς followed by ἄν, which means "anyone" or "whoever" (BDAG 56.1bβ; 727.1jα). **Syntactically,** ὅ introduces a dependent indefinite relative clause. The entire clause also functions adjectivally. It modifies "him" (αὐτῷ) in 3:17d. It is translated either at "anyone" (NIV ESV CNT) or "whoever" (KJV ASV NASB NET).

ἔχῃ: The Greek word ἔχῃ is a third singular present active subjunctive from the verb ἔχω that means, "I own" or "I possess" indicating that something is under one's control (BDAG 420.1aα). **Syntactically,** ἔχῃ is the first governing verb of the compound relative clause. It modifies the personal pronoun "him" (αὐτῷ). The subject is the indefinite relative pronoun, "whoever" (ὅς . . . ἄν), which refers to anyone who professes Christ yet refuses to help those in need. The verb is in the subjunctive mood because it is part of a ἄν clause. **Semantically,** ἔχῃ is a gnomic present: "possesses" (*contra* "has"; cf. KJV NASB ESV NIV NET etc.). The verb points to a timeless fact (Wallace 1996, 523). The word "resources" (τὸν βίον; BDAG 177.2) is used instead of the more specific word "riches" (πλοῦτον) to show that it is not just the rich who have resources but everyone (Culy 2004, 88). John draws attention to anyone who possesses the resources to help those in need but does not do so, that person cannot possibly be filled with the love of God.

3:17b καί [ὅς ἄν]: The Greek word καί is a conjunction that means "and" (BDAG 494.1b). **Syntactically,** καί introduces the second part of the indefinite relative clause: "*and* perceives his brother and sister possessing a need" (καὶ θεωρῇ τὸν ἀδελφὸν αὐτοῦ χρείαν ἔχοντα). It modifies the personal pronoun "him" (αὐτῷ). **Semantically,** καί is a coordinating conjunction joining two dependent clauses together: "and" (cf. KJV NASB ESV NIV NET etc.). It provides some additional information about the one who possess worldly resources. The additional information is found in the rest of the clause.

θεωρῇ: The Greek word θεωρῇ is a third singular present active subjunctive from the verb θεωρέω that means, "I see" or "I observe" or "I perceive" or "to observe something with sustained attention" (BDAG 454.1). The verb is in the subjunctive mood because it is part of a ἄν clause and thereby connected to the previous clause. **Syntactically,** θεωρῇ is the second verb of the indefinite relative clause. It modifies the personal pronoun "him" (αὐτῷ). The subject is the indefinite relative pronoun, "whoever" (ὅς . . . ἄν), which refers to anyone who professes Christ yet refuses to help those in need. **Semantically,** θεωρῇ is a gnomic present: "perceives," though most render as "sees" (cf. KJV NASB ESV NIV NET etc.). John is about to make another timeless fact about anyone who sees another in need (Wallace 1996, 523).

ἔχοντα: The Greek word ἔχοντα is an accusative singular masculine present active participle from the verb ἔχω that means, "I own" or "I possess" (BDAG 420.1aα). **Syntactically,** ἔχοντα serves as a double accusative as an object-complement to the direct object "need" (χρείαν), modifying the verb "whoever notices" (θεωρῇ). **Semantically,** ἔχοντα is a gnomic present: "possesses" (*contra* "has"; cf. KJV NASB ESV NIV NET etc.). John continues to specify a timeless fact about anyone who sees a person in need.

3:17c καί [ὅς ἄν]: The Greek word καί is a conjunction that means "and" (BDAG 494.1b). **Syntactically,** καί introduces the third part of the compound dependent indefinite relative clause, "and shuts off his heart against him" (καὶ κλείσῃ τὰ σπλάγχνα αὐτοῦ ἀπ᾽ αὐτοῦ), modifying the personal pronoun "him" (αὐτῷ). **Semantically,** καί is a coordinating conjunction joining two dependent clauses together:

"and" (KJV ASV NASB NET), though some (ESV NIV NLT CNT) render καί as though it introduces a surprising or unexpected event (cf. BDAG 495.1bη). It provides some additional information about the one who possess worldly resources.

κλείσῃ: The Greek word κλείσῃ is a third singular aorist active subjunctive from the verb κλείω that means, "I close" or "close one's heart against someone" (BDAG 547.2) or "shut down their intestines"; LN 25:55). The verb is in the subjunctive mood because it is part of a ἂν clause. **Syntactically**, κλείσῃ is the third governing verb of the compound dependent indefinite relative clause, modifying the personal pronoun "him" (αὐτῷ). The subject is the indefinite relative pronoun, "whoever" (ὃς . . . ἂν), which refers to anyone who professes Christ yet refuses to help those in need. **Semantically**, κλείσῃ is a gnomic aorist rendered various ways: "closes" (NASB ESV CNT), "has no pity" (NIV), "shows no compassion" (NLT), "refuses help" (NRSV), and "shut off" (KJV ASV NET). The gnomic aorist is rendered in the present tense presenting a timeless fact (Wallace 1996, 562). Regardless of how κλείσῃ is rendered the point remains the same: people who shut down their emotions and refuse to help others have a problem. This phrase goes further than just to say that they would not help, but that they shut down their natural instict of compassion as well (Brown 1982, 450).

3:17d πῶς: The Greek word πῶς is a conjunction that means, "how" (BDAG 901.1a δ). **Syntactically**, πῶς introduces an independent interrogative clause, "*how* can the love of God remain in him" (πῶς ἡ ἀγάπη τοῦ θεοῦ μένει ἐν αὐτῷ;). **Semantically**, πῶς introduces a rhetorical question which denies that that a person who has the means to help someone, yet refuses, can possibly have a relationship with the self-giving Christ.

μένει: The Greek word μένει is a third singular present active indicative from the verb μένω that means, "I remain," "I continue," "I abide" or of someone does not leave a certain realm or sphere (BDAG 631.1aβ). **Syntactically**, μένει serves as the main verb of the independent interrogative clause. The subject is the nominal phrase "the love of God" (ἡ ἀγάπη τοῦ θεοῦ). **Semantically**, μένει is a customary present: "remain" (NET), "abide" (ASV NASB NRSV ESV), "in" (CNT NLT). It speaks of an ongoing state (Wallace 1996, 521). John's point is this: the love God does not have a home in the heart of a person that refuses to show compassion to those in need.

1 John 3:18–24

Verb Recognition for 1 John 3:18–24

¹⁸Τεκνία, μὴ ἀγαπῶμεν λόγῳ μηδὲ τῇ γλώσσῃ ἀλλὰ ἐν ἔργῳ καὶ ἀληθείᾳ. ¹⁹[Καὶ] ἐν τούτῳ γνωσόμεθα ὅτι ἐκ τῆς ἀληθείας ἐσμέν, καὶ ἔμπροσθεν αὐτοῦ πείσομεν τὴν καρδίαν ἡμῶν ²⁰ὅτι ἐὰν καταγινώσκῃ ἡμῶν ἡ καρδία, ὅτι μείζων ἐστὶν ὁ θεὸς τῆς καρδίας ἡμῶν καὶ γινώσκει πάντα. ²¹Ἀγαπητοί, ἐὰν ἡ καρδία μὴ καταγινώσκῃ ἡμῶν, παρρησίαν ἔχομεν πρὸς τὸν θεόν, ²²καὶ ὃ ἐὰν αἰτῶμεν λαμβάνομεν ἀπ' αὐτοῦ, ὅτι τὰς ἐντολὰς αὐτοῦ τηροῦμεν καὶ τὰ ἀρεστὰ ἐνώπιον αὐτοῦ ποιοῦμεν. ²³καὶ αὕτη ἐστὶν ἡ ἐντολὴ αὐτοῦ, ἵνα πιστεύσωμεν τῷ ὀνόματι τοῦ υἱοῦ αὐτοῦ Ἰησοῦ Χριστοῦ καὶ ἀγαπῶμεν ἀλλήλους, καθὼς ἔδωκεν ἐντολὴν ἡμῖν. ²⁴καὶ ὁ τηρῶν τὰς ἐντολὰς αὐτοῦ

ἐν αὐτῷ <mark>μένει</mark> καὶ αὐτὸς ἐν αὐτῷ· καὶ ἐν τούτῳ <mark>γινώσκομεν</mark> ὅτι μένει ἐν ἡμῖν, ἐκ τοῦ πνεύματος οὗ ἡμῖν ἔδωκεν.

Clausal Outline Translated for 1 John 3:18–24

3:18a Τεκνία, μὴ <u>**ἀγαπῶμεν**</u> λόγῳ μηδὲ τῇ γλώσσῃ
3:18a Little children, **let us** not **love** with word or with tongue

3:18b <u>**ἀλλὰ**</u> [<u>ἀγαπῶμεν</u>] ἐν ἔργῳ καὶ ἀληθείᾳ.
3:18b **but** [*let us love*] in deed and truth.

3:19a [Καὶ] ἐν τούτῳ <u>**γνωσόμεθα**</u> (<u>ὅτι</u> ἐκ τῆς ἀληθείας <u>ἐσμέν</u>),
3:19a [And *so*] by this **we will know** (<u>that</u> we are of the truth),

> **3:19b** (καὶ [<u>ὅτι</u>] ἔμπροσθεν αὐτοῦ <u>**πείσομεν**</u> τὴν καρδίαν ἡμῶν)
> **3:19b** (and [that] **we will convince** our heart before him)

> > **3:20a** <u>ὅτι</u> <u>**ἐὰν καταγινώσκῃ**</u> ἡμῶν ἡ καρδία,
> > **3:20a** **that whenever** our heart **condemns** us,

> > **3:20b** <u>ὅτι</u> μείζων <u>**ἐστὶν**</u> ὁ θεὸς τῆς καρδίας ἡμῶν
> > **3:20b** **that** God **is** greater than our heart

> > **3:20c** καὶ [<u>ὅτι</u>] <u>**γινώσκει**</u> πάντα.
> > **3:20c** and [*that*] **he knows** all things.

> **3:21a** Ἀγαπητοί, <u>**ἐὰν**</u> ἡ καρδία μὴ <u>**καταγινώσκῃ**</u> ἡμῶν,
> **3:21a** Beloved, **if** our heart **does** not **condemn** us,

3:21b παρρησίαν <u>**ἔχομεν**</u> πρὸς τὸν θεόν,
3:21b **we *feel*** confident before God,

3:22a καὶ (<u>**ὃ ἐὰν αἰτῶμεν**</u>) <u>**λαμβάνομεν**</u> ἀπ᾽ αὐτοῦ,
3:22a and *so* (**whatever we ask for**) **we *will* receive** from him (= God),

> **3:22b** <u>ὅτι</u> τὰς ἐντολὰς αὐτοῦ <u>**τηροῦμεν**</u>
> **3:22b** **because** **we *persist* in keeping** his (= God's) commands

> **3:22c** καὶ [<u>ὅτι</u>] τὰ ἀρεστὰ ἐνώπιον αὐτοῦ <u>**ποιοῦμεν**</u>.
> **3:22c** and [*because*] **we *persist* in doing** *the things* that are pleasing in his sight.

3:23a καὶ αὕτη <u>**ἐστὶν**</u> ἡ ἐντολὴ αὐτοῦ,
3:23a And this **is** his (= God's) commandment

|
3:23b ἵνα **πιστεύσωμεν** τῷ ὀνόματι τοῦ υἱοῦ αὐτοῦ Ἰησοῦ Χριστοῦ
3:23b *namely* **that we believe** in the name of his Son Jesus, who is the Christ

|
3:23c καὶ [ἵνα] **ἀγαπῶμεν** ἀλλήλους,
3:23c and [*that*] **we** *persist* **in loving** one another,

|
v23d **καθὼς** **ἔδωκεν** ἐντολὴν ἡμῖν.
3:23d **just as he gave** us *the* command

3:24a καὶ ὁ τηρῶν τὰς ἐντολὰς αὐτοῦ ἐν αὐτῷ **μένει**
3:24a and the one who *persists* in keeping his commandments **abides** with him (= God)

3:24b καὶ [*μένει*] αὐτὸς ἐν αὐτῷ·
3:24b and this one [*abides*] with him (= God);

3:24c καὶ ἐν τούτῳ **γινώσκομεν** (ὅτι μένει ἐν ἡμῖν),
3:24c And by this **we know** (that God abides in us),

|
3:24d ἐκ τοῦ πνεύματος (οὗ ἡμῖν ἔδωκεν).
3:24d by the Spirit whom he has given us.

Syntax Explained for 1 John 3:18–24

3:18a ἀγαπῶμεν: The Greek word ἀγαπῶμεν is a first plural present active subjunctive from the verb ἀγαπάω that means, "I love" or "I cherish" or "to practice/express love" (BDAG 6.3). **Syntactically**, ἀγαπῶμεν is the main verb of the independent clause, "Children, *let us* not *love* in word or tongue" (τεκνία, μὴ ἀγαπῶμεν λόγῳ μηδὲ τῇ γλώσσῃ). **Semantically**, the negated (μὴ) ἀγαπῶμεν is a hortatory subjunctive: "let us not love" (cf. KJV NASB ESV NIV NET etc.). It functions as a first person imperative in the present tense indicating something that ought to be a regular practice (Wallace 1996, 465). Believers are not to love with mere words.

3:18b ἀλλά: The Greek word ἀλλά is a conjunction that means "but" or "rather" (BDAG 44.1a). **Syntactically**, ἀλλά is an independent conjunctive clause: "but [let us love] in deed and truth" (ἀλλὰ ἐν ἔργῳ καὶ ἀληθείᾳ). It introduces the second part of the compound independent clause. It seems best to insert "let us love" (ἀγαπῶμεν) from the first part of the clause, in order to make the best sense out of this compound sentence. **Semantically**, ἀλλά, after the negative "let us not love" (μὴ ἀγαπῶμεν), is contrastive. It contrasts love that merely loves with mere words with real love. John tells his readers what real love is in the rest of this clause.

[ἀγαπῶμεν]: The Greek word ἀγαπῶμεν is a first plural present active subjunctive from the verb ἀγαπάω that means, "I love" or "I cherish" or "to practice/express love" (BDAG 6.3). **Syntactically**, ἀγαπῶμεν is an elliptical verb functioning as the main verb of the second independent clause. **Semantically**, ἀγαπῶμεν is a hortatory subjunctive: "let us love" (cp. NLT). It too functions as a first person imperative in the present tense indicating something that ought to be a regular practice (Wallace 1996, 464). In contrast to people who love in mere words, true love manifests itself through self-less actions.

³:¹⁹ᵃ [Καί]: The Greek word καί is an elliptical conjunction that means "and so" (BDAG 495.1bζ). **Syntactically**, καί is introduces an independent conjunctive clause: "[and so] by this we will know" ([Καὶ] ἐν τούτῳ γνωσόμεθα). The brackets around [καί] indicate that there is a textual problem. καί is an inferential connective: "and so." It provides a conclusion about the followers of Jesus who love through self-less action demonstrates something. That something is evident in the rest of the clause.

ἐν τούτῳ: The Greek word ἐν is a preposition, which means "by" (BDAG 328.5b). The Greek word τούτῳ is declined as a dative singular neuter from the demonstrative pronoun τοῦτο that means "this one" (BDAG 741.1bα). **Syntactically**, ἐν τούτῳ introduces an independent prepositional clause: "[and so] *by this* we will know" ([Καὶ] ἐν τούτῳ γνωσόμεθα). The construction, "by this" (ἐν τούτῳ) is very important in 1 John (2:3, 4, 5 [twice], 3:10, 16, 19, 24; 4:2, 9, 10, 13, 17; 5:2). **Semantically**, ἐν τούτῳ can either be anaphoric, pointing back to the preceding discussion, or cataphoric, pointing forward. Here the phrase is anaphoric and points back to the previous verse and its discussion on how to be assured that you belong to God (cf. BDAG 741.1bα). Followers of Jesus have assurance by showing love with self-less action rather than just with empty words. Brown puts it this way, "The exterior deed shows the interior reality" (Brown 1982, 454).

Syntactical Nugget: The usual rule is that the prepositional phrase is cataphoric, if it is followed by a subordinating conjunction that epexegetically provides us with the content of the demonstrative. Although there is a ὅτι clause immediately following, the clause "that we are of the truth and we have assured our hearts before him" (ὅτι ἐκ τῆς ἀληθείας ἐσμέν) is not functioning epexegetically, but rather substantivally as the direct object of "we will know" (γνωσόμεθα). Therefore, there is no expexegetical clause that can explicate the content of the demonstrative pronoun.

γνωσόμεθα: The Greek word γνωσόμεθα is a first plural future middle indicative from the verb γινώσκω that means, "I know" or "to arrive at a knowledge of someone or something" (BDAG 199.1c). **Syntactically**, γνωσόμεθα is the main verb of the independent clause. The subject of the verb is an implied "we" embedded in the verb and refers to the orthodox readers of the letter who live in love for other believers. **Semantically**, γνωσόμεθα is a predictive future: "we will know" (NASB NRSV NET) or "we shall know" (ASV ESV CNT). It indicates that something will take place (Wallace 1996, 568). Followers of Jesus who love in self-less action like Jesus will know something. That something is evident in the next ὅτι clause.

ὅτι: The Greek word ὅτι is a conjunction, which means "that" (BDAG 731.1c). **Syntactically**, ὅτι introduces the compound dependent conjunctive clause: "*that* we are of the truth" (ὅτι ἐκ τῆς ἀληθείας ἐσμέν). The entire ὅτι clause is substantival. It is the direct object of the verb "we will know" (γνωσόμεθα). The clause is placed in parenthesis in order to visualize its contribution to the independent clause. **Semantically**, ὅτι is an indirect discourse: "we know *that*" (KJV ASV NASB NRSV ESV NIV NET). It provides us with the content of what the believer should know (Wallace 1996, 454-55). The specifics of the ὅτι clause is found in the next verb.

ἐσμέν: The Greek word ἐσμέν is first plural present active indicative from the verb εἰμί that means, "is" or "to be in close connection (with)" (BDAG 283.2b). **Syntactically**, ἐσμέν is the governing verb of the dependent ὅτι clause. The subject of the verb is an implied "we" embedded in the verb and refers to the orthodox readers/hearers of the letter. **Semantically**, ἐσμέν is an equative present: "are" (cf. KJV NASB ESV NIV NET etc.). It equates a believer's selfless acts of love with being "of the truth," so that they can have assurance they have a relationship with God.

3:19b καὶ [ὅτι]: The Greek word καί is a conjunction which means "and" (BDAG 494.1bα). **Syntactically**, καί introduces another dependent conjunctive clause: "*and [that] we will convince our heart before him*" (καὶ *[ὅτι]* ἔμπροσθεν αὐτοῦ πείσομεν τὴν καρδίαν ἡμῶν). The clause is placed in parenthesis in order to visualize its contribution to the independent clause as well as view its parallel to the previous ὅτι clause. **Semantically**, καί is a connective ("and") that introduces an additional thought about the assurance that we can have, namely, our faith is genuine. A ὅτι is inserted to make better sense of this compound clause.

Syntactical Nugget: It is possible that this καὶ [ὅτι] clause is not the second part of a compound thought, but that this clause begins a new series of thoughts, however, since the verb in the previous clause is future and so is this one, it seems clear that they should be read together as parallel clauses.

πείσομεν: The Greek word πείσομεν is a first plural future active indicative from the verb πείθω that means, "I convince" or "to be so convinced that one puts confidence in something" (BDAG 792.2b). **Syntactically**, πείσομεν is the governing verb of the conjunctive dependent ὅτι clause. **Semantically**, πείσομεν is a predictive future: "we will convince" (NET) or "assure" (KJV ASV NASB CNT) or "reassure" (NRSV ESV). It indicates that something will take place (Wallace 1996, 568). When believers exhibit selfless acts of love for their fellow Christians, they can have assurance that one day they will stand before Jesus confident in their relationship with God.

3:20a ὅτι: The Greek word ὅτι is a conjunction, which means "that" (BDAG 731.1e). **Syntactically**, ὅτι introduces a dependent conjunctive clause, "*that whenever our hearts condemn us*" (ὅτι ἐὰν καταγινώσκῃ ἡμῶν ἡ καρδία). It functions adverbially to "is" (ἐστίν) in 20b. **Semantically**, the conjunctive ὅτι clause is epexegetical and modifies the entire previous clause: "*and [that] we will assure our heart before him*" (καὶ *[ὅτι]* ἔμπροσθεν αὐτοῦ πείσομεν τὴν καρδίαν ἡμῶν). Thus the entire clause that expresses a believer's emotional state is bracketed (|_____|; cf. BDAG 731.1e). This option parallels a subsequent usage in 1 John 5:14 where a conjunctive ὅτι clause modifies an entire preceding clause (see NET note for an extended discussion). John assures his readers that they belong to God and he does so with the next conjunctive ὅτι clause (v. 20b).

Syntactical Nugget: The conjunctive ὅτι clause could be classifed one of three ways with three different English translations: epexegetical ("that if"), adverbial ("because if"), or redivide the Greeks words ὅτι ἐὰν into an indefinite relative clause ὅ τι ἐὰν ("in whatever"). If epexegetical "that if our hearts condemn us" (NET), it could be giving us the content of the "by this" (ἐν τούτῳ) or could be explicating the noun "heart" (καρδίαν). We have already concluded in 3:19a that the prepostional phrase (ἐν τούτῳ) refers back to the previous context rather than pointing forward to an epexegetical clause. If adverbial "because if our hearts condemn us" (KJV ASV), it could be either modifying the verb "know" (γνωσόμεθα) giving us the reason that the believer knows, or the verb "persuade" (πείσομεν) providing us with the reason that the believer can have assurance. If an indefinite relative clause, the Greek letters would be redivided from ὅτι ἐὰν to ὅ τι ἐὰν, then translated as "whenever our hearts condemn us" (NRSV NIV ESV; cf. NASB). The author, however, seems to use the indefinite relative clause "whatever" (ὅ ἐὰν) elsewhere (3:22) and therefore out of stylistic character to use ὅ τι ἐὰν. Of all the options, the best is the epexegetical whereby the conjunctive ὅτι clause modifies the entire previous clause: "*and [that] we will assure our heart before him*" (καὶ *[ὅτι]* ἔμπροσθεν αὐτοῦ πείσομεν τὴν καρδίαν ἡμῶν).

ἐάν: The Greek word ἐάν is a conjunction, which means "whenever" (BDAG 268.2). **Syntactically**, the conjunction ἐάν is a conjunction marker of time for the dependent ὅτι clause: "that *whenever* our heart condemns us" (ἐὰν καταγινώσκῃ ἡμῶν ἡ καρδία). **Semantically**, ἐάν is a marker of the *prospect* *of an action*, namely the heart or condemning conscience at any given point of time (cp. ESV, "for whenever"). It approaches closely to that of ὅταν. Since the believer has assurance of their standing before God due to their selfless acts, at any given point of time when their conscience brings doubt, believers can know that God is greater than their conscience.

καταγινώσκῃ: The Greek word καταγινώσκῃ is a third singular present active subjunctive from the verb καταγινώσκω that means, "I condemn" or "I convict" (BDAG 515). The verb is in the subjunctive because it is part of the ἐάν clause. **Syntactically**, καταγινώσκῃ is the governing verb of the dependent epexegetical clause. The subject is the nominal phrase "our heart" (ἡμῶν ἡ καρδία) and is a metaphor for the believer's conscience. **Semantically**, καταγινώσκῃ is a conative present whereby the present tense portrays the subject (ἡμῶν ἡ καρδία) as desiring to do something, namely condemn (Wallace 1996, 534). Whenever the believer's conscience (e.g., ἡμῶν ἡ καρδία) brings guilt, they can still have assurance of their faith because God is greater than their hearts.

3:20b ὅτι: The Greek word ὅτι is a conjunction, which means "that" (BDAG 731.1e). **Syntactically**, ὅτι introduces a conjunctive dependent clause: "*that* God is greater than our hearts" (ὅτι μείζων ἐστὶν ὁ θεὸς τῆς καρδίας ἡμῶν). It modifies the believer's emotional state, which is bracketed (|_____|; cf. BDAG 731.1e). Any **semantical** decision about this conjunctive ὅτι clause is dependent upon the decision made concerning the first ὅτι clause of 20a. Based upon our decision for the conjunctive ὅτι clause of 20a, this ὅτι clause is classified as epexegetical of verse 20a and thereby a technical way (though an ungrammatical way) to underscore God's knowing the depths of our heart (Brown 1982, 457; Culy 2004, 94). Believers should know by their self-less imitation of the love of Jesus, that even if their consciences condemn them, that God is greater than their hearts and knows everything about them. The NLT captures the author's core theological concern for verse 20 the best: "Even if we feel guilty, God is greater than our feelings . . ."

Syntactical Nugget: If we assume that the first ὅτι is epexegetical, then this ὅτι would be classified as epexegetical: "*that God is greater than our heart*" is epexegetical to "*that whenever our heart condemns us*" (see NET note). If we assume the first ὅτι is causal, then this ὅτι could also be causal acting resumptively as well "because if our hearts condemn us, *because* I repeat, God is greater than our hearts," or it could be indirect discourse following an elliptical verb "because if our hearts condemn us, *we know that* God is greater than our hearts" (KJV ASV; cf. NASB). Finally, if we redivide the first clause into an indefinite relative pronoun, then this second ὅτι would be classified as causal, "whenever our hearts condemn us; *for* God is greater than our hearts. All of these options are grammatically possible (NRSV NIV ESV). Yet the best option is to classify this ὅτι clause as epexegetical of verse 20a and thereby a technical way (though an ungrammatical way) to underscore God's knowing the depths of our heart (Brown 1982, 457; Culy 2004, 94).

ἐστίν: The Greek word ἐστίν is third singular present active indicative from the verb εἰμί that means, "is" or "to show how something is to be understood" (BDAG, 282.2cα). **Syntactically**, ἐστίν is the governing verb of this compound dependent conjunctive epexegetical clause. The subject of the verb is the noun "God" (ὁ θεός). **Semantically**, ἐστίν is a gnomic present: "is" (cf. KJV NASB ESV NIV NET etc.). John reveals a timeless fact (Wallace 1996, 523). God is greater than our conscience.

3:20c καὶ [ὅτι] The Greek word καί is a conjunction which means "and" (BDAG, 494.1b). **Syntactically**, καί introduces a dependent conjunctive clause that links two compound dependent. adverbial clauses: "and *that* he knows all things" (καὶ [ὅτι] γινώσκει πάντα) is linked to "that God is greater than our heart" The elliptical [ὅτι] is inserted to visualize John's second reason why God answers a believer's prayer. **Semantically**, καί is a coordinating conjunction that introduces additional information about God's awareness.

γινώσκει: The Greek word γινώσκει is a third singular present active indicative from the verb γινώσκω that means, "I have come to know" or "I know" or to have come to the knowledge of something (BDAG 200.6aα). **Syntactically**, γινώσκει is the governing verb of this compound dependent conjunctive epexegetical clause. The subject of the verb is the noun "God" (ὁ θεός). **Semantically**, γινώσκει is a gnomic present: "he knows" (NRSV ESV NIV CNT NLT). John reveals a timeless fact about God (Wallace 1996, 523). God knows all things, including the heart and lifestyle of the believer.

3:21a   ἐάν: The Greek word ἐάν is a conjunction that means "if" (BDAG 267.1aα). **Syntactically**, ἐάν identifies the clause as a dependent conjunctive clause. The entire clause, "Beloved, *if* our heart does not condemn us" (Ἀγαπητοί, ἐὰν ἡ καρδία μὴ καταγινώσκῃ ἡμῶν), functions adverbially. It modifies the verb, "we have" (ἔχομεν). **Semantically**, ἐάν introduces the protasis of a third class condition: "if" (cf. KJV NASB ESV NIV NET etc.). The third class conditional clause has a level of uncertainly (Wallace 1996, 696). There remains a possibility that while a believer's conscience doesn't condemn them, they can still have assurance when they stand before God.

καταγινώσκῃ: The Greek word καταγινώσκῃ is a third singular present active subjunctive from the verb καταγινώσκω that means, "I condemn" or "I convict" (BDAG 515). The verb is in the subjunctive because it is part of the ἐάν clause. **Syntactically**, καταγινώσκῃ serves as the governing verb of the dependent adverbial clause. The subject is "heart" (ἡ καρδία) and is a metaphor for the believer's conscience. **Semantically**, καταγινώσκῃ is a customary present: "*persistently* condemn" (Wallace 1996, 521) or "condemn" (KJV NASB ESV NIV NET etc.). When the believer's conscience does not bring guilt, they can still have assurance of their faith, because God is greater than their hearts. God's opinion is what matters.

3:21b   ἔχομεν: The Greek word ἔχομεν is a first plural present active indicative from the verb ἔχω that means, "I have" or to experience in inner condition (BDAG 421.7aβ). **Syntactically**, ἔχομεν is the main verb of the independent clause: "we *feel* confident before God" (παρρησίαν ἔχομεν πρὸς τὸν θεόν). The subject is an implied "we" embedded in the verb and refers to the readers who exhibit the self-less love of Jesus. The inner emotion experienced or felt is "confidence" (BDAG 781.3b). **Semantically**, ἔχομεν is a gnomic present: "we *feel*" or "we have" (KJV NASB ESV NIV NET etc.). Thus John discloses another timeless fact (Wallace 1996, 523). The believer whose conscience does not condemn feels confident before God. (For the first timeless fact, return to 3:20b.)

3:22a   καί: The Greek word καί is a conjunction which means "and so" (BDAG 495.1bζ). **Syntactically**, καί introduces an independent conjunctive clause: "*and so* whatever we ask for we will receive from him" (καὶ ὃ ἐὰν αἰτῶμεν λαμβάνομεν ἀπ' αὐτοῦ). **Semantically**, καί is inferential: "and so" or "and" (cf. KJV NASB ESV NIV NET etc.). It introduces a conclusion about the believer's confidence before God, which is fleshed out in the rest of the clause.

ὃ ἐάν: The Greek word ὃ is a neuter singular accusative from the relative pronoun ὅς that means, "what" (BDAG 727.1jα). The Greek word ἐάν is a conjunction that means, "ever" (BDAG 268.3). Together ὃ ἐάν is translated "whatever." **Syntactically**, the Greek construction ὃ ἐάν is a dependent indefinte relative clause. The entire clause "whatever we ask" (ὃ ἐὰν αἰτῶμεν) is the direct object of the verb "we receive" (λαμβάνομεν). So the ὃ ἐάν clause is placed in parenthesis in order to visualize its contribution to the independent clause. The rest of this clause is rather significant.

αἰτῶμεν: The Greek word αἰτῶμεν is a first plural present active subjunctive from the verb αἰτέω that means, "I ask," "I ask for" or "to ask for, with a claim on receipt of an answer" (BDAG 30). The verb is in the subjunctive because it is part of the ἐάν clause. **Syntactically**, αἰτῶμεν is the governing verb of the dependent indefinite relative clause. The subject is an implied "we" embedded in the verb and refers to the orthodox readers. **Semantically**, αἰτῶμεν is an instantaneous present: "We ask for" or "we ask" (cf. KJV NASB ESV NIV NET, etc.). The act of asking is completed at the moment of praying (Wallace 1996, 517). What is rather significant is God's response evident in the next verb.

λαμβάνομεν: The Greek word λαμβάνομεν is a first plural present active indicative from the verb λαμβάνω that means, "I receive" or "I get" or "I obtain" or "to be a receiver" (BDAG 585.10c). **Syntactically**, λαμβάνομεν is the main verb of the independent clause "And (whatever we ask for) *we will receive* from him" (λαμβάνομεν ἀπ' αὐτοῦ). **Semantically**, λαμβάνομεν is a futuristic present: "will receive" (NLT) or "we receive" (cf. KJV NASB ESV NIV NET, etc.). John describes "an event that is *wholly* subsequent to the time of speaking" (Wallace 1996, 536). Followers of Jesus *will* receive whatever we ask.

3:22b   ὅτι: The Greek word ὅτι is a conjunction, which means "because" (BDAG 732.4a). **Syntactically**, ὅτι introduces a dependent conjunctive clause: "*because* we persist in keeping his commands" (ὅτι τὰς ἐντολὰς αὐτοῦ τηροῦμεν). The entire clause functions adverbially. It modifies the verb, "we receive" (λαμβάνομεν). **Semantically**, ὅτι is causal: "because" (cf. KJV NASB ESV NIV NET etc.). It provides the reason why God considers the request of the believer (Wallace 1996, 460), which is highlighted in the next verb.

τηροῦμεν: The Greek word τηροῦμεν is a first plural present active indicative from the verb τηρέω that means, "I keep" or "I observe" or "to persist in obedience" (BDAG 1002.3). **Syntactically**, τηροῦμεν is the governing verb of the compound dependent adverbial ὅτι clause. The subject of the verb is an implied "we" embedded in the verb and refers to John and any believer who follows Jesus' example of self-less love. **Semantically**, τηροῦμεν is a customary present: "we *persist* in keeping" or "we keep" (KJV ASV NASB ESV NET CNT) or "we obey" (NRSV NIV NLT). It describes a pattern of behavior (Wallace 1996, 521). The reason God answers a believer's prayer is because they *continually strive to obey* God in their life. The theme of keeping (τηρέω) God's commands first appeared in chapter 2 (vv. 3a, 4a, 5a).

3:22c   καὶ [ὅτι]: The Greek word καί is a conjunction which means "and" (BDAG, 494.1b). **Syntactically**, καί introduces a dependent conjunctive clause that links together two compound dependent adverbial clauses: "*because* we persist in keeping his commands" (ὅτι τὰς ἐντολὰς αὐτοῦ τηροῦμεν) is linked to "[*because*] we persist in doing the things that are pleasing to him" (καὶ [ὅτι] τὰ ἀρεστὰ ἐνώπιον αὐτοῦ ποιοῦμεν). The elliptical [ὅτι] is inserted to visualize John's second reason why God answers a believer's prayer. **Semantically**, καί is a coordinating conjunction that introduces additional information about why God answers prayer.

ποιοῦμεν: The Greek word ποιοῦμεν is a first plural present active indicative from the verb ποιέω that means, "I do" or "I bring about" or to undertake or do something that brings about an event (BDAG, 840.2e), **Syntactically**, ποιοῦμεν is the governing verb of the conjunctive dependent adverbial [ὅτι] clause. The subject of the verb is an implied "we" embedded in the verb and refers to John and any other believer who follows Jesus' example of self-less love. **Semantically**, ποιοῦμεν is a customary present: "we persist in doing" or "do" (cf. KJV NASB ESV NIV NET etc.). It describes a pattern of behavior (Wallace 1996, 521). The prayers are answered for any believer who undertakes or makes it a practice to follow Jesus' example of selflessnes.

Syntactical Nugget: The two clauses: "we persist in keeping his commands" (τὰς ἐντολὰς αὐτοῦ τηροῦμεν) and "we persist in doing what is pleasing in his sight" (τὰ ἀρεστὰ ἐνώπιον αὐτοῦ ποιοῦμεν) are figures of speech called a synonymous parallelism. Therefore, to keep God's love commands is to do what is pleasing to him (Brown 1982, 462; see also Bateman 2008, 406).

3:23a καί: The Greek word καί is a conjunction that means "and" (BDAG 494.1b). **Syntactically**, καί introduces a conjunctive independent clause: "*And* this is his command" (καὶ αὕτη ἐστὶν ἡ ἐντολὴ αὐτοῦ). **Semantically**, καί is a marker that introduces additional information about the commandments of God with loose connections with the previous independent clause. The translation of καί appears in most translations as "and" (KJV ASV NASB NRSV ESV NIV NLT CNT), but at least one transation interprets καί as a transitional conjuction, "now" (NET). Nevertheless, John adds information about God's command.

ἐστίν: The Greek word ἐστίν is third singular present active indicative from the verb εἰμί that means, "is" or "to be in close connection with" (BDAG 283.2a). **Syntactically**, ἐστίν is the main verb of the independent conjunctive clause. The subject of the verb is the demonstrative pronoun "this" (αὕτη), due to the grammatical priority of pronouns (Wallace 1996, 42-43). **Semantically**, ἐστίν is a gnomic statement: "is" (cf. KJV NASB ESV NIV NET etc.). It reveals a timeless commandment (Wallace 1996, 523). This construction (αὕτη ἐστὶν) occurs often in 1 John. It is a way John highlights his main ideas (Brown 1982, 192). It is cataphoric in that what John says in the following ἵνα clauses is rather important because while the theme of keeping (τηρέω) God's commands first appeared in chapter 2 (vv. 3a, 4a, 5a). John now specifies what those commands are via these two ἵνα clauses.

3:23b ἵνα: The Greek word ἵνα is a conjunction, which means "that" (BDAG 476.2e). **Syntactically**, ἵνα introduces a conjunctive dependent clause, "*namely that* we will believe in the name of his son, Jesus, who is the Christ, and persist in loving one another" (ἵνα πιστεύσωμεν τῷ ὀνόματι τοῦ υἱοῦ αὐτοῦ Ἰησοῦ Χριστοῦ καὶ ἀγαπῶμεν ἀλλήλους). The entire ἵνα clause is substantival. It clarifies the demonstrative pronoun "this" (αὕτη). **Semantically**, ἵνα is an appositional conjunction: "*namely* that" (KJV ASV NASB NRSV ESV NET CNT). It clarifies the demonstrative pronoun "this" (αὕτη). It is almost idiomatic within Johannine literature (Wallace 1996, 475). God's command is that believers place their faith in Jesus and love one another (cp. 3:11c ἵνα).

πιστεύσωμεν: The Greek word πιστεύσωμεν is a first plural aorist active subjunctive from the verb πιστεύω that means, "I believe" or "I trust" or "to entrust oneself to an entity in complete confidence" (BDAG 817.2aα). "I believe" is in the subjunctive because ἵνα takes a subjunctive verb. **Syntactically**, πιστεύσωμεν is the governing verb of the dependent adjectival ἵνα clause. The verb is in the subjunctive mood because it follows a ἵνα. **Semantically**, πιστεύσωμεν is a constative aorist: "we believe" (cf. NASB ESV NET). Others render πιστεύσωμεν as "we should believe" (KJV ASV NRSV CNT), or "we must believe" (NLT) or "to believe" (NIV). The rendering "we believe" as a constative aorist, suggests that John views belief as an event that covers a multitude of actions (Wallace 1996, 557). John tells his readers that the first part of God's command is belief. The actual object of belief is the "name of Jesus" (τῷ ὀνόματι τοῦ υἱοῦ αὐτοῦ Ἰησοῦ Χριστοῦ), which is in the dative case rather than the accusative. This is because the verb πιστεύω takes a direct object in the dative case.

3:23c καὶ [ἵνα]: The Greek word καί is a conjunction that means "and" (BDAG 494.1b). **Syntactically**, καί introduces a second dependent ἵνα clause: "*and* [*that*] we love one another" (καὶ [ἵνα] ἀγαπῶμεν ἀλλήλους). An elliptical [ἵνα] is inserted to visualize John's second substantival comment. **Semantically**, καί is a marker to indicate additional information about God's command. It links two content clauses together: *"that* we believe in the name of his son, Jesus Christ and *"[that]* we love one another." This second aspect of the command underscores the love expected within the family of God. When belief in Jesus and love for others are paired together, then the individual can have assurance when they stand before God.

ἀγαπῶμεν: The Greek word ἀγαπῶμεν is a first plural present active subjunctive from the verb ἀγαπάω that means, "I love" or "to have a warm regard for and interest in another" person (BDAG 5.1aα). The subjunctive, "we love" (ἀγαπῶμεν), signals this is a second epexegetical clause. Thus a ἵνα is inserted. **Syntactically**, ἀγαπῶμεν is the governing verb of the dependent adjectival [ἵνα] clause. The subject is an implied "we" embedded in the verbal ending and refers to John and the believers who put their faith in the name of Jesus. **Semantically**, ἀγαπῶμεν is a customary present: "we persist in loving" or "love" (cf. KJV NASB ESV NIV NET etc.). It indicates a pattern of behavior (Wallace 1996, 521). Together the two ἵνα clauses emphasize two expectations: Believers are to trust in Jesus and continually love each other with sincere actions.

3:23d καθώς: The Greek word καθώς is a conjunction, which means "just as" or "as" (BDAG 493.1). **Syntactically**, καθώς introduces a dependent conjunctive clause. The entire dependent καθώς clause, "just as he gave us the command to us" (καθὼς ἔδωκεν ἐντολὴν ἡμῖν) functions adverbially modifying the verb "we love" (ἀγαπῶμεν). **Semantically**, καθώς is comparative: "just as" (NASB NRSV ESV NET CNT NLT). Believers who trust in Jesus and continually love each other with sincere actions are compared with being obedient to God.

ἔδωκεν: The Greek word δέδωκεν is a third person singular aorist active indicative from the verb δίδωμι that means, "I give" (BDAG 242.8) or "I command" where the translation of ἔδωκεν is determined by the object ἐντολὴν (see BDAG 243.17a). **Syntactically**, δέδωκεν is the main verb of the dependent adverbial καθώς clause. The subject is an implied "he" embedded in the verb and can either refer to the God, the Father or Jesus (see note 3:23 above). **Semantically**, δέδωκεν is a constative aorist: "he gave" (KJV ASV NET) or "he commanded" (NASB NIV NLT). It describes an event as a whole (Wallace 1996, 557). John points to multiple actions in the past that are ultimately summed up with the simple statement: God gave us *the* command.

3:24a καί: The Greek word καί is a conjunction that means "and" (BDAG, 494.1b). **Syntactically**, καί introduces an independent conjunctive clause: "and *the one who persists in keeping* his commands abides in him" (καὶ ὁ τηρῶν τὰς ἐντολὰς αὐτοῦ ἐν αὐτῷ μένει). While a translation of καί appears in some translations (KJV ASV NET), others leave καί untranslated (NASB NRSV ESV NIV NLT). **Semantically**, καί is connective and introduces some additional thoughts about the believer who keeps the commands of God. The believer can know that when they believe in Jesus and love their fellow believers they also have an abiding relationship with God.

τηρῶν: The Greek word τηρῶν is a nominative masculine singular present active participle from the verb τηρέω that means, "I keep" or "I observe" or "to persist in obedience" (BDAG 1002.3). **Syntactically**, τηρῶν, "the one who persists in keeping," functions substantivally as the subject of the verb "remains" (μένει). **Semantically**, τηρῶν is a gnomic present with a customary present force: "the one who persists in keeping" or "the one who keeps" (KJV ASV NASB ESV NET CNT) or "who obeys" (NRSV NIV NLT). John presents a timeless maxim about people (Wallace 1996, 521, 523). People who "keep" or "live" a lifestyle of obedience continue to have a relationship with God.

μένει: The Greek word μένει is a third singular present active indicative from the verb μένω that means, "I remain" or "I abide" or "I continue" or of "someone who does not leave" (BDAG 631.1aβ).

Syntactically, μένει is the main verb of the independent clause. The subject is participial phrase, "the one who *continually keeps* his commands" (ὁ τηρῶν τὰς ἐντολὰς αὐτοῦ). John speaks of the believer who persists in keeping God's commands. The referent, however, is ambiguous (see Theological Nugget 3:23b). **Semantically**, μένει is a gnomic present with a customary present force: "*continues to* remain" or "remains" (NLT). Some render as μένει "abides" (KJV ASV NASB ESV CNT) or "lives" (NIV). Regardless of how its rendered: John once again shares a timeless truth (Wallace 1996, 521, 523). The one who habitually loves other believers can have assurance that they have an abiding relationship with God.

3:24b καί: The Greek word καί is a conjunction that means "and" (BDAG 494.1b). **Syntactically**, καί introduces an independent conjunctive clause: "*and* the one who *persists* in keeping his commandments abides with God" (καὶ ὁ τηρῶν τὰς ἐντολὰς αὐτοῦ ἐν αὐτῷ μένει). **Semantically**, καί is a marker that introduces additional information about those who persist in keeping God's command. Not only do believers have prayers answered (v. 23), they have a relationship (μένει) with God.

[μένει]: The Greek word μένει is a third singular present active indicative from the verb μένω that means, "I remain" or "I abide" or "I continue" or of "someone who does not leave" (BDAG 631.1aβ). **Syntactically**, μένει is an ellipsis assumed from the previous clause and serves as the main verb of the independent conjunctive clause. The subject is the emphatic pronoun, "this one" (αὐτός), and refers to the readers who keep the love command of God. The pronoun is already embedded in the elliptical verb and therefore does not need to be explicitly stated. Its presence heightens the intimacy of the relationship between God and the one who loves others. **Semantically**, μένει is again a gnomic present with a customary present force: "*continues to* remain." John shares a timeless truth (Wallace 1996, 521, 523). God is continually present in the life of the one who follows his commands.

3:24c καί: The Greek word καί is a conjunction that means "and" (BDAG 494.1b). **Syntactically**, καί introduces a conjunctive independent clause, "*and* by this we know that God abides in us" (καὶ ἐν τούτῳ γινώσκομεν ὅτι μένει ἐν ἡμῖν). **Semantically**, καί is connective and introduces some additional information about the assurance that a believer can have in his intimate relationship with God. While a translation of καί appears in some translations (NRSV NLT), others leave it untranslated (KJV ASV NASB ESV NIV). At least one translation renders it as a transitional καί similar to that found in 1:5a (NET). Regardless of the presence of καί, the point is that they can also be assured by the conintual presence of the Spirit of God in their life.

ἐν τούτῳ: The Greek word ἐν is a preposition that means "in" (BDAG 328.5b). The Greek word τούτῳ is declined as a dative singular neuter from the demonstrative pronoun τοῦτο, which means "this one" (BDAG 741.1ba). **Syntactically**, ἐν τούτῳ introduces an independent prepositional clause: "by this we know" (ἐν τούτῳ γινώσκομεν). As noted before, this prepositional construction occurs frequently in 1 John (2:3, 4, 5 [twice], 3:10, 16, 19, 24; 4:2, 9, 10, 13, 17; 5:2) and is an important structural marker. **Semantically**, ἐν τούτῳ can either be anaphoric, pointing back to a preceding discussion, or cataphoric, pointing forward. Since there is an prepositional phrase "by the Spirit" (ἐκ τοῦ πνεύματος) immediately following our current clause, the phrase is cataphoric and points forward to the prepositional phrase in 3:24d ἐκ τοῦ πνεύματος, which gives us the content of the demonstrative pronoun "this" (τούτῳ; Brown 1982, 464; Culy 2004, 98).

γινώσκομεν: The Greek word γινώσκομεν is a first plural present active indicative from the verb γινώσκω that means, "I know" or "to arrive at a knowledge of someone or something" (BDAG 200.1c). **Syntactically**, γινώσκομεν is the main verb of the independent clause. The subject of the verb is an implied "we" embedded in the verb and refers to the orthodox readers of the letter who live in love for other believers. **Semantically,** γινώσκομεν is a customary present: "we know" (cf. KJV NASB ESV NIV NET etc.). John's focus is on an on-going awareness that believers have (Wallace 1996, 521). That awareness or knowledge concerns the status of a believer's relationship with God.

ὅτι: The Greek word ὅτι is a conjunction, which means "that" or to identify content after a verb of mental perception (BDAG 731.1c). **Syntactically,** ὅτι introduces a dependent conjunctive clause: "that he abides in us" (ὅτι μένει ἐν ἡμῖν). The entire ὅτι clause functions substantivally as the direct object of the verb, "we know" (γινώσκομεν; cf. Wallace 1996, 454). The clause is placed in parenthesis in order to visualize its contribution to the independent clause. **Semantically,** ὅτι is an indirect discourse: "that" (cf. KJV NASB ESV NIV NET etc.; cf. Wallace 1996, 456). The entire ὅτι clause provides the content of the verb "we know" (γινώσκομεν). What is known is found in the governing verb of this ὅτι clause.

μένει: The Greek word μένει is a third singular present active indicative from the verb μένω that means, "I remain" or "I abide" or "I continue" or of "someone who does not leave" (BDAG 631.1aβ). **Syntactically,** μένει serves as the governing verb of the dependent substantival ὅτι clause. The subject is an implied "he" embedded in the verb and refers to God. **Semantically,** μένει is a customary present: "abides." It emphasizes an on-going state (Wallace 1996, 521). While some render μένει as "abides" (KJV ASV NASB NRSV ESV CNT), others prefer "lives" (NIV NLT) or "resides" (NET). Regardless of how μένει is rendered, John underscores that his readers are aware that God abides in them. Note that in 3:24a, John speaks of Christians relating to God, but here God is relating to Christians. The source of this awareness is identified in the next clause.

3:24d ἐκ: The Greek word ἐκ is a preposition, which means "from" or "of" or to denote origin (BDAG 297.3cβ). **Syntactically,** ἐκ τοῦ πνεύματος is a prepositional phrase that functions adjectivally. It modifies the demonstrative pronoun "this" (τούτῳ) that provides information or insight. **Semantically,** ἐκ indicates means: "by" (cf. KJV NASB ESV NIV NET etc.). It tells how believers can know they have an abiding relationship with God (For the semantical categories of the preposition ἐκ, cf. Wallace 1996, 371-372). So the source of a believer's assurance is through the presence of God's Spirit in their lives, a point John underscores earlier in the letter (cf. 2:20, 27).

οὗ: The Greek word οὗ is a genitive singular neuter from the relative pronoun ὅς which means, "who" (BDAG 726.1aα). **Syntactically,** οὗ introduces a dependent adjectival relative clause, "whom he has given us" (οὗ ἡμῖν ἔδωκεν), which modifies its antecedent "the Spirit" (τοῦ πνεύματος). Technically, the relative pronoun should be in the accusative case, since it serves as the direct object of the verb "he gave" (ἔδωκεν). However, it's is the genitive case. Sometimes a relative pronoun takes on the case of its antecedent rather than its grammatical case. This is called attraction. This occurs over 50 times in the New Testament and seems to be an idiomatic phenomenon with no linguistic impact (cf. BDAG 726.1aα; Culy 2004, 99; Wallace 1996, 337-339). The relative clause gives us some additional information about the Spirit of God. God himself gave us the Spirit.

ἔδωκεν: The Greek word ἔδωκεν is a third singular aorist active indicative from the verb δίδωμι that means, "I give" or "to give something out" (BDAG 242.2). Syntactically, ἔδωκεν is the governing verb of the dependent adjectival relative clause. The subject of the verb is an implied "he" embedded in the verb and refers to God. Semantically, ἔδωκεν is a consummative aorist: "he has given" (KJV NASB NRSV ESV NET CNT). The stress is on the cessation of God's giving the Spirit because the act was already presented as having happened in 2:20, 27 (Wallace 1996, 559). John then draws attention once again to an event, namely the time when God anointed his readers with his Spirit.

1 John 4:1–6

Verb Recognition for 1 John 4:1–6

¹Ἀγαπητοί, μὴ παντὶ πνεύματι πιστεύετε, ἀλλὰ δοκιμάζετε τὰ πνεύματα εἰ ἐκ τοῦ θεοῦ ἐστιν, ὅτι πολλοὶ ψευδοπροφῆται ἐξεληλύθασιν εἰς τὸν κόσμον. ²ἐν τούτῳ γινώσκετε τὸ πνεῦμα τοῦ θεοῦ· πᾶν πνεῦμα ὃ ὁμολογεῖ Ἰησοῦν Χριστὸν ἐν σαρκὶ ἐληλυθότα ἐκ τοῦ θεοῦ ἐστιν, ³καὶ πᾶν πνεῦμα ὃ μὴ ὁμολογεῖ τὸν Ἰησοῦν ἐκ τοῦ θεοῦ οὐκ ἔστιν· καὶ τοῦτό ἐστιν τὸ τοῦ ἀντιχρίστου, ὃ ἀκηκόατε ὅτι ἔρχεται, καὶ νῦν ἐν τῷ κόσμῳ ἐστὶν ἤδη. ⁴ὑμεῖς ἐκ τοῦ θεοῦ ἐστε, τεκνία, καὶ νενικήκατε αὐτούς, ὅτι μείζων ἐστὶν ὁ ἐν ὑμῖν ἢ ὁ ἐν τῷ κόσμῳ. ⁵αὐτοὶ ἐκ τοῦ κόσμου εἰσίν· διὰ τοῦτο ἐκ τοῦ κόσμου λαλοῦσιν καὶ ὁ κόσμος αὐτῶν ἀκούει. ⁶ἡμεῖς ἐκ τοῦ θεοῦ ἐσμεν· ὁ γινώσκων τὸν θεὸν ἀκούει ἡμῶν, ὃς οὐκ ἔστιν ἐκ τοῦ θεοῦ οὐκ ἀκούει ἡμῶν. ἐκ τούτου γινώσκομεν τὸ πνεῦμα τῆς ἀληθείας καὶ τὸ πνεῦμα τῆς πλάνης.

Clausal Outline Translated for 1 John 4:1–6

⁴ː¹ᵃἈγαπητοί, μὴ παντὶ πνεύματι πιστεύετε,
⁴ː¹ᵃ Beloved, **do** not **believe** every spirit,

⁴ː¹ᵇ ἀλλὰ δοκιμάζετε τὰ πνεύματα
⁴ː¹ᵇ **but test** the spirits
       |
       ⁴ː¹ᶜ εἰ ἐκ τοῦ θεοῦ ἐστιν,
       ⁴ː¹ᶜ *to determine* **whether they are** from God,
       |
       ⁴ː¹ᵈ ὅτι πολλοὶ ψευδοπροφῆται ἐξεληλύθασιν εἰς τὸν κόσμον.
       ⁴ː¹ᵈ **because** many false prophets **have gone out** into the world.

            ⁴ː²ᵃ ἐν τούτῳ γινώσκετε τὸ πνεῦμα τοῦ θεοῦ·
            ⁴ː²ᵃ By this **you know** the Spirit of God'
            |
⁴ː²ᵇ πᾶν πνεῦμα . . . ἐκ τοῦ θεοῦ ἐστιν,
⁴ː²ᵇ every spirit . . . **is** from God,
   |
       ⁴ː²ᶜ ὃ ὁμολογεῖ Ἰησοῦν Χριστὸν ἐν σαρκὶ ἐληλυθότα,
       ⁴ː²ᶜ **who** *repeatedly* **acknowledges** Jesus *to be* the Christ <u>who has come</u> in flesh,

⁴ː³ᵃ καὶ πᾶν πνεῦμα . . . ἐκ τοῦ θεοῦ οὐκ ἔστιν·
⁴ː³ᵃ **but** every spirit . . . **is** not from God;
   |
       ⁴ː³ᵇ ὃ μὴ ὁμολογεῖ τὸν Ἰησοῦν [ἐν σαρκὶ ἐληλυθότα]
       ⁴ː³ᵇ **who** does not *repeatedly* **claim** Jesus [*has come in the flesh*]

^{4:3c} καὶ τοῦτό ἐστιν τὸ [πνεῦμα] τοῦ ἀντιχρίστου,
^{4:3c} <u>and</u> this **is** the *spirit* of the antichrist,

> ^{4:3d} ὃ ἀκηκόατε (ὅτι ἔρχεται),
> ^{4:3d} *about* **which you have heard** (that it is coming),

> ^{4:3e} καὶ [ὃ] νῦν ἐν τῷ κόσμῳ ἐστὶν ἤδη.
> ^{4:3e} <u>and</u> [*which*] **is** now already in the world.

^{4:4a} ὑμεῖς ἐκ τοῦ θεοῦ ἐστε, τεκνία,
^{4:4a} **You** *yourselves* **are** from God, little children,

^{4:4b} καὶ νενικήκατε αὐτούς,
^{4:4b} and **you have overcome** them (= these antichrists),

> ^{4:4c} ὅτι μείζων ἐστὶν (ὁ ἐν ὑμῖν) ἢ (ὁ ἐν τῷ κόσμῳ).
> ^{4:4c} **because** the one who [*is*] in you **is** greater than the one who [*is*] in the world

^{4:5a} αὐτοὶ ἐκ τοῦ κόσμου εἰσίν·
^{4:5a} **They** *themselves* **are** from the world;

^{4:5b} διὰ τοῦτο ἐκ τοῦ κόσμου λαλοῦσιν
^{4:5b} **Therefore they speak** *regualarly* from the world's perspective

^{4:5c} καὶ ὁ κόσμος αὐτῶν ἀκούει.
^{4:5c} and the world **listens** *regularly* to them.

^{4:6a} ἡμεῖς ἐκ τοῦ θεοῦ ἐσμεν·
^{4:6a} **We are** from God;

^{4:6b} ὁ γινώσκων τὸν θεὸν ἀκούει ἡμῶν,
^{4:6b} the person who knows God **listens** to us,

^{4:6c} (ὃς οὐκ ἔστιν ἐκ τοῦ θεοῦ) οὐκ ἀκούει ἡμῶν.
^{4:6c} (whoever is not from God) does not **listen** to us.

^{4:6d} ἐκ τούτου γινώσκομεν τὸ πνεῦμα τῆς ἀληθείας καὶ τὸ πνεῦμα τῆς πλάνης.
^{4:6d} <u>From this</u> **we know** the spirit of truth and the spirit of deceit.

Syntax Explained for 1 John 4:1–6

^{4:1a} πιστεύετε: The Greek word πιστεύετε is a second plural present active imperative from the verb πιστεύω that means, "I believe" or "to consider something to be true and therefore worthy of one's trust" (BDAG 816.1b). **Syntactically**, πιστεύετε is the main verb of the independent clause: "Beloved, do not *believe* every spirit" (Ἀγαπητοί, μὴ παντὶ πνεύματι πιστεύετε). The subject of the

imperative is an implied "you" and refers to the readers of the letter. In this case the vocative "Beloved" (Ἀγαπητοί) plus the imperative clearly marks off the beginning of a new paragraph and a new train of thought, stressing the responsibility that believers have to discern true teaching from false teaching (Culy 2004, 100). This is the second of three times that this particular vocative of direct address is employed to begin a new section (see also 3:21 and 4:7). **Semantically**, πιστεύετε is an imperative of prohibiton due to the presence of not" (μὴ; Wallace 1996, 487): "do not *believe*" (cf. KJV NRSV ESV NIVE NET etc.). John forbids his readers to believe every spirit. Perhaps he is telling them not to be naïve. The present tense is meant to communicate that John's command is to be an ongoing process (Wallace 1996, 715). John's readers are to be persistant in discerning what to believe.

4:1b ἀλλά: The Greek word ἀλλά is a conjunction that means "but" (BDAG 44.1a). **Syntactically**, ἀλλά identifies the clause as a conjunctive independent clause: "but test the spirits" (ἀλλὰ δοκιμάζετε τὰ πνεύματα). It typically follows after a negative like "do not believe" (μὴ . . . πιστεύετε). **Semantically**, ἀλλά is contrastive: "but" (cf. KJV NRSV ESV NIVE NET etc.). The clause contrasts his command against spiritually naivety with another command.

δοκιμάζετε: The Greek word δοκιμάζετε is a second plural present active imperative from the verb δοκιμάζω that means, "I put to the test" or "to make a critical examination of something to determine genuineness" (BDAG 255.1). This is the only time "test" (δοκιμάζω) is found in Johannine literature. It has the idea of evaluating or discerning what is true from what is false. **Syntactically**, δοκιμάζετε is the main verb of the conjunctive independent clause. The subject of the imperative is an implied "you" embedded in the verb and refers to the readers of the letter. **Semantically**, δοκιμάζετε is an imperative of command: "test" (cf. KJV NRSV ESV NIVE NET etc.). Believers are expected not to be spiritually naïve but to think critically about the message from God. Believers have a responsibility to not to believe every teaching about Christ, but to put those teachings to a test so that they do not fall into theological error about Jesus.

4:1c εἰ: The Greek word εἰ is a conjunction, which means "whether" (BDAG 278.5bα). **Syntactically**, εἰ identifies the clause as a conjunction dependent clause. The entire dependent clause, "if they are from God" (εἰ ἐκ τοῦ θεοῦ ἐστιν) functions adverbially. It modifies the verb, "test" (δοκιμάζετε). Translated "whether" (KJV ASV) or "to see whether" (NASB NARSV ESV NIV CNT), it serves as a marker of an indirect question (BDAG 278. 5bα; cf. Culy 2004, 100). John exhorts or expects (δοκιμάζετε) his readers to test the spirits by asking the question, "Is this prophecy or teaching from God?"

ἐστιν: The Greek word ἐστιν is third singular present active indicative from the verb εἰμί that means, "be" or to have a point of origin, to come from somewhere (BDAG 285.8). **Syntactically**, ἐστιν is the governing verb of the dependent adverbial conjunctive clause. The subject of the verb is an elliptical [τὰ πνεύματα] implied from the previous clause. The subject is plural and the verb is singular because neuter plural nouns always take a singular verb (Wallace 1996, 399-400). **Semantically**, ἐστιν is a verb of origin: "be from" or "are from" (cf. KJV NASB ESV NIV NET etc.). John expects believers to question the origin of a teaching or prophecy. Is it from God?

4:1d ὅτι: The Greek word ὅτι is a conjunction that means "because" (BDAG 732.4a). **Syntactically**, ὅτι introduces a dependent conjunctive ὅτι clause: "*because* many false prophets have gone out into the world" (ὅτι πολλοὶ ψευδοπροφῆται ἐξεληλύθασιν εἰς τὸν κόσμον). The entire clause functions adverbially. It modifies the verb "test" (δοκιμάζετε). **Semantically**, ὅτι is causal: "because" (cf. KJV ASV NASB NIV NET) or "for" (NRSV ESV NLT). John provides the reason why the believer should not believe every teaching or prophecy. It seems the necessity of discernment stems from the abundance of false teachers who have made their way throughout the world.

ἐξεληλύθασιν: The Greek word ἐξεληλύθασιν is a third plural perfect active indicative from the verb ἐξέρχομαι that means, "I go out" or "to move out of or away from an area" (BDAG 348.1aα). **Syntactically**, ἐξεληλύθασιν is the governing verb of the dependent adverbial ὅτι clause. The subject of the verb is the nominal phrase "many false prophets" (πολλοὶ ψευδοπροφῆται). **Semantically**, ἐξεληλύθασιν is an extensive perfect: "have gone out" (NASB NRSV ESV NIV NET CNT). The focus is on the completed action of the false teachers (Wallace 1996, 577). They have rejeceted the true teachings of God and left the church. Their association with the world, requires believers to discern and evaluate doctine and teaching. When comparing this verse with 2:29, there is a noted difference in tense. In 1 John 2:19 the aorist tense is used, while here we find the perfect. While John may be emphasizing the permanent departure of these false teachers, perhaps this is just an example of John's linguistic variety similar to that in chapter one where John vacillated between the aorist and perfect tenses for stylistic reasons (Brown 1982, 490).

⁴:²ᵃ ἐν τούτῳ: The Greek word ἐν is a preposition that means "in" (BDAG 328.5). The Greek word τούτῳ is declined as a dative singular neuter from the demonstrative pronoun τοῦτο, which means "this one" (BDAG 741.1bα). **Syntactically**, ἐν τούτῳ introduces an independent prepositional clause: *"by this* you know the Spirit of God" (ἐν τούτῳ γινώσκετε τὸ πνεῦμα τοῦ θεοῦ). The construction, "by this" (ἐν τούτῳ) is discussed several times in 1 John (2:3, 4, 5, 3:10, 16, 19, 24; 4:9, 10, 13, 17; 5:2 below). **Semantically**, ἐν τούτῳ means: "by this" (NASB ESV NET CNT). The clause can either be anaphoric, pointing back to the preceding discussion, or cataphoric, pointing forward. "This" (τούτῳ) is cataphoric. The believer can know if a teaching is true or false by whether or not it confesses that Jesus is God in human flesh.

γινώσκετε: The Greek word γινώσκετε is a second plural present active indicative from the verb γινώσκω that means, "I know" or "I know about" or "to arrive at a knowledge of someone or something" (BDAG 199.1a). **Syntactically**, γινώσκομεν is the main verb of the independent clause. The subject of the verb is an implied "you" embedded in the verb and refers to the orthodox readers of the letter. It is possible that this could be an imperative rather than an indicative (see the KJV ASV). If an imperative, John exhorts his readers to test the prophets rather than suggesting a way in which they can discern teachings. Since the context seems to be a gentle reminder of something that they should already know, it is more likely to be an indicative (Bateman 2008, 424). **Semantically**, γινώσκετε is a customary present: "know" (cf. KNV NASB ESV NIV NET etc.). John's focus is on the conintual knowledge believers possess about a teaching's origin (Wallace 1996, 521). If from God, it will cohere with the teaching about Jesus espoused in John's letter. In this context our author repeatedly contrasts the one Spirit of God (or God's Spirit) with the spirits of the antichrist. It is the Holy Spirit who animates those who belong to God (Culy 2004, 101).

⁴:²ᵇ ἐστιν: The Greek word ἐστιν is third singular present active indicative from the verb εἰμί that means, "is" or "to be in close connection (with)" (BDAG 283.2b). **Syntactically**, ἐστιν is the main verb of the independent asyndeton clause (πᾶν πνεῦμα ὃ ὁμολογεῖ Ἰησοῦν Χριστὸν ἐν σαρκὶ ἐληλυθότα ἐκ τοῦ θεοῦ ἐστιν). The subject of the verb is the nominal phrase "πᾶν πνεῦμα" along with the relative clause that amplifies it. **Semantically**, ἐστιν is a gnomic present: "is" (cf. KJV NASB ESV NIV NET etc.). John reveals a timeless truth about teaching (Wallace 1996, 523). Anyone who provides *correct teaching* (πᾶν πνεῦμα) is speaking *from God*. The correct teaching is is found in the next clause.

^{4:2c} ὅ: The Greek word ὅ is nominative singular neuter from the relative pronoun ὅς, which means, "that" (BDAG 725.1a). **Syntactically**, ὅ introduces a dependent adjectival relative clause: "*who* repeatedly acknowledges Jesus to be the Christ who has come in flesh" (ὃ ὁμολογεῖ Ἰησοῦν Χριστὸν ἐν σαρκὶ ἐληλυθότα). The gender agreement with the noun "spirit" (πνεῦμα) reveals that the entire realitive clause modifies "spirit" (πνεῦμα). This relative pronoun is in the nominitve case because is serves as the subject of the verb "confesses" (ὁμολογεῖ). The relative clause then underscores a specific Christological teaching from God.

ὁμολογεῖ: The Greek word ὁμολογεῖ is a third singular present active indicative from the verb ὁμολογέω that means, "I acknowledge" or "I claim" or "I profess" or "to acknowledge something, ordinarily in public" (BDAG 708.4b). **Syntactically**, ὁμολογεῖ is the governing verb of the dependent relative clause. The subject of the verb is the relative pronoun "that" (ὅ). **Semantically**, ὁμολογεῖ is an iterative present: "*regularly* acknowledge" (cf. NIV) or "claims" (NLT) or "confesses" (KJV ASV NASB NRSV ESV NET CNT). The person who repeatedly acknowleges in his or her teaching that Jesus was human and is God's Messiah reveals that that teaching is from God.

ἐληλυθότα: The Greek word ἐληλυθότα is an accusative masculine singular perfect active participle from the verb ἔρχομαι that means, "I come" or "of making an appearance before the public" (BDAG 394.1bα). **Syntactically**, ἐληλυθότα is part of a double accusative object complement. "Jesus" (Ἰησοῦν) is the direct object of the verb "acknowledges" (ὁμολογεῖ). "Christ" (Χριστὸν) is the first object complement. The participle "having come" (ἐληλυθότα) is a second object complement. Thus translated: "that *repeatedly* acknowledges Jesus *to be* the Christ who has come in flesh." "In flesh" (ἐν σαρκὶ) is a figure of speech called a synecdoche where a part is used to reference the whole. Here the idea of flesh is used to indicate the full bodily incarnation of Jesus. John underscores here that Jesus, as the Messiah, has come in the flesh (cf. NET note on this verse). **Semantically**, ἐληλυθότα is an extensive perfect: "who has come" (cf. NASB NRSV ESV NIV NET CNT). John's focus is on the completed action upon which the present confession is based (Wallace 1996, 577). Thus the past action of Jesus' incarnation has present effects for those who put their faith in him. The correct Christological confession then is based upon the historical realtity of Jesus's humanity and messiahship.

^{4:3a} καί: The Greek word καί is a conjunction that can mean either "and" or "but" (BDAG 494.1bε). **Syntactically**, καί introduces an independent conjunctive clause: "*but* every spirit who does not confess Jesus is not from God" (καὶ πᾶν πνεῦμα ὃ μὴ ὁμολογεῖ τὸν Ἰησοῦν ἐκ τοῦ θεοῦ οὐκ ἔστιν). **Semantically**, καί is adversative: "but" (NIV NET NLT) even though some translations prefer "and" (KJV ASV NASB NRSV ESV CNT). John's contrastive καί heightens the Christological affirmative. Regardless of how one translates καί, it introduces the second part of the confessional test of a false teacher (Brown 1982, 494).

ἔστιν: The Greek word ἔστιν is third singular present active indicative from the verb εἰμί that means, "is" or "to be in close connection (with)" (BDAG 283.2b). **Syntactically**, ἔστιν is the main verb of the independent clause (πᾶν πνεῦμα ὃ ὁμολογεῖ Ἰησοῦν Χριστὸν ἐν σαρκὶ ἐληλυθότα ἐκ τοῦ θεοῦ ἐστιν). The subject of the verb is the nominal phrase "πᾶν πνεῦμα" along with the relative clause that amplifies it. **Semantically**, ἔστιν is a gnomic present: "is" (cf. KJV NASB ESV NIV NET etc.). John reveals a timeless truth about teaching (Wallace 1996, 523). Anyone who offers *incorrect teaching* (πᾶν πνεῦμα) is *not from God*. That incorrect teaching is found in the next clause.

^{4:3b} ὅ: The Greek word ὅ is nominative singular neuter from the relative pronoun ὅς, which means "that" (BDAG 725.1a). **Syntactically**, ὅ introduces a dependent relative clause: "*who* does not repeatedly

acknowledge Jesus to be the Christ [who has come in the flesh] (ὃ μὴ ὁμολογεῖ τὸν Ἰησοῦν [ἐληλυθότα]). The entire realtive clause modifies the noun "spirit" (πνεῦμα). The relative pronoun is in the nominitve case because it serves as the subject of the verb "confesses" (ὁμολογεῖ). The use of the negative particle "not" (μὴ) with the indicative mood is grammatically unusual since it is typically used with subjunctive and imperatival moods (Wallace 1996, 469, 487). Culy suggests that the presence of "not" (μὴ) is an aberration and could be a classical Greek holdover that was used to express an assertion with no exceptions (Culy 2004, 102). Regardless of which particle is used the point remains the same: no one who refuses to hold an orthodox belief in the incarnation of Jesus can possibly be speaking from God.

ὁμολογεῖ: The Greek word ὁμολογεῖ is a third singular present active indicative from the verb ὁμολογέω that means, "I acknowledge" or "I claim" or "I profess" or "to acknowledge something, ordinarily in public" (BDAG 708.4b). **Syntactically**, ὁμολογεῖ is the governing verb of the dependent relative clause. The subject of the verb is the relative pronoun "who" (ὃ). **Semantically**, ὁμολογεῖ is a iterative present: *regularly* claim" (cf. NLT) or "acknowledge" (NIV) or "confess" (KJV ASV NASB NRSV ESV NET CNT). It speaks of something that happens on a regular basis (Wallace 1996, 520). Anyone who repeatedly teaches that Jesus was not human and is not God's Messiah reveals that their teaching is not from God.

[ἐληλυθότα]: The Greek word ἐληλυθότα is an accusative masculine singular perfect active participle from the verb ἔρχομαι "I come" or "of making an appearance before the public" (BDAG 394.1ba). **Syntactically**, ἐληλυθότα is an elliptical participle implied from the previous clause. As was the case in 4:2c, [ἐληλυθότα] is a substantival double accusative object complement. "Jesus" (Ἰησοῦν) is the direct object of the verb "claims" (ὁμολογεῖ). "Christ" (Χριστόν) is the first object complement, and the substantival participle, "having come" (ἐληλυθότα), is the second object complement: "that *regularly* claims Jesus *to be* the Christ who has come in flesh." The ellipsis has led many scribes to make explicit what was implied. **Semantically**, ἐληλυθότα is an extensive perfect: "who has come" (Wallace 1996, 577). Translations, however, tend to leave out translating the ellipsis (cf. NASB NRSV ESV NIV NET CNT). Regardless John's focus is on the ones who do not acknowledge the historical realtity of Jesus having come in the flesh as Messiah.

4:3c καί: The Greek word καί is a conjunction which means "and" (BDAG 494.1ba). **Syntactically**, καί introduces an independent conjunctive clause: "*and* this one is the [spirit] of the antichrist" (καὶ τοῦτό ἐστιν τὸ τοῦ ἀντιχρίστου). **Semantically**, καί is a coordinating conjunction. While some translate καί as "and" (KJV ASV NASB NRSV NET), others leave καί untranslated (ESV NLT CNT). It not only joins two independent clauses together, it also provides additional information about those who do not acknowledge the incarnation of Jesus.

ἐστιν: The Greek word ἐστιν is third singular present active indicative from the verb εἰμί that means, "is" or "to be in close connection (with)" (BDAG 283.2b). **Syntactically**, ἐστιν is the main verb of the independent conjunctive clause. The subject of the verb is the demonstrative pronoun "this one" (τοῦτό) due to the grammatical priority of pronouns (Wallace 1996, 43). While the definite article (τό) positioned before "of the antichrist" (τοῦ ἀντιχρίστου) could indicate it is a substantival predicate nominative phrase (Culy 2004, 103), it seems more likely that the article is anaphoric modifying an elliptical "spirit" [πνεῦμα] (Wallace 1996, 217). Thus the article and the implied "spirit" [πνεῦμα] is the predicate nominative (cf. NASB NRSV ESV NIV NET CNT). **Semantically**, ἐστιν is a equative present: "is" (cf. KJV NASB ESV NIV NET etc.). The one who does not confess the humanity of Jesus who is Messiah (Χριστόν) has a close connection with the antichrist.

^{4:3d} ὅ: The Greek word ὅ is accusative singular neuter from the relative pronoun ὅς that means, "which" (BDAG 725.1bβ). **Syntactically**, ὅ introduces a dependent relative clause: *about which* you have heard is coming" (ὃ ἀκηκόατε ὅτι ἔρχεται). Some translations render ὅ as "which" (ESV NIV NET NLT) others "of which" (NASB NRSV CNT). Regardless, the entire clause is adjectiveal. It modifies the elliptical noun "spirit" (τὸ [πνεῦμα]) and provides additional information about the spirit of the antichrist. He is the one whose coming had been predicted. The relative pronoun is in the accusative case because it serves as the direct object of the verb "you have heard" (ἀκηκόατε).

ἀκηκόατε: The Greek word ἀκηκόατε is a second plural perfect active indicative from the verb ἀκούω that means, "I hear" or "to receive news or information about something, to learn something" (BDAG 38.3e). **Syntactically**, ἀκηκόατε is the governing verb of the dependent relative clause: "about which *you have heard* is coming" (ὃ ἀκηκόατε ὅτι ἔρχεται). The subject of the verb is an implied "you" embedded in the verb and refers to the readers of the letter. **Semantically**, ἀκηκόατε is an extensive perfect: "you have heard" (KJV ASV NASB NRSV NIV NET CNT). The focus is on the completed action upon which John's present comment is based (Wallace 1996, 577). John's readers had heard that an antichrist was coming, resulting in a state of their expectation that continues to be relevant.

ὅτι: The Greek word ὅτι is a conjunction, which means "that" (BDAG 731.1b). **Syntactically**, ὅτι introduces a dependent conjunctive clause: "that he is coming" (ὅτι ἔρχεται). The entire clause is substantival. It functions as the direct object of the verb "you have heard" (ἀκηκόατε). Thus the entire clause is placed in parenthesis in order to visualize its contribution to the dependent relative clause. **Semantically**, ὅτι is an indirect discourse ὅτι: "that" (NASV NRSV). The clause provides the content of the message that believers had received about the antichrist and his coming (Wallace 1996, 456).

ἔρχεται: The Greek word ἔρχεται is a third singular present middle indicative from the verb ἔρχομαι that means, "I come" or with a focus on an approach of a forerunner from the author's perspective (BDAG 394.1bβ). **Syntactically**, ἔρχεται is the governing verb of the dependent conjunctive ὅτι clause. The subject of the verb is an implied "he" embedded in the verb and refers to the spirit of the antichrist that the believers had heard was coming. **Semantically**, ἔρχεται is a *mostly* futuristic present: "is coming" (NIV NET NLT). "The present tense describes an event *begun* in present time but completed in the furture" (Wallace 1996, 537), and it has validaton in the next clause with the presence of "and [who] now is" (καὶ [ὅ] νῦν . . . ἐστίν). John underscores the immediacy or certain coming of false messiahs (cf. 1 John 2:18; Mark 13:6; Matt 24:5; Luke 21:8).

^{4:3e} καὶ [ὅ] νῦν: The Greek word καί is a conjunction which means "and" (BDAG 494.1ba). Similarly, the Greek word νῦν is a conjunction, but it means "now" (BDAG 681.1aa). **Syntactically**, καὶ [ὅ] νῦν introduces a second conjunctive dependent relative clause, "and [who] is now in the world already" (καὶ [ὅ] νῦν ἐν τῷ κόσμῳ ἐστὶν ἤδη). The entire relative clause is adjectival. It modifies the elliptical noun "spirit" (τὸ [πνεῦμα]). **Semantically**, καὶ [ὅ] νῦν is a coordinating connection with temporal force: "and now" (NASB NRSV ESV NET) or "and indeed" (NIV). Together the two conjunctions provide additional information about the spirit of the antichrist with a focus on the immediate present. John's readers have heard that an Antichrist figure was coming, but now he warns that antichrist's teachings are already present among them.

[ὅ]: The Greek word ὅ is nominative singular neuter from the relative pronoun ὅς that means, "which" (BDAG 725.1bβ). **Syntactically**, [ὅ] introduces a dependent adjectival relative clause: "and [*which*] is now in the world already" (καὶ [ὅ] νῦν ἐν τῷ κόσμῳ ἐστὶν ἤδη). Like the previous relative clause, it too modifies the elliptical noun "spirit" (τὸ [πνεῦμα]). This relative pronoun is in the nominative case because is serves as the subject of the verb "is" (ἐστίν). Due to the presence of καὶ [ὅ] νῦν, the relative clause reveals that antichrist like teachings are already present in the false teaching of the secessionists.

ἐστίν: The Greek word ἐστίν is third singular present active indicative from the verb εἰμί that means, "is" or "to be in close connection (with)" (BDAG 283.2b). **Syntactically**, ἐστιν is the main verb of the second dependent adjectival relative clause. The subject of the verb is an implied relative pronoun "which" ([ὅ]). **Semantically**, ἐστίν is a equative present: "is" (cf. KJV NASB ESV NIV NET etc.). The people in John's churches, those who are spreading teachings against the humanity of Jesus the Messiah, have a close connection (ἐστίν) with the teachings of the forthcoming Antichrist.

4:4a ἐστε: The Greek word ἐστε is second plural present active indicative from the verb εἰμί that means, "is" or "to be in close connection (with)" (BDAG 283.2b). **Syntactically**, ἐστε is the main verb of the independent asyndeton clause, "you, yourselves *are* of God" (ὑμεῖς ἐκ τοῦ θεοῦ ἐστε). The subject of the verb is the emphatic personal pronoun "you" (ὑμεῖς). While an explicit pronoun is not often seen as emphatic with a verb of being, here it is. It is set in stark contrast to the third person masculine pronoun that serves as the direct object of the next clause (Bateman 2008, 434). John strengthens the distinction between those who belong to God and the false teachers who belong to the world system. The Johannie letters are characterized by a stark dualism. The lines are vividly drawn, and every human either belongs to God or to his enemy. **Semantically**, ἐστε is an equative present: "are" (cf. KJV NASB ESV NIV NET etc.). John once again underscores the close connection his readers have with God (cf. 3:1–2).

4:4b καί: The Greek word καί is a conjunction that means "and" (BDAG 494.1ba). **Syntactically**, καί introduces a conjunctive independent clause: "*and* you have overcome them" (καὶ νενικήκατε αὐτούς). **Semantically**, καί is a coordinating connection: "and" (KJV ASV NASB NRSV ESV NIV). The conjunction connects an additional idea about his readers's relationship with God (Wallace 1996, 671). John's readers not only belong to God, but the καί signals that some additional information about the believer's status with God is coming.

νενικήκατε: The Greek word νενικήκατε is a second plural perfect active indicative from the verb νικάω that means, "I conquer" or "I overcome" or "to overcome someone" (BDAG 673.2a). **Syntactically**, νενικήκατε is the main verb of the independent conjunctive clause. The subject of the verb is an implied "you" embedded in the verb and refers to the readers of the letter. **Semantically**, νενικήκατε is an extensive perfect: "you have overcome" (cf. KJV NASB ESV NIV NET etc.). The focus is on the completed action upon which John's present comment is based (Wallace 1996, 577). John focuses attention on the past victory believers have over people of the world who spread information that is against Jesus that has continuing results in the present. The NLT captures the force of this clause the best: "You have already won a victory over those people."

4:4c ὅτι: The Greek word ὅτι is a conjunction that means "because" (BDAG 732.4a). **Syntactically**, ὅτι introduces the dependent conjunctive clause: "*because* the one who [is] in you is greater than the one who [is] in the world" (ὅτι μείζων ἐστὶν ὁ ἐν ὑμῖν ἢ ὁ ἐν τῷ κόσμῳ). The entire clause functions adverbially. It modifies the verb "overcome" (νενικήκατε). **Semantically**, ὅτι is causal: "because" (KJV ASV NASB NIV NET CNT NLT) or "for" (NRSV ESV). John provides the reason why the believer has overcome the world: God's presence in believers (e.g. his spirit) is greater than the spirit of the antichrist who abides in those who teach against Jesus.

ἐστίν: The Greek word ἐστίν is third singular present active indicative from the verb εἰμί that means, "be" or to be in reference a condition (BDAG 284.3c). **Syntactically**, ἐστίν is the governing verb of the dependent conjunctive ὅτι clause. The entire clause functions substantivally. It modifies the verb "overcome" (νενικήκατε). The subject of the verb is "the one in you" (ὁ ἐν ὑμῖν). The articles preceding both prepositional phrases are equivalent to a relative pronoun in force (Wallase 1996, 213) that nominalize and serve to identify the phrases as subjective. The first functions as the nominative of the verb "is" (ἐστίν): "(the one who [is] in you) **is**" (NRSV ESV NIV NET). **Semantically**, ἐστίν is an equative present that is part of an explanation disclosing the spirit in a believer to be greater than the spirits who are in the world (= spirit of the antichrist). The NLT captures this interpretation: "because the *Spirit* who lives in you is greater than the *spirit* who lives in the world" (emphasis ours).

4:5a εἰσίν: The Greek word εἰσίν is third plural present active indicative from the verb εἰμί that means, "to be" or "I come from somewhere" or "to have a point of derivation or origin" (BDAG 285.8). **Syntactically**, εἰσίν is the main verb of the independent asyndeton clause: "they themselves *are* of the world" (αὐτοὶ ἐκ τοῦ κόσμου εἰσίν). The subject of the verb is the emphatic personal pronoun "they" (αὐτοί). The presence of an explicit pronoun emphasizes the dualism that has been prevalent throughout the letter and in this section specifically. John distinguishes between those who are of the world and those who belong to God (Culy 2004, 104). **Semantically**, εἰσίν is an equative present: "are" (cf. KJV NASB ESV NIV NET etc.). Those who are against Jesus are not from God but from the evil world system.

4:5b διὰ τοῦτο: The Greek word διὰ is a preposition, which means "therefore" (BDAG 223.B2a). The Greek word τοῦτο is declined as an accusative singular neuter from the demonstrative pronoun τοῦτο, which means "this one" (BDAG 741.1ba). **Syntactically**, διὰ τοῦτο introduces an independent prepositional clause: "*therefore* they speak from the world *and* the world listens to them" (διὰ τοῦτο ἐκ τοῦ κόσμου λαλοῦσιν καὶ ὁ κόσμος αὐτῶν ἀκούει). The prepositional phrase is common in 1 John (3:1; 4:5). **Semantically**, διὰ τοῦτο can either be anaphoric, pointing back to the preceding discussion, or cataphoric, pointing forward. The usual rule is that the prepositional phrase is cataphoric, if it is followed by a subordinating conjunction. Since there is no subordinating conjunction it points back as a summary of the previous statements. People who speak against Jesus are animated by the spirit of the antichrist and have their origin in the world system, which John builds upon in the next verb.

λαλοῦσιν: The Greek word λαλοῦσιν is a third plural present active indicative from the verb λαλέω that means, "I talk" or "I speak" or "to utter words" (BDAG 582.2aδ). **Syntactically**, λαλοῦσιν is the main verb of the independent clause introduced by a prepositional phrase. The subject of the verb is an implied "they" embedded in the word and refers to the secessionists. **Semantically**, λαλοῦσιν is a customary present: "they speak *regularly*" (cf. KJV ASV NASB ESV NET NLT). It speaks of a pattern of behavior (Wallace 1996, 521). People who are of the world system speak the world's language.

4:5c καί: The Greek word καί is a conjunction which means "and" (BDAG 494.1ba). **Syntactically**, καί introduces an independent conjunctive clause: "*and* the world listens to them" (καὶ ὁ κόσμος αὐτῶν ἀκούει). **Semantically**, καί is a coordinating conjunction: "and" (KJV ASV NASB NRSV ESV NIV NLT CNT). The conjunction connects an additional element about those who speak against Jesus's humanity and Messiahship (Wallace 1996, 671). John builds upon his two previous statements about people who are part of the world's system (v. 5a) and who speak the world's language (v. 5b), which John builds upon in the next verb.

ἀκούει: The Greek word ἀκούει is a third singular present active indicative from the verb ἀκούω that means, "I hear" or "I listen to" or "to have or exercise the faculty of hearing" (BDAG 37.1c). **Syntactically**, ἀκούει is the main verb of independent conjunctive clause. The subject of the verb is the noun "world" (ὁ κόσμος). **Semantically**, ἀκούει is a customary present: "listens *regularly*" (NASB NRSV ESV NIV NET CNT NLT). John stresses the continual receptivity that the people of the world system have to the teachings against Jesus's humanity and Messiahship (Wallace 1996, 521). John continues to build on his statement about people who are part of the world's system (v. 5s), who speaks the world's language (v.5b), and the world's system is attracted to what they have to say (v. 5c).

4:6a ἐσμεν: The Greek word ἐσμεν is first plural present active indicative from the verb εἰμί that means, "is" or "to be in close connection (with)" (BDAG 283.2b). **Syntactically**, ἐσμεν is the main verb of the independent asyndeton clause: "We ourselves *are* from God" (ἡμεῖς ἐκ τοῦ θεοῦ ἐσμεν). The subject of the verb is emphatic personal pronoun "we" (ἡμεῖς). Again the explicit presence of the personal pronoun highlights the dualistic contrast between John and his readers (ἡμεῖς) and the false teachers (Culy 2004, 105). **Semantically**, ἐσμεν is an equative present: "are" (cf. KJV NASB ESV NIV NET etc.). In contrast to the false teachers whose origin is from the world system, believers have their origin in God.

4:6b γινώσκων: The Greek word γινώσκων is a nominative masculine singular present active participle from the verb γινώσκω that means, "I know" or "I know about" or "to arrive at a knowledge of someone or something" (BDAG 199.1a). **Syntactically**, ὁ γινώσκων and its object τὸν θεόν functions substantivally as the subject of the verb "listens" (ἀκούει). **Semantically**, γινώσκων is a gnomic present: "the person who knows God" or "whoever knows God" (NRSV ESV NIV NET CNT) or "those who know God" (NLT). The stress is on a timeless fact about those who claim to have a relationship with God (Wallace 1996, 523), which is defined with the following.

ἀκούει: The Greek word ἀκούει is a third singular present active indicative from the verb ἀκούω that means, "I hear" or "I listen to" or "to have or exercise the faculty of hearing" (BDAG 37.1c). **Syntactically**, ἀκούει is the main verb of the independent asyndeton clause: "the person who knows God listens to us" (ὁ γινώσκων τὸν θεὸν ἀκούει ἡμῶν). The subject of the verb is the substantival participial phrase, "the person who knows God" (ὁ γινώσκων τὸν θεόν). The "to us" is John and the eyewitnesses. This string of asyndeton clauses without conjunctions creates a stacatto effect that very powerfully illustrates a teaching style (Bateman 2008, 441). **Semantically**, ἀκούει is a gnomic present: "listens" (NASB NRSV ESV NIV NET CNT NLT). John presents a timeless truth (Wallace 1996, 523). People who claim to know God will be receptive to the teaching about Jesus's humanity and Messiahship.

4:6c ὅς: The Greek word ὅς is nominative singular masculine from the relative pronoun ὅς that means, "the one who" (BDAG 725.1bα). **Syntactically**, ὅς introduces a dependent relative clause: "*whoever* is not of God" (ὃς οὐκ ἔστιν ἐκ τοῦ θεοῦ). The relative pronoun (ὅς) is in the nominative case because it is the subject of the verb "is" (ἔστιν). The entire clause functions as the subject of the verb "listens" (ἀκούει) and is placed in parenthesis in order to visualize its contribution as the subject of the independent clause. Technically, this relative pronoun conceals a demonstrative pronoun and is called an "embedded demonstrative" (Wallace 1996, 240). The clause demonstrates that anyone whose origin is not from God will not be receptive to the teaching about Jesus.

ἔστιν: The Greek word ἔστιν is third singular present active indicative from the verb εἰμί that means, "is" or "to be in close connection (with)" (BDAG 283.2b). **Syntactically**, ἔστιν is the governing verb of the dependent substantival relative clause. The subject of the verb is the relative pronoun "whoever" (NRSV ESV NIV NET). In order to heighten the implied contrast, some translations insert "but" (NIV NET). Yet any inserted conjunction seems to take away from John's stacatto effect (see

1:6b ἀκούει). **Semantically**, ἔστιν is an equative present pointing out that the one whose origin is not from God will not be receptive to the true teaching about the nature of Jesus.

ἀκούει: The Greek word ἀκούει is a third singular present active indicative from the verb ἀκούω that means, "I hear" or "I listen to" or "to have or exercise the faculty of hearing" (BDAG 37.1c). **Syntactically**, ἀκούει serves as the main verb of the independent clause, "Whoever is not from God does not *listen* to us" (ὃς οὐκ ἔστιν ἐκ τοῦ θεοῦ οὐκ ἀκούει ἡμῶν). The subject of the verb is the relative clause "whoever is not from God" (ὃς οὐκ ἔστιν ἐκ τοῦ θεοῦ). **Semantically**, ἀκούει is a gnomic present: "listens" (NASB NRSV ESV NIV NET CNT NLT). John continues to stress a timeless fact (Wallace 1996, 523). Anyone who do not have an abiding relationship with God will not be receptive to the true teaching about Jesus and his nature.

4:6d   ἐκ τούτου: The Greek word ἐκ is a preposition, which means "from" or "of" or a marker denoting origin (BDAG 296.3a). The Greek word τοῦτο is declined as an accusative singular neuter from the demonstrative pronoun τοῦτο, which means "this one" (BDAG 741.1ba). **Syntactically**, ἐκ τούτου introduces an independent prepositional clause: "*from this* we know the Spirit of truth and the spirit of deceit" (ἐκ τούτου γινώσκομεν τὸ πνεῦμα τῆς ἀληθείας καὶ τὸ πνεῦμα τῆς πλάνης). **Semantically**, ἐκ τούτου can either be anaphoric, pointing back to the preceding discussion, or cataphoric, pointing forward. Since there is no subsequent clause to further define ἐκ τούτου, it is anaphoric. It summarizes the previous statements (Culy 2004, 106). On the one hand, some people are animated by the spirit of the antichrist and have their origin in the world system, therefore they speak the world's language, and the world is attracted to their message. On the other hand, others are animated by the Spirit of God and have their origins in him, therefore, when they speak, those who belong to God listen to them. John concludes that believers can discern who those people are by observing who are attracted to their message.

γινώσκομεν: The Greek word γινώσκομεν is a first plural present active indicative from the verb γινώσκω that means, "I know" or "I know about" or "to arrive at a knowledge of someone or something" (BDAG 199.1a). **Syntactically**, γινώσκομεν is the main verb of the independent clause. The subject of the verb is an implied "we" embedded in the verb and refers to John and his readers of the letter. **Semantically**, γινώσκομεν is a customary present: "we know" (cf. KJV NASB ESV NET etc.; Wallace 1996, 521). John underscores that believers can continually assess the difference between individuals who are attracted to the message about Jesus's humanity and Messiahship and those who are not.

1 John 4:7–10

Verb Recognition for 1 John 4:7–10

⁷Ἀγαπητοί, ἀγαπῶμεν ἀλλήλους, ὅτι ἡ ἀγάπη ἐκ τοῦ θεοῦ ἐστιν, καὶ πᾶς ὁ ἀγαπῶν ἐκ τοῦ θεοῦ γεγέννηται καὶ γινώσκει τὸν θεόν. ⁸ὁ μὴ ἀγαπῶν οὐκ ἔγνω τὸν θεόν, ὅτι ὁ θεὸς ἀγάπη ἐστίν. ⁹ἐν τούτῳ ἐφανερώθη ἡ ἀγάπη τοῦ θεοῦ ἐν ἡμῖν, ὅτι τὸν υἱὸν αὐτοῦ τὸν μονογενῆ ἀπέσταλκεν ὁ θεὸς εἰς τὸν κόσμον ἵνα ζήσωμεν δι᾽ αὐτοῦ. ¹⁰ἐν τούτῳ ἐστὶν ἡ ἀγάπη, οὐχ ὅτι ἡμεῖς ἠγαπήκαμεν τὸν

θεόν, ἀλλ᾽ ὅτι αὐτὸς ἠγάπησεν ἡμᾶς καὶ ἀπέστειλεν τὸν υἱὸν αὐτοῦ ἱλασμὸν περὶ τῶν ἁμαρτιῶν ἡμῶν.

Clausal Outline Translated for 1 John 4:7–10

^{4:7a} Ἀγαπητοί, **ἀγαπῶμεν** ἀλλήλους,
^{4:7a} Beloved, **let us** *persist in* **love** *for* one another,

|
^{4:7b} **ὅτι** ἡ ἀγάπη ἐκ τοῦ θεοῦ **ἐστιν**,
^{4:7b} **because** love **is** from God,

^{4:7c} καὶ πᾶς ὁ ἀγαπῶν ἐκ τοῦ θεοῦ **γεγέννηται**
^{4:7c} and everyone who loves **has been fathered** by God

^{4:7d} καὶ [πᾶς ὁ ἀγαπῶν ἐκ τοῦ θεοῦ] **γινώσκει** τὸν θεόν.
^{4:7d} and [*everyone who loves*] **knows** God.

^{4:8a} ὁ μὴ ἀγαπῶν οὐκ **ἔγνω** τὸν θεόν,
^{4:8a} The person who does not love does not **know** God,

|
^{4:8b} **ὅτι** ὁ θεὸς ἀγάπη **ἐστίν**.
^{4:8b} **because** God **is** love.

^{4:9a} **ἐν τούτῳ ἐφανερώθη** ἡ ἀγάπη τοῦ θεοῦ ἐν ἡμῖν,
^{4:9a} **By this** the love of God **was made known** among us,

|
^{4:9b} **ὅτι** τὸν υἱὸν αὐτοῦ τὸν μονογενῆ **ἀπέσταλκεν** ὁ θεὸς εἰς τὸν κόσμον
^{4:9b} **that** God **sent** his one and only Son into the world

|
^{4:9c} **ἵνα ζήσωμεν** δι᾽ αὐτοῦ.
^{4:9c} **in order that we may live** through him.

^{4:10a} **ἐν τούτῳ ἐστὶν** ἡ ἀγάπη,
^{4:10a} **In this is** love,

|
^{4:10b} οὐχ **ὅτι** ἡμεῖς **ἠγαπήκαμεν** τὸν θεόν,
^{4:10b} not **that we loved** God,

|
^{4:10c} ἀλλ᾽ **ὅτι** αὐτὸς **ἠγάπησεν** ἡμᾶς
^{4:10c} but **that he loved** us

|
^{4:10d} καὶ [**ὅτι**] **ἀπέστειλεν** τὸν υἱὸν αὐτοῦ ἱλασμὸν περὶ τῶν ἁμαρτιῶν ἡμῶν.
^{4:10d} and [*that*] **he sent** his Son to be the atoning sacrifice for our sins.

Syntax Explained for 1 John 4:7–10

^{4:7a} ἀγαπῶμεν: The Greek word ἀγαπῶμεν is a first plural present active subjunctive from the verb ἀγαπάω that means, "I love" or "to have a warm regard for and interest in another" person (BDAG 5.1aα). **Syntactically**, ἀγαπῶμεν is the main verb of the independent clause: "*Beloved*, let us persist in love for one another" (Ἀγαπητοί, ἀγαπῶμεν ἀλλήλους). The subject of the verb is an implied "we" embedded in the word and refers to John and the readers of the letter. The noun that begins this sentence, "beloved" (Ἀγαπητοί) is a vocative of direct address and serves to mark out a new paragraph and train of thought. The pronoun "one another" (ἀλλήλους) is a reciprocal pronoun. **Semantically**, ἀγαπῶμεν is a hortatory subjunctive and a customary present: "let us *persist in* love *for*" (cf. KJV NASB ESV NIV NET etc.). While the hortatory subjunctive urges John readers, the customary present signals an urging that will occur on a regular basis (Wallace 1996, 464, 521). John, then, urges believers to persist in their love for fellow believers.

^{4:7b} ὅτι The Greek word ὅτι is a conjunction, which means "because" (BDAG 732.4a). **Syntactically**, ὅτι introduces a dependent conjunctive ὅτι clause: "*because* love is from God" (ὅτι ἡ ἀγάπη ἐκ τοῦ θεοῦ ἐστιν). The entire clause is functioning adverbially modifying the verb, "let us love" (ἀγαπῶμεν). **Semantically**, ὅτι is causal: "because" (NRSV NET) or "for" (KJV ASV NASB ESV NIV CNT NLT; cf. Wallace 1996, 460). John provides the reason why believers should demonstrate love for each other, which is evident in the next verb.

ἐστιν: The Greek word ἐστιν is third singular present active indicative from the verb εἰμί that means, "is" or "to be in close connection (with)" (BDAG 284.2ca). **Syntactically**, ἐστιν is the governing verb of the dependent adverbial ὅτι clause. The subject of the verb is the noun "love" (ἡ ἀγάπη). **Semantically**, ἐστιν is equative: "is" (cf. KJV NAS ESV NIV NET). John equates a believer's persistant love with God's love. All true love finds its origin in God (cf. 1:5; 3:10; 4:7–8, 16).

^{4:7c} καί: The Greek word καί is a conjunction that means "and" (BDAG 494.1ba). **Syntactically**, καί introduces an independent conjunctive clause that joins two independent clauses together: "*and* everyone who loves has been fathered by God" (καὶ πᾶς ὁ ἀγαπῶν ἐκ τοῦ θεοῦ γεγέννηται). **Semantically**, καί is a coordinating connective that introduces additional information undergirding John's urging to love others (Wallace 1996, 671). While most translations translate καί (KJV ASV NASB NET ESV), others leave it untranslated (NRSV NIV NLT). John builds upon his statement about his expectation for believers to persist in love.

ἀγαπῶν: The Greek word ἀγαπῶν is a nominative masculine singular present active participle from the verb ἀγαπάω that means, "I love" or "I cherish" or "to have a warm regard for and interest in another" (BDAG 5.1aα). **Syntactically**, the πᾶς ὁ ἀγαπῶν functions substantivally as the subject of the verbs "has been born" (γεγέννηται) and "knows" (γινώσκει). **Semantically**, ἀγαπῶν is a gnomic present: "everyone who loves" (KJV ASV NASB NRSV NIV NET CNT) or "whoever" (ESV) or "anyone" (NLT). This generic reference conveys a gnomic idea (Wallace 1996, 521, 615). John is describing any person who loves or does not love, a description that is noted in the next verb.

γεγέννηται: The Greek word γεγέννηται is a third singular perfect passive indicative from the verb γεννάω that means, "I become the parent of" or "to exercise the role of a parental figure" (BDAG 193.1b). **Syntactically**, γεγέννηται serves as the first of two main verbs in the independent conjunctive καί clause. The subject of γεγέννηται is the phrase "everyone who loves" (πᾶς ὁ ἀγαπῶν). **Semantically**, γεγέννηται is both a gnomic and extensive perfect: "has been fathered" (NET) or "has been born" (NIV ESV). It is gnomic because of the generic subject (πᾶς) while extensive in that the focus is on the decisive relationship between God and the believer (Wallace 1996, 580). This generic or proverbial force may also be rendered as an intensive: "is born" (KJV NASB NRSV CNT; cf. ASV NLT) with an emphasis on the results of the present condition of the believer. Regardless of where one places the emphasis of the perfect, John's point is simply this: believers have been fathered by God in the past and that past event has continuing results in the present (cf. 2:29; 3:9; 5:1, 4, 18). The focus is upon those who practice righteousness: they have had an on-going relationship with God.

^{4:7d} καί: The Greek word καί is a conjunction that means "and" (BDAG 494.1ba). **Syntactically**, καί introduces an independent conjunctive clause that joins two independent clauses together: *"and* everyone who loves knows God" (καὶ [πᾶς ὁ ἀγαπῶν] γινώσκει τὸν θεόν). **Semantically**, καί is a coordinating connective: "and." It that introduces additional information undergirding John's urging to love others (Wallace 1996, 671). While most translations translate καί (KJV ASV NASB ESV NET ESV), others leave it untranslated (NRSV NIV NLT). John builds upon his statement about his expectation for believers to persist in love.

γινώσκει: The Greek word γινώσκει is a third singular present active indicative from the verb γινώσκω that means, "I know" or to have come to the knowledge of a person (BDAG 200.6c). **Syntactically**, γινώσκει is the main verbs in the independent conjunctive καί clause. The subject is the elliptical phrase "everyone who loves" (πᾶς ὁ ἀγαπῶν). **Semantically**, γινώσκει is a customary present: "know" or "knows" (cf. KJV NASB ESV NET etc.). It describes an on-going state (Wallace 1996, 521). John once again stresses that people who demonstrate love for their fellow Christians show that they have an abiding knowledge of God and his nature.

^{4:8a} ἀγαπῶν: The Greek word ἀγαπῶν is a nominative masculine singular present active participle from the verb ἀγαπάω that means, "I love" or "I cherish" or "to have a warm regard for and interest in another" (BDAG 5.1aα). **Syntactically**, ἀγαπῶν is a substantival participle ("the person who loves") that functions as the subject of the verb "know" (ἔγνω). The entire phrase is negated with μή. **Semantically**, ἀγαπῶν is a gnomic present negated with μή: "the person who does not love" (cf. KJV NASB ESV NIV NET etc.). John presents a timeless statement about people who refuse to love their brothers and sisters in Christ (Wallace 1996, 521). John underscores the neglect of a certain type of affection (cf. 4:20d).

ἔγνω: The Greek word ἔγνω is a third singular aorist active indicative from the verb γινώσκω that means, "I know" or to have come to the knowledge of a person (BDAG 200.6c). **Syntactically**, ἔγνω is the main verb of the independent clause, "the one who does not love does not *know* God" (ὁ μὴ ἀγαπῶν οὐκ ἔγνω τὸν θεόν). The subject of the verb is the participial phrase: "The one who does not love" (ὁ μὴ ἀγαπῶν). **Semantically**, ἔγνω is a gnomic aorist negated with μή: "does not know" (cf. KJV NASB ESV NIV NET etc.). John speaks a timeless or general truth (Wallace 1996, 562). Any person who claims to be a believer but refuses to demonstrate love, cannot possibly have the relationship with the God that they claim (cf. 1 John 1:9–11).

^{4:8b} ὅτι: The Greek word ὅτι is a conjunction, which means "because" (BDAG 732.4a). **Syntactically**, ὅτι introduces the dependent clause, *"because* God is love" (ὅτι ὁ θεὸς ἀγάπη ἐστίν). The entire dependent clause functions adverbially. It modifies the verb of perception, "know" (ἔγνω). **Semantically**, ὅτι is causal: "because" (ESV NIV NET) or "for" (KJV ASV NASB NRSV CNT NLT; cf. Wallace 1996, 460). John underscores the reason why someone who claims to know God, yet refuses to love, does not have a relationship with God. How can anyone who refuses to imitate God's character truly have a relationship with him?

ἐστίν: The Greek word ἐστίν is third singular present active indicative from the verb εἰμί that means, "is" or "to be in close connection (with)" (BDAG 284.2cα). **Syntactically**, ἐστίν is the main verb of the dependent adverbial ὅτι clause. The subject of the verb is the proper noun "God" (ὁ θεὸς). **Semantically**, ἐστίν an equative present: "is." John equates God with a qualatative noun "love" (ἀγάπη; cf. Wallace 1996, 245). By his very nature, God is love. Love is but one description of God's character. He is also Spirit (John 4:24) and light (see 1:5). Similarly in 1 John, John describes God as light and love because he encourages believers to follow God's ethical demand for love which springs from his very character (Bateman 2008, 454-455; see also Brown 1982, 515).

4:9a ἐν τούτῳ: The Greek word ἐν is a preposition, which means "by" (BDAG 328.5b). The Greek word τούτῳ is declined as a dative singular neuter from the demonstrative pronoun τοῦτο, which means "this one" (BDAG 741.1bβ). **Syntactically**, ἐν τούτῳ introduces an independent prepositional clause: "*by this* the love of God is revealed in us" (ἐν τούτῳ ἐφανερώθη ἡ ἀγάπη τοῦ θεοῦ ἐν ἡμῖν). "By this" (ἐν τούτῳ) occurs frequently in 1 John (2:3, 4, 5, 3:10, 16, 19, 24; 4:2, 10, 13, 17; 5:2). **Semantically**, ἐν τούτῳ can either be anaphoric, pointing back to the preceding discussion, or cataphoric, pointing forward. Here "by this" is cataphoric pointing forward to the subordinating conjunctive clause (ὅτι . . . . . τὸν κόσμον). The content of "by this" is found in the ὅτι clause below in 4:9b.

ἐφανερώθη: The Greek word ἐφανερώθη is a third singular aorist passive indicative from the verb φανερόω that means, "I make known" or "I show" or "to cause to become known" (BDAG 1048.2αβ). **Syntactically**, ἐφανερώθη is the main verb of the independent clause. It is a passive with an intransitive sense. The subject is the nominal phrase "the love of God" (ἡ ἀγάπη τοῦ θεοῦ). **Semantically**, ἐφανερώθη is a constative aorist: "was made known" or "was manifested" (KJV ASV NASB ESV) or "was revealed" (NRSV NET CNT) or "was showed" (NIV NLT). John stresses the cessation of a state (Wallace 1996, 559). God's great sacrificial love was shown to us through the coming of Jesus.

Syntactical Nugget: The prepositional phrase "among us" (ἐν ἡμῖν) is difficult and could be rendered referentially as "for us" emphasizing that God's love has been directed at the believing community through the work of Jesus (KJV; cf. Brown 1982, 516), as sphere "in us" (NET) indicating God's presence within believers or locatively, as "among us" indicating that God's love is revealed in the midst of the believing community (ESV NIV CNT; Culy 2004, 107).

4:9b ὅτι: The Greek word ὅτι is a conjunction, which means "that" (BDAG 732.2a). **Syntactically**, ὅτι introduces the dependent clause, "*that* God sent his one and only son into the world" (ὅτι τὸν υἱὸν αὐτοῦ τὸν μονογενῆ ἀπέσταλκεν ὁ θεὸς εἰς τὸν κόσμον). The entire ὅτι clause is functioning adjectivally modifying the demonstrative pronoun "this" (τούτῳ). **Semantically**, ὅτι is epexegetical: "that" (ASV NASB ESV NET CNT). The ὅτι clause explains or clarifies the demonstrative, τούτῳ (Wallace 1996, 459). The way believers know the love of God is by looking back at the selfless giving of his son. This ὅτι clause is very important. The first indication of its importance is in explaining the demonstrative. The second is the direct object of this clause "the son" (τὸν υἱόν). It is emphatic because it is at the beginning of the ὅτι clause. The final reason is that the verb tense switches from an aorist to a perfect tense. All of these factors point out that John fervently desired to proclaim to his readers that God sent his son into the world to give his life for those created in his image (Culy 2004, 107-108).

ἀπέσταλκεν: The Greek word ἀπέσταλκεν is a third singular perfect active indicative from the verb ἀποστέλλω that means, "I send" or is to dispatch someone for the achievement of some objective" (BDAG 120.1αβ). **Syntactically**, ἀπέσταλκεν is the governing verb of the dependent adjectival ὅτι clause. The subject is the proper noun "God" (ὁ θεὸς). **Semantically**, ἀπέσταλκεν is an intensive perfect: "sent" (KJV NRSV ESV NIV CNT). The emphasis is on the results of God's past action (Wallace 1996, 574). God dispatches Jesus into the world to achieve something specific. What he achieved is evident in the next clause.

4:9c ἵνα: The Greek word ἵνα is a conjunction, which means "in order that" or "that" or "to denote purpose, aim, or goal" (BDAG 475.1aβ). **Syntactically**, ἵνα introduces the conjunctive dependent adverbial clause: "in order that we might live through him" (ἵνα ζήσωμεν δι᾽ αὐτοῦ). The entire ἵνα clause modifies the verb "sent" (ἀπέσταλκεν). **Semantically**, ἵνα indicates purpose: "in order that" or "that" (KJV ASV). It indicates God's intention behind his sending Jesus into the world (Wallace 1996, 472). That intention is found in the governing verb of the ἵνα clause.

ζήσωμεν: The Greek word ζήσωμεν is a first plural present active subjunctive from the verb ζάω that means, "I live" or "of the sanctified life of a child of God" or "to live in a transcendent sense" (BDAG 425.2bβ). The verb is in the subjunctive mood because ἵνα takes the subjunctive mood. **Syntactically**, ζήσωμεν is the governing verb of the dependent adverbial ἵνα clause. The assumed subject "we" refers to John and the readers. **Semantically**, ζήσωμεν is a customary present: "we might live" (KJV ASV NSB NRSV ESV NIV CNT). God's intention for sending Jesus into the world was so that believers might *continually* live (Wallace 1996, 521).

4:10a ἐν τούτῳ: The Greek word ἐν is a preposition, which means "by" (BDAG 328.5b). The Greek word τούτῳ is declined as a dative singular neuter from the demonstrative pronoun τοῦτο, which means "this one" (BDAG 741.1bβ). **Syntactically**, ἐν τούτῳ is a prepositional phrase introducing an independent prepositional clause, *"by this* is love" (ἐν τούτῳ ἐστὶν ἡ ἀγάπη). "By this" (ἐν τούτῳ) occurs frequently in 1 John (2:3, 4, 5, 3:10, 16, 19, 24; 4:2, 9, 13, 17; 5:2). **Semantically**, ἐν τούτῳ can either be anaphoric, pointing back to the preceding discussion, or cataphoric, pointing forward. "By this" (ἐν τούτῳ) is cataphoric pointing forward to the two subordinating ὅτι clauses, "not *that* we loved God" (οὐχ ὅτι ἡμεῖς ἠγαπήκαμεν τὸν θεόν) and "but that he loved us and sent his lon to be the atoning sacrifice for our sins" (ἀλλ᾽ ὅτι αὐτὸς ἠγάπησεν ἡμᾶς καὶ ἀπέστειλεν τὸν υἱὸν αὐτοῦ ἱλασμὸν περὶ τῶν ἁμαρτιῶν ἡμῶν) in 4:10b and 4:10c and thereby provide the content of the demonstrative pronoun.

ἐστίν: The Greek word ἐστίν is third singular present active indicative from the verb εἰμί that means, "is" or "to show how something is to be understood" (BDAG 284.2cα). **Syntactically**, ἐστίν is the main verb of the independent clause introduced by a prepositional phrase. The subject of the verb is the noun "love" (ἡ ἀγάπη). **Semantically**, ἐστίν is an equative present: "is" (cf. KJV NASB ESV NIV NET etc.). It serves to introduce John's explanation about real love, which is spelled out in the next three clauses.

4:10b ὅτι: The Greek word ὅτι is a conjunction, which means "that" (BDAG 732.2a). **Syntactically**, ὅτι introduces a dependent conjunctive clause: *"not that* we ourselves have loved God" (οὐχ ὅτι ἡμεῖς ἠγαπήκαμεν τὸν θεόν). It modifies the demonstrative pronoun "this" (τούτῳ). **Semantically**, ὅτι is epexegetical negated with οὐχ: "not that" (cf. KJV NASB ESV NIV NET etc.). The ὅτι clause explains or clarifies the demonstrative (Wallace 1996, 459). Real love is not seen in the believer reaching out in love for God, but in his reaching out to them by sending his son as a sacrifice for sin.

ἠγαπήκαμεν: The Greek word ἠγαπήκαμεν is a first plural perfect active indicative from the verb ἀγαπάω that means, "I cherish" or "I have affection for" or "I love" or "to have a warm regard for and interest in another" (BDAG 5.1bα). **Syntactically**, ἠγαπήκαμεν is the governing verb of the dependent adjectival ὅτι clause. The subject is the emphatic personal pronoun "we" (ἡμεῖς) which does not need to be present since it is already embedded in the verbal ending. **Semantically**, ἠγαπήκαμεν is an intensive perfect: "we loved" (KJV ASV NASB NRSV NIV NLT). The emphasis is on the present state of a past or in this case the lack of a past action (Wallace 1996, 574). So John's first explanation is presented in the negative: Real love is not evident in mankind's love for God.

4:10c ἀλλ': The Greek word ἀλλά is a conjunction, which means "but" (BDAG 44.1a). **Syntactically**, ἀλλά identifies the clause as a conjunctive dependent clause: "*but* that God loved us and sent his son to be the atoning sacrifice for our sins" (ἀλλ' ὅτι αὐτὸς ἠγάπησεν ἡμᾶς καὶ ἀπέστειλεν τὸν υἱὸν αὐτοῦ ἱλασμὸν περὶ τῶν ἁμαρτιῶν ἡμῶν). This clause also modifies the demonstrative pronoun "this" (τούτῳ). **Semantically**, ἀλλά is contrastive: "but" (cf. KJV NASB ESV NIV NET etc.). It contrasts with the previous οὐχ ὅτι clause (Wallace 1996, 671). The specifics of the contrast are evident in the ὅτι clause.

ὅτι: The Greek word ὅτι is a conjunction, which means "that" (BDAG 732.2a). **Syntactically**, ὅτι is a dependent conjunctive clause: "*that* he loved us and sent his son to be the atoning sacrifice for our sins" (ὅτι αὐτὸς ἠγάπησεν ἡμᾶς καὶ ἀπέστειλεν τὸν υἱὸν αὐτοῦ ἱλασμὸν περὶ τῶν ἁμαρτιῶν ἡμῶν). This clause also modifies the demonstrative pronoun "this" (τούτῳ). **Semantically**, ὅτι is epexegetical negated with ἀλλά: "but that" (cf. KJV NASB ESV NIV NET etc.). The ὅτι clause explains or clarifies the demonstrative (Wallace 1996, 459). Real love is exemplified in God's sending of his son into the world to become its atoning sacrifice. John emphasizes here that a believer's love begins with God and not with mankind.

ἠγάπησεν: The Greek word ἠγάπησεν is a third singular aorist active indicative from the verb ἀγαπάω that means, "I cherish" or "I have affection for" or "I love" or "to have a warm regard for and interest in another" (BDAG 5.1bα). **Syntactically**, ἠγάπησεν is the governing verb of the second dependent adjectival conjunctive ὅτι clause. The subject is the emphatic personal pronoun "he" (αὐτὸς) referring to God. The contrast between the first person plural emphatic pronoun and this third person emphatic pronoun highlights the main idea here. Believers did not love God first. Instead, God reached out to ordinary human beings when they least deserved it. **Semantically**, ἠγάπησεν is a constative aorist: "he loved" (cf. KJV NASB ESV NIV NET etc.). The verb describes God's act of loving as a whole in a summary fashion without any specifics (Wallace 1996, 557). God loved ordinary people, which is in contrast to ordinary people loving God.

4:10d καί: The Greek word καί is a conjunction which means "and" (BDAG 494.1a). **Syntactically**, καί introduces another part of the compound dependent adjectival ὅτι clause: "*and* he sent his son to be the atoning sacrifice for our sins" (καὶ ἀπέστειλεν τὸν υἱὸν αὐτοῦ ἱλασμὸν περὶ τῶν ἁμαρτιῶν ἡμῶν). **Semantically**, καί is a coordinating connective of two dependent clauses: "and" (cf. KJV NASB ESV NIV NET etc.). It introduces some additional information about God's love (Wallace 1996, 671). John builds upon his previous statement about God and his love.

ἀπέστειλεν: The Greek word ἀπέστειλεν is a third singular aorist active indicative from the verb ἀποστέλλω that means, "I send" or to dispatch someone for the achievement of some objective" (BDAG 121. 1bγ). **Syntactically**, ἀπέστειλεν is the governing verb of the dependent adjectival ὅτι clause. The subject is also the emphatic personal pronoun "he" (αὐτὸς). We have here another double accusative object-complement construction. The direct object of the verb "sent" (ἀπέστειλεν) is the noun "son" (τὸν υἱὸν). The second accusative functions as the complement for the noun "atoning sacrifice" (ἱλασμὸν). This type of construction is often translated with the words "to be." Therefore, we should translate this, "and he sent his son *to be* the atoning sacrifice for our sins" (Wallace 1996,

181-186). **Semantically**, ἀπέστειλεν is a constative aorist: "he sent" or "sent" (cf. KJV NASB ESV NIV NET etc.). The verb describes God's act of sending Jesus into the world as a whole in a summary fashion without any specifics (Wallace 1996, 557). God showed his love for ordinary people when he sent Jesus into the world as an atoning sacrifice (cf. 1 John 2:2).

1 John 4:11-16c

Verb Recognition for 1 John 4:11–16c

¹¹Ἀγαπητοί, εἰ οὕτως ὁ θεὸς ἠγάπησεν ἡμᾶς, καὶ ἡμεῖς ὀφείλομεν ἀλλήλους ἀγαπᾶν. ¹²θεὸν οὐδεὶς πώποτε τεθέαται· ἐὰν ἀγαπῶμεν ἀλλήλους, ὁ θεὸς ἐν ἡμῖν μένει καὶ ἡ ἀγάπη αὐτοῦ τετελειωμένη ἐν ἡμῖν ἐστιν. ¹³Ἐν τούτῳ γινώσκομεν ὅτι ἐν αὐτῷ μένομεν καὶ αὐτὸς ἐν ἡμῖν, ὅτι ἐκ τοῦ πνεύματος αὐτοῦ δέδωκεν ἡμῖν. ¹⁴καὶ ἡμεῖς τεθεάμεθα καὶ μαρτυροῦμεν ὅτι ὁ πατὴρ ἀπέσταλκεν τὸν υἱὸν σωτῆρα τοῦ κόσμου. ¹⁵ὃς ἐὰν ὁμολογήσῃ ὅτι Ἰησοῦς ἐστιν ὁ υἱὸς τοῦ θεοῦ, ὁ θεὸς ἐν αὐτῷ μένει καὶ αὐτὸς ἐν τῷ θεῷ. ¹⁶καὶ ἡμεῖς ἐγνώκαμεν καὶ πεπιστεύκαμεν τὴν ἀγάπην ἣν ἔχει ὁ θεὸς ἐν ἡμῖν.

Clausal Outline Translated for 1 John 4:11–16c

^4:11a Ἀγαπητοί, **εἰ** οὕτως ὁ θεὸς **ἠγάπησεν** ἡμᾶς,
^4:11a Beloved, **if** God so loved us,

|

^4:11b **καὶ** ἡμεῖς **ὀφείλομεν** ἀλλήλους **ἀγαπᾶν**.
^4:11b *then* **we** ourselves **are obligated** to love one another.

^4:12a θεὸν οὐδεὶς πώποτε **τεθέαται**·
^4:12a No one **has seen** God at any time;

    ^4:12b **ἐὰν ἀγαπῶμεν** ἀλλήλους,
    ^4:12b **if we** *persist in* **loving** one another,

    |

^4:12c ὁ θεὸς ἐν ἡμῖν **μένει**
^4:12c God **abides** in us,

^4:12d καὶ ἡ ἀγάπη αὐτοῦ **τετελειωμένη** ἐν ἡμῖν **ἐστιν**.
^4:12d and his love **is perfected** in us.

^4:13a Ἐν τούτῳ **γινώσκομεν** (ὅτι ἐν αὐτῷ **μένομεν** καὶ αὐτὸς [**μένει**] ἐν ἡμῖν)
^4:13a **By this** **we know** (that we remain in God and he [*remains*] in us),

^{4:13c} ὅτι ἐκ τοῦ πνεύματος αὐτοῦ **δέδωκεν** ἡμῖν.
^{4:13c} **that he has given** to us *a portion of* his spirit.

^{4:14} καὶ ἡμεῖς **τεθεάμεθα** καὶ **μαρτυροῦμεν** (ὅτι ὁ πατὴρ ἀπέσταλκεν τὸν υἱὸν σωτῆρα τοῦ κόσμου).
^{4:14} And **we have seen** and **we** *now* **testify** (that the Father sent the Son to be the savior of the world).

^{4:15a} ὃς ἐὰν ὁμολογήσῃ (ὅτι Ἰησοῦς ἐστιν ὁ υἱὸς τοῦ θεοῦ),
^{4:15a} **Whoever professes** (that Jesus is the Son of God),

^{4:15b} ὁ θεὸς ἐν αὐτῷ **μένει**
^{4:15b} God **remains** in him,

^{4:15c} καὶ αὐτὸς [**μένει**] ἐν τῷ θεῷ.
^{4:15c} and he [*remains*] in God.

^{4:16a} καὶ ἡμεῖς **ἐγνώκαμεν**
^{4:16a} And *so* we **have come to know**

^{4:16b} καὶ **πεπιστεύκαμεν** τὴν ἀγάπην
^{4:16b} and **have** *come to* **believe** the love

^{4:16c} ἣν **ἔχει** ὁ θεὸς ἐν ἡμῖν.
^{4:16c} **which** God **has** for us.

Syntax Explained for 1 John 4:11–16c

^{4:11a} εἰ: The Greek word εἰ is a conjunction, which means "if" or "since" (BDAG 278.3). **Syntactically**, εἰ identifies the clause as a dependent conjunction clause. The entire clause, "Beloved, if God so loved us" (Ἀγαπητοί, εἰ οὕτως ὁ θεὸς ἠγάπησεν ἡμᾶς) functions adverbially. It modifies the verb, "we ought" (ὀφείλομεν). The word "so" (οὕτως) here seems to be a linguistic link to John 3:16 where we learn that God *so* loved the world that he gave his one and only son. The noun "beloved" is a vocative of direct address and serves as a paragraph break. **Semantically**, εἰ is a marker of a cause: "since" (NRSV NIV NLT) or "if" KJV ASV NASB ESV NET CNT). The rendering "since" appears appropriate because John has affirmed the truth of the protasis elsewhere in his letter, yet "if" is preferred to discourage the idea that John is lecturing (Wallace 1996, 694). What John affirms is evident in the accompanying verb.

ἠγάπησεν: The Greek word ἠγάπησεν is a third singular aorist active indicative from the verb ἀγαπάω that means, "I cherish" or "I have affection for" or "I love" or "to have a warm regard for and interest in another" (BDAG 5.1bα). **Syntactically**, ἠγάπησεν is the governing verb of the dependent adverbial εἰ clause. **Semantically**, ἠγάπησεν is a constative aorist: "loved" (cf. KJV NASB ESV NIV NET etc.). As in 4:10, ἠγάπησεν once again describes God's act of loving as a whole in a summary fashion without any specifics (Wallace 1996, 557). God loved ordinary people. He loved them enough that he gave Jesus to atone for their sins (1 John 3:10).

⁴·¹¹ᵇ καί: The Greek word καί is a conjunction that means "then" (BDAG 494.1bδ). **Syntactically**, καί introduces an independent conjunctive clause: "*then* we ourselves ought to love one another (καὶ ἡμεῖς ὀφείλομεν ἀλλήλους ἀγαπᾶν). The entire clause serves as the apodosis of the first class condition. **Semantically**, καί introduces the apodosis of the preceding clause: "then" (NET). While many translations consider καί to be a continuative connective, "also" (KJV ASV NASB NRSV ESV NIV CNT), the presence of the previous εἰ clause favors the translation "then." So based upon the assumption that God loved ordinary people, *then* some sort of conclusion is expected and is found in the next two verbs.

ὀφείλομεν: The Greek word ὀφείλομεν is a first plural present active indicative from the verb ὀφείλω that means, "I am obligated" or to be under obligation to meet certain social and moral expectation (BDAG 743.2aβ). **Syntactically**, ὀφείλομεν is the main verb of the independent conjunctive καί clause that serves as an apodosis. The subject is the emphatic personal pronoun "we" (ἡμεῖς) and refers to John and the orthodox readers of the letter. The presence of this emphatic pronoun is to emphasize the point that what God has done, we should imitate (Culy 2004, 110). **Semantically**, ὀφείλομεν is a customary present: "we are obligated" or "we must" or "we ought" (cf. KJV NASB ESV NIV NET etc). While the word "ought" indicates the believer's obligation, the customary present indicates an ongoing action (Wallace 1996, 521). John underscores a believers ongoing obligation. That obligation is revealed in the infinitive (ἀγαπᾶν).

ἀγαπᾶν: The Greek word ἀγαπᾶν is a present active infinitive from the verb ἀγαπάω that means, "I love" or "to have a warm regard for and interest in another" person (BDAG 5.1aα). **Syntactically**, is part of the main verb. **Semantically**: ἀγαπᾶν is a complementary infinitive: "to love" (cf. KJV NASB ESV NIV NET etc). The infinitive completes the thought of the verb "ought" (ὀφείλομεν; cf. Wallace 1996, 598). Since God loved ordinary people enough that he gave Jesus to atone for their sins then those who believe in him ought to show a similar kind of love to fellow believers.

⁴·¹²ᵃ τεθέαται: The Greek word τεθέαται is third singular perfect middle indicative from the verb θεάομαι that means, "I see" or "I look at" or "to have an intent look at something" (BDAG 445.1a). **Syntactically**, τεθέαται is the main verb of the independent clause: "No one *has seen* God at any time" (θεὸν οὐδεὶς πώποτε τεθέαται). The subject of the verb is the indefinite pronoun "no one" (οὐδείς). **Semantically**, τεθέαται is an gnomic perfect: "has seen" (cf. KJV NASB ESV NIV NET etc). "No one" (οὐδείς) indicates a timeless truth about all people (Wallace 1996, 580). Unlike John's usage of this verb to describe his seeing Jesus (1 John 1:1), here John emphasizes that no one has seen God. So God must be made known in other ways.

⁴·¹²ᵇ ἐάν: The Greek word ἐάν is a conjunction, which means "if" (BDAG 267.1aα). **Syntactically**, ἐάν identifies the clause as a dependent conjunctive clause. The entire dependent ἐάν clause: "*if* we love one another" (ἐὰν ἀγαπῶμεν ἀλλήλους) functions adverbially, modifying the verb "remains (μένει) and the periphrastic construction "is perfected" (τετελειωμένη . . . ἐστιν). **Semantically**, ἐάν introduces a third class conditional clause of probability: "if" (cf. KJV NASB ESV NIV NET etc). The condition is uncertain of fulfillment but still likely (Wallace 1996, 696). What that uncertain condition is is found in the next verb.

ἀγαπῶμεν: The Greek word ἀγαπῶμεν is a first plural present active subjunctive from the verb ἀγαπάω that means, "I love" or "to have a warm regard for and interest in another" person (BDAG 5.1aα). The verb is in the subjunctive mood because ἐάν takes the subjunctive. **Syntactically**, ἀγαπῶμεν is the governing verb of the dependent adverbial ἐάν clause. The subject of the verb is the implied "we" embedded in the verb and refers to John and his readers. The direct object of the verb is the reciprocal pronoun "one another" (ἀλλήλους), indicating the type of love that is evidence of God existence within the community. **Semantically**, ἀγαπῶμεν is a customary present: "we *persist* in love" or "we love" (cf. KJV NASB ESV NIV NET etc.). The present underscores a pattern of behavior (Wallace 1996, 521). In the likelihood that a person persists in love toward other believers, a certain fact may be concluded. That fact is found in the next clause.

4:12c μένει: The Greek word μένει is a third singular present active indicative from the verb μένω that means, "I remain" or "I abide" or "I continue" or of "someone who does not leave" (BDAG 631.1αβ). **Syntactically**, μένει is the main verb of independent clause: "God *abides* in us" (ὁ θεὸς ἐν ἡμῖν μένει). It is the first of two clauses that function as an apodosis of the third class ἐάν adverbial clause. The subject is the noun, "God" (ὁ θεὸς). **Semantically**, μένει is a customary present: "remains" or "abides" (ASV NASB ESV CNT) or "lives" (NRSV NIV NLT; cf. KJV) or "resides" (NET). The present tense underscores God's continual presence in the lives of those who love others (Wallace 1996, 521). The relationship between the protasis (adverbial ἐάν clause) and the apodosis (independent μένει clause) is an evidence-inference construction. When believers love each other, it is evidence that God and his love abide in them and their community. And yet there is another apodosis.

4:12d καί: The Greek word καί is a conjunction that means "and" (BDAG 494.1a). **Syntactically**, καί introduces an independent conjunctive clause: "*and* his love is perfected in us" (καὶ ἡ ἀγάπη αὐτοῦ τετελειωμένη ἐν ἡμῖν ἐστιν). It too is an apodosis to the third class ἐάν adverbial clause. **Semantically**, καί is a coordinating connective: "and" (cf. KJV NASB ESV NIV NET etc). It introduces an additional element to John's inference drawn from a loving community of believers (Wallace 1996, 671), which is evident in the next verb.

τετελειωμένη . . . ἐστιν: The Greek word τετελειωμένη is a nominative singular feminine perfect middle participle from the verb τελειόω that means, "I perfect" or to overcome an imperfect state (BDAG 996.2eβ). The Greek word ἐστιν is third singular present active indicative from the verb εἰμί that acts as an auxiliary verb (BDAG 285.11a). **Syntactically**, τετελειωμένη . . . ἐστιν is a *perfect* periphrastic construction where a participle and a verb of being work together to form a finite verbal idea. This two verb construction is "a *round-about* way of saying what could be expressed by a single verb" (Wallace 1996, 647). The periphrasis is the main verb of the independent clause that is functioning as the second part of apodosis of the ἐάν clause. The subject is the nominal phrase "his love" (ἡ ἀγάπη αὐτοῦ). **Semantically**, τετελειωμένη . . . ἐστιν is an intensive perfect: "is perfected" (KJV ASV NASB NRSV ESV NET CNT). The perfect is used to emphasize the results or present state produced by a past action, namely perfection (Wallace 1996, 574). When believers love one another, they are imitating the selfless love of Jesus and God's love is manifested and completed among them. They are in the process of overcoming their imperfect state and thereby being perfected. So not only can it be seen that God abides in them, but also that God's love is perfected among them.

Syntactical Nugget: The gentive pronoun "his" (αὐτοῦ) in the nominal phrase "his love" (ἡ ἀγάπη αὐτοῦ) modifying the articular noun "love" (ἡ ἀγάπη) can be a subjective gentive (God's love) or an objective genitive (love for God). The difference between the two is substantial. Are believers manifesting God's love when they love one another or are they manifesting their love for God. Since God is the subject of the previous clause (God lives in us), it seems likely that this should be taken as a subjective genitive (Brown 1982, 521). Culy, however, suggests that it could be intentional ambiguity or "semantic density" on the part of John (Culy 2004, 111), meaning that we shouldn't make a choice, because John is being ambiguous. Nevertheless, classifying "his" (αὐτοῦ) as a subjective genitive seems best. God's love is seen in the life of the believer when they love others. And this self-less imitation of God is evidence that God has an abiding relationship with them (see 1

John 3:24; also 2:5, 20, 27). All of this is perhaps an answer to Jesus' prayer in John 17:23 that his followers might be perfected into one (Bateman 2008, 471).

4:13a ἐν τούτῳ: The Greek word ἐν is a preposition, which means "by" (BDAG 328.5b). The Greek word τούτῳ is declined as a dative singular neuter from the demonstrative pronoun τοῦτο, which means "this one" (BDAG 741.1bβ). **Syntactically,** ἐν τούτῳ introduces an independent prepositional clause: *"by this* we know that we remain in him and he [remains] in us" (Ἐν τούτῳ γινώσκομεν ὅτι ἐν αὐτῷ μένομεν καὶ αὐτὸς ἐν ἡμῖν). "By this" (ἐν τούτῳ) occurs frequently in 1 John (2:3, 4, 5, 3:10, 16, 19, 24; 4:2, 9, 10, 17; 5:2). **Semantically,** ἐν τούτῳ can either be anaphoric, pointing back to the preceding discussion, or cataphoric, pointing forward. Here *"by this"* is cataphoric, and points forward to the ὅτι clause. The content of the prepositional phrase is found in the ὅτι clause (v. 13b).

γινώσκομεν: The Greek word γινώσκομεν is a first plural present active indicative from the verb γινώσκω that means, "I know" or "I know about" or to arrive at a knowledge of something" (BDAG 200.1). **Syntactically,** γινώσκομεν is the main verb of the independent clause. The subject of the verb is an implied "we" embedded in the verb and refers to the orthodox readers of the letter who live in love for other believers. **Semantically,** γινώσκομεν is a customary present: "I know" (cf. KJV NASB ESV NET NIV etc.). It points out that believers have a consistent knowledge (Wallace 1996, 521). It's not a "secret" knowledge because John provides the content of what all believers know in the ὅτι clause.

ὅτι: The Greek word ὅτι is a conjunction, which means "that" (BDAG 731.1c). **Syntactically,** ὅτι introduces a dependent conjunctive clause: *"that* we remain in him and he [remains] in us" (ὅτι ἐν αὐτῷ μένομεν καὶ αὐτὸς ἐν ἡμῖν). It functions substantivally as the direct object of the verb of perception "we know" (γινώσκομεν). The entire ὅτι clause is placed in parenthesis in order to visualize its grammatical contribution to the independent clause. **Semantically,** ὅτι is indirect discourse: "that" (cf. KJV NASB ESV NET NIV). It provides the content of the believer's knowledge (Wallace 1996, 456). Believers can know on a regular basis they have an abiding relationship with God.

μένομεν: The Greek word μένομεν is a first plural present active indicative from the verb μένω that means, "I remain" or "I abide" or "I continue" or of "someone who does not leave" (BDAG 631.1αβ). **Syntactically,** μένομεν is the governing verb of the first part of the compound dependent substantival ὅτι clause. The subject is an implied "we" embedded in the verb and references John and his readers. **Semantically,** μένομεν is a customary present: "remains" or "abides" (ASV NASB ESV CNT) or "lives" (NRSV NIV NLT) or "resides" (NET). The present tense underscores our continual relationship with God (Wallace 1996, 521). Believers can have a definitive knowledge that they have an abiding relationship with God.

καί: The Greek word καί is a conjunction that means "and" (BDAG 494.1a). **Syntactically,** καί introduces the second part of the substantival conjunctive clause: *"and* he [remains] in us" (καὶ αὐτὸς ἐν ἡμῖν). **Semantically,** καί is a coordinating connective of two clauses within the dependent substantival ὅτι clause: "and" (cf. KJV NASB ESV NIV NET etc.). It introduces some additional information about their relationship (Wallace 1996, 671). John adds more information to the simple fact that his readers have a relationship with God. That information is found in the next verb.

[μένει]: The Greek word μένει is a third singular present active indicative from the verb μένω that means, "I remain" or "I abide" or "I continue" or of "someone who does not leave" (BDAG 631.1αβ). **Syntactically,** μένει is an ellipsis and serves as the governing verb of the second part of the dependent substantival ὅτι clause. The subject is the emphatic pronoun "he" (αὐτὸς). **Semantically,** "remains" or "abides" (ASV NASB NRSV ESV CNT) or "lives" (NIV; cf. NLT) or "resides" (NET). The present tense underscores God's continual relationship with believers (Wallace 1996, 521). So not only do his readers abide in God, John adds here that God abides in them as well. It is not a one way relationship.

4:13b ὅτι: The Greek word ὅτι is a conjunction, which means "that" (BDAG 732.2a). **Syntactically,** ὅτι serves to introduce the dependent conjunctive clause: *"that* he has given us of his Spirit" (ὅτι ἐκ τοῦ πνεύματος αὐτοῦ δέδωκεν ἡμῖν). It modifies the demonstrative pronoun, "this" (τοῦτο). **Semantically,** ὅτι is epexegetical: "that" (NET; cf. NLT). The ὅτι clause explains or clarifies the demonstrative (Wallace 1996, 459). The evidence of an abiding relationship with Jesus is highlighted in the next verb.

δέδωκεν: The Greek word δέδωκεν is a third singular perfect active indicative from the verb δίδωμι that means, "I give" or "I grant" (BDAG 243.17b). **Syntactically,** δέδωκεν is the governing verb of the dependent adjectival ὅτι clause. The subject is an implied "he" embedded in the verb and is a reference to God. **Semantically,** δέδωκεν is an extensive perfect: "he has given" (cf. KJV NASB ESV NIV NET etc). It emphasizes the completed action of God's giving of his spirit (Wallace 1996, 577). John's readers can be assured that they have relationship with God because he has given them his Spirit (cf. 2:20, 27; 3:24; 4:13). The evidence is the presence of God's Spirit in our lives.

Sematical Nugget: The prepositional phrase ἐκ τοῦ πνεύματος αὐτοῦ has a few challenges. On the one hand, a literal rendering of the phrase *"of* his Spirit" (ἐκ τοῦ πνεύματος αὐτοῦ) seems like a strange way to describe the believer's relationship with Jesus. On the other hand, the preposition ἐκ could be classifed as source (*from* the Spirit). However it seems more reasonable to classify ἐκ as partitive (*a portion* of the Spirit). Although it seems strange to think that God has only given us a portion of his Spirit and not his entire Spirit, Culy, following Fee, argues that this is the best way to understand it (Culy 2004, 112). The idea is not that John's readers were once for all given the Spririt at conversion, but that God constantly provides them with empowerment from the Spirit throughout the course of their spiritual lives. Therefore, the presence of God's spiritual empowering in their daily lives is evidence that they have an abiding relationship with God.

4:14 καί: The Greek word καί is a conjunction that means "and" (BDAG 495.1a). **Syntactically,** καί introduces the independent conjunctive clause: *"and* we have seen *and* testify that the father sent the son to be the savior of the world" (καὶ ἡμεῖς τεθεάμεθα καὶ μαρτυροῦμεν ὅτι ὁ πατὴρ ἀπέσταλκεν τὸν υἱὸν σωτῆρα τοῦ κόσμου). **Semantically,** καί is a coordinating connective of two independent clauses: "and" (KJV ASV NASB NRSV ESV NET NIV). It introduces some additional information about the reader's reciplicated abiding relationship with God (Wallace 1996, 671). There is the sense that John echoes the beginning of the letter where he focused on eyewitness accounts to the life of Jesus. They beheld the selfless love of the father which was manifested through the sending of his Son into the world in order to save it from sin.

τεθεάμεθα: The Greek word τεθεάμεθα is first plural perfect middle indicative from the verb θεάομαι that means, "I see" or "I behold" or "to perceive something above and beyond what is merely seen with the eye" (BDAG 445.3a). **Syntactically,** τεθεάμεθα is the first main verb of the independent conjunctive clause. The subject of the verb is the emphatic personal pronoun "we" (ἡμεῖς). **Semantically,** τεθεάμεθα is an extensive perfect: "we have seen" (cf. KJV NASB ESV NIV NET etc). It emphasizes the completed action of what John saw in the past from which his current message is founded (Wallace 1996, 577). Since John and other eyewitnesses have seen the life, death, and resurrection of Jesus, they are able to testify that God indeed sent his son into the world to save it.

μαρτυροῦμεν: The Greek word μαρτυροῦμεν is a first plural present active indicative from the verb μαρτυρέω that means, "I bear witness" or to confirm or attest something to be true based upon personal knowledge (BDAG 618.1αβ). **Syntactically**, μαρτυροῦμεν is the second main verb of the compound independent conjunctive clause joined with a καί. The subject is also the emphatic personal pronoun "we" (ἡμεῖς). **Semantically**, μαρτυροῦμεν is a progressive present: "*now* testify" (NLT) or "do testify" (KJV NRSV). It emphasizes John's continuous proclamation (Wallace 1996, 518). John and other eyewitnesses are right now bearing witness to what they have seen (cf. 1:2c). The specifics of their witness is disclosed in the next dependent ὅτι clause.

ὅτι: The Greek word ὅτι is a conjunction, which means "that" (BDAG 731.1a). **Syntactically**, ὅτι introduces a dependent conjunctive clause: "*that* the father sent his son to be the savior of the world" (ὅτι ὁ πατὴρ ἀπέσταλκεν τὸν υἱὸν σωτῆρα τοῦ κόσμου). It functions substantivally as the direct object of the compound verbs of perception: "we have seen" (τεθεάμεθα) and "we bear witness" (μαρτυροῦμεν). The entire ὅτι clause is placed in parenthesis in order to visualize its contribution to the independent clause. **Semantically**, ὅτι is an indirect discourse: "that" (cf. KJV NASB ESV NIV NET etc). The ὅτι clause provides the content of what John and other eyewitnesses testify (Wallace 1996, 456). The content of their message is evident in the next discussion about ἀπέσταλκεν.

ἀπέσταλκεν: The Greek word ἀπέσταλκεν is a third singular perfect active indicative from the verb ἀποστέλλω that means, "I send" or to dispatch someone for the achievement of some objective" (BDAG 121. 1bγ). **Syntactically**, ἀπέσταλκεν is the governing verb of the dependent substantival clause. The subject is the proper noun "the Father" (ὁ πατὴρ). We have here another double accusative object-complement construction. The direct object of the verb "sent" (ἀπέσταλκεν) is the noun "son" (τὸν υἱὸν). The second accusative functions as a complementary noun, "the savior" (σωτῆρα). This type of construction is often translated with the words "to be." Therefore, we should translate this, "that the Father has sent the son *to be* the savior of the world" (Wallace 1996, 181–186). **Semantically**, ἀπέσταλκεν is an extensive perfect: "he sent" (KJV ASV NLT) or "has sent" (NASB NRSV ESV NIV NET CNT). It emphasizes a past action from which a present state emerges (Wallace 1996, 577). Since the father sent the son into the world, its inhabitants are now able to experience salvation. They saw with their eyes and now bear witness to the fact that Jesus came to save the world.

4:15a ὃς ἐάν: The Greek word ὃς is a nominative singular neuter from the relative pronoun ὅς which means, "who" (BDAG 727.1ja). The Greek word ἐάν is a conjunction, which means "when" or "whoever" (BDAG 268.2). It is typically rendered "whoever" (NASB ESV cf. KJV ASV) or "anyone" (NIV NET CNT). **Syntactically**, the Greek construction ὃς ἐάν is an indefinite relative pronoun. It identifies the clause as a dependent pronominal clause. The entire clause "*whoever* confesses that Jesus is the son of God" (ὃς ἐὰν ὁμολογήσῃ ὅτι Ἰησοῦς ἐστιν ὁ υἱὸς τοῦ θεοῦ) functions adjectivally. It modifies the personal pronouns "him" (αὐτῷ) and "he" (αὐτὸς), located in the subsequent independent clause (4:15b). The entire ὃς ἐάν clause provides further information about the person within whom God remains.

ὁμολογήσῃ: The Greek word ὁμολογήσῃ is a third singular aorist active subjunctive from the verb ὁμολογέω that means, "I confess" or "I profess" or to acknowledge something ordinarily in public (BDAG 708.4b). **Syntactically**, ὁμολογήσῃ is the governing verb of the dependent adjectival indefinite relative ὃς ἐάν clause. The subject is the indefinite relative pronoun "whoever" (ὃς ἐάν).

Semantically, ὁμολογήσῃ is a gnomic aorist: "professes" or "confesses" (NASB ESV) or "confess" (NRSV NET CNT). It presents a timeless or general fact about anyone who professes Jesus (Wallace 1996, 562). In 1 John 1:9, this particular verb occurs in the present tense "if we confess our sin," while here it is in the aorist tense. Why the shift in tense? In 1:9 there is the expressesd need for every believer to habitually confess their sins, while here John merely describes a generic one time event.

ὅτι: The Greek word ὅτι is a conjunction, which means "that" (BDAG 731.1a). **Syntactically**, ὅτι introduces a dependent conjunctive clause: "*that* Jesus is God's son" (ὅτι Ἰησοῦς ἐστιν ὁ υἱὸς τοῦ θεοῦ). It functions substantivally as the direct object of the verb, "professes" (ὁμολογήσῃ). The entire ὅτι clause is placed in parenthesis in order to visualize its contribution as the dependent indefinite relative ὃς ἐάν clause. **Semantically**, ὅτι is an indirect discourse: "that" (cf. KJV NASB ESV NIV NET etc). It provides the content of the profession or confession (Wallace 1996, 456). The profession is about Jesus as God's son (= God's Messiah).

Theological Nugget: The content of ὁμολογέω is rather consistent in Johannine literature. In 1 John 2:23, John underscores that the person who persists in their confession about *Jesus as Messiah* has a relationship with God. In 1 John 4:2–3, the emphasis is the person who repeatedly acknowleges in his or her teaching that *Jesus was human and is God's Messiah* reveals that their teaching is from God versus the person who does not profess that *Jesus was human and is God's Messiah*. In 1 John 4:15, there is once again the emphasis on professing *Jesus as God's Son* (= God's Messiah) and God's remaining within that person. This confession of Jesus' identity is very significant in 1 John. It is a must to believe that Jesus is indeed the Messiah for a relationship with God the Father to exist.

ἐστιν: The Greek word ἐστιν is third singular present active indicative from the verb εἰμί that means, "is" or "to be in close connection with" (BDAG 283.2a). **Syntactically**, ἐστιν is the governing verb of the dependent substantival ὅτι clause. The subject of the verb is the proper noun "Jesus" (Ἰησοῦς). This is an example where a proper name assumes the position of the subject of an εἰμί verb over an articular noun or messianic title, "son of God" (Wallace 1996, 45). **Semantically**, ἐστιν is an equative present: "is" (cf. KJV NASB ESV NIV NET etc). John equates Jesus with God's Son (= Messiah).

4:15b μένει: The Greek word μένει is a third singular present active indicative from the verb μένω that means, "I remain" or "I abide" or "I continue" or of "someone who does not leave" (BDAG 631.1aβ). **Syntactically**, μένει is the first main verb of the compound independent clause: "God *remains* in him and he remains in God" (ὁ θεὸς ἐν αὐτῷ μένει καὶ αὐτὸς ἐν τῷ θεῷ). The subject is the proper noun "God" (ὁ θεὸς). **Semantically**, μένει is a customary present: "remains" or "dwells" (KJV) or "abides" (ASV NASB NRSV ESV CNT) or "lives" (NIV; cf. NLT) or "resides" (NET). The present tense underscores God's continual relationship (Wallace 1996, 521). John tells his readers that God has a continual relationship with those who profess that Jesus is God's Messiah.

4:15c καί: The Greek word καί is a conjunction that means "and" (BDAG 494.1ba). **Syntactically**, καί introduces another independent conjunctive clause: "*and* he remains in God" (καὶ αὐτὸς ἐν τῷ θεῷ). **Semantically**, καί is coordinating connective: "and" (cf. KJV NASB ESV NIV NET etc). It links two independent clauses together and provides additional information (Wallace 1996, 671). More specifically, John expands his previous thoughts on God's relationship with those who profess Jesus to be Messiah.

[μένει]: The Greek word μένει is a third singular present active indicative from the verb μένω that means, "I remain" or "I abide" or "I continue" or of "someone who does not leave" (BDAG 631.1aβ). **Syntactically**, μένει serves as the elliptical main verb of the second part of the compound independent clause. The subject is the emphatic personal pronoun "he" (αὐτὸς). **Semantically**, μένει is a customary present: "remains." Most translations do not indicate the presence of an elliptical [μένει]. It's understood. The present tense underscores for his readers their continual relationship with God (Wallace 1996, 521). In this additional information (καί), John underscores that the one who confesses that Jesus is God's son has an abiding relationship with God.

4:16a καί: The Greek word καί is a conjunction which means "and so" or "indeed" or "to introduce a result that comes from what precedes" (BDAG 495.1bζ). **Syntactically**, καί introduces an independent conjunctive clause: "*and* we have come to know and have believed the love" (καὶ ἡμεῖς ἐγνώκαμεν καὶ πεπιστεύκαμεν τὴν ἀγάπην). **Semantically**, καί is inferential: "and so" (NIV) or "so" (NRSV ESV CNT). While most translations translate καί as "and" (KJV ASV NET), it seems more reasonable to also suggest that καί is inferential and underscores John's concluding remarks (Wallace 1996, 673).

ἐγνώκαμεν: The Greek word ἐγνώκαμεν is a first plural perfect active indicative from the verb γινώσκω that means, "I know" or "I have come to know" (BDAG 200.6aα). **Syntactically**, ἐγνώκαμεν is one of two main verbs of an independent conjunctive καί clause. The subject of the verb is the emphatic pronoun "we" (ἡμεῖς) and refers to John and readers who have an abiding relationship with God. The accusative "love" (τὴν ἀγάπην) serves as an accusative for both "we have come to know" and "we have believed" (ἐγνώκαμεν and πεπιστεύκαμεν). **Semantically**, ἐγνώκαμεν is an extensive perfect: "we have come to know" (NASB ESV NET) or "we have known" (KJV NRSV). It emphasizes a past act of knowledge from which a present state of understanding exists (Wallace 1996, 577). John's readers have come to *know* of God's love.

4:16b πεπιστεύκαμεν: The Greek word πεπιστεύκαμεν is a first plural perfect active indicative from the verb πιστεύω that means, "I believe" or "to consider something to be true and therefore worthy of one's trust" (BDAG 816.1ba). **Syntactically**, πεπιστεύκαμεν is the second verb of this independent conjunctive καί clause. The subject of the verb is the emphatic pronoun "we" (ἡμεῖς) that refers to John and readers who have a relationship with God. **Semantically**, πεπιστεύκαμεν is an extensive perfect: "have *come to* believe" or "have believed" (NASB). It empasizes a past action from which a present state emerges (Wallace 1996, 577). John's readers have also come to *believe* the message about God's love.

4:16c ἥν: The Greek word ἥν is accusative singular feminine from the relative pronoun ὅς that means, "which" (BDAG 725.1a). **Syntactically**, ἥν introduces a relative clause: "*which* God has for us" (ἥν ἔχει ὁ θεὸς ἐν ἡμῖν). It funtions adjectivally modifying the noun "love" (ἀγάπην) This relative pronoun is in the accusative case because is serves as the direct object of the verb "has" (ἔχει). It provides the further information about the love of God.

ἔχει: The Greek word ἔχει is a third singular present active indicative from the verb ἔχω that means, "I have" or "I possess" (BDAG 420.1a). **Syntactically**, ἔχει is the governing verb of the dependent relative clause. The subject is the articular proper noun "God" (ὁ θεὸς). **Semantically**, ἔχει is a customary present: "has" (cf. KJV NASB ESV NIV NET etc). It emphasizes ongoing state for believers (Wallace 1996, 521). God has an on-going love relationship with believers.

Syntactical Nugget: In order to figure out exactly what John had in mind we have a choice to make on how to translate the prepositional phrase ἐν ἡμῖν. Brown translates it spatially: "in us." He argues that it refers to God's love which is expressed in believers when they love each other (Brown 1982, 525-526). In 4:12, John points out that when the believer shows self-less love, they prove that God abides in them. Most translations and commentators, however, translate ἐν ἡμῖν referentially: "for us." Thus John references God's love for us as demonstrated in the self-less sending of Jesus, the Messiah. In 4:9, God's love is revealed among us through the sending of his one and only son into the world. John's broader context underscores that we have come to know what selfless love is through the example of the Father sending Jesus into the world to save ordinary people from their sin. Based upon this selfless example, believers who have a relationship with God, should imitate that same selfless love (see Bateman 2008, 485).

1 John 4:16d–21

Verb Recognition for 1 John 4:16d–21

¹⁶ᵈὉ θεὸς ἀγάπη **ἐστίν**, καὶ ὁ **μένων** ἐν τῇ ἀγάπῃ ἐν τῷ θεῷ **μένει** καὶ ὁ θεὸς ἐν αὐτῷ **μένει**. ¹⁷ἐν τούτῳ **τετελείωται** ἡ ἀγάπη μεθ' ἡμῶν, ἵνα παρρησίαν **ἔχωμεν** ἐν τῇ ἡμέρᾳ τῆς κρίσεως, ὅτι καθὼς ἐκεῖνός **ἐστιν** καὶ ἡμεῖς **ἐσμεν** ἐν τῷ κόσμῳ τούτῳ. ¹⁸φόβος οὐκ **ἔστιν** ἐν τῇ ἀγάπῃ, ἀλλ' ἡ τελεία ἀγάπη ἔξω **βάλλει** τὸν φόβον, ὅτι ὁ φόβος κόλασιν **ἔχει**, ὁ δὲ **φοβούμενος** οὐ **τετελείωται** ἐν τῇ ἀγάπῃ. ¹⁹ἡμεῖς **ἀγαπῶμεν**, ὅτι αὐτὸς πρῶτος **ἠγάπησεν** ἡμᾶς. ²⁰ἐάν τις **εἴπῃ** ὅτι Ἀγαπῶ τὸν θεόν, καὶ τὸν ἀδελφὸν αὐτοῦ **μισῇ**, ψεύστης **ἐστίν**· ὁ γὰρ μὴ **ἀγαπῶν** τὸν ἀδελφὸν αὐτοῦ ὃν **ἑώρακεν**, τὸν θεὸν ὃν οὐχ **ἑώρακεν** οὐ **δύναται** **ἀγαπᾶν**. ²¹καὶ ταύτην τὴν ἐντολὴν **ἔχομεν** ἀπ' αὐτοῦ, ἵνα ὁ **ἀγαπῶν** τὸν θεὸν **ἀγαπᾷ** καὶ τὸν ἀδελφὸν αὐτοῦ.

Clausal Outline for Translating 1 John 4:16d–21

⁴:¹⁶ᵈ Ὁ θεὸς ἀγάπη **ἐστίν**,
⁴:¹⁶ᵈ God **is** love,

⁴:¹⁶ᵉ καὶ ὁ μένων ἐν τῇ ἀγάπῃ ἐν τῷ θεῷ **μένει**
⁴:¹⁶ᵉ and the one who abides in love **abides** in God

⁴:¹⁶ᶠ καὶ ὁ θεὸς ἐν αὐτῷ **μένει**.
⁴:¹ᶠᶜ and God **abides** in him.

⁴:¹⁷ᵃ ἐν τούτῳ τετελείωται ἡ ἀγάπη μεθ' ἡμῶν,
⁴:¹⁷ᵃ **By this**, love **is perfected** with us,

⁴:¹⁷ᵇ ἵνα παρρησίαν ἔχωμεν ἐν τῇ ἡμέρᾳ τῆς κρίσεως,
⁴:¹⁷ᵇ **so that we may have** confidence in the day of judgment,

⁴:¹⁷ᶜ ὅτι . . . καὶ ἡμεῖς ἐσμεν ἐν τῷ κόσμῳ τούτῳ.
⁴:¹⁷ᶜ **because** . . . so also **are we** in this world

|
4:17d **καθὼς** ἐκεῖνός **ἐστιν**
4:17d **just as** he (=Jesus) **is**

4:18a φόβος οὐκ **ἔστιν** ἐν τῇ ἀγάπῃ,
4:18a There **is** no fear in love,

4:18b ἀλλ᾽ ἡ τελεία ἀγάπη ἔξω **βάλλει** τὸν φόβον,
4:18b but perfect love **expels** fear,

|
4:18c **ὅτι** ὁ φόβος κόλασιν **ἔχει**,
4:18c **because** fear **includes** punishment,

4:18d ὁ δὲ [ὅτι] φοβούμενος οὐ **τετελείωται** ἐν τῇ ἀγάπῃ.
4:18d and [*because*] the one who fears **is** not **perfected** in love.

4:19a ἡμεῖς **ἀγαπῶμεν**,
4:19a As for us **we** *persist in* **love**
|
4:19b **ὅτι** αὐτὸς πρῶτος **ἠγάπησεν** ἡμᾶς.
4:19b **because** **he** first **loved** us.

4:20a **ἐάν** τις **εἴπῃ** (ὅτι Ἀγαπῶ τὸν θεόν),
4:20a **If** someone **says**, "I love God,"
|
4:20b καὶ [**ἐάν** τις] τὸν ἀδελφὸν αὐτοῦ **μισῇ**,
4:20b and [*that someone*] **hates** his brother or sister
|
4:20c ψεύστης **ἐστίν·**
4:20c he **is** a liar;

4:20d ὁ **γὰρ** μὴ ἀγαπῶν τὸν ἀδελφὸν αὐτοῦ . . . , τὸν θεὸν . . . οὐ **δύναται** ἀγαπᾶν.
4:20d **for** the one who does not love his brother or sister . . . **is unable** to love God.

| |
4:20e **ὃν ἑώρακεν**   4:20f **ὃν** οὐχ **ἑώρακεν**
4:20e whom **he has seen**   4:20f whom **he has** not **seen**

4:21a **καὶ** ταύτην τὴν ἐντολὴν **ἔχομεν** ἀπ᾽ αὐτοῦ,
4:21a **And** this commandment **we have** from him (= God),
|
4:21b **ἵνα** ὁ ἀγαπῶν τὸν θεὸν **ἀγαπᾷ** καὶ τὸν ἀδελφὸν αὐτοῦ.
4:21b *namely* **that** the one who loves God **should love** his brother and sister also.

Syntax Explained for 1 John 4:16d–21

^{4:16d} ἐστίν: The Greek word ἐστίν is third singular present active indicative from the verb εἰμί that means "is" or "to be in close connection with" (BDAG 283.2a). **Syntactically**, ἐστίν is the main verb of the independent anacoluthon clause: "God is love" (Ὁ θεὸς ἀγάπη ἐστίν). The subject of the verb is the articular proper noun "God" (Ὁ θεὸς). **Semantically**, ἐστιν is a gnomic present: "is" (cf. KJV NASB ESV NIV NET etc.). It identifies a timeless fact about God (Wallace 1996, 523). The verb equates God with his abiding character (cf. 1:5d). The equative nature of the verb of being here does not mean that this definition can go both ways (for more information, see note 4:8b).

^{4:16e} καί: The Greek word καί is a conjunction that means "and" (BDAG 494.1bα). **Syntactically**, καί introduces the independent conjunctive clause: "*and* the one who remains in love remains in God" (καὶ ὁ μένων ἐν τῇ ἀγάπῃ ἐν τῷ θεῷ μένει). **Semantically**, καί is a coordinating connective: "and" (KJV ASV NASB NRSV ESV NIV NET NLT). The entire conjunctive clause links two independent clauses together and provides additional information about those who share God's character (Wallace 1996, 671). That additional information is found in the discussions about the next two Greek terms in the clause.

μένων: The Greek word μένων is a nominative masculine singular present active participle from the verb μένω that means, "I remain" or "I abide" or "I continue" or of "someone who does not leave" (BDAG 631.1αβ). **Syntactically**, μένων is functioning substantially: "the one who remains" or "the one who abides" (NASB; cf. NASB) or "the one who resides" (NET) or "whoever lives" (NIV; cf. NLT). The entire phrase, "the one who remains in love" (ὁ μένων ἐν τῇ ἀγάπῃ) is functioning as the subject of the verb "remains" (μένει). **Semantically**, μένων is a gnomic present: "abides" (ASV NASB NRSV ESV CNT) or "lives" (NIV NLT; cf. NLT). It describes a timeless fact about a generic believer (Wallace 1996, 523, 615), ordinary people who have a relationship with God.

μένει: The Greek word μένει is a third singular present active indicative from the verb μένω that means, "I remain" or "I abide" or "I continue" or of "someone who does not leave" (BDAG 631.1αβ). **Syntactically**, μένει is the main verb of the independent conjunctive καί clause. The subject is the participial phrase: *"The one who remains* in love" (ὁ μένων ἐν τῇ ἀγάπῃ). **Semantically**, μένει is a gnomic present: "abides" (ASV NASB NRSV ESV CNT) or "lives" (NIV NLT; cf. NLT). It describes a timeless fact (Wallace 1996, 523). Believers who demonstrate love show that they have a relationship with God.

^{4:16f} καί: The Greek word καί is a conjunction which means "and" (BDAG 494.1bα). **Syntactically**, καί introduces the independent conjunctive clause: "*and* God remains in him" (καὶ ὁ θεὸς ἐν αὐτῷ μένει). **Semantically**, καί is coordinating connective: "and" (KJV ASV NASB NRSV ESV NIV NET NLT). The entire conjunctive clause provides additional information about those who have relationship with God (Wallace 1996, 671).

μένει: The Greek word μένει is a third singular present active indicative from the verb μένω that means "I remain" or "I abide" or "I continue" or of "someone who does not leave" (BDAG 631.1αβ). **Syntactically**, μένει is the main verb of the independent conjunctive clause. The subject is the articular proper noun "God" (ὁ θεὸς). **Semantically**, μένει is a gnomic present: "abides" (ASV NASB NRSV ESV CNT) or "lives" (NIV NLT; cf. NLT). It describes a timeless fact (Wallace 1996, 523). The believer who demonstrates self-less love has a continual abiding relationship with God.

4:17a ἐν τούτῳ: The Greek word ἐν is a preposition that means "by" (BDAG 328.5b). The Greek word τούτῳ is declined as a dative singular neuter from the demonstrative pronoun τοῦτο that means "this one" (BDAG 741.1bβ). **Syntactically**, ἐν τούτῳ introduces an independent prepositional clause: "*by this* love has been perfected with us" (ἐν τούτῳ τετελείωται ἡ ἀγάπη μεθ᾽ ἡμῶν). "By this" (ἐν τούτῳ) occurs frequently in 1 John (2:3, 4, 5, 3:10, 16, 19, 24; 4:2, 9, 10, 13; 5:2). **Semantically**, ἐν τούτῳ can either be anaphoric, pointing back to the preceding discussion, or cataphoric, pointing forward. Here "by this" ἐν τούτῳ points back (anaphoric). It is a summary of the previous material. God's love is perfected in a believer when they imitate it in their own values and behavior, providing the believer with confidence when they stand before God's judgment.

Semantical Nugget: The usual rule is that the prepositional phrase is cataphoric, if it is followed by a subordinating conjunction. So some classify the phrase as cataphoric either pointing forward to the ἵνα clause or the subsequent ὅτι clause. If ἐν τούτῳ points forward to the ἵνα clause, then God perfects love in the life of the believer so that they can be confident when they are judged by him. It seem odd though to suggest that love is perfect already in a future event. If ἐν τούτῳ points forward to the ὅτι clause, then love is perfected in us when we love just like Jesus loved when he was in the world. Having a ὅτι clause explicating a demonstrative is common in 1 John, but the intervening ἵνα clause makes this difficult. The best option seems to be that ἐν τούτῳ points back and serves as a summary of the previous material (anaphoric). Thus John summarizes that if believers continue in their abiding relationship with God by imitating his selfless love, then love itself has come to maturity in them (Strecker, 1996, 162). This option would seem to fit with the author's emphasis in 4:12 that God's love is perfected in us when we love others (cf. Bateman 2008, 488-189; also Culy 2004, 115-116).

τετελείωται: The Greek word τετελείωται is a third singular perfect passive indicative from the verb τελειόω that means, "I perfect" or to overcome and imperfect state (BDAG 996.2eβ). **Syntactically**, τετελείωται is the main verb of the independent clause. The subject is the articular noun "love" (ἡ ἀγάπη). **Semantically**, τετελείωται is an intensive perfect: "is perfected" (NASB NET CNT; cf. ESV). It emphasizes the present state of love within the believer which emerges from a past action (Wallace 1996, 574). John's summarized point is that love is being perfected in the believer due to God, who is love, abiding in us.

4:17b ἵνα: The Greek word ἵνα is a conjunction, which means "so that" (BDAG 477.3). **Syntactically**, ἵνα introduces a conjunctive dependent clause: "*so that* we might have confidence in the day of judgment" (ἵνα παρρησίαν ἔχωμεν ἐν τῇ ἡμέρᾳ τῆς κρίσεως). While it is possible to view the ἵνα clause as epexegetical to "this" (τούτῳ; KJV ASV NRSV NET CNT; BDAG 476.2e), it seems the entire ἵνα clause is adverbial. It modifies the verb "is perfected" (τετελείωται). See the discussion above for 4:17a ἐν τούτῳ. **Semantically**, ἵνα is a result: "so that" (NASB ESV NIV). It is a substitute for the infinitive of result (BDAG 477.3) and thereby expresses the result of the verb τετελείωται (Wallace 1996, 473). The result of God's love being perfected in the believer is found in their confidence.

ἔχωμεν: The Greek word ἔχωμεν is a first plural present active subjunctive from the verb ἔχω that means, "I have" or to experience an inner condition (BDAG 421.7aβ). The verb is in the subjunctive mood because ἵνα takes the subjunctive. **Syntactically**, ἔχωμεν is the governing verb of the dependent adverbial ἵνα clause. The subject is the pronoun "we" embedded in the verb and refers to John and his readers. **Semantically**, ἔχωμεν is an ingressive future present: "we may have" (KJV ASV NASB NRSV ESV NET CNT) or "we will have" (NIV; cf. NLT). It describes a condition (e.g. confidence) begun in the present time but will be experienced fully in the future (Wallace 1996, 537). Believers who exhibit God's love in their lives will have confidence when they stand before him on judgment day (cf. 5:14).

^{4:17c} ὅτι: The Greek word ὅτι is a conjunction, which means "because" (BDAG 732.4a). **Syntactically**, ὅτι introduces a dependent conjunctive clause: "*because* just as he is, so also are we in this world" (ὅτι καθὼς ἐκεῖνός ἐστιν καὶ ἡμεῖς ἐσμεν ἐν τῷ κόσμῳ τούτῳ). The entire clause functions adverbially. It modifies "we may have" (ἔχωμεν). **Semantically**, ὅτι is causal: "because" (cf. KJV NASB ESV NIV NET etc.). It provides the reason (Wallace 1996, 460) why believers can have confidence when we stand before God on judgment day. It's because of Jesus's example.

Syntactical Nugget: We have three options when it comes to classifying this ὅτι. First as discussed above, the clause could be functioning adjectivally providing us with the content of the demonstrative (for reasons why that does not seem to be the best option, see note 4:17a above). The next two options understand the force of the phrase to be causal, but which main verb, "is perfected" (τετελείωται) or "we have" (ἔχωμεν), does it modify? If the ὅτι modifies the verb "is perfected" (τετελείωται), then John would be telling us that the reason why love is perfected in the believer who has an abiding relationship with God is because they are imitating the selfless example of love that Jesus lived out while he was here. If, however, it modifies the verb, "we have" (ἔχωμεν), then John is providing us with a reason why we can be confident on judgment day.

ἐσμεν: The Greek word ἐσμεν is first plural present active indicative from the verb εἰμί that means, "is" or "to be in close connection with" (BDAG 283.2a). **Syntactically**, ἐσμεν is the governing verb of the dependent conjunctive ὅτι clause. The subject of the verb is an implied "we" embedded in the verb and refers to John and anyone else who has a relationship with God. The καὶ in this clause is not a coordinating connector but rather an adjunctive (so also; BDAG 495.2a; NASB ESV NET) that provides additional emphasis on the comparison between the believer who loves and the selfless life of Jesus (Wallace 1996, 671). **Semantically**, ἐσμεν is an equative present: "we are" (cf. KJV NASB ESV NIV NET etc.). It is an identifying statement that underscores the believer's close connection with the world, namely that believers live in this physical world.

^{4:17d} καθώς: The Greek word καθώς is a conjunction, which means "as" (BDAG 493.1). **Syntactically**, καθώς introduces a dependent conjunctive clause. The entire καθώς clause: "*just* as that one is" (καθὼς ἐκεῖνός ἐστιν) is functioning adverbially modifying the verb "we are" (ἐσμεν). **Semantically**, καθώς is comparative: "as" (KJV ASV NASB NRSV ESV CNT). It serves to make a comparison between Jesus and believers (Wallace 1996, 675). Believers who have a relationship with God are similar to Jesus in that they too live in the world.

ἐστιν: The Greek word ἐστιν is third singular present active indicative from the verb εἰμί that means, "is" or "to be in close connection with" or "to be in reference to location" (BDAG 283.2a or 284.3b). **Syntactically**, ἐστιν is the governing verb of the dependent conjunctive καθώς clause. The subject of the verb is the demonstrative pronoun "that one" (ἐκεῖνός). This particular demonstrative is virtually a technical term for Jesus throughout 1 John (2:6; 3:3, 5, 16; 4:17). **Semantically**, ἐστιν is equative: "is" (KJV ASV NASB NRSV ESV NET CNT). It underscores Jesus's historical presence in the world.

^{4:18a} ἐστιν: The Greek word ἐστιν is third singular present active indicative from the verb εἰμί that means, "is" or in reference to a person's condition (BDAG 284.3c). **Syntactically**, ἐστιν is the main verb of the independent clause: "no fear *is* in love" (φόβος οὐκ ἔστιν ἐν τῇ ἀγάπῃ). The subject of the verb is the noun "fear" (φόβος). **Semantically**, ἐστιν is gnomic present in that it is part of a generic statement that describes something that is true at any time (Wallace 1996, 523). John underscores that real love does not contain fear.

⁴ᐟ¹⁸ᵇ ἀλλ': The Greek word ἀλλά is a conjunction, which means "but" (BDAG 45.3). **Syntactically**, ἀλλά introduces an independent conjunctive clause: "*but* perfect love expels fear" (ἀλλ᾿ ἡ τελεία ἀγάπη ἔξω βάλλει τὸν φόβον). **Semantically**, ἀλλά is contrastive: "but" (cf. KJV NASB ESV NIV NET etc.). It introduces a strong contrast to underscore something that is true all the time. In this case, it contrasts John's depiction about love.

βάλλει: The Greek word βάλλει is a third singular present active indicative from the verb βάλλω that means, "I drive out" or "I expel" or "to force out" (BDAG 163.2). **Syntactically**, βάλλει is the main verb of the independent clause. The subject is the nominal phrase "perfect love" (ἡ τελεία ἀγάπη). **Semantically**, βάλλει is a gnomic present: "expels" (NLT) or "casts out" (KJV ASV NASB NRSV ESV CNT) or "drives out" (NIV NET). It too is part of a generic statement that describes something that is true at any time (Wallace 1996, 523). John is emphasizing a timeless truth about perfect love, namely that there is no fear in perfect love.

⁴ᐟ¹⁸ᶜ ὅτι: The Greek word ὅτι is a conjunction that means, "because" (BDAG 732.4a). **Syntactically**, ὅτι introduces two dependent conjunctive clauses: "*because* fear involves punishment and [*because*] the one who fears is not perfected in love" (ὅτι ὁ φόβος κόλασιν ἔχει [ὅτι] ὁ δὲ φοβούμενος οὐ τετελείωται ἐν τῇ ἀγάπῃ). Both ὅτι clauses function adverbially. They modify the verb "casts out" (βάλλει). **Semantically**, ὅτι is causal: "because" (KJV ASV NASB NIV NET CNT) or "for" (NRSV ESV NLT). It answers the question "why?" (cf. Wallace 1996, 460). John provides the first of two reasons why perfect love drives away fear as evident in the rest of the clause.

ἔχει: The Greek word ἔχει is a third singular present active indicative from the verb ἔχω that means, "I have" or "I bring about" or "I include" (BDAG 422.8). **Syntactically**, ἔχει is the governing verb of the first part of the dependent adverbial ὅτι clause. The subject is "fear" (ὁ φόβος). **Semantically**, ἔχει is a gnomic present: "includes" or "involves" (NASB) or "has to do with" (NASB ESV NIV NET CNT). It too is a generic statement that describes something that is true at any time (Wallace 1996, 523). Behind the idea of fear is the prospect of punishment (κόλασιν).

⁴ᐟ¹⁸ᵈ δέ: The Greek word δέ is a conjunction, which means "but" or "rather" (BDAG 213.1). **Syntactically**, δέ is in the post-positive position and introduces the second part of the compound dependent adverbial clause: "*and* [because] the one who fears is not perfected in love" (ὁ δὲ φοβούμενος οὐ τετελείωται ἐν τῇ ἀγάπῃ). **Semantically**, δέ is coordinating connective: "and" (ASV NASB NRSV ESV NIV NLT). The entire conjunctive clause provides an additional reason (ὅτι) about those who fear (Wallace 1996, 671).

φοβούμενος: The Greek word φοβούμενος is a nominative masculine singular present middle participle from the verb φοβέομαι that means, "I fear" or "to be in an apprehensive state" (BDAG 1060.1a). **Syntactically**, φοβούμενος is a substantival participle: "the one who fears" (NASB NIV NET) or "whoever" (NRSV ESV) or "he that fears" (KJV ASV). It functions as the subject of the verb "is perfected" (τετελείωται). **Semantically**, φοβούμενος is a gnomic present describing a timeless truth due to its generic subject (Wallace 1996, 523, 615). John underscores the truth about anyone who fears.

τετελείωται: The Greek word τετελείωται is a third singular perfect passive indicative from the verb τελειόω that means, "I perfect" or to overcome an imperfect state (BDAG 996.2eα). **Syntactically**, τετελείωται is the governing verb of the second part of the compound dependent ὅτι clause. The subject is the substantival participle "the one who fears" (ὁ . . . φοβούμενος). **Semantically**, τετελείωται is a gnomic and extensive perfect negated with οὐ: "has not been perfected" (ESV NET cf. NRSV). It too speaks of a general truth with a focus on the lack of a decisive act of experiencing God's love (cf. Wallace 1996, 580).

4:19a ἀγαπῶμεν: The Greek word ἀγαπῶμεν is a first plural present active indicative from the verb ἀγαπάω that means, "I cherish" or "I have affection for" or "I love" or "to have a warm regard for and interest in another" (BDAG 5.1ba). **Syntactically**, ἀγαπῶμεν is the main verb of the independent clause. The subject of the verb is the emphatic personal pronoun "we" (ἡμεῖς). The emphatic pronoun emphasizes the distinction between those who need to fear and those whose love has been brought to maturity. Brown suggests we highlight this contrast by translating it *"as for us, we love . . ."* (Brown 1982, 532). **Semantically**, is a customary present: "we *persist* in love" or "we love" (cf. KJV NASB ESV NIV NET etc.). It illustrates an ongoing state (Wallace 1996, 521). Believers persist in or exhibit a pattern of behavior in that they love other believers.

4:19b ὅτι: The Greek word ὅτι is a conjunction that means, "because" (BDAG 732.4a). Syntactically, ὅτι serves to introduce the dependent conjunctive clause: *"because he first loved us"* (ὅτι αὐτὸς πρῶτος ἠγάπησεν ἡμᾶς). The entire ὅτι clause functions adverbially modifying the verb "we love" (ἀγαπῶμεν). **Semantically**, ὅτι is causal: "because" (cf. KJV NASB ESV NIV NET etc.). It answers the question "why?" (cf. Wallace 1996, 460). John provides the reason why believers perstst in love.

ἠγάπησεν: The Greek word ἠγάπησεν is a third singular aorist active indicative from the verb ἀγαπάω that means, "I cherish" or "I have affection for" or "I love" or "to have a warm regard for and interest in another" (BDAG 5.1ba). **Syntactically**, ἠγάπησεν is the governing verb of the dependent adverbial clause. The subject of the verb is an emphatic personal pronoun "he" (αὐτὸς) and refers to God. The direct object of the verb is the personal pronoun "us" (ἡμᾶς), and refers to the believing community. **Semantically**, ἠγάπησεν is a constative aorist qualified with πρῶτος: "he first loved" (cf. KJV NASB ESV NIV NET etc.). It describe an historical act as a whole (Wallace 1996, 557). God loved ordinary people first.

4:20a ἐάν: The Greek word ἐάν is a conjunction, which means "if" (BDAG 267.1aβ). **Syntactically**, ἐάν identifies the clause as a dependent conjunctive clause: *"if anyone says, "I love God," yet hates his brother or sister"* (ἐάν τις εἴπῃ ὅτι Ἀγαπῶ τὸν θεόν, καὶ τὸν ἀδελφὸν αὐτοῦ μισῇ). The entire ἐάν clause functions adverbially, modifying the verb "is" (ἐστίν). **Semantically**, ἐάν introduces a third class conditional clause of probability: "if" (cf. KJV NASB ESV NIV NET etc). The condition is uncertain of fulfillment but still likely (Wallace 1996, 696). That uncertain condition is found in the next verb.

εἴπῃ: The Greek word εἴπῃ is a third singular aorist active subjunctive from the verb λέγω that means, "I say" or "to express oneself orally" (BDAG 588.1aβ). **Syntactically**, εἴπῃ is functioning as the governing verb of the first part of the dependent adverbial ἐάν clause. The verb is in the subjunctive mood because ἐάν takes only a subjunctive mood. The subject of the verb is the indefinite pronoun "anyone" (τις). **Semantically**, εἴπῃ is a constative aorist: "says" (NASB ESV NIV NET CNT NLT) or "say" (KJV ASV NRSV). It describes a hypothetical event as a whole (Wallace 1996, 557). It underscores a person's assumed claim to love God.

ὅτι: The Greek word ὅτι is a conjunction, which is not translated (BDAG 732.3). **Syntactically**, ὅτι serves to introduce the dependent conjunctive clause: "I love God" (ὅτι Ἀγαπῶ τὸν θεόν). The entire clause is functioning substantivally as the direct object of the verb "we love" (ἀγαπῶμεν). The ὅτι clause is placed in parenthesis in order to visualize its contribution to the independent clause. **Semantically**, ὅτι is direct discourse, which is not translated in English (cf. KJV NASB ESV NIV

NET etc.; cf. Wallace 1996, 454). It provides the words of the hypothetical believer's claim to know God.

ἀγαπῶ: The Greek word ἀγαπῶ is a first singular present active indicative from the verb ἀγαπάω that means, "I love" or to have a warm regard for and interest in another person (BDAG 5.1aα). **Syntactically,** Syntactically, ἀγαπῶ is functioning as the main verb of the dependent substantival ὅτι clause. The subject of the verb is the pronoun "I" embedded in the verb and refers to the hypothetical believer who is making a claim to know God. **Semantically,** ἀγαπῶ is a gnomic present: "I love" (cf. KJV NASB ESV NIV NET etc.). John draws attention to a timeless truth about anyone's claim (Wallace 1996, 523). It draws attention to a hypothetical claim of anyone who loves God.

4:20b καί [ἐάν τις]: The Greek word καί is a conjunction which means "and" (BDAG 494.1bε). **Syntactically,** καί introduces the second part of the compound dependent adverbial clause, "and hates his brother or sister" (καὶ τὸν ἀδελφὸν αὐτοῦ μισῇ). **Semantically,** καί is coordinating connective: "and" (KJV NASB NRSV ESV CNT etc.). It provides additional information about the hypothetical [ἐάν] believer who claims to know God (Wallace 1996, 671). Even though they say that they love God, they despise their fellow believers. Some translations use a contrastive conjunction "yet" (NIV NET; cf. NLT). It highlights a person's hypocrisy. The contextual idea, however, is connective and thereby rendered "and."

μισῇ: The Greek word μισῇ is a third singular present active subjunctive from the verb μισέω that means, "I hate" " or "I detest" or "to have a strong aversion to" (BDAG 652.1a). **Syntactically,** μισῇ serves as the governing verb of the second part of the compound dependent adverbial clause. The verb is in the subjunctive mood because ἐάν takes only a subjunctive mood. The subject of the verb is an implied pronoun "he" embedded in the verb and refers to the hypothetical [ἐάν] believer who claims to know God. **Semantically,** μισῇ is a gnomic present: "he hates" (NASB ESV NIV NET CNT NLT). John draws attention to a timeless truth about anyone's claim whose action does not follow (Wallace 1996, 523). It illustrates a hypothetical claim of any believer whose talk does not match their walk.

4:20c ἐστίν: The Greek word ἐστίν is third singular present active indicative from the verb εἰμί that means, "is" or "to be in close connection with" (BDAG 283.2a). **Syntactically,** ἐστίν is the main verb of the independent clause "he *is* a liar" (ψεύστης ἐστίν). The subject of the verb is an implied "he" embedded in the verb and refers back to the hypothetical believer who claims to have a relationship with God. **Semantically,** ἐστίν is a gnomic present: "is" (cf. KJV NASB ESV NIV NET etc.). It points out a timeless reality (Wallace 1996, 523). Anyone who claims to love God and hates their follow believer is equated with being a liar. They have no relationship with God (cf. 1:9; 3:10; 4:8).

4:20d γάρ: The Greek word γάρ is a conjunction that means "for" or "you see" (BDAG 189.2). **Syntactically,** γάρ is the post-positive position that identifies the clause as a independent conjunctive clause: "*for* the one who does not love his brother or sister whom he has seen is not able to love God whom he has not seen" (ὁ γὰρ μὴ ἀγαπῶν τὸν ἀδελφὸν αὐτοῦ ὃν ἑώρακεν, τὸν θεὸν ὃν οὐχ ἑώρακεν οὐ δύναται ἀγαπᾶν). **Semantically,** γάρ is a marker of clarification: "for" (KJV ASV NASB NRSV ESV CNT NLT; cf. Wallace 1996, 658). John explains why the believer who claims to know God yet hates his brother or sister is a liar.

ἀγαπῶν: The Greek word ἀγαπῶν is a nominative masculine singular present active participle from the verb ἀγαπάω that means, "I love" or to have a warm regard for and interest in another person (BDAG 5.1aα). **Syntactically,** ἀγαπῶν is a substantival participle functioning as the subject of the verb "is not able" (δύναται). **Semantically**, ἀγαπῶν is a gnomic present negated with μή: "the one who does not love" (NASB NET; cf. ESV CNT) or "anyone who does not have" (NIV) or "those who do not have" (NRSV). John is presenting a timeless fact about people who refuse to love their brothers and sisters in Christ (cf. 4:8a; Wallace 1996, 521), which is clarified with the next verbal and verb.

δύναται: The Greek word δύναται is a third singular present middle indicative from the verb δύναμαι that means, "I can" or "I am able" or "I am capable" or "to possess capability (whether because of personal or external factors) for experiencing or doing something" (BDAG 262.aα). **Syntactically**, δύναται is the main verb of the independent clause. The subject of the verb is the substantival participial clause "the one who does not love his brother and sister" (ὁ . . . μὴ ἀγαπῶν τὸν ἀδελφὸν αὐτοῦ). **Semantically**, δύναται is a gnomic present negated with μή. John is explaining a timeless fact about people who refuse to love their brothers and sisters in Christ (cf. 4:8a; Wallace 1996, 521).

ἀγαπᾶν: The Greek word ἀγαπᾶν is a present active infinitive from the verb ἀγαπάω that means, "I love" or to have a warm regard for and interest in another person (BDAG 5.1aα). **Syntactically**, ἀγαπᾶν is the complementary infinitive for δύναται negated with μή: "cannot love" (ASV NASB NRSB ESV NIV NET CNT). It completes the thought of the verb "is not able" (δύναται; Wallace 1996, 598). The one who does not love his fellow believers cannot possibly love God.

4:20e ὅν: The Greek word ὅν is accusative singular masculine from the relative pronoun ὅς that means, "who" (BDAG 725.1a). **Syntactically**, ὅν introduces a dependent relative clause: "*whom* he sees" (ὅν ἑώρακεν). It is adjectival modifying the noun "brother" (ἀδελφὸν). The relative pronoun is in the accusative case because it is the direct object of the verb "he has seen" (ἑώρακεν). The entire relative clause provides information about the hypothetical Christian who does not love.

ἑώρακεν: The Greek word ἑώρακεν is a third singular perfect active indicative from the verb ὁράω that means, "I see" or "I notice" or "to perceive by the eye" (BDAG, 719.A1b). **Syntactically**, ἑώρακεν is the governing verb of the dependent relative clause. The subject of the verb is an implied "he" embedded in the verb that refers to the hypothetical believer who claims to love God. **Semantically**, ἑώρακεν is a gnomic and extensive perfect: "he has seen" (NASB ESV NIV NET CNT). It contributes to John's generic proclamation about many individuals that focuses on the decisive act of noticing another believer (Wallace 1996, 580). If a believer does not love fellow Christians that he has encountered in his everyday life, they cannot possibly love God, whom they have not seen.

4:20f ὅν: The Greek word ὅν is accusative singular masculine from the relative pronoun ὅς that means, "who" (BDAG 725.1a). **Syntactically**, ὅν introduces a dependent relative clause: "*whom* he has not seen" (ὅν οὐχ ἑώρακεν). It is adjectival modifying the noun "God" (θεὸν) The relative pronoun is in the accusative case because is serves as the direct object of the verb "he has seen" (ἑώρακεν). The entire relative clause provides information about God whom the hypothetical believer claims to know.

ἑώρακεν: The Greek word ἑώρακεν is a third singular perfect active indicative from the verb ὁράω that means, "I see" or "I notice" or "to perceive by the eye" (BDAG, 719.A1b). **Syntactically**, ἑώρακεν functions as the governing verb of the dependent relative clause. The subject of the verb is an implied "he" embedded in the verb and refers to the hypothetical believer who claims to love God. **Semantically**, ἑώρακεν is a gnomic and extensive perfect negated with μή: "whom he has not seen" (NASB ESV NIV NET CNT). It contributes to John's generic proclamation about many individuals that focuses on the decisive act of noticing another believer (Wallace 1996, 580). A believer who cannot love fellow Christians that he has encountered in his everyday life, cannot possibly love God, whom he has not seen.

4:21a καί: The Greek word καί is a conjunction which means "and" (BDAG 494.1aα). **Syntactically**, καί introduces the independent conjunctive clause: "*and* we have this commandment from him" (καὶ ταύτην τὴν ἐντολὴν ἔχομεν ἀπ' αὐτοῦ). **Semantically**, καί is a coordinating connective: "and" (KJV ASV NASB ESV NIV NET NLT). It provides additional information about the loving lifestyle that God expects from those who claim to have a relationship with him.

4:21b ἔχομεν: The Greek word ἔχομεν is a first plural present active indicative from the verb ἔχω that means, "I have" or to experience something in the sense of an obligation (BDAG 421.7aδ). **Syntactically**, ἔχομεν is the main verb of the independent clause. The subject of the verb is an implied "we" embedded in the verb and refers to John and the readers. **Semantically**, ἔχομεν is a customary present: "we have" (NASB NRSV ESV NET CNT). It illustrates that the command to love is something that believers continually possess (cf. Wallace 1996, 521).

4:21b ἵνα: The Greek word ἵνα is a conjunction, which means "that" (BDAG 476.2e). **Syntactically**, ἵνα serves to introduce a conjunctive dependent clause: "*namely that* the one who loves God also loves his brother and sister" (ἵνα ὁ ἀγαπῶν τὸν θεὸν ἀγαπᾷ καὶ τὸν ἀδελφὸν αὐτοῦ). The entire ἵνα clause is adjectival, modifying the demonstrative pronoun "this" (ταύτην). **Semantically**, ἵνα is an appositional conjunction: "*namely* that" (KJV ASV NASB NET CNT). It clarifies the demonstrative pronoun "this" (αὕτη). It is almost idiomatic within Johannine literature (Wallace 1996, 475). The content of the command is that God expects that those who love him will also make a lifestyle out of self-lessly loving fellow believers (cp. 3:11c ἵνα, 3:23b ἵνα).

ἀγαπῶν: The Greek word ἀγαπῶν is a nominative masculine singular present active participle from the verb ἀγαπάω that means, "I love" or to have a warm regard for and interest in another person (BDAG 5.1aα). **Syntactically**, ἀγαπῶν is a substantival participle that functions as the subject of the verb "loves" (ἀγαπᾷ). **Semantically**, ἀγαπῶν is a gnomic present: "the one who loves" (NASB NET), "he who loves" (KJV ASV CNT), "those who love" (NASB NLT), "whoever loves" (ESV NIV). It refers to a general, timeless fact that is universally true and envisioned for many people (Wallace 1996, 523). John describes a universal truth about people who love God.

ἀγαπᾷ: The Greek word ἀγαπᾷ is a third singular present active subjunctive from the verb ἀγαπάω that means, "I love" or to have a warm regard for and interest in another person (BDAG 5.1aα). The verb is in the subjunctive mood because ἵνα takes only a subjunctive mood. **Syntactically**, ἀγαπᾷ is the governing verb of the dependent adjectival clause. The subject of the verb is the substantival participial phrase "the one who loves God" (ὁ ἀγαπῶν τὸν θεὸν). **Semantically**, ἀγαπᾷ is a gnomic present: "also loves" (NASB). It illustrates a timeless truth about believers in general who love (Wallace 1996, 523). However, some translations appear to render it as an expectation: "must also love" (ESV NIV NLT) or "should love" (NASB NET).

1 John 5:1-4

Verb Recognition for 1 John 5:1–4

¹Πᾶς ὁ πιστεύων ὅτι Ἰησοῦς ἐστιν ὁ Χριστὸς ἐκ τοῦ θεοῦ γεγέννηται, καὶ πᾶς ὁ ἀγαπῶν τὸν γεννήσαντα ἀγαπᾷ [καὶ] τὸν γεγεννημένον ἐξ αὐτοῦ. ²ἐν τούτῳ γινώσκομεν ὅτι ἀγαπῶμεν τὰ

τέκνα τοῦ θεοῦ, ὅταν τὸν θεὸν ἀγαπῶμεν καὶ τὰς ἐντολὰς αὐτοῦ ποιῶμεν. ³αὕτη γάρ ἐστιν ἡ ἀγάπη τοῦ θεοῦ, ἵνα τὰς ἐντολὰς αὐτοῦ τηρῶμεν· καὶ αἱ ἐντολαὶ αὐτοῦ βαρεῖαι οὐκ εἰσίν, ⁴ᵃὅτι πᾶν τὸ γεγεννημένον ἐκ τοῦ θεοῦ νικᾷ τὸν κόσμον· ⁴ᵇκαὶ αὕτη ἐστὶν ἡ νίκη ἡ νικήσασα τὸν κόσμον, ἡ πίστις ἡμῶν.

Clausal Outline for Translating 1 John 5:1–4

⁵:¹ᵃ Πᾶς ὁ πιστεύων (ὅτι Ἰησοῦς ἐστιν ὁ Χριστὸς) ἐκ τοῦ θεοῦ γεγέννηται,
⁵:¹ᵃ Everyone who *persists in* believing (**that** Jesus **is** the Christ) **has been fathered** by God,

⁵:¹ᵇ καὶ πᾶς ὁ ἀγαπῶν τὸν γεννήσαντα ἀγαπᾷ [καὶ] τὸν γεγεννημένον ἐξ αὐτοῦ.
⁵:¹ᵇ and everyone who *persists in* loving the father **loves** [also] those who have been fathered by him.

⁵:²ᵃ ἐν τούτῳ γινώσκομεν (ὅτι ἀγαπῶμεν τὰ τέκνα τοῦ θεοῦ),
⁵:²ᵃ By this **we know** (that **we love** the children of God),

    |
    ⁵:²ᵇ ὅταν τὸν θεὸν ἀγαπῶμεν
    ⁵:²ᵇ **whenever** we *persist* **in loving** God

        |
        ⁵:²ᶜ καὶ [ὅταν] τὰς ἐντολὰς αὐτοῦ ποιῶμεν.
        ⁵:²ᶜ and [*whenever*] **we** *persist* **in carrying out** his commandments.

⁵:³ᵃ αὕτη γάρ ἐστιν ἡ ἀγάπη τοῦ θεοῦ,
⁵:³ᵃ **For** this **is** the love *for* God,

    |
    ⁵:³ᵇ ἵνα τὰς ἐντολὰς αὐτοῦ τηρῶμεν·
    ⁵:³ᵇ *namely* **that** **we** *persist* **in keeping** his commandments;

⁵:³ᶜ καὶ αἱ ἐντολαὶ αὐτοῦ βαρεῖαι οὐκ εἰσίν,
⁵:³ᶜ and his commandments **are** not difficult to carry out,

            |
            ⁵:⁴ᵃ ὅτι πᾶν τὸ γεγεννημένον ἐκ τοῦ θεοῦ νικᾷ τὸν κόσμον·
            ⁵:⁴ᵃ **because** everyone who has been fathered by God
                                        overcomes the world;

⁵:⁴ᵇ καὶ αὕτη ἐστὶν ἡ νίκη ἡ νικήσασα τὸν κόσμον, ἡ πίστις ἡμῶν.
⁵:⁴ᵇ and this **is** the victory that overcame the world, our faith.

Syntax Explained for 1 John 5:1–4

⁵:¹ᵃ πιστεύων: The Greek word πιστεύων is a nominative masculine singular present active participle from the verb πιστεύω that means, "I believe" or "to consider something to be true and therefore worthy of one's trust" (BDAG 816.1aβ). **Syntactically**, πιστεύων is an adjectival participle. It modifies the

adjective, "each" (πᾶς). The entire phrase, "*everyone* who believes that Jesus is the Christ" (πᾶς ὁ πιστεύων ὅτι Ἰησοῦς ἐστιν ὁ Χριστὸς) functions as the subject of the verb "has been born" (γεγέννηται). **Semantically**, πιστεύων is a gnomic present with a customary present force: "everyone who *persists in* believing" (cf. NRSV ESV NIV NET CNT NLT) or "whoever believes" (NASB; cf. KJV ASV). It draws attention to a timeless fact about something that is currently happening" (Wallace 1996, 521, 523, 615). John draws attention to a timeless truth about any person who persists in believing that Jesus is the Christ (= Messiah).

ὅτι: The Greek word ὅτι is a conjunction that means "that" (BDAG 731.1c). **Syntactically**, ὅτι introduces a dependent conjunctive clause: "*that* Jesus is the Christ" (ὅτι Ἰησοῦς ἐστιν ὁ Χριστὸς). The entire clause functions substantivally as the direct object of the participle "believes" (πιστεύων). The ὅτι clause is placed in parenthesis in order to visualize its contribution to the independent clause. **Semantically**, ὅτι is an indirect discourse: "that" (cf. KJV NASB ESV NIV NET etc.). It provides the content of what the generic "everyone" *persists in* believing (Wallace 1996, 456).

ἐστιν: The Greek word ἐστιν is third singular present active indicative from the verb εἰμί that means, "is" or "to be in close connection with" (BDAG 282.2a). **Syntactically**, ἐστιν is the verb of the dependent ὅτι clause. The subject of the verb is the proper name "Jesus" (Ἰησοῦς). Even though the articular noun is normally the subject in an equative clause, a proper noun normally takes precedence (Wallace 1996, 44-45; Culy 2004, *55*). **Semantically**, ἐστιν is an equative present: "is" (cf. KJV NASB ESV NIC NET etc.). It equates Jesus or identifies Jesus to be the Messiah

γεγέννηται: The Greek word γεγέννηται is a third singular perfect passive indicative from the verb γεννάω that means, "I become the parent of" or "to exercise the role of a parental figure" (BDAG 193.1b). **Syntactically**, γεγέννηται is the main verb of the independent clause: "everyone who believes that Jesus is the Christ is born of God" (Πᾶς ὁ πιστεύων ὅτι Ἰησοῦς ἐστιν ὁ Χριστὸς ἐκ τοῦ θεοῦ γεγέννηται). The subject is the participial phrase "everyone who believes that Jesus is the Christ" (Πᾶς ὁ πιστεύων ὅτι Ἰησοῦς ἐστιν ὁ Χριστὸς). **Semantically**, γεγέννηται is both gnomic and an extensive perfect: "has been fathered" (NET) or "has been born" (NRSV ESV; cf. NLT). It is gnomic because of the generic subject (πᾶς) while extensive in that the focus is on the decisive relationship between the God and the believer (Wallace 1996, 580). This generic or proverbial force may also be rendered intensive: "is born" (KJV NASB NIV CNT; cf. ASV) with an emphasis on the results of the present condition of the believer. Regardless of where one places the emphasis of the perfect, John's point is that believers have been fathered by God in the past and that past event has continuing results in the present (cf. 2:29; 3:9; 5:1, 4, 18). The focus is upon those who practice righteousness: they have an on-going relationship with God.

5.1b καί: The Greek word καί is a conjunction which means "and" (BDAG 494.1bα). **Syntactically**, καί introduces a conjunctive independent clause: "*and* everyone who loves the father [also] loves the one who is born of him" (καὶ πᾶς ὁ ἀγαπῶν τὸν γεννήσαντα ἀγαπᾷ [καὶ] τὸν γεγεννημένον ἐξ αὐτοῦ). **Semantically**, καί is a coordinating connective: "and" (KJV ASV NASB NRSV ESV NIV NET NLT CNT). It provides additional information about the generic person who is part of God's family (Wallace 1996, 671). The added information is found in the rest of the clause.

ἀγαπῶν: The Greek word ἀγαπῶν is a nominative masculine singular present active participle from the verb ἀγαπάω that means, "I love" or "I cherish" or "to have a warm regard for and interest in another" (BDAG 5.1aα). **Syntactically**, ἀγαπῶν is an adjectival participle modifying the substantival adjective "each" (πᾶς). The first form of γεννάω, τὸν γεννήσαντα functions as the *object of the participle* ἀγαπῶν ("who loves"). The entire πᾶς + participial phrase, "everyone who loves the father" (πᾶς ὁ ἀγαπῶν τὸν γεννήσαντα) is functioning as the subject of the verb "loves" (ἀγαπᾷ). **Semantically**, the participle ἀγαπῶν is a gnomic present with a customary present force: "everyone who *persists in* loving" (cf. NRSV ESV NIV NET CNT NLT) or "whoever loves" (NASB; cf. ASV). It draws attention to a timeless fact about a generic "anyone" who persists in loving God which in turn translates into loving other people (Wallace 1996, 521, 523, 615).

γεννήσαντα: The Greek word γεννήσαντα is an accusative masculine singular aorist active participle from the verb γεννάω that means, "I become the parent of" or "to exercise the role of a parental figure" (BDAG 193.1b). **Syntactically,** γεννήσαντα is the object of "everyone who loves" (πᾶς ὁ ἀγαπῶν). **Semantically**, γεννήσαντα is a constative aorist: "has been fathered" (NET; cf. NRSV ESV). John draws attention to an example from everyday life (Brown 1982, 566). As a general rule if someone loves the parent, usually they also love the children of that parent.

ἀγαπᾷ: The Greek word ἀγαπᾷ is a third singular present active indicative from the verb ἀγαπάω that means, "I love" or "I cherish" or "to have a warm regard for and interest in another" (BDAG 5.1aα). **Syntactically,** ἀγαπᾷ is the main verb of the independent clause: "and everyone who loves the father [also] *loves* the one who is born of him" (καὶ πᾶς ὁ ἀγαπῶν τὸν γεννήσαντα ἀγαπᾷ [καὶ] τὸν γεγεννημένον ἐξ αὐτοῦ). **Semantically**, ἀγαπᾷ is a gnomic present: "loves" (cf. KJV NASB ESV NIV NET etc.). John draws attention to an example from everyday life (Wallace 1996, 523). As a general rule if someone loves the parent, usually they also love the children of that parent (Brown 1982, 566). People who claim God to be their father will love him, and they will love other believers whom he has fathered.

γεγεννημένον: The Greek word γεγεννημένον is an accusative masculine singular perfect passive participle from the verb γεννάω that means, "I become the parent of" or "to exercise the role of a parental figure" (BDAG 193.1b). **Syntactically,** γεγεννημένον functions substantivally. It is a *direct object* of the main verb. The entire participial phrase "the one who has been fathered by him" (τὸν γεγεννημένον ἐξ αὐτοῦ) is the direct object of the verb "loves" (ἀγαπᾷ). **Semantically**, γεγέννηται is both gnomic and an extensive perfect: "has been fathered" (NET) or "has been born" (ESV). It is gnomic because of the generic subject (πᾶς) while extensive in that the focus is on the decisive relationship between God and the believer (Wallace 1996, 580). This generic or proverbial force may also be rendered intensive: "is born" (cf. KJV ASV NASB) with an emphasis on the results of the present condition of the believer. Regardless of where one places the emphasis of the perfect, John's point is simply this: believers have been fathered by God in the past and that past event has continuing results in the present (cf. 2:29; 3:9; 4:7; 5:4, 18). The focus is upon those who practice righteousness: they have an on-going relationship with God.

5:2a ἐν τούτῳ: The Greek word ἐν is a preposition, which means "by" (BDAG 328.5b). The Greek word τούτῳ is declined as a dative singular neuter from the demonstrative pronoun τοῦτο, which means "this one" (BDAG 741.1bβ). **Syntactically,** ἐν τούτῳ introduces an independent prepositional clause: "By this we know that we love the children of God" (ἐν τούτῳ γινώσκομεν ὅτι ἀγαπῶμεν τὰ τέκνα τοῦ θεοῦ). "By this" (ἐν τούτῳ) occurs frequently in 1 John (2:3, 4, 5, 3:10, 16, 19, 24; 4:2, 9, 10, 13, 17). **Semantically,** ἐν τούτῳ can either be anaphoric, pointing back to the preceding discussion, or cataphoric, pointing forward. In this instance, the phrase is cataphoric. It points forward to the conjunction ὅταν (5:2b), which provides the content of the test by which believers can know that they really love the children of God.

γινώσκετε: The Greek word γινώσκετε is a first plural present active indicative from the verb γινώσκω that means, "I know" or "I know about" or "to arrive at a knowledge of someone or something"

(BDAG 200.6c). **Syntactically**, γινώσκομεν is the main verb of the independent clause. The subject of the verb is an implied "we" embedded in the verb and refers to the orthodox readers of the letter. **Semantically**, γινώσκετε is a customary present: "we know" (cf. KJV NASB ESV NIV NET etc.). It focuses on the conintual knowledge that a believer can possess. The content of that knowledge is found in the following ὅτι clause.

ὅτι: The Greek word ὅτι is a conjunction, which means "that" (BDAG 731.1c). **Syntactically**, ὅτι introduces a substantival dependent clause: "*that* we love the children of God" (ὅτι ἀγαπῶμεν τὰ τέκνα τοῦ θεοῦ), functioning as the direct object of the verb, "we know" (γινώσκομεν). The entire ὅτι clause is placed in parenthesis in order to visualize its contribution to the independent clause. **Semantically**, ὅτι completes a verb of cognition and therefore is an indirect discourse conjunction (Wallace 1996, 456). It provides the content of what is known (cf. KJV NASB ESV NIV NET etc.), which evident in the rest of the clause.

ἀγαπῶμεν: The Greek word ἀγαπῶμεν is a first plural present active indicative from the verb ἀγαπάω that means, "I love" or "I cherish" or "to have a warm regard for and interest in another" (BDAG 5.1aα). **Syntactically**, ἀγαπῶμεν is the governing verb of the dependent substantival clause. The subject of the verb is an implied "we" embedded in the verb and refers to the readers. **Semantically**, ἀγαπῶμεν is a customary present: "we love" (cf. KJV NASB ESV NIV NET etc.). It points out that the love for God's children that believers should be looking for is a habitual love that is grounded in action (Wallace 1996, 521).

5:2b ὅταν: The Greek word ὅταν is a conjunction that means "at the time that" or "whenever" or "when" or "pertaining to an action that is conditional, possible, and, in many instances, repeated" (BDAG, 730.1aα). **Syntactically**, ὅταν introduces a dependent conjunctive clause: "*whenever* we love God and practice his commands" (ὅταν τὸν θεὸν ἀγαπῶμεν καὶ τὰς ἐντολὰς αὐτοῦ ποιῶμεν). The entire ὅταν clause modifies the demonstrative pronoun, "this" (τούτῳ). **Semantically**, ὅταν is temporal: "whenever" (NET) or "when" (KJV ASV NASB NRSV ESV CNT). It is when a believer knows that he or she has a relationship with God (Wallace 1996, 677). The evidence of sincere love for other children of God is in the sincere affection for God and concrete acts of obedience to God's love commands.

ἀγαπῶμεν: The Greek word ἀγαπῶμεν is a first plural present active subjunctive from the verb ἀγαπάω that means, "I love" or "I cherish" or "to have a warm regard for and interest in another" (BDAG 5.1aα). **Syntactically**, ἀγαπῶμεν is the governing verb of the dependent conjunctive ὅταν clause. The subject of the verb is an implied "we" embedded in the verb and refers to the orthodox readers of the letter. **Semantically**, ἀγαπῶμεν is a customary present: "we *persist* in loving" or "we love" (cf. KJV NASB ESV NIV NET etc.). It points out that continual love for God is evidence of genuine love for his children (Wallace 1996, 521). But it doesn't end there.

5:2c καὶ [ὅταν]: The Greek word καί is a conjunction that means "and" (BDAG 494.1bα). **Syntactically**, καί introduces the second part of the compound dependent conjunctive ὅταν clause. Thus the inclusion of "whenever" [ὅταν] is in brackets. **Semantically**, καὶ is coordinating connective: "and" (cf. KJV NASB ESV NIV NET etc.). It provides further information about a believer and when they can know that they have genuine love for God's children.

ποιῶμεν: The Greek word ποιῶμεν is first plural present active subjunctive from the verb ποιέω that means, "I do" or "I keep" or "I carry out" or "I practice" or to carry out an obligation of a moral or social nature" (BDAG 840.3a). **Syntactically**, ποιῶμεν is the second verb of the dependent conjunctive ὅταν clause. The subject of the verb is an implied "we" embedded in the verb and refers to the orthodox readers of the letter. **Semantically,** ποιῶμεν is an customary present: "we *persist* in carrying out" or "we obey" (NASV ESV NET CNT NLT). It stresses that repeated acts of practicing the love commands of Jesus evidence that a believer loves God's children (Wallace 1996, 521). The love for God and the practice of his love commands are not necessarily two separate proofs of love for God's children. Most likely this is an example of a figure of speech called a hendiadys where to separate acts form one idea (See Smally 1984, 268). Thus the evidence for a genuine love of other children of God is a sincere affection for God that results in repeated demonstrations of faithfulness to his love commands.

5:3a   γάρ: The Greek word γάρ is a conjunction that means "for" or "because" (BDAG 189.1a). **Syntactically,** γάρ introduces an independent conjunctive clause: *"for* this is the love of God" (αὕτη γάρ ἐστιν ἡ ἀγάπη τοῦ θεοῦ). **Semantically,** γάρ is explanatory: "for" (KJV NASB NRSV ESV NIV CNT NLT) or "because" (NET). It explains how a believer can determine if they truly love other believers (cf. Culy 2004, 49; 122).

ἐστιν: The Greek word ἐστιν is third singular present active indicative from the verb εἰμί that means, "is" or "to be in close connection with" (BDAG 282.2a). **Syntactically,** ἐστιν is the main verb of the independent clause: "for this *is* God's love" (αὕτη γάρ ἐστιν ἡ ἀγάπη τοῦ θεοῦ). The subject of the verb is the demonstrative pronoun "this" (αὕτη) due to the grammatical priority of pronouns (Wallace 1996, 42-43). **Semantically,** ἐστιν is a gnomic: "is" (cf. KJV NASB ESV NIV NET etc.). It is a timeless fact about the one who follows the love commandments of Jesus (Wallace 1996, 523).

5:3b   ἵνα: The Greek word ἵνα is a conjunction, which means "that" (BDAG 476.2e). **Syntactically,** ἵνα introduces a dependent conjunctive clause: *"that* we keep his commands" (ἵνα τὰς ἐντολὰς αὐτοῦ τηρῶμεν). The entire ἵνα clause is substantival. It clarifies the demonstrative pronoun "this" (αὕτη). **Semantically,** ἵνα is an appositional conjunction: *"namely* that" (KJV NASB NRSV ESV NET CNT). It clarifies the demonstrative pronoun "this" (αὕτη). It is almost idiomatic within Johannine literature (Wallace 1996, 475). The basis for love is found in the next verb.

τηρῶμεν: The Greek word τηρῶμεν is a first plural present active subjunctive from the verb τηρέω that means, "I keep" or "I observe" or "to persist in obedience" (BDAG 1002.3). It is in the subjunctive mood because it follows an ἵνα. **Syntactically,** τηρῶμεν is the governing verb of the dependent conjunctive ἵνα clause. It explains the content of the demonstrative pronoun, "this" (αὕτη). The assumed subject "we" refers to any believer who desires to demonstrate their love for God. **Semantically,** τηρῶμεν is a customary present: "we *persist* in keeping" or "we keep" (KJV ASV ESV NET; cf. NLT). It describes a pattern of behavior (Wallace 1996, 521). It describes believers who persist in keeping God's commands, especially the command to love others (cf. 2:3).

5:3c   καί: The Greek word καί is a conjunction which means "and" (BDAG 494.1bβ). **Syntactically,** καί introduces a independent conjunctive clause: *"And* his commands are not difficult to carry out" (καὶ αἱ ἐντολαὶ αὐτοῦ βαρεῖαι οὐκ εἰσίν). **Semantically,** καί is connective drawn from Hebrew where καί is used as a *waw* consecutive that begins a new sentence (cf. NRSV ESV NIV NET CNT). It joins two sentences together that expands the information about God's commands to love. These commands are not difficult for the genuine believer to keep because they have conquered the world in their hearts through their faith in the work of Jesus.

εἰσίν: The Greek word εἰσίν is third plural present active indicative from the verb εἰμί that means, "is" or "to be in close connection with" (BDAG 283.2a). **Syntactically,** εἰσίν is the main verb of the independent clause. The subject of the verb is the nominal phrase "his commands" (αἱ ἐντολαὶ αὐτοῦ) referring to the love commands of God given through Jesus. The predicate nominative βαρεῖαι pertains to being a source of difficulty (BDAG 167.2a). **Semantically**, εἰσίν is an equative present: "is" (cf. KJV NASB ESV NIV NET etc.). It underscores for the reader who has God in their life the command to love others is not a burden. Matthew also describes the regulaions and rules of the Pharisees as heavy burdens (23:4), but God's command to love is easy, because the genuine believer has conquered the world in their heart.

5:4a ὅτι: The Greek word ὅτι is a conjunction that means "because" (BDAG 732.4a). **Syntactically**, ὅτι serves to introduce the dependent conjunctive clause: "*because* everyone who is born of God conquers the world" (ὅτι πᾶν τὸ γεγεννημένον ἐκ τοῦ θεοῦ νικᾷ τὸν κόσμον). The entire clause is functioning adverbially, modifying the verb "casts out" (εἰσίν). **Semantically**, ὅτι is causal: "because" (NET; cf. NRSV NIV), though many translate ὅτι as "For" indicating perhaps a loose connection with the preceding clause (KJV ASV NASB ESV CNT NLT; BDAG 732.4b). It provides the reason why God's love commands are not burdesome for those who believe (Wallace 1996, 460). The reason is pointed out in the next verb.

γεγεννημένον: The Greek word γεγεννημένον is an nominative neuter singular perfect passive participle from the verb γεννάω that means, "I become the parent of" or "to exercise the role of a parental figure" (BDAG 193.1b). **Syntactically**, the entire participial phrase, "the one who is born of God" (τὸ γεγεννημένον ἐκ τοῦ θεοῦ), modifies the substantival adjective (πᾶν). The neuter gender here is difficult. Why refer to a group of individuals by the neuter? Perhaps John is influenced by the gender of "children" (τεκνία,) or perhaps it emphasizes a quality (conquering the world) rather than the individual (cf. BDF § 138). **Semantically**, γεγέννηται is both gnomic and an extensive perfect: "has been fathered" (NET) or "has been born" (ESV). It is gnomic because of the generic subject (πᾶν) while extensive in that the focus is on the decisive relationship between God and the believer (Wallace 1996, 580). This generic or proverbial force may also be rendered intensive: "is born" (KJV NASB NRSV CNT cf. ASV) with an emphasis on the results of the present condition of the believer. Regardless of where one places the emphasis of the perfect, John's point is simply this: believers have been fathered by God in the past and that past event has continuing results in the present (cf. 2:29; 3:9; 4:7; 5:4, 18). The focus is upon those who practice righteousness: they have had an on-going relationship with God.

νικᾷ: The Greek word νικᾷ is a third singular present active indicative from the verb νικάω that means, "I vanquish" or "I overcome" or "to overcome someone" (BDAG 673.2a). **Syntactically**, νικᾷ is the governing verb of the dependent adverbial ὅτι clause. The subject of the verb is the substantival phrase "everyone who is born of God" (πᾶν τὸ γεγεννημένον ἐκ τοῦ θεοῦ). **Semantically**, νικᾷ is a gnomic present: "overcomes" (KJV ASV NASB ESV CNT) or "conquers" (NRSV NET). It emphasizes a timeless reality (Wallace 1996, 523) concerning the believer's victory over the world (cf. NLT).

5:4b καί The Greek word καί is a conjunction that means "and" (BDAG 494.1ba). **Syntactically**, καί introduces a conjunctive independent clause, "and this is the victory that overcame the world, our faith" (καὶ αὕτη ἐστὶν ἡ νίκη ἡ νικήσασα τὸν κόσμον, ἡ πίστις ἡμῶν). Semantically, καί is coordinating connective and gives us additional information about the victory that believers have over the world system. While most translations translate καί as "and" (KJV ASV NASB ESV NET NLT), the NIV leaves the καί untranslated that heightens the author's point that it is faith in the work of Jesus that enables the believers to achieve victory.

ἐστίν The Greek word ἐστίν is third singular present active indicative from the verb εἰμί that means, "is" or "to be in close connection with" (BDAG 283.2a). **Syntactically**, ἐστίν is the main verb of the independent clause. The subject of the verb is the demonstrative pronoun "this" (αὕτη) due to the grammatical priority of pronouns (Wallace 1996, 42-43). **Semantically**, ἐστίν is an equative present: "is" (cf. KJV NASB ESV NIV NET etc.). It equates the victory that believers have over the world as something that is gained through their faith in the work of Jesus.

νικήσασα: The Greek word νικήσασα is a nominative singular feminine aorist active participle from the verb νικάω that means, "I vanquish" or "I overcome" or "to overcome someone" (BDAG 673.2a). **Syntactically**, ἡ νικήσασα is adjectivally in the attributive position with "victory" (ἡ νίκη). The entire participial phrase, "that overcame the world" (ἡ νικήσασα τὸν κόσμον), modifies the noun "victory" (ἡ νίκη). **Semantically**, νικήσασα is a constative aorist: "overcame," though most translations render it as a consummative aorist: "has overcome" (NASB ESV NIV NET, cf. KJV ASV). The constative aorist describes the action as a whole (Wallace 1996, 557). This participial phrase echoes the noun that it modifies and is difficult to translate due to John's use of cognates (see also 1 John 2:25). Nevertheless, the phrase serves to emphasize the power that believers possess to overcome the world. This victory is explained by another nominative phrase also set in apposition to the demonstrative pronoun, "our faith" (ἡ πίστις ἡμῶν). This addditional phrase points out that the origin of the believer's victory comes from their faith that Jesus is God's son.

1 John 5:5–12

Verb Recognition for 1 John 5:5–12

⁵τίς [δέ] ἐστιν ὁ νικῶν τὸν κόσμον εἰ μὴ ὁ πιστεύων ὅτι Ἰησοῦς ἐστιν ὁ υἱὸς τοῦ θεοῦ; ⁶Οὗτός ἐστιν ὁ ἐλθὼν δι' ὕδατος καὶ αἵματος, Ἰησοῦς Χριστός· οὐκ ἐν τῷ ὕδατι μόνον ἀλλ' ἐν τῷ ὕδατι καὶ ἐν τῷ αἵματι· καὶ τὸ πνεῦμά ἐστιν τὸ μαρτυροῦν, ὅτι τὸ πνεῦμά ἐστιν ἡ ἀλήθεια. ⁷ὅτι τρεῖς εἰσιν οἱ μαρτυροῦντες, ⁸τὸ πνεῦμα καὶ τὸ ὕδωρ καὶ τὸ αἷμα, καὶ οἱ τρεῖς εἰς τὸ ἕν εἰσιν. ⁹εἰ τὴν μαρτυρίαν τῶν ἀνθρώπων λαμβάνομεν, ἡ μαρτυρία τοῦ θεοῦ μείζων ἐστίν, ὅτι αὕτη ἐστὶν ἡ μαρτυρία τοῦ θεοῦ, ὅτι μεμαρτύρηκεν περὶ τοῦ υἱοῦ αὐτοῦ. ¹⁰ὁ πιστεύων εἰς τὸν υἱὸν τοῦ θεοῦ ἔχει τὴν μαρτυρίαν ἐν αὐτῷ· ὁ μὴ πιστεύων τῷ θεῷ ψεύστην πεποίηκεν αὐτόν, ὅτι οὐ πεπίστευκεν εἰς τὴν μαρτυρίαν ἣν μεμαρτύρηκεν ὁ θεὸς περὶ τοῦ υἱοῦ αὐτοῦ. ¹¹καὶ αὕτη ἐστὶν ἡ μαρτυρία, ὅτι ζωὴν αἰώνιον ἔδωκεν ἡμῖν ὁ θεός, καὶ αὕτη ἡ ζωὴ ἐν τῷ υἱῷ αὐτοῦ ἐστιν. ¹²ὁ ἔχων τὸν υἱὸν ἔχει τὴν ζωήν· ὁ μὴ ἔχων τὸν υἱὸν τοῦ θεοῦ τὴν ζωὴν οὐκ ἔχει.

Clausal Outline Translated for 1 John 5:5–12

⁵·⁵ᵃτίς [δέ] ἐστιν ὁ νικῶν τὸν κόσμον
⁵·⁵ᵃ <u>Now</u> who **is** overcoming the world

^{5:5b} εἰ μὴ ὁ πιστεύων (ὅτι Ἰησοῦς **ἐστιν** ὁ υἱὸς τοῦ θεοῦ);
^{5:5b} **except** the one who believes (that Jesus **is** the Son of God)?

^{5:6a}Οὗτός **ἐστιν** ὁ ἐλθὼν δι᾽ ὕδατος καὶ αἵματος, Ἰησοῦς Χριστός·
^{5:6a} "this **is** the one who came by water and blood, Jesus, *who is the* Christ"

^{5:6b}οὐκ [*ἦλθεν*] ἐν τῷ ὕδατι μόνον
^{5:6b} [*Jesus came*] not by water only

^{5:6c}ἀλλ᾽ [*ἦλθεν*] ἐν τῷ ὕδατι καὶ ἐν τῷ αἵματι·
^{5:6c} **but** [*he came*] by the water and the blood;

^{5:6d}καὶ τὸ πνεῦμά **ἐστιν** τὸ μαρτυροῦν,
^{5:6d} **and** the Spirit **is** the one who testifies,

        ^{5:6e}ὅτι τὸ πνεῦμά **ἐστιν** ἡ ἀλήθεια.
        ^{5:6e} **because** the Spirit **is** the truth,

^{5:7}ὅτι τρεῖς **εἰσιν** οἱ μαρτυροῦντες
^{5:7} For the ones that testify **are** three,

^{5:8a}τὸ πνεῦμα καὶ τὸ ὕδωρ καὶ τὸ αἷμα [**ἐστιν**],
^{5:8a} [***they are***] Spirit and the water and the blood,

^{5:8b}καὶ οἱ τρεῖς εἰς τὸ ἕν **εἰσιν**.
^{5:8b} and these three **are** in agreement.

        ^{5:9a}εἰ τὴν μαρτυρίαν τῶν ἀνθρώπων **λαμβάνομεν**,
        ^{5:9a} **If we receive** the testimony of men,

^{5:9b}ἡ μαρτυρία τοῦ θεοῦ μείζων **ἐστίν**,
^{5:9b} God's testimony **is** greater,

        ^{5:9c}ὅτι αὕτη **ἐστὶν** ἡ μαρτυρία τοῦ θεοῦ,
        ^{5:9c} **because** this **is** the testimony of God,

            ^{5:9d}ὅτι **μεμαρτύρηκεν** περὶ τοῦ υἱοῦ αὐτοῦ.
            ^{5:9d} **that he has testified** concerning his Son.

^{5:10a}ὁ πιστεύων εἰς τὸν υἱὸν τοῦ θεοῦ **ἔχει** τὴν μαρτυρίαν ἐν αὐτῷ·
^{5:10a} The one who believes in the Son of God **has** the testimony in himself;

^{5:10b}ὁ μὴ πιστεύων τῷ θεῷ ψεύστην **πεποίηκεν** αὐτόν,
^{5:10b} the one who does not believe God has made him a liar,

^{5:10c} ὅτι οὐ **πεπίστευκεν** εἰς τὴν μαρτυρίαν

^{5:10c} **because** he **has** not **believed** in the testimony

^{5:10d} ἣν **μεμαρτύρηκεν** ὁ θεὸς περὶ τοῦ υἱοῦ αὐτοῦ.

^{5:10d} **that** God **has testified** concerning his Son.

^{5:11a} καὶ αὕτη **ἐστὶν** ἡ μαρτυρία,

^{5:11a} And this **is** the testimony,

^{5:11b} ὅτι ζωὴν αἰώνιον **ἔδωκεν** ἡμῖν ὁ θεός,

^{5:11b} **that** God **has granted** us eternal life,

^{5:11c} καὶ αὕτη ἡ ζωὴ ἐν τῷ υἱῷ αὐτοῦ **ἐστιν**.

^{5:11c} and this life **is** in his Son.

^{5:12a} ὁ ἔχων τὸν υἱὸν **ἔχει** τὴν ζωήν·

^{5:12a} The one who has the Son **has** eternal life;

^{5:12b} ὁ μὴ ἔχων τὸν υἱὸν τοῦ θεοῦ τὴν ζωὴν οὐκ **ἔχει**.

^{5:12b} the one who does not have the Son of God does not **have** eternal life.

Syntax Explained for 1 John 5:5–12

^{5:5a} [δέ]: The Greek word δέ is a conjunction in the postpositive position that means "now" (BDAG 213.2). **Syntactically**, if [δέ] is authentic, it introduces an independent conjunctive clause: "[*now*] who is the one who conquers the world" (τίς [δέ] ἐστιν ὁ νικῶν τὸν κόσμον). **Semantically**, δέ is a transitional conjunction: "now" (NET; cf. CNT), though some translate it as a coordinating connective (ASV NLT). Even though some translatons seemingly reject [δέ] as an authentic reading (KJV NASB NRSV NIV NLT), the acceptance and rendering of [δέ] as "now" indicates a change to a new topic of discussion (Wallace 1996, 674). The new topic is disclosed in the subsequent clauses.

ἐστιν: The Greek word ἐστιν is third singular present active indicative from the verb εἰμί that means, "is" or "in explanations to show how something is to be understood" (282.2cβ). **Syntactically**, ἐστιν is the main verb of the independent clause. The subject of the verb is the interrogative pronoun "who" (τίς) due to the grammatical priority of pronouns over articular nouns (Wallace 1996, 42-43). **Semantically**, ἐστιν is an equative present demonstrating the close connection with the interrogative pronoun "who" (τίς) that explains someone's identity. That identity is raised in the following participle.

νικῶν: The Greek word νικῶν is a nominative singular masculine present active participle from the verb νικάω that means, "I vanquish" or "I overcome" or "to overcome someone" (BDAG 673.2a). **Syntactically**, ὁ νικῶν is a substantival participle functioning as the direct object of the verb "is" (ἐστιν). **Semantically**, ὁ νικῶν is a gnomic present: "is overcoming" (cf. KJV ASV NASB ESV NIV CNT). The participle makes a generic statement (Wallace 1996, 523, 615). John is presenting a timeless truth about the person who overcomes the world. That timeless truth is clarified in the next clause.

5:5b εἰ μὴ: The Greek construction εἰ + μὴ is a subcategory of the conditional conjunction that means "except" or "but" (BDAG 278.6iα). **Syntactically**, εἰ μὴ introduces a dependent conjunctive clause, which is functioning adverbially modifying the elliptical verb "[is]" ([ἐστιν]). **Semantically**, εἰ μὴ expresses a contrast or an exception: "except" (ESV NET) or "but" (KJV ASV NASB NRSV CNT). The exception is clearified in the clauses verb and subsequent ὅτι clause.

πιστεύων: The Greek word πιστεύων is a nominative masculine singular present active participle from the verb πιστεύω that means, "I believe" or "to consider something to be true and therefore worthy of one's trust" (BDAG 816.1αβ). **Syntactically**, πιστεύων is a substantival participle. The entire participial phrase, "the one who believes that Jesus is the son of God" (ὁ πιστεύων ὅτι Ἰησοῦς ἐστιν ὁ υἱὸς τοῦ θεοῦ) is functioning as the subject of the elliptical verb "[is]" ([ἐστιν]). These εἰ + μὴ constructions often are elliptical which means that the entire participial phrase would be the subject of an elliptical "[is the one who conquers the world]" ([ἐστιν ὁ νικῶν τὸν κόσμον]) (cf. Culy 2004, 124). **Semantically**, ὁ πιστεύων is a gnomic present: "the one who believes" (NRSV ESV NET) or "he who" (NASB NIV CNT). The participle makes a generic statement (Wallace 1996, 523, 615). If anyone has conquered the world, it is definitely the one who beleives that Jesus is God's son.

ὅτι: The Greek word ὅτι is a conjunction, which means "that" (BDAG 731.1d). **Syntactically**, ὅτι introduces a dependent conjunctive clause: "*that* Jesus is the son of God" (ὅτι Ἰησοῦς ἐστιν ὁ υἱὸς τοῦ θεοῦ). The entire clause functions substantively as the object of the participle "the one who believes" (μὴ ὁ πιστεύων). The clause is placed in parenthesis in order to visualize its contribution to the participle. **Semantically**, ὅτι is indirect discourse: "that" (cf. KJV NASB ESV NIV NET etc.). It provides the content of what the person who overcomes the world believes.

ἐστιν: The Greek word ἐστιν is third singular present active indicative from the verb εἰμί that means, "is" or "to be in close connection with" (BDAG 283.2a). **Syntactically**, ἐστιν is the governing verb of the dependent conjunctive ὅτι clause. The subject of the verb is the proper noun "Jesus" (Ἰησοῦς), even though articular nouns and proper names hold the same weight when it comes to determining which substantive is the subject and which is the predicate nominative. Wallace points out that when two substantives have equal weight, word order should be the determining factor (Wallace 1996, 44). **Semantically**, ἐστιν is an equative present: "is" (cf. KJV NASB ESV NIV NET etc.). It equates Jesus with being the Messiah.

5:6a ἐστίν: The Greek word ἐστίν is third singular present active indicative from the verb εἰμί that means, "is" or "to be in close connection with" (BDAG 283.2a). **Syntactically**, ἐστίν is the main verb of the independent clause: "this *is* the one who came by water and blood, Jesus Christ" (οὗτός ἐστιν ὁ ἐλθὼν δι' ὕδατος καὶ αἵματος, Ἰησοῦς Χριστός). The subject of the verb is the demonstrative pronoun "this one" (οὗτός), due to the grammatical priority of demonstratives (Wallace 1996, 42-43). The pronoun anaphorically points back to its referent, the proper noun "Jesus" (Ἰησοῦς) found in verse 5. The demonstrative is also further clarified by a subsequent appositional phrase, "Jesus Christ" (Ἰησοῦς Χριστός). **Semantically**, ἐστίν is an equative present: "is" (cf. KJV NASB ESV NIV NET etc.). It equates Jesus with being human (e.g. "by water and blood").

ἐλθὼν: The Greek word ἐλθὼν is a nominative masculine singular aorist active participle from the verb ἔρχομαι, which means, "I come" or to make a public appearance (BDAG, 394.1bα). **Syntactically**, ἐλθὼν functions substantivally as the predicate nominative of the verb "is" (ἐστίν). **Semantically**, ἐλθὼν is a constative aorist: "the one who came" (NASB NRSV NIV NET). It describes an event as a whole (Wallace 1996, 559). John describes Jesus's historical presence as a human being (e.g. "by water and blood").

5:6b [ἦλθεν]: The implied Greek word ἦλθεν is a third singular aorist active indicative from the verb ἔρχομαι, which means, "I come" or to make a public appearance (BDAG, 394.1bα). **Syntactically**, [ἦλθεν] is an elliptical verb that governs the independent anacoluthon clause. The subject of [ἦλθεν] is Jesus: "*Jesus* came not by water only" (οὐκ ἐν τῷ ὕδατι μόνον). **Semantically**, the ellipsis [ἦλθεν] is a constative aorist negated with οὐκ: "[*Jesus* came] not." It points out the general historical act as a whole that Jesus did not come by water alone (Wallace 1996, 557). These images serve as a metonymy pointing to events associated with Jesus's incarnation (birth and death).

5:6c ἀλλ': The Greek word ἀλλά is a conjunction that means "but" (BDAG 44.1a). **Syntactically**, ἀλλά introduces a dependent conjunctive clause. **Semantically**, ἀλλά is contrastive: "But" (cf. KJV NASB ESV NIV NET etc.). It emphasizes a contrast. The content of that contrast is found in the prepositional phrase: "by water and blood" (ἐν τῷ ὕδατι καὶ ἐν τῷ αἵματι).

[ἦλθεν]: The implied Greek word ἦλθεν is a third singular aorist active indicative from the verb ἔρχομαι, which means, "I come" or to make a public appearance (BDAG, 394.1bα). **Syntactically**, [ἦλθεν] is an elliptical verb that governs the independent clause. The subject of [ἦλθεν] is Jesus: "but *Jesus* came by water and by blood" (ἀλλ' ἐν τῷ ὕδατι καὶ ἐν τῷ αἵματι). **Semantically**, ἦλθεν is a constative aorist: "[*Jesus* came]." It points out the general historical act as a whole that Jesus did not come by water alone (Wallace 1996, 557). Once again, these images serve as a metonymy pointing to events associated with Jesus's incarnation (birth and death).

5:6d καί: The Greek word καί is a conjunction that means "and" (BDAG 494.1bα). **Syntactically**, καί introduces a conjunctive independent clause: "*and* the Spirit is the one who testifies" (καὶ τὸ πνεῦμά ἐστιν τὸ μαρτυροῦν). **Semantically**, καί is coordinating connective: "and" (cf. KJV NASB ESV NIV NET etc.). It provides additional information (Wallace 1996, 671). The additional information is found in the remainder of the clause.

ἐστιν: The Greek word ἐστιν is third singular present active indicative from the verb εἰμί that means, "is" or "to be in close connection with" (BDAG 283.2a). **Syntactically**, ἐστιν is the main verb of the independent conjunctive clause. Both the subject and the verb in this clause happen to have an article. The subject is the articular noun "Spirit" (τὸ πνεῦμά), since it is a proper designation, the participle requires an article to nominalize it, and it is the subject of the next clause as well (Culy 2004, 126; see also Wallace 1996, 42–46). **Semantically**, ἐστίν is an equative present: "is" (cf. KJV NASB ESV NIV NET etc.). It equates the Spirit as the one who bears witness to the coming of Jesus as a human being.

μαρτυροῦν: The Greek word μαρτυροῦν is a neuter nominative singular present active participle from the verb μαρτυρέω that means, "I bear witness" or "I testify" or "to confirm or attest something on the basis of personal knowledge or belief" (BDAG 617.1aα). **Syntactically**, μαρτυροῦν is functioning substantivally as the predicate nominative of the verb "is" (ἐστιν). **Semantically**, μαρτυροῦν is a customary present: "who testifies" (cf. NASB ESV NIV NET etc.). It illustrates a pattern of behavior (Wallace 1996, 521). The Spirit always bears witness to the incarnation of Jesus.

5:6e ὅτι: The Greek word ὅτι is a conjunction that means "because" (BDAG 732.4a). **Syntactically**, ὅτι introduces the dependent conjunctive clause: "*because* the Spirit is truth" (ὅτι τὸ πνεῦμά ἐστιν ἡ ἀλήθεια). The entire clause is functioning adverbially, modifying the verb "is" (ἐστιν). **Semantically**, ὅτι is causal: "because" (KJV NASB ESV NIV NET CNT). It provides the reason why the Spirit's testimony is valid (Wallace 1996, 460). The reason for the Spirit's testimony being valid is evident in the remainder of the clause.

ἐστίν: The Greek word ἐστίν is third singular present active indicative from the verb εἰμί that means, "is" or "to be in close connection with" (BDAG 283.2a). **Syntactically**, ἐστιν is the main verb of the dependent conjunctive ὅτι clause. The subject of the verb is the articular noun "Spirit" (τὸ πνεῦμά). **Semantically**, ἔστιν is an equative present: "is" (cf. KJV NASB ESV NIV NET etc.). It equates the Spirit's identity with truth. The Spirit speaks truth because he is by nature truthful.

5:7 ὅτι: The Greek word ὅτι is a conjunction that means "for" or "so" (BDAG 732.4b). **Syntactically**, ὅτι introduces the dependent conjunctive clause: "*For* the ones that testify are three" (ὅτι τρεῖς εἰσιν οἱ μαρτυροῦντες). **Semantically**, ὅτι is classified as explanatory: "for" (KJV NASB ESV NIV NET). It explains the previous discussion (Wallace, 1996, 673).

Semantical Nugget: ὅτι could be taken in a few different ways. It could be classified as a second causal clause also dependent on the verb "is" (ἐστὶν) (cf. Culy 2004, 127). It could also be classified adjectivally, epexegetically explaining the nature of the "truth" (ἀλήθεια). Finally, it could be classified as substantival, loosely connected with the previous verses. The best option seems to be the third option: a loosely connected conjunction to the previous clause: "*for* the ones that testify are three" (ὅτι τρεῖς εἰσιν οἱ μαρτυροῦντες).

εἰσιν: The Greek word εἰσιν is third plural present active indicative from the verb εἰμί that means, "is" or "to be in close connection with" (BDAG 283.2a). **Syntactically**, εἰσιν is the main verb of the independent clause. The subject of the verb is the articular participle "the ones that testify" (οἱ μαρτυροῦντες), due to the grammatical priority of articular nouns over adjectives (Wallace 1996, 42-44). **Semantically**, εἰσιν is an equative present: "are" (cf. KJV NASB ESV NIV NET etc.). It equates the substantival participle "the ones that testify" (οἱ μαρτυροῦντες) with "three" (τρεῖς). It equates those who testify with the number three. The significance of this equation is explained in the next word (cf. Wallace 1996, 332 n44).

μαρτυροῦντες: The Greek word μαρτυροῦντες is a nominative plural masculine present active participle from the verb μαρτυρέω that means, "I declare" or "I bear witness to" or to attest to something based upon personal knowledge (BDAG 618.1b). **Syntactically**, μαρτυροῦντες is functioning substantivally as the subject of the verb "are" (εἰσιν). **Semantically**, μαρτυροῦντες is a customary present: "the ones who testify" (Wallace 1996, 615). It underscores the existence of three seperate witnesses to the incarnation of Jesus. All three witnesses mentioned point to the incarnation of Jesus: the Spirit, the water, and the blood.

Textual Nugget: The majority text contains an additional reading known as the *Comma Johanneum*, "The ones who testify in heaven, the Father, the word, and the Holy Spirit and these three are one. And there are three that testify on earth," which occurs after the participle "testify" and before the nouns "the Spirit, the water, and the blood." The eclectic text favors the shorter reading which does not include the Johannine Comma. In spite of the fact that such a passage could be a clear prooftext for the orthodox view of the Trinity, it was never cited by the early church fathers as such in their extensive Trinitarian debates. The obvious conclusion is that it was not at that time part of the textual tradition. In fact, the *Comma Johanneum* does not appear in any Greek text until 1215 CE. It also doesn't fit into the immediate context of 1 John 5 either. For this reason we will not be analyizng its syntax (see Metzger, *A Textual Commentary of the Greek New Testament*, 715-716; see also the note on the Comma in the NET Bible).

5:8a [ἐστιν] The Greek word ἐστιν is third singular present active indicative from the verb εἰμί that means, "is" or "to be in close connection with" (BDAG 283.2a). **Syntactically**, the ellipsis [ἐστιν] is the governing verb of an independent clause. The subject of the verb is an implied "they." In keeping with John's usage elsewhere, the subject is plural and the verb is singular because neuter plural nouns always take a singular verb (Wallace 1996, 399-400). **Semantically**, the ellipsis [ἐστιν] is an equative present "they are" (cf. KJV NASB ESV NIV NET etc.). It equates the implied subject that refers back to "three" (τρεῖς) in 5:7a with three predicate nominatives: the Spirit, water, and blood.

5:8b καί: The Greek word καί is a conjunction that means "and" (BDAG 494.1ba). **Syntactically**, καί introduces a conjunctive independent clause: "*and* these three are one" (καὶ οἱ τρεῖς εἰς τὸ ἕν εἰσιν). **Semantically**, καί is coordinating connective: "and" (KJV ASV NASB NRSV ESV NIV NET NLT CNT). It provides additional information (Wallace 1996, 671) about the three witnesses: Spirit, the water, and the blood.

εἰσιν: The Greek word εἰσιν is third plural present active indicative from the verb εἰμί that means, "take place" or "occur" or "be in" or "to take place as a phenomenon or event" (BDAG 285.6). **Syntactically**, εἰσιν is the main verb of the independent clause. The subject of the verb is the substantival adjective "the three" (οἱ τρεῖς). The prepositional phrase "into one" (εἰς τὸ ἕν) is the predicate nominative due to word order and the contextual clue that "the three" has been the subject of previous discussion. This type of prepositional construction used as a predicate nominative is rare. It is used most often in Old Testament quotations, which may mean that it reflects Semitic influence (Bateman 2008, 539). **Semantically**, εἰσιν is an equative present: "are" (cf. KJV NASB ESV NIV NET etc.). It underscores a phenomenon or an event, namely that the testimony of the Spirit, the water, and the blood unite together as a powerful witness to the incarnation of Jesus. The idea behind the phrase is not that the three witnesses are one in identity, but that they are in agreement about the nature of Jesus (Smalley 1984, 282).

5:9a εἰ: The Greek word εἰ is a conjunction that means "if" (BDAG 277.1a). **Syntactically** εἰ identifies the clause as a dependent conjunctive clause. The entire dependent clause, "If we receive the testimony of men" (εἰ τὴν μαρτυρίαν τῶν ἀνθρώπων λαμβάνομεν), is functioning adverbially as the protasis of a conditional clause which modifies the verb, "is" (ἐστίν). **Semantically**, εἰ introduces a first class conditional clause: "if" (KJV ASV NASB NRSV ESV NET CNT). Some translations, however, appear to view the conjunction as an assertion without an apodosis (NIV NLT; BDAG 278.4). Nevertheless, the best option is to consider the entire εἰ clause as an assertion for the sake of argument (Wallace 1996, 690–694). John's assumption is identified in the next verb.

λαμβάνομεν: The Greek word λαμβάνομεν is a first plural present active indicative from the verb λαμβάνω that means, "I receive" or "I get" or "I obtain" or "to be a receiver" (BDAG, 584.10b). **Syntactically**, λαμβάνομεν is the governing verb of the dependent conditional conjunctive εἰ clause. The subject is an embedded "we." **Semantically**, λαμβάνομεν is a customary present: "we receive" (KJV ASV NASB NRSV ESV CNT). It expresses an ongoing acceptance (Wallace 1996, 521; cf. NIV NET rendering). John's ongoing assumption is a person's comfort level of accepting the testimony of men as truth. Based upon an assumption his readers would agree to be true, John makes a point about God's testimony in the next clause (Wallace 1996, 694 see Romans 8:9 example).

5:9b ἐστίν: The Greek word ἐστίν is third singular present active indicative from the verb εἰμί that means, "take place" or "occur" or "be in" or "to take place as a phenomenon or event" (BDAG 285.6). **Syntactically**, ἐστίν is the main verb of the independent clause "God's testimony *is* greater" (ἡ μαρτυρία τοῦ θεοῦ μείζων ἐστίν). It is the apodosis of the conditional thought. The subject of the verb is the articular noun "testimony" (ἡ μαρτυρία) due to the presence of the article. The genitive "of God" (τοῦ θεοῦ) is subjective (Wallace 1996, 115). **Semantically**, ἐστίν is an equative present: "is" (cf. KJV NASB ESV NIV NET etc.). It underscores a phenomenon or an event about God's testimony, namely that God's testimony is greater and thus more reliable than the testimony of ordinary people.

5:9c ὅτι: The Greek word ὅτι is a conjunction that means "because" (BDAG 732.4a). **Syntactically**, ὅτι introduces the dependent conjunctive clause: "*because* this is God's testimony" (ὅτι αὕτη ἐστὶν ἡ μαρτυρία τοῦ θεοῦ). The entire clause is functioning adverbially, modifying the verb "is" (ἐστίν). **Semantically**, ὅτι is causal: "because" (KJV NASB ESV NIV NET CNT). It provides the reason why God's testimony is greater than the testimony of any person (Wallace 1996, 460).

ἐστίν: The Greek word ἐστίν is third singular present active indicative from the verb εἰμί that means, "is" or "to be in close connection with" (BDAG 282.2a). **Syntactically**, ἐστίν is the governing verb of the dependent adverbial clause. The subject of the verb is the demonstrative pronoun "this" (αὕτη) due to the grammatical priority of demonstratives over articular noun (Wallace 1996, 42-44). **Semantically**, ἐστίν is an equative present: "is" (cf. KJV NASB ESV NIV NET etc.). It elucidates the idea that the Spirit's testimony is actually God's testimony.

5:9d ὅτι: The Greek word ὅτι is a conjunction, which means "that" (BDAG 732.2a). **Syntactically**, ὅτι introduces the dependent conjunction clause: "*that* he has testified concerning his son" (ὅτι μεμαρτύρηκεν περὶ τοῦ υἱοῦ αὐτοῦ). Yet some translations separate the letters in the conjunction to form an indefinite relative pronoun "which" (ὅ τι; cf. KJV NIV NET). Thus ὅ τι is an indefinite relative clause that removes the awkward repitition of ὅτι. One might take the ὅτι clause adverbially like the previous ὅτι. In this case, John provides the reason for God's testmony because it is about Jesus, his son. It might also be resumptive to the previous clause and explaining it further. Simply saying that the testimony of God is cocerning his son. The best option, however, is to understand this entire ὅτι clause as modifying the demonstrative pronoun "this" (αὕτη). We have seen this construction over and over again throughout 1 John (cf. 3:1, 5, 16; 4:9, 10, 13). **Semantically**, ὅτι then would be epexegetical: "that" (NASB CNT). The ὅτι clause explains or clarifies the demonstrative (Wallace 1996, 459). That content is clarified with the next verb.

μεμαρτύρηκεν: The Greek word μεμαρτύρηκεν is a third singular perfect active indicative from the verb μαρτυρέω that means, "I bear witness to" or to attest to something based upon personal knowledge (BDAG 617.1aα). **Syntactically**, μεμαρτύρηκεν is the governing verb of the dependent conjunctive ὅτι clause. The subject is an implied "he" embedded in the verb. **Semantically**, μεμαρτύρηκεν is an extensive perfect: "he has testified" (KJV NASB NRSV NET NLT). It focuses on the past action from which a present state emerges (Wallace 1996, 577). God's past testimony about his son has certainty in the present. God testified about his son, namely that he is the Messiah who has conquered the world (cf. Bateman 2008, 545-546).

5:10a πιστεύων: The Greek word πιστεύων is a nominative masculine singular present active participle from the verb πιστεύω that means, "I believe" or "to entrust oneself to an entity in complete confidence" (BDAG 817.2aβ). **Syntactically**, πιστεύων is substantival and begins a parenthesis in John's argument (NET). The entire phrase, "the one who believes in the Son of God" (ὁ πιστεύων εἰς τὸν υἱὸν τοῦ θεοῦ) is functioning nominally as the subject of the verb "has" (ἔχει). The object of belief is God. **Semantically**, πιστεύων is a gnomic present: "the one who believes" (NASB NET). Some translations reveal the gnomic sense of this singular participle with "those who do not believe" (NRSV) or "anyone" (NIV). It points out a generic truth about anyone who does not believe (Wallace 1996, 523, 615). That gnomic or timeless truth is evident in the next verb.

ἔχει: The Greek word ἔχει is a third singular present active indicative from the verb ἔχω that means, "I have" or "I possess" or "to have within oneself" (BDAG 420.1d). **Syntactically**, ἔχει is the main verb of the independent clause: "The one who believes in the Son of God *has* this testimony in him" (ὁ πιστεύων εἰς τὸν υἱὸν τοῦ θεοῦ ἔχει τὴν μαρτυρίαν ἐν αὐτῷ). The subject is the participial phrase "the one who believes in the Son of God" (ὁ πιστεύων εἰς τὸν υἱὸν τοῦ θεοῦ). **Semantically**, ἔχει is a gnomic present: "has" (KJV NASB ESV NIV NET CNT). It emphasizing a timeless fact (Wallace 1996, 523). Anyone who believes in Jesus as God's Son has God's testimony within them and thereby life.

5:10b πιστεύων: The Greek word πιστεύων is a nominative masculine singular present active participle from the verb πιστεύω that means, "I believe" or "to consider something to be true and therefore worthy of one's trust" (BDAG 816.1b). **Syntactically**, πιστεύων is a substantival participle. The entire phrase, "the one who does not believe God" (ὁ μὴ πιστεύων τῷ θεῷ) is functioning as the subject of the verb "makes" (πεποίηκεν). The dative case is used because πιστεύω takes a direct object in the dative. The negative particle "not" (μὴ) is used instead of the normal "not" (οὐ) simply because μὴ negates non-indicatives, such as participles, infinitives, and verbs that appear in the subjunctive or optative mood. **Semantically**, πιστεύων is a gnomic present negated with μὴ: "the one who does not believe" (NASB NET). Some translations try to reveal the gnomic sense of the singular participle with "those who do not believe" (NRSV NLT) or "anyone" (NIV). It speaks generically of any person who does not believe (Wallace 1996, 615). It is a timeless truth more pointedly defined with the next verb.

πεποίηκεν: The Greek word πεποίηκεν is a third singular perfect active indicative from the verb ποιέω that means, "I do" or "I bring about" or "to undertake or do something that brings about a state or condition" (BDAG 840.2nβ). **Syntactically**, πεποίηκεν is the main verb of the independent clause: "the one who does not believe God *has made* him out to be a liar" (ὁ μὴ πιστεύων τῷ θεῷ ψεύστην πεποίηκεν αὐτόν). The subject is the participial phrase, "the one who does not believe God" (ὁ μὴ πιστεύων τῷ θεῷ). This is a double accusative object-complement construction. The direct object of the verb "has made" (πεποίηκεν) is the pronoun "him" (αὐτόν). The second accusative "liar" (ψεύστην) functions as the complement. This type of construction is often translated with the words "to be." Therefore, it is translated "the one who does not believe God has made him *to be* a liar" (Wallace 1996, 181-186). **Semantically**, πεποίηκεν is a gnomic perfect with an extensive perfect: "has made" (KJV ASV NASB ESV NIV NET CNT). The generic subject is in view with a focus on the decisive act having been carried out (Wallace 1996, 580). The one who has disbelieved God has labeled him a liar.

Theological Nugget: John has insinuated that anyone who denies God's main claims are liars. The one who claims that he has never sinned (1:10), the one who says they know God but experiences no life change (2:4), the one who denies that Jesus is the Messiah (2:22), the one who says they love God but refuses to love other believers (4:20), and the one who does not believe in God's testimony about Jesus (5:10) are all called liars. These may be laid out chiastically whereby the ultimate liar is the one who denies that Jesus is the Christ.

1:10   If we say, "We have not sinned," we make God a liar . . .
2:4   The one who says "I have known God," yet does not keep his commandments is a liar . . .

2:22   Who is the liar but the person who denies that Jesus is the Christ?
4:20   If anyone says, "I love God," but hates his fellow Christian, he is a liar . . .
5:10   The one who does not believe God has made him (God) a liar . . .

5:10c ὅτι: The Greek word ὅτι is a conjunction that means "because" (BDAG 732.4a). **Syntactically,** ὅτι introduces the dependent conjunctive clause, "since he has not believed in the testimony" (ὅτι οὐ πεπίστευκεν εἰς τὴν μαρτυρίαν). The entire ὅτι clause functions adverbially. It modifies the verb "has made" (πεποίηκεν). **Semantically,** ὅτι is causal: "because" (KJV ASV NASB ESV NIV NET CNT NLT). It provides the reason why the one who does not believe makes God out to be a liar. That reasons is found in the next verb.

πεπίστευκεν: The Greek word πεπίστευκεν is a third singular perfect active indicative from the verb πιστεύω that means, "I believe" or "to consider something to be true and therefore worthy of one's trust" (BDAG 816.1aε). **Syntactically,** πεπίστευκεν is the governing verb of the dependent conjunctive ὅτι clause. The subject of the verb is an implied "he." It refers to "the one who does not believe God" (ὁ μὴ πιστεύων τῷ θεῷ). **Semantically,** πεπίστευκεν gnomic perfect with an extensive perfect negated with οὐ: "he has not believed" (cf. KJV NASB ESV NIV NET cf.). It focuses on the past event from which a current state emerges (Wallace 1996, 577). The generic subject is in view with a focus on the decisive act of disbelief (Wallace 1996, 580). Anyone who simply does not trust what God has said is labelled as a liar.

5:10d ἥν: The Greek word ἥν is accusative singular feminine from the relative pronoun ὅς, which means, "that" (BDAG 725.1a). **Syntactically,** ἥν introduces a dependent relative clause: "*that* God has testified about his son" (ἥν μεμαρτύρηκεν ὁ θεὸς περὶ τοῦ υἱοῦ αὐτοῦ). It is an adjectival clause. It modifies the noun "testimony" (μαρτυρίαν). This relative pronoun is in the accusative case because it is the direct object of the verb "has" (μεμαρτύρηκεν). The entire relative clause closes John's parenthesis in his argument and gives us some concluding information about God's testimony, which is identified in the next verb.

μεμαρτύρηκεν: The Greek word μεμαρτύρηκεν is a third singular perfect active indicative from the verb μαρτυρέω that means, "I bear witness" or "to confirm or attest something on the basis of personal knowledge or belief" (BDAG 618.1b). **Syntactically,** μεμαρτύρηκεν is the governing verb of the dependent relative clause. The subject is the proper noun "God" (ὁ θεὸς). **Semantically,** μεμαρτύρηκεν is an extensive perfect: "has testified" (KJV ASV NASB NRSV ESV NET CNT). It focuses on a past event from which a current state emerges (Wallace 1996, 577). God has bore witness about the identity of his son and that testimony remains valid.

5:11a καί: The Greek word καί is a conjunction that means "and" (BDAG 494.1c). **Syntactically,** καί introduces a conjunctive independent clause: "*and* this is the testimony" (καὶ αὕτη ἐστὶν ἡ μαρτυρία). **Semantically,** καί is coordinating connective: "and" (cf. KJV NASB ESV NIV NET etc.). It is a coordinating explicative that serves to explain God's greater testimonty introdcued in 5:9b. It provides additional information about God's testimony, which is underscored with the equative verb and subsequent ὅτι clause.

ἐστίν: The Greek word ἐστίν is third singular present active indicative from the verb εἰμί that means, "is" or "to be in close connection with" (BDAG 283.2a). **Syntactically,** ἐστίν is the main verb of the independent clause. The subject of the verb is the demonstrative pronoun "this" (αὕτη) due to the grammatical priority of pronouns (Wallace 1996, 42-44). **Semantically,** ἐστίν is an equative present:

"is" (cf. KJV NASB ESV NIV NET etc.). It equates the demonstrative pronoun "this" (αὕτη) with the testimony. The meaning of the demonstrative pronoun is clarified in the next ὅτι clause.

^{5:11b} ὅτι: The Greek word ὅτι is a conjunction, which means "that" (BDAG 732.2a). **Syntactically,** ὅτι introduces the compound dependent clause: "*that* God has given us eternal life" (ὅτι ζωὴν αἰώνιον ἔδωκεν ἡμῖν ὁ θεός). The entire clause is functioning adjectivally, modifying the demonstrative "this" (αὕτη). **Semantically,** ὅτι is epexegetical: "that" (KJV ASV NASB ESV CNT). The ὅτι clause explains or clarifies the demonstrative "that" (αὕτη; Wallace 1996, 459). The testimony of God is clearly defined in the remainder of the clause.

ἔδωκεν: The Greek word ἔδωκεν is a third singular aorist active indicative from the verb δίδωμι that means, "I give" or "I bestow" or "I grant" or "to give something out" (BDAG 242.2). **Syntactically,** ἔδωκεν is the governing verb of the first part of the compound dependent adjectival clause. The subject of the verb is the proper noun "God" (ὁ θεός). **Semantically,** ἔδωκεν is a constative aorist: "granted" or "gave" (ASV NRSV ESV). It focuses on the event as a whole (Wallace 1996, 557). God granted eternal life to all those who trust in his testimony about Jesus.

^{5:11c} καί: The Greek word καί is a conjunction that means "and" (BDAG 494.1c). **Syntactically,** καί introduces a independent conjunctive clause: "*and* that life is through his son" (καὶ αὕτη ἡ ζωὴ ἐν τῷ υἱῷ αὐτοῦ ἐστιν). **Semantically,** καί is coordinating connective: "and" (cf. NRSV ESV NIV NET CNT). It is a coordinating connector that explains from whence eternal life comes. The expanded information is identified in the remainder of the clause.

ἐστιν: The Greek word ἐστιν is third singular present active indicative from the verb εἰμί that means, "is" or "to be in close connection with" (BDAG 283.2a). **Syntactically,** ἐστιν is the governing verb of independent conjunctive clause. The subject of the verb is the nominal phrase "this life" (αὕτη ἡ ζωή). The demonstrative pronoun "this" (αὕτη) is anaphorical and refers back to the eternal life mentioned in the previous clause. **Semantically,** ἐστιν is an equative present: "is" (cf. KJV NASB ESV NIV NET etc.). It equates "this life" (αὕτη ἡ ζωή) that refers back to "eternal life" (ζωὴν αἰώνιον) with Jesus.

^{5:12a} ἔχων: The Greek word ἔχων is a nominative masculine singular present active participle from the verb ἔχω that means, "I have" or to experience an emotion or inner possession (BDAG 421.7aβ). **Syntactically,** ἔχων is a substantival participle. The entire phrase, "the one who has the son" (ὁ ἔχων τὸν υἱὸν) functions as the subject of the verb "has" (ἔχει). **Semantically,** ἔχων is a gnomic present: "the one who" (NET CNT) or "whoever" (NRSV ESV NLT). The participle is being used in generic utterances (Wallace 1996, 615). John describes a timeless fact about people in general. The timeless fact is described within the remaining portion of the clause beginning with the next verb.

ἔχει: The Greek word ἔχει is a third singular present active indicative from the verb ἔχω that means, "I have" or to experience an emotion or inner possession (BDAG 421.7aβ). **Syntactically,** ἔχει is the main verb of the independent asyndeton clause. The subject is the entire participial phrase "the one who has the son" (ὁ ἔχων τὸν υἱὸν). **Semantically,** ἔχει is a gnomic present: "has" (cf. KJV NASB ESV NIV NET etc.). The verb is part of the generic statement that was introduced with the generic participle (Wallace 1996, 523). John underscores a timeless truth about a person's possession of eternal life in the here and now.

^{5:12b} ἔχων: The Greek word ἔχων is a nominative masculine singular present active participle from the verb ἔχω that means, "I have" or to experience an emotion or inner possession (BDAG 421.7aβ).

Syntactically, ἔχων is a substantival participle. The entire phrase, "the one who does not have the son" (ὁ μὴ ἔχων τὸν υἱὸν τοῦ θεοῦ) is functioning as the subject of the verb "has" (ἔχει). The negative particle "not" (μή) is used instead of the normal "not" (οὐ) simply because μή negates non-indicatives, such as participles, infinitives, and verbs that appear in the subjunctive or optative mood. **Semantically**, ἔχων is a gnomic present: "the one who" (NET CNT) or "whoever" (NRSV ESV NLT). The participle is being used in generic utterances (Wallace 1996, 615). John describes a timeless fact about people in general. The timeless fact is described within the remaining of portion of the clause.

ἔχει: The Greek word ἔχει is a third singular present active indicative from the verb ἔχω that means, "I have" or to experience an emotion or inner possession (BDAG 421.7aβ). **Syntactically**, ἔχει is the main verb of the independent asyndeton clause. The subject is the entire participial phrase "the one who does not have the son of God does not have this life" (ὁ μὴ ἔχων τὸν υἱὸν τοῦ θεοῦ τὴν ζωὴν οὐκ ἔχει.). The NET Bible translates the article here as "this" since it anaphorically points back to the eternal life previously mentioned. **Semantically**, ἔχει with the negated μή is a gnomic present: "has not" or "does not have" (NRSV ESV NIV NET CNT NLT). The verb is part of the generic statement that was introduced with the generic participle (Wallace 1996, 523). With this thought John summarizes what he has been saying in the previous verses. Eternal life is based on receiving, agreeing with, and firmly believing in the true identity of Jesus, and not buying into the false teaching of the secessionists.

1 John 5:13-21

Verb Recognition for 1 John 5:13–21

¹³Ταῦτα ἔγραψα ὑμῖν ἵνα εἰδῆτε ὅτι ζωὴν ἔχετε αἰώνιον, τοῖς πιστεύουσιν εἰς τὸ ὄνομα τοῦ υἱοῦ τοῦ θεοῦ. ¹⁴καὶ αὕτη ἐστὶν ἡ παρρησία ἣν ἔχομεν πρὸς αὐτόν, ὅτι ἐάν τι αἰτώμεθα κατὰ τὸ θέλημα αὐτοῦ ἀκούει ἡμῶν. ¹⁵καὶ ἐὰν οἴδαμεν ὅτι ἀκούει ἡμῶν ὃ ἐὰν αἰτώμεθα, οἴδαμεν ὅτι ἔχομεν τὰ αἰτήματα ἃ ᾐτήκαμεν ἀπ᾽ αὐτοῦ. ¹⁶Ἐάν τις ἴδῃ τὸν ἀδελφὸν αὐτοῦ ἁμαρτάνοντα ἁμαρτίαν μὴ πρὸς θάνατον, αἰτήσει, καὶ δώσει αὐτῷ ζωήν, τοῖς ἁμαρτάνουσιν μὴ πρὸς θάνατον. ἔστιν ἁμαρτία πρὸς θάνατον· οὐ περὶ ἐκείνης λέγω ἵνα ἐρωτήσῃ. ¹⁷πᾶσα ἀδικία ἁμαρτία ἐστίν, καὶ ἔστιν ἁμαρτία οὐ πρὸς θάνατον. ¹⁸Οἴδαμεν ὅτι πᾶς ὁ γεγεννημένος ἐκ τοῦ θεοῦ οὐχ ἁμαρτάνει, ἀλλ᾽ ὁ γεννηθεὶς ἐκ τοῦ θεοῦ τηρεῖ αὐτόν, καὶ ὁ πονηρὸς οὐχ ἅπτεται αὐτοῦ. ¹⁹οἴδαμεν ὅτι ἐκ τοῦ θεοῦ ἐσμεν, καὶ ὁ κόσμος ὅλος ἐν τῷ πονηρῷ κεῖται. ²⁰οἴδαμεν δὲ ὅτι ὁ υἱὸς τοῦ θεοῦ ἥκει, καὶ δέδωκεν ἡμῖν διάνοιαν ἵνα γινώσκομεν τὸν ἀληθινόν· καὶ ἐσμὲν ἐν τῷ ἀληθινῷ, ἐν τῷ υἱῷ αὐτοῦ Ἰησοῦ Χριστῷ. οὗτός ἐστιν ὁ ἀληθινὸς θεὸς καὶ ζωὴ αἰώνιος. ²¹Τεκνία, φυλάξατε ἑαυτὰ ἀπὸ τῶν εἰδώλων.

Clausal Outline Translated for 1 John 5:13–21

^{5:13a} Ταῦτα **ἔγραψα** ὑμῖν . . . (τοῖς πιστεύουσιν εἰς τὸ ὄνομα τοῦ υἱοῦ τοῦ θεοῦ).
^{5:13a} I have written these things to you . . . (who believe in the name of the Son of God).

|

     ^{5:13b} ἵνα **εἰδῆτε** (ὅτι ζωὴν **ἔχετε** αἰώνιον),
     ^{5:13b} **so that you may know** (that you have eternal life),

^{5:14a} **καὶ** αὕτη **ἐστὶν** ἡ παρρησία
^{5:14a} and this **is** the confidence

     |

     ^{5:14b} **ἣν ἔχομεν** πρὸς αὐτόν,
     ^{5:14b} **that we have** before him:

       |

       ^{5:14c} **ὅτι** . . . **ἀκούει** ἡμῶν.
       ^{5:14c} **that** . . . **he hears** us.

          |

          ^{5:14d} **ἐάν** τι **αἰτώμεθα** κατὰ τὸ θέλημα αὐτοῦ
          ^{5:14d} **whatever we ask** anything accoding to his will

^{5:15a} **καὶ ἐὰν οἴδαμεν** (ὅτι ἀκούει ἡμῶν)
^{5:15a} and **if we know** (that he hears us)

          |

          ^{5:15b} [**ἀκούει**] (ὃ **ἐὰν αἰτώμεθα**),
          ^{5:15b} *namely*, [he listens to] (**whatever we ask**),

   |

^{5:15c} **οἴδαμεν** (ὅτι **ἔχομεν** τὰ αἰτήματα)
^{5:15c} **we know** (that we have the requests)

       |

       ^{5:15d} **ἃ ἠτήκαμεν** ἀπ᾽ αὐτοῦ.
       ^{5:15d} **that we have asked** from him

^{5:16a} **Ἐάν** τις **ἴδῃ** τὸν ἀδελφὸν αὐτοῦ ἁμαρτάνοντα ἁμαρτίαν μὴ πρὸς θάνατον,
^{5:16a} **If** anyone **sees** his *fellow follower of Jesus* committing a sin not *leading* to death,

|

^{5:16b} **αἰτήσει**,
^{5:16b} **he should ask**,

^{5:16c} καὶ **δώσει** αὐτῷ ζωήν, (τοῖς ἁμαρτάνουσιν μὴ πρὸς θάνατον),
^{5:16c} And God **will grant** life (to the one who does not commit a sin *leading* to death).

^{5:16d} **ἔστιν** ἁμαρτία πρὸς θάνατον·
^{5:16d} there **is** a sin *leading* to death;

^{5:16e} οὐ (περὶ ἐκείνης) **λέγω** (ἵνα **ἐρωτήσῃ**).
^{5:16e} **I do** not **say** (that he should ask) (about that).

^{5:17a} πᾶσα ἀδικία ἁμαρτία **ἐστίν**,
^{5:17a} All unrighteousness **is** sin,

^{5:17b} καὶ **ἔστιν** ἁμαρτία οὐ πρὸς θάνατον.
^{5:17b} and yet there **is** a sin not *leading* in death.

^{5:18a} **Οἴδαμεν** (ὅτι πᾶς ὁ γεγεννημένος ἐκ τοῦ θεοῦ οὐχ **ἁμαρτάνει**,
^{5:18a} **We know** (that everyone fathered by God does not *persist in* sin,

  ^{5:18b} ἀλλ᾽ [ὅτι] ὁ γεννηθεὶς ἐκ τοῦ θεοῦ **τηρεῖ** αὐτόν,
  ^{5:18b} but the one fathered by God **he preserves** him

  ^{5:18c} καὶ [ὅτι] ὁ πονηρὸς οὐχ **ἅπτεται** αὐτοῦ).
  ^{5:18c} and the evil one cannot **harm** him).

^{5:19a} **οἴδαμεν** (ὅτι ἐκ τοῦ θεοῦ **ἐσμεν**,
^{5:19a} **We know** (that we are of God,

  ^{5:19b} καὶ [ὅτι] ὁ κόσμος ὅλος ἐν τῷ πονηρῷ **κεῖται**).
  ^{5:19b} and [that] the whole world **lies** in the power of the evil *one*).

^{5:20a} **οἴδαμεν** δὲ (ὅτι ὁ υἱὸς τοῦ θεοῦ **ἥκει**,
^{5:20a} And **we know** (that the son of God has come,

  ^{5:20b} καὶ [ὅτι] **δέδωκεν** ἡμῖν διάνοιαν
  ^{5:20b} and [that] **he has given** us understanding
    |
    ^{5:20c} ἵνα **γινώσκωμεν** τὸν ἀληθινόν)·
    ^{5:20c} **in order that we may know** the truth);

^{5:20d} καὶ **ἐσμὲν** ἐν τῷ ἀληθινῷ, ἐν τῷ υἱῷ αὐτοῦ Ἰησοῦ Χριστῷ.
^{5:20d} and **we are** in the true one, in his son Jesus, who is the Christ.

^{5:20e} οὗτός **ἐστιν** ὁ ἀληθινὸς θεὸς καὶ ζωὴ αἰώνιος.
^{5:20e} This one **is** the true God and eternal life.

^{5:21} Τεκνία, **φυλάξατε** ἑαυτὰ ἀπὸ τῶν εἰδώλων.
^{5:21} Children, **guard** yourselves from idols.

Syntax Explained for 1 John 5:13–21

^{5:13a} ἔγραψα: The Greek word ἔγραψα is a first singular aorist active indicative from the verb γράφω that means "I write" or "I compose" with reference to composing a letter (BDAG 207.2d). **Syntactically,**

ἔγραψα is the main verb of the independent clause "*I have written* these things to you" (Ταῦτα ἔγραψα ὑμῖν). The assumed subject "I" refers to the author. **Semantically**, ἔγραψα is an epistolary aorist: "I have written" (NASB NET NLT; cf. Wallace 1996, 562).

Lexical Nugget: This gets at the idea of what the referent of "these things" (Ταῦτα) truly is. It could simply be a reference to the preceding discussion (5:11-12 or 5:1-12), but it seems to be more than that. In a similar way to John 20:31, our author appears to be referring to his entire work. Notice the parallel to the ending of the prologue in 1 John 1:4 "and we have written these things" (καὶ ταῦτα γράφομεν ἡμεῖς). John is summarizing the intention behind the letter as a whole (Brown 1984, 607; Bateman 2008, 557).

πιστεύουσιν: The Greek word πιστεύουσιν is a dative masculine plural present active participle from the verb πιστεύω that means, "I believe" or "I trust" or "to entrust oneself to an entity in complete confidence" (BDAG 817.2αβ). **Syntactically**, πιστεύουσιν is a substantival participle. The entire phrase, "*who believe* in the name of the Son of God" (τοῖς πιστεύουσιν εἰς τὸ ὄνομα τοῦ υἱοῦ τοῦ θεοῦ) is in apposition to the personal pronoun "you" (ὑμῖν) which is the indirect object of the verb "I wrote" (ἔγραψα). John writes to those who believe that Jesus is the Son of God to assure them of their salvation and destiny. The phrase is placed in parenthesis in order to visualize its contribution to the independent clause. **Semantically**, πιστεύουσιν is a customary present: "who believe" (NASB NRSV ESV NIV NET CNT NLT). Since the participle is substantival, its aspect has less force (Wallace 1996, 527, 615). It describes the one who has eternal life as the one who continually holds to the truth about the true identity of Jesus as God's son.

5:13b ἵνα: The Greek word ἵνα is a conjunction that means "that" or "in order that" (BDAG 475.a) or "so that" (BDAG 477.3). **Syntactically**, ἵνα introduces a conjunctive dependent clause: "*so that* you might know that you have eternal life" (ἵνα εἰδῆτε ὅτι ζωὴν ἔχετε αἰώνιον). **Syntactically**, the clause is adverbial modifying the verb "I wrote" (ἔγραψα). **Semantically**, ἵνα is classified as purpose: "in order that" or "that" (KJV ASV ESV; cf. NET note), though some translations seem to indicate result: "so that" (NASB NRSV NIV CNT NLT). However, the ἵνα clause indicates John's purpose for writing.

εἰδῆτε: The Greek word εἰδῆτε is a second plural perfect active subjunctive from the verb οἶδα that means, "I know" or "to have information about" (BDAG 693.1e). It is in the subjunctive mood because it follows an ἵνα. **Syntactically**, εἰδῆτε is the governing verb of the dependent conjunctive ἵνα clause. It functions adverbially modifying the verb, "I wrote" (ἔγραψα). The assumed subject "you" refers to the recipients of the letter. The word is in the subjunctive because it follows a ἵνα. **Semantically**, εἰδῆτε is a perfect with present force: "may know" (cf. KJV NASB ESV NIV NET etc.). It is a verb in the "perfect tense without the usual aspectual significance" (Wallace 1996, 579). John's intention for writing this letter to his readers is for them to come to know something. That something is found in the ὅτι clause.

ὅτι: The Greek word ὅτι is a conjunction that means "that" (BDAG 731.1c). **Syntactically**, ὅτι introduces a dependent conjunctive clause: "*that* you have eternal life" (ὅτι ζωὴν ἔχετε αἰώνιον). The entire clause is functioning substantivally as the direct object of the verb "you might know" (εἰδῆτε). **Semantically**, ὅτι is indirect discourse: "that" (cf. KJV NASB ESV NIV NET etc.). The entire ὅτι clause provides the content of the knowledge (Wallace 1996, 456), which is clearly expressed in the next verb.

ἔχετε: The Greek word ἔχετε is a second plural present active indicative from the verb ἔχω that means, "I have" or to experience an emotion or inner possession (BDAG 421.7aβ). **Syntactically**, ἔχετε is the governing verb of the dependent substantival clause. The subject is the implied "you" embedded in the verb and refers to the orthodox readers of the letter. **Semantically**, ἔχετε is a customary present: "you have" (cf. KJV NASB ESV NIV NET etc.). It underscores an on-going action (Wallace 1996, 521). John underscores to his readers their possession of eternal life.

5:14a καί: The Greek word καί is a conjunction that means "and" (BDAG 494.1b). **Syntactically**, καί introduces a conjunctive independent clause: "*and* this is the confidence" (καὶ αὕτη ἐστὶν ἡ παρρησία). **Semantically**, καί is a coordinating connective: "and" (KJV ASV NRSV ESV NET NLT CNT), even though two do not translate καί (NASB NIV). It provides additonal information (Wallace 1996, 671) about the assurance believers can have about eternal life which is clarified in the subsequent verb and dependent clauses.

ἐστιν: The Greek word ἐστίν is third singular present active indicative from the verb εἰμί that means, "is" or "to be in close connection with" (BDAG 283.2a). **Syntactically**, ἐστίν is the main verb of the independent clause: "this *is* the confidence" (καὶ αὕτη ἐστὶν ἡ παρρησία). The subject of the verb is the demonstrative pronoun "this" (αὕτη), due to the grammatical priority of demonstratives (Wallace 1996, 42-43). **Semantically**, ἐστίν is an equative present: "is" (cf. KJV NASB ESV NIV NET etc.). It equates "this" (αὕτη), which is defined in the next two clause, with confidence.

5:14b ἥν: The Greek word ἥν is accusative singular feminine from the relative pronoun ὅς that means, "which" (BDAG 725.1a). **Syntactically**, ἥν introduces a relative clause: "*which* we have from him" (ἥν ἔχομεν πρὸς αὐτόν). It modifies the predicate nominative, "confidence" (ἡ παρρησία) and is thereby adjectival. This relative pronoun is in the accusative case because is serves as the direct object of the verb "has" (ἔχομεν).

ἔχομεν: The Greek word ἔχομεν is a first plural present active indicative from the verb ἔχω, which means, "I have" or to experience an inner condition (BDAG 421.7aβ). **Syntactically**, ἔχομεν is the governing verb of the dependent relative clause. The subject of the verb is an implied "we" embedded in the verb and refers to the readers who have placed their faith in Jesus as the Son of God. **Semantically**, ἔχομεν is a customary present: "we have" (cf. KJV NASB ESV NIV NET etc.). It points out a continual state of being Wallace 1996, 521). Believers have their confidence bestowed on them by God himself (cf. 4:17).

5:14c ὅτι: The Greek word ὅτι is a conjunction that means, "that" (BDAG 732.2a). **Syntactically**, ὅτι introduces the dependent conjunctive clause: "*that* if we ask for anything according to his will, he listens to us" (ὅτι ἐάν τι αἰτώμεθα κατὰ τὸ θέλημα αὐτοῦ ἀκούει ἡμῶν). The entire ὅτι clause functions adjectivally, modifying the demonstrative pronoun "this" (αὕτη). **Semantically**, ὅτι is expexegetical: "that" (cf. KJV NASB ESV NIV NET etc.). It clarifies or completes the demonstrative pronoun "this" (αὕτη; cf. Wallace 1996, 459). The details of that clarification are found in the next verb and ἐάν clause.

ἀκούει: The Greek word ἀκούει is a third singular present active indicative from the verb ἀκούω that means, "I listen" or "to pay attention to by listening" (BDAG 38.5). **Syntactically**, ἀκούει is the main verb of the independent clause. It is the apodosis of the conditional idea: "he *listens* to us" (ἀκούει ἡμῶν). The subject of the verb is an implied "he" embedded in the verb and refers to God. The pronoun is genitive because ἀκούω takes an object in the genitive case. The preposition here should be translated as standard rather than as purpose. **Semantically**, ἀκούει is a customary present: "he listens" or "he hears" (seemingly BDAG 38.1c). It stresses the continual nature of God's desire to listen to believers (Wallace 1996, 521). Yet what is to be asked is qualified in the ἐάν clause.

5:14d ἐάν: The Greek word ἐάν is a conjunction that means, "whenever" (BDAG 268.2). **Syntactically**, ἐάν identifies the clause as a dependent conjunctive clause. The entire dependent clause: "*whenever* we ask for anything according to his will" (ἐάν τι αἰτώμεθα κατὰ τὸ θέλημα αὐτοῦ). It functions adverbially, modifying the verb, "he listens" (ἀκούει). **Semantically**, ἐάν introduces a third class conditional clause: "whenever" (NET), though a popular alternative is "if" (seemingly BDAG 267.1aα). It presents a condition as uncertain of fulfillment, but still likely (Wallace 1996, 696). The conjunction ἐάν is a marker that coordinates the likelihood of God's listening as long as it occurs with the action presented in the next verb.

αἰτώμεθα: The Greek word αἰτώμεθα is a first plural present middle subjunctive from the verb αἰτέω that means, "I ask" or "to ask for, with a claim on receipt of an answer" (BDAG 30). It is in the subjunctive mood because it follows an ἐάν. **Syntactically**, αἰτώμεθα is the governing verb of the dependent conditional clause. The verb is in the subjunctive mood because it is part of an ἐάν clause. **Semantically**, αἰτώμεθα is an iterative present: "we ask" (cf. KJV NASB ESV NIV NET etc.). It describes an event that repeatedly happens (Wallace 1996, 520). John underscores that whenever a believer asks God for something that is in agreement with his will, he will hear them. The believer is to ask in correspondance with the will of God (Culy 2004, 133).

Syntactical Nugget: The fact that αἰτώμεθα is in the middle voice should be noted. John has previously used the same verb in the active voice, so there must be a special nuance in this context. The classical middle voice is normally used when the action is both performed by the subject and the subject receives some sort of benefit from that action. We can see both apects here in this passage. The petitioner is the one making the request from God, but is also the beneficiary of God's sympathetic audience (cf. Culy 2004, 133).

5:15a καί: The Greek word καί is a conjunction that means "and" (BDAG 494.1bβ). **Syntactically**, καί introduces an independent conjunctive clause: "*and* if we know that he listens to us" (καὶ ἐὰν οἴδαμεν ὅτι ἀκούει ἡμῶν). **Semantically**, καί is a coordinating connective: "and" (NIV NET CNT NLT). It is a common feature drawn from Hebrew. Many translations do not translate καί (KJV ASV NASB NRSV ESV). Nevertheless it provides additional comments on the confidence evident in the ἐάν clause.

ἐάν: The Greek word ἐάν is a conjunction that means, "if" (BDAG 267.1bβ). **Syntactically**, ἐάν identifies the clause as a dependent conjunctive clause. The entire ἐάν clause: "*if* we know that he listens to us" (ἐὰν οἴδαμεν ὅτι ἀκούει ἡμῶν) functions adverbially, modifying the verb, "he knows" (οἴδαμεν). **Semantically**, ἐάν introduces a third class conditional clause of probability: "if" (cf. KJV NASB ESV NIV NET etc). The condition is uncertain of fulfillment but still likely (Wallace 1996, 696). What that uncertain condition is evident in the next verb.

οἴδαμεν: The Greek word οἴδαμεν is a first plural perfect active indicative from the verb οἶδα that means, "I know" or "to have information about" (BDAG 693.1e). **Syntactically**, οἴδαμεν is the governing verb of the dependent conditional clause. The assumed subject "we" refers to John and the readers of the letter. The appearance of οἴδαμεν in the indicative mood is rare after the conjunction ἐάν. Perhaps a first class condition is intended with an anomalous switch in conjuction from εἰ to ἐάν. If so, then instead of a hypothetical, John is assuming for the sake of argument that God does listen and that believers have whatever we ask (NET note). Culy calls this strange usage of ἐάν + indicative solecistic, but the usage is not unheard of (Culy 2004, 134; Zerwick 1963, §330-331; Brown 1984, 609-610). **Semantically**, οἴδαμεν is a perfect with present force: "may know" (cf. KJV NASB ESV NIV NET etc.). It is a verb in the "perfect tense without the usual aspectual significance" (Wallace 1996, 579). John's hypothetical of knowledge is found in the ὅτι clause.

ὅτι: The Greek word ὅτι is a conjunction, which means "that" (BDAG 731.1c). **Syntactically**, ὅτι introduce a dependent conjunctive clause: "*that* he listens to us" (ὅτι ἀκούει ἡμῶν). The entire clause is functioning substantivally as the direct object of the verb "know" (οἴδαμεν). The clause is placed in parenthesis in order to visualize its contribution to the independent clause. **Semantically**, ὅτι is an indirect discourse: "that" (cf. KJV NASB ESV NIV NET etc.). The entire ὅτι clause provides the content of the knowledge (Wallace 1996, 456), which is clearly expressed in the next verb.

ἀκούει: The Greek word ἀκούει is a third singular present active indicative from the verb ἀκούω that means, "I listen" or "to pay attention to by listening" (BDAG 38.5). **Syntactically**, ἀκούει is the governing verb of the dependent ὅτι clause. The assumed subject "we" refers to John and the readers of the letter. **Semantically**, ἀκούει is a customary present: "he listens" or "he hears" (seemingly BDAG 38.1c). It stresses the continual nature of God's desire to listen to believers (Wallace 1996, 521). Yet John's assurance that God listens is underscored in next clause.

5:15b ὃ ἐάν: The Greek word ὃ is a neuter singular accusative from the relative pronoun ὅς that means, "what" (BDAG 727.1jα). The Greek word ἐάν is a conjunction, which means "ever" (BDAG 268.3). Together ὃ ἐάν is translated "whatever" (see previous occurrence 3:22): "*namely*, [he listens] to whatever we ask" **Syntactically**, the Greek construction ὃ ἐάν is an indefinte relative pronoun that is classified as a dependent pronominal clause. The entire clause "whatever we ask" (ὃ ἐὰν αἰτῶμεν) most likely functions as the direct object of an elliptical verb "he listens" ([ἀκούει]). The entire thought is in apposition to the previous clause "he hears us" (ἀκούει ἡμῶν; cf. Culy 2004, 134). The relative pronoun itself is in the accusative case because it is functioning as the direct object of the verb "we ask" (αἰτώμεθα).

αἰτώμεθα: The Greek word αἰτῶμεν is a first plural present active subjunctive from the verb αἰτέω that means, "I ask" or "to ask for, with a claim on receipt of an answer" (BDAG 30). It is in the subjunctive mood because it follows an ἐάν. **Syntactically**, αἰτῶμεν is the governing verb of the dependent indefinite relative ὃ ἐάν clause. **Semantically**, αἰτῶμεν is an iterative present: "we ask" (cf. KJV NASB ESV NIV NET etc.). It describes an event that repeatedly happens (Wallace 1996, 521). John points out that whenever a believer asks God for anything, God will consider it.

5:15c οἴδαμεν: The Greek word οἴδαμεν is a first plural perfect active indicative from the verb οἶδα that means, "I know" or "to have information about" (BDAG 693.1e). **Syntactically**, οἴδαμεν is the main verb of the independent clause: "*we know* that we have the requests" (οἴδαμεν ὅτι ἔχομεν τὰ αἰτήματα). The assumed subject "we" refers to John and the readers of the letter who believe in Jesus. This clause serves as the apodosis of the conditional phrase. **Semantically**, οἴδαμεν is a perfect with present force: "know" (cf. KJV NASB ESV NIV NET etc.). It is in the "perfect tense without the usual aspectual significance" (Wallace 1996, 579). The content of what John's readers know appears in the ὅτι clause.

ὅτι: The Greek word ὅτι is a conjunction, which means "that" (BDAG 731.1c). **Syntactically**, ὅτι introduces the dependent clause: "*that* we have the requests" (ὅτι ἔχομεν τὰ αἰτήματα). The entire clause is functioning substantivally. It is the direct object of the verb "we know" (οἴδαμεν). The clause is placed in parenthesis in order to visualize its contribution to the independent clause.

Semantically, ὅτι is an indirect discourse: "that" (cf. KJV NASB ESV NIV NET etc.). The entire ὅτι clause provides the content of the knowledge (Wallace 1996, 456), which is clearly expressed in the next verb.

ἔχομεν: The Greek word ἔχομεν is a first plural present active indicative from the verb ἔχω, which means, "I have" or to experience a benefit (BDAG 421.7aγ). Syntactically, ἔχομεν serves as the governing verb of the dependent substantival clause. The subject of the verb is an implied "we" embedded in the verb and refers to John and the orthodox readers who believe that Jesus is God's son. Semantically, ἔχομεν is an customary present: "we have" (cf. KJV NASB ESV NIV NET etc.). It describes an event that occurs regularly (Wallace 1996, 521). Believers always and repeatedly have requests of God.

5:15d ἅ: The Greek word ἅ is accusative plural neuter from the relative pronoun ὅς, which means, "that" (BDAG 725.1a). **Syntactically**, ἅ introduces a dependent relative clause: "*that* we have asked from him" (ἅ ᾐτήκαμεν ἀπ᾽ αὐτοῦ). It is an adjectival clause in that the entire clause modifies the noun "requests" (αἰτήματα). This relative pronoun is in the accusative case because it is the direct object of the verb "we have asked" (ᾐτήκαμεν). The clause provides more information about a believer's continual request.

ᾐτήκαμεν: The Greek word ᾐτήκαμεν is a first plural perfect active indicative from the verb αἰτέω that means, "I ask" or "to ask for, with a claim on receipt of an answer" (BDAG 30). **Syntactically**, ᾐτήκαμεν functions as the governing verb of the dependent relative clause. The subject of the verb is an implied "we" embedded in the verb. John refers to the readers who believe that Jesus is God's son. **Semantically**, ᾐτήκαμεν is an extensive perfect: "we have asked" (ASV NASB NET CNT). It emphasizes the completed action from which a present state emerges (Wallace 1996, 577). When believers ask God for things in accordance with his will, they can expect that they will receive them.

5:16a ἐάν: The Greek word ἐάν is a conjunction, which means "if" (BDAG 267b 1aβ). **Syntactically**, ἐάν identifies the clause as a dependent conjunctive clause. The entire dependent clause: "if anyone sees his brother or sister sinning a sin that does not lead to death" (Ἐάν τις ἴδῃ τὸν ἀδελφὸν αὐτοῦ ἁμαρτάνοντα ἁμαρτίαν μὴ πρὸς θάνατον) functions adverbially. It modifies the verbs "he should ask" (αἰτήσει) and "he will give" (δώσει). **Semantically**, ἐάν introduces a third class conditional clause: "if" (cf. KJV NASB ESV NIV NET etc.). It presents a condition as uncertain of fulfillment, but still likely (Wallace 1996, 696). That uncertain condition is appears in the next verb.

ἴδῃ: The Greek word ἴδῃ is a third singular aorist active subjunctive from the verb ὁράω that means, "I see" or "to be mentally or spiritually perceptive" (BDAG 720.4b). It is in the subjunctive mood because it follows an ἐάν. **Syntactically**, ἴδῃ is the governing verb of the dependent conditional ἐάν clause. The verb is in the subjunctive mood because it is part of an ἐάν clause. The subject of the verb is the indefinite pronoun "anyone" (τις). **Semantically**, ἴδῃ is a gnomic aorist: "sees" (cf. KJV NASB ESV NIV NET etc.). It presents a timeless fact about a generic person (τις; Wallace 1996, 562). The general fact of which John speaks is clarified with the next verb.

ἁμαρτάνοντα: The Greek word ἁμαρτάνοντα is an accusative singular masculine plural active participle from the verb ἁμαρτάνω that means, "I sin" or "to commit a wrong" (BDAG 50c). **Syntactically**, ἁμαρτάνοντα is a substantival participle. The entire phrase, "sinning a sin not *leading* to death" (ἁμαρτάνοντα ἁμαρτίαν μὴ πρὸς θάνατον) is a complement to the noun "brother" (ἀδελφὸν). This is a double accusative object-complement construction (Wallace 1996, 182–86). The direct object of the verb "sees" (ἴδῃ) is "his brother" (τὸν ἀδελφὸν αὐτοῦ). The second accusative, which functions as the complement, is the participial phrase "sinning a sin not leading to death" (ἁμαρτάνοντα ἁμαρτίαν μὴ πρὸς θάνατον). This type of construction is often translated with the words "to be." Therefore, we should translate this, "if anyone sees his brother *to be* sinning a sin not leading to death." **Semantically**, ἁμαρτάνοντα is a progressive present: "sinning" (NLT) or "sin" (KJV). It describes an event in progress (Wallace 1996, 518). When a believer sees a fellow Christian in the process of sinning a sin that is not the outright denial of Jesus, then he or she should pray for that individual and God will listen.

5:16b αἰτήσει: The Greek word αἰτήσει is a third singular future active indicative from the verb αἰτέω that means, "I ask" or "to ask for, with a claim on receipt of an answer" (BDAG 30). **Syntactically**, αἰτήσει is the main verb of the independent clause "he must ask" (αἰτήσει). It is the first part of the compound apodosis of the conditional ἐάν clause. The subject of the verb is an implied "he" embedded in the verb and refers to the one in the protasis who sees a fellow believer caught in sin. **Semantically**, αἰτήσει is an imperatival future: "he should ask" (NET; cf. NLT) or "he shall ask" (KJV ASV NASB ESV). While not common outside of Matthew, "he should ask" issues an indirect command (Wallace 1996, 569). The believer, who sees a brother or sister caught in sin, has a moral obligation to offer prayers on their behalf (Culy 2004, 135).

5:16c καί: The Greek word καί is a conjunction that means "and" (BDAG 494.1b). **Syntactically**, καί introduces the independent conjunctive clause: "*and* he will give him life" (καὶ δώσει αὐτῷ ζωήν). It serves as the second part of the compound apodosis. **Semantically**, καί is coordinating connective: "and" (cf. KJV NASB ESV NIV NET etc.). It provides additonal information (Wallace 1996, 671) about the prayer offered on behalf of the erring believer. That additonal information is found in the rest of the clause.

δώσει: The Greek word δώσει is a third singular future active indicative from the verb δίδωμι that means, "I give" or "I grant" or "to give something out" (BDAG 242.2). The verb is in the subjunctive mood because it is part of an ἐάν clause. **Syntactically**, δώσει is the main verb of the independent conjunctive καί clause. It is the second part of the compound apodosis of the conditional ἐάν clause. The subject of the verb is an implied "God" assumed from context. **Semantically**, δώσει is a predictive future: "God will grant" (NET) or "God will give" (KJV ASV NRSV ESV NIV CNT NLT). It describes something that will take place (Wallace 1996, 568). God will grant life, but to whom? The next verbal is important in answering this question.

ἁμαρτάνουσιν: The Greek word ἁμαρτάνουσιν is a dative plural masculine plural active participle from the verb ἁμαρτάνω that means, ἁμαρτάνω that means, "I sin" or "to commit a wrong" (BDAG 50e). **Syntactically**, ἁμαρτάνουσιν is a substantival participle. The entire phrase: "*to the one who does not commit a sin* leading to death" (τοῖς ἁμαρτάνουσιν μὴ πρὸς θάνατον) is set in apposition to the pronoun "him" (αὐτῷ). **Semantically**, ἁμαρτάνουσιν is a gnomic present negated with μή: "to the one who does not commit a sin" or "to those who commit a sin not" (NASB ESV NIV CNT). It is another generic utterance (Wallace 1996, 615). The phrase is placed in parenthesis in order to visualize its contribution to the independent clause. John presents a timeless truth about a petitioner who prays for a person who is caught in the middle of a sin, which does not lead to spiritual separation from God.

5:16d ἔστιν: The Greek word ἔστιν is third singular present active indicative from the verb εἰμί that means, "be" or "exist", or "be on hand" (BDAG 283.1). **Syntactically**, ἔστιν serves as the main verb of the independent clause "there is a sin that leads to death" (ἔστιν ἁμαρτία πρὸς θάνατον). The subject of the verb is the nominal phrase "a sin leading to death" (ἁμαρτία πρὸς θάνατον). **Semantically**, ἔστιν is an gnomic present: "is" (cf. KJV NASB ESV NIV NET etc.). It presents a gnomic truth about sin, more specifically a sin exists that leads to a separation from God.

^{5:16e} λέγω: The Greek word λέγω is a first person singular present active indicative from the verb λέγω that means, "I say" or "to express oneself in a specific way" (BDAG 589.2c). **Syntactically**, λέγω is the main verb of the independent clause: "*I* do not *say* that he should ask about that" (οὐ περὶ ἐκείνης λέγω ἵνα ἐρωτήσῃ). The subject of the verb is an implied "I" embedded in the verbal ending and refers to John. **Semantically**, λέγω is an instantaneous present negated with οὐ: "I do not say" (KJV NASB NRSV ESV NET CNT). It indicates that John's statement is completed at the moment to writing (Wallace 1996, 517). John is clarifying what he means or what he is saying. That clarity appears in the ἵνα clause.

ἵνα: The Greek word ἵνα is a conjunction, which means "that" (BDAG 476.2aα). **Syntactically**, ἵνα introduces a conjunctive dependent clause: "*that* he should ask" (ἵνα ἐρωτήσῃ). **Syntactically**, the clause is substantival functioning as the direct object of the verb "I am saying" (λέγω). The clause is placed in parenthesis in order to visualize its contribution to the independent clause. **Semantically**, ἵνα is an indirect discourse: "that" (cf. KJV NASB ESV NIV NET etc.). It provides the content of the author's clarified saying, which is evident in the verb of the ἵνα clause.

ἐρωτήσῃ: The Greek word ἐρωτήσῃ is a third singular aorist active subjunctive from the verb ὁράω that means, "I ask" or "I request" or "to ask for something" (BDAG 395.2). It is in the subjunctive mood because it follows an ἵνα. **Syntactically**, ἐρωτήσῃ is the governing verb of the dependent substantival clause. It is in the subjunctive mood because it follows an ἵνα. The subject of the verb is an implied "he" embedded in the verb and refers to the one who is petitioning God for life for the sinner. The object of ἐρωτήσῃ is the prepositional phrase, "about that" (περὶ ἐκείνης). **Semantically**, ἐρωτήσῃ is an constative aorist: "he should ask" (NET) or "he should pray" (NIV CNT). It describes an action as a whole (Wallace 1996, 557). It focuses attention on what ought not be requested in a prayer.

^{5:17a} ἐστίν: The Greek word ἐστίν is third singular present active indicative from the verb εἰμί that means, "is" or "to be in close connection with" (BDAG 282.2a). **Syntactically**, ἐστίν is the main verb of the independent asyndeton clause: "all unrighteousness *is* sin" (πᾶσα ἀδικία ἁμαρτία ἐστίν). The subject of the verb is the nominal phrase "all unrighteousness" (πᾶσα ἀδικία). Although both the subject and the predicate nominative in this clause are anarthrous, "unrighteousness" (ἀδικία) is clearly the subject because of the presence of the adjectival qualifier (Wallace 1996, 42–44). **Semantically**, ἐστίν is a gnomic present: "is" (cf. KJV NASB ESV NIV NET etc.). It points out the timeless principle (Wallace 1996, 523): unrigtheousness is sin.

^{5:17b} καί: The Greek word καί is a conjunction that means "and yet" (BDAG 495.1bη). Syntactically, καί introduces a coordinating independent clause: "*and yet* there is sin that does not lead to death" (καὶ ἔστιν ἁμαρτία οὐ πρὸς θάνατον). **Semantically**, καί is adversative: "and yet" or "but" (NRSV NET ESV NLT). It emphasizes an unexpected fact. That noteworthy fact is identified in the rest of the clause.

ἐστίν: The Greek word ἐστίν is third singular present active indicative from the verb εἰμί that means, "be" or "exist", or "be on hand" (BDAG 283.1). **Syntactically**, ἐστίν is the main verb of the independent clause. The subject of the verb is the nominal phrase "a sin not leading to death" (ἁμαρτία οὐ πρὸς θάνατον). **Semantically**, ἐστίν is a gnomic present: "is" (cf. KJV NASB ESV NIV NET etc.). It presents a gnomic truth about sin (Wallace 1996, 523). There is a sin exists that does not lead to a separation from God.

5:18a Οἴδαμεν: The Greek word οἴδαμεν is a first plural perfect active indicative from the verb οἶδα that means, "I know" or "to have information about" (BDAG 693.1e). **Syntactically**, οἴδαμεν is the main verb of the independent clause: "*We know* that everyone who is born of God does not sin" (Οἴδαμεν ὅτι πᾶς ὁ γεγεννημένος ἐκ τοῦ θεοῦ οὐχ ἁμαρτάνει). The subject of the verb is an implied "we" embedded in the verb and refers to John and the readers of the letter. **Semantically**, οἴδαμεν is a perfect with present force: "we know" (cf. KJV NASB ESV NIV NET etc.). It is a verb in the "perfect tense without the usual aspectual significance" (Wallace 1996, 579). That information is found in the ὅτι clause.

ὅτι: The Greek word ὅτι is a conjunction, which means "that" (BDAG 731.1c). **Syntactically**, ὅτι introduces a dependent conjunctive clause: "*that* everyone born of God does not sin" (ὅτι πᾶς ὁ γεγεννημένος ἐκ τοῦ θεοῦ οὐχ ἁμαρτάνει). The entire ὅτι clause is functioning substantivally as the direct object of the verb "casts out" (οἴδαμεν). It is placed in parenthesis in order to visualize its contribution to the independent clause. **Semantically**, ὅτι is indirect discourse: "that" (cf. KJV NASB ESV NIV NET etc.). The entire ὅτι clause provides the content of the knowledge (Wallace 1996, 456), which is clearly expressed in the next verb.

γεγεννημένος: The Greek word γεγεννημένος is a nominative masculine singular perfect passive participle from the verb γεννάω that means, "I become the parent of" or "to exercise the role of a parental figure" (BDAG 193.1b). **Syntactically**, γεγεννημένος is functioning adjectivally. It modifies the substantival adjective "each" (Πᾶς). The entire participial phrase "Everyone who is born of God" (πᾶς ὁ γεγεννημένος ἐκ τοῦ θεοῦ) is the subject of the verb "does" (ἁμαρτάνει). **Semantically**, γεγέννηται is both a gnomic and extensive perfect: "has been fathered" (cf. NET) or "has been born" (ESV). It is gnomic because of the generic subject (πᾶς) while extensive in that the focus is on the decisive relationship between God and believer (Wallace 1996, 580). This generic or proverbial force may also be rendered intensive: "is born" (KJV NASB; cf. ASV NRSV) with an emphasis on the results of the present condition of the believer. Regardless of where one places the emphasis of the perfect, John's point is simply that believers have been fathered by God in the past and that has continuing results in the present (cf. 2:29; 3:9; 4:7; 5:1, 4). The focus is upon those who practice righteousness: they have had an on-going relationship with God.

ἁμαρτάνει: The Greek word ἁμαρτάνει is a third singular present active indicative from the verb ἁμαρτάνω that means, "I sin" or "to commit a wrong" (BDAG 49.a). **Syntactically**, ἁμαρτάνει is the governing verb of the dependent substantival clause. The subject is the substantial adjective πᾶς plus the entire participial phrase that modifies it, "*everyone* who is born of God" (πᾶς ὁ γεγεννημένος ἐκ τοῦ θεοῦ). **Semantically**, ἁμαρτάνει negated with οὐχ is a customary present: "does not *persist* in sin" or "does not keep on sinning" (ESV) or "does not continue to sin" (NIV) or "does not sin" (NET CNT). It speaks of something that occurs regularly (Wallace 1996, 521). John says the one who has God as their father is unable to deny Jesus.

5:18b ἀλλ' [ὅτι]: The Greek word ἀλλά is a conjunction that means "but" (BDAG 44.1a). **Syntactically**, ἀλλά identifies a dependent conjunctive clause: "*but* [that] the one fathered by God he preserves him" (ἀλλ' [ὅτι] ὁ γεννηθεὶς ἐκ τοῦ θεοῦ τηρεῖ αὐτόν). It is also part of the direct object of "we know" (οἴδαμεν). **Semantically**, ἀλλά is contrastive: "but" (KJV ASV NASB NRSV ESV NET CNT). It introduces a contrast to the previous οὐχ clause (Wallace 1996, 671). The significance of the contrast is evident in next verb.

γεννηθεὶς: The Greek word γεννηθεὶς is a nominative masculine singular aorist passive participle from the verb γεννάω that means, "I beget" or "become the parent of" (BDAG 193.1b). **Syntactically**, γεννηθεὶς is functioning as a pendant nominative and serves to further describe the direct object of the clause "him" (αὐτόν). It is the logical rather than the syntactical subject (Wallace 1996, 51-53). **Semantically,** ὁ γεννηθεὶς is a gnomic aorist: "the one fathered" or "the one who was born" (NRSV NIV). It presents a generic statement that reflects a timeless truth (Wallace 1996, 615). John focuses on a general fact about the one whom God has fathered. The specifics are found in the next verb.

τηρεῖ: The Greek word τηρεῖ is a third singular present active indicative from the verb τηρέω that means, "I keep" or "I preserve" or to cause a condition or activity to continue (BDAG 1002.2b). **Syntactically,** τηρεῖ is the main verb of the independent clause. The subject of the verb is an implied "he" embedded in the verbal ending and refers to God. **Semantically,** τηρεῖ is a customary present: "he preserves" or "keeps" (NASB CNT) or "he protects" (NRSV ESV NET). It is an action that happens regularly (Wallace 1996, 521). God *continually* preserves or protects those whom he has fathered.

5:18c καὶ [ὅτι]: The Greek word καί is a conjunction that means "and" (BDAG 494.1ba). **Syntactically,** καί introduces another dependent conjunctive clause: "*and* [that] the evil one cannot touch him" (καὶ [ὅτι] ὁ πονηρὸς οὐχ ἅπτεται αὐτοῦ). It also is part of the direct object of "we know" (οἴδαμεν). **Semantically,** καί is a coordinating connective: "and" (KJV ASV NASB NRSV ESV NIV NET NLT CNT). The conjunctive καί clause provides more information about the one whom God protects, which is clearly stated in the next verb.

ἅπτεται: The Greek word ἅπτεται is a third singular present middle indicative from the verb ἅπτω that means, "I harm" or "to make contact with a view to causing harm" (BDAG 126.5). **Syntactically,** ἅπτεται is the main verb of the independent clause. The subject is the substantival adjective is "the evil one" (ὁ πονηρὸς). **Semantically,** ἅπτεται negated with οὐχ is a customary present: "cannot harm" (NIV) or "cannot touch" (KJV ASV NASB NRSV ESV NET CNT NLT). It presents an ongoing or habitual action (Wallace 1996, 521). The Devil is not able to harm the true believer because God himself protects them.

5:19a οἴδαμεν: The Greek word οἴδαμεν is a first plural perfect active indicative from the verb οἶδα that means, "I know" or "to have information about" (BDAG 693.1e). **Syntactically,** οἴδαμεν is the main verb of the independent clause: "*we know* that we are of God" (οἴδαμεν ὅτι ἐκ τοῦ θεοῦ ἐσμεν). The assumed subject "we" refers to John and the orthodox readers of the letter. **Semantically,** οἴδαμεν is a perfect with present force: "we know" (cf. KJV NASB ESV NIV NET etc.). It is a verb in the "perfect tense without the usual aspectual significance" (Wallace 1996, 579). That information is found in the ὅτι clause.

ὅτι: The Greek word ὅτι is a conjunction, which means "that" (BDAG 731.1c). **Syntactically,** ὅτι introduces a dependent conjunctive clause: "*that* we are of God" (ὅτι ἐκ τοῦ θεοῦ ἐσμεν). The entire clause is functioning substantivally as the direct object of the verb "we know" (οἴδαμεν) and is placed in parenthesis in order to visualize its contribution to the independent clause. **Semantically,** ὅτι is indirect discourse: "that" (cf. KJV NASB ESV NIV NET etc.). The entire ὅτι clause provides the content of the knowledge (Wallace 1996, 456), which is clearly expressed in the next verb.

ἐσμεν: The Greek word ἐσμεν is first plural present active indicative from the verb εἰμί that means, "is" or "to be in close connection (with)" (BDAG 283.2b). **Syntactically,** ἐσμεν is the governing verb of the dependent substantival clause. The subject of the verb is an implied "we" and refers to John and his readers of the letter. **Semantically,** ἐσμεν is an equative present: "is" (cf. KJV NASB ESV NIV NET etc.). It describes a special connection between the subject (e.g. the readers) and the predicate (e.g. God). pointing out that the person who believes that Jesus is God's son can have assurance that they have been fathered by God.

5:19b καὶ [ὅτι]: The Greek word καί is a conjunction that means "and" (BDAG 494.1e). **Syntactically**, καί introduces a dependent conjunctive clause: "*and* [that] the whole world is under the control of the evil one" (καὶ [ὅτι] ὁ κόσμος ὅλος ἐν τῷ πονηρῷ κεῖται). It is also part of the direct object of "we know" (οἴδαμεν). **Semantically**, καί is a coordinating conjunction: "and" (cf. KJV NASB ESV NIV NET etc.). It introduces something new with a loose connection to the previous ὅτι clause (BDAG 494.1e; Wallace 1996, 671). The conjunctive καὶ [ὅτι] clause then provides more information about what is known by the reader.

κεῖται: The Greek word κεῖται is third singular present middle indicative from the verb κεῖμαι that means, "I exist" or "I am there" or "to find oneself, be, in a certain state or condition" (BDAG 437.3d). **Syntactically**, κεῖται is the governing verb of the second dependent [ὅτι] clause. The subject of the nominal phrase, "the whole world" (ὁ κόσμος ὅλος) and refers to the world system in opposition to God and his values (cf. 2:15–17). **Semantically**, κεῖται is a customary present: "*continually* lies *in the power of*" (NASB NRSV ESV NET) or "under the control of" (NIV NLT; cf. CNT). It describes an ongoing occurance (Wallace 1996, 521). The world system continually lies under Satan's power.

5:20a οἴδαμεν: The Greek word οἴδαμεν is a first plural perfect active indicative from the verb οἶδα that means, "I know" or "to have information about" (BDAG 693.1e). **Syntactically**, οἴδαμεν serves as the main verb of the independent clause: "but *we know* that the son of God has come" (οἴδαμεν δὲ ὅτι ὁ υἱὸς τοῦ θεοῦ ἥκει). The assumed subject "we" refers to John and the orthodox readers of the letter. **Semantically**, οἴδαμεν is a perfect with present force: "we know" (cf. KJV NASB ESV NIV NET etc.). It is a verb in the "perfect tense without the usual aspectual significance" (Wallace 1996, 579). That information is found in the ὅτι clause.

δέ: The Greek word δέ is a conjunction in the post-positive position which means "and" (BDAG 213.1). **Syntactically**, δέ introduces an independent conjunctive clause. **Semantically**, δέ is a coordinating connective: "and" (cf. KJV NASB ESV NIV NET etc.). It connects yet another clause about what John claims his readers know (Wallace 1996, 671).

ὅτι: The Greek word ὅτι is a conjunction, which means "that" (BDAG 731.1c). **Syntactically**, ὅτι introduces a dependent conjunctive clause: "*that* the son of God comes and has gives us insight" (ὅτι ὁ υἱὸς τοῦ θεοῦ ἥκει, καὶ δέδωκεν ἡμῖν διάνοιαν). The entire clause is functioning substantivally as the direct object of the verb "we know" (οἴδαμεν) and is placed in parenthesis in order to visualize its contribution to the independent clause. **Semantically**, ὅτι is indirect discourse: "that" (cf. KJV NASB ESV NIV NET etc.). The entire ὅτι clause provides the content of the knowledge (Wallace 1996, 456), which is clearly expressed in the next verb.

ἥκει: The Greek word ἥκει is a third singular present active indicative from the verb ἥκω that means, "I have come" or "to be in a place as the result of movement" (BDAG 435.1c). **Syntactically**, ἥκει is the governing verb of the dependent [ὅτι] clause. The subject of the verb is the nominal phrase "the son of God" (ὁ υἱὸς τοῦ θεοῦ) and is a reference to Jesus. **Semantically**, ἥκει is a perfective present: "has come" (NASB NRSV ESV NIV NET CNT NLT). It emphasizes the results of a past action that are still continuing (Wallace 1996, 532). Jesus the Messiah has come, and yet there is more that is known by John's readers as evident in the next clause.

5:20b καὶ [ὅτι]: The Greek word καί is a conjunction that means "and" (BDAG 494.1ba). **Syntactically**, καί introduces a dependent clause: "*and* [that] he has given to us insight" (καὶ [ὅτι] δέδωκεν ἡμῖν διάνοιαν). It is also part of the direct object of "we know" (οἴδαμεν). **Semantically**, καί is a coordinating conjunction: "and" (cf. KJV NASB ESV NIV NET etc.). It introduces something new with a loose connection to the previous ὅτι clause (BDAG 494.1e; Wallace 1996, 671). The conjunctive καὶ [ὅτι] clause once again provides more information about what is known by the reader.

δέδωκεν: The Greek word δέδωκεν is a third singular perfect active indicative from the verb δίδωμι that means, "I give" or "to give something out" (BDAG 242.2). **Syntactically**, δέδωκεν is the governing verb of the second part of the compound dependent clause. The subject of the verb is an implied "he" and refers back to the son of God. **Semantically**, δέδωκεν is an extensive perfect: "has given" (cf. KJV NASB ESV NIV NET etc.). It emphasizes a past event from which a present state emerges (Wallace 1996, 577). Since Jesus came as God in flesh, we have gained insight. God's intention for revealing insight is clarified in the next clause.

5:20c ἵνα: The Greek word ἵνα is a conjunction, which means "that" or "in order that" (BDAG 475.1c). **Syntactically**, ἵνα introduces the dependent conjunctive clause: "*in order that* we may know the true one" (ἵνα γινώσκωμεν τὸν ἀληθινόν). **Syntactically**, the clause is adverbial modifying the verb "he has given" (δέδωκεν). **Semantically**, ἵνα denotes purpose: "in order that" or "that" (KJV ASV). It indicates John's intention (Wallace 1996, 472). That intention is clearly provided in the next verb.

γινώσκωμεν: The Greek word γινώσκωμεν is a first plural present active subjunctive from the verb γινώσκω that means, "I know" or "to arrive at a knowledge of someone or something" (BDAG 199.1b). It is in the subjunctive mood because it follows an ἵνα. **Syntactically**, γινώσκομεν serves as the governing verb of the dependent clause. It appears in the subjunctive because ἵνα takes the subjunctive. The subject of the verb is an implied "we" embedded in the verb and refers to John and his readers. **Semantically**, γινώσκομεν is a customary present: "we may know" (KJV NASB NRSV ESV NIV CNT). It signals something that occurs regularly. John's intention for writing this letter is in order that believers may know the truth, ultimately the truth about Jesus as the human Messiah and God's expectation to love other believers.

5:20d καί: The Greek word καί is a conjunction which means "and" (BDAG 494.1aα). **Syntactically**, καί introduces a conjunctive independent clause: "*and* we are in the true one, in his son, Jesus Christ" (καὶ ἐσμὲν ἐν τῷ ἀληθινῷ, ἐν τῷ υἱῷ αὐτοῦ Ἰησοῦ Χριστῷ). **Semantically**, καί is a coordinating connective: "and" (cf. KJV NASB ESV NIV NET etc.). It adds additional information about what believers know (Wallace 1996, 671). That additional information is evident in the rest of the conjunctive καί clause.

ἐσμέν: The Greek word ἐσμέν is first plural present active indicative from the verb εἰμί that means, "be" or to be in reference to a person (BDAG 284.3b). **Syntactically**, ἐσμέν is the main verb of the independent clause. The subject of the verb is an implied "we" embedded in the verb and refers back to John and his readers. **Semantically**, ἐσμέν is an instantaneous present: "we are" (cf. KJV NASB ESV NIV NET etc.). It reveals something that is completed (Wallace 1996, 517). Believers have a relationship with Jesus who is the Christ.

5:20e ἐστιν: The Greek word ἐστιν is third singular present active indicative from the verb εἰμί that means, "and" (BDAG 494.1aα). **Syntactically**, ἐστιν is the main verb of the independent clause "this one *is* the true God and eternal life": (οὗτός ἐστιν ὁ ἀληθινὸς θεὸς καὶ ζωὴ αἰώνιος). The subject is the demonstrative pronoun "this one" (οὗτός) and refers back to Jesus, God's son. **Semantically**, ἐστιν is an equative present pointing out that Jesus, the Messiah, God's son, is also truly God himself and eternal life personified.

5:21 φυλάξατε: The Greek word φυλάξατε is a second plural aorist active imperative from the verb φυλάξάω that means, "I guard" or "I protest" or "to protect by taking careful measures" (BDAG 1068.2b). **Syntactically**, φυλάξατε is the main verb of the independent clause: "children, *keep* yourselves from idols" (Τεκνία, φυλάξατε ἑαυτὰ ἀπὸ τῶν εἰδώλων). The subject of the verb is an implied "you" hidden in the verb and refers to the orthodox readers/hearers of the letter. **Semantically**, φυλάξατε is an imperative of request with the personal pronoun, ἑαυτά: "I guard yourselves" (SV NASB NET). It is an imperative from a leader to his readers (Wallace 1996, 488). John admonishes readers to avoid following after idolatrous views of God, namely heterodox teachings about the nature of Jesus.

Interpretive Translation for 1 John

1:1That which was from the beginning, which we have heard, which we have seen with our eyes, which we have looked at, and which our hands have touched about the word, which is life — 2for the life was revealed, and we have seen, and we now testify and proclaim to you eternal life, which was with the Father and was revealed to us — 3that which we have seen and heard we now proclaim to you also in order that even you may have fellowship with us. And indeed our fellowship is with the Father and with his Son, Jesus, who is the Christ. 4Therefore we are writing these things in order that our joy may be complete.

5Now this is the gospel message, which we have heard from him and which we now proclaim to you, namely that God is light and that in him there is no darkness at all. 6If we say, "We have fellowship with him" yet if we persist on living in the darkness, we lie and we are not practicing the truth; 7 but if we make it a point to live in the light as he is in the light, we have fellowship with one another and the blood of Jesus, his son, cleanses us from all sins.

8If we say, "We have no sin", we deceive ourselves and the truth is not in us. 9But if we confess our sins, he is faithful and righteous to pardon our sins and to declare us purified from all unrighteousness. 10If we say "We have not sinned," we make him a liar and his word is not in us. 2:1My children, I now write these things to you in order that you may not sin. But if anyone does sin, we have an advocate with the Father, Jesus who is the Christ, the righteous one; and he himself is the atoning sacrifice for our sins, and not only is he the atonig sacrifice for our sins, but he is also the atoning sacrifice for the whole world.

3Now by this we know that we have known him, If we persist in keeping his commandments. 4The one who says, "I know him," but does not persist in keeping his commands, is a liar, and the truth is not in this person. 5But whoever persists in keeping his word, truly, in this person, our love for God has been perfected. By this, we know that we are in him; 6The one who says that God abides in him must also persist in living just as Jesus lived. 7Beloved, I write no new command to you, but I now write an old command, which you have had as an obligation from the beginning. The old command is the word, which you have heard, which is true in Jesus and in you. 8On the other hand, I now write to you a new command because the darkness is passing away and true light is already shining. [9]The one who claims to be in the light and yet persists in hating his brother and sister is still in the darkness until now. [10] In contrast, the one who persists in loving his brother and sister abides in the light, and in that person, there is no cause for stumbling. [11]But the one who persists in hating his brother and sister is in the darkness and so he is walking in the darkness and he does not know where he is going because the darkness has blinded his eyes.

[12] I now write to you, children, that for your benefit your sins have been pardoned because of Jesus's name. [13]I now write to you, fathers, that you have known him who is from the beginning. I now write to you, young people, that you have overcome the evil one. [14]I have written to you, children, that you have known the Father. I have written to you, fathers, that you have known the Father from the beginning. I have written to you, young people, that you are strong, and that the Word of God abides in you and that you have conquered the Evil One.

[15]Do not love the world nor the things in the world. If anyone persists in loving the world, the love of the Father is not in him; [16]For this reason all that is in the world, the flesh that desires and the eyes that desire and the boastful pride about one's life, is not from the Father but from the world. [17]And the world is passing away, and also its lusts; [2:17b] but the one who does the will of God remains forever.

[18]Children, it is the last hour, and as you heard that the antichirst is coming, even now many antichrists have appeared; whereby we now know that it is the last hour. [19]They went out from us, but they were not of us; for you see if they had been of us, they would have remained with us; but they did go out, so that it would be shown that they all are not of us. [20]But you have an anointing from the Holy One, and you know all things. [21]I have not written to you because you do not know the truth, but rather I have written to you because you know it, and because you know that no lie is of the truth. [22]Who is the liar except the one who persists in denying that Jesus is the Christ; This is the antichrist, namely the one who persists in denying the Father and the Son. [23]Whoever persists in denying the Son does not have the Father; [yet] the one who persists in their confession of the Son has the Father also.

[24]Let what you yourselves have heard from the beginning remain in you; if what you have heard from the beginning remains in you, you also will remain in the Son and in the Father. [25]Now this is the promise, which God himself made to us: eternal life. [26]I have written these things to you concerning those who persist in their attempts to mislead you.

[27]Now as for you, the anointing that you have received from him remains continually in you. And you have no need that anyone teach you; but now the anointing is true and not a lie, as his anointing continually teaches you about all things, and just as he has taught you, make it a practice to remain in him. —— [28]Even now, children, make it a practice to remain in him, so that we may have confidence when he appears and may not shrink away from him at his coming. [29]If you know that he is righteous, you also know that everyone who practices righteousness has been fathered by him.

[3:1]Consider what sort of love the Father has granted to us that we should be called children of God; indeed we really are called children of God. For this reason, the world does not know us, that the world did not know him. Beloved, we are God's children, [2]and what we will be whenever he comes has not been revealed. We know that we will be like him when he appears, because we will see him as he is. [3]And so everyone who has this hope in him purifies himself even as Jesus is pure. [4]Everyone who practices sin also practices lawlessness, indeed sin is lawlessness. [5]And you know that Jesus appeared in order to take away sin. And you know that in Jesus there is no sin. [6]Everyone who abides in him does not persist in sin; [yet] everyone who makes it a practice to sin has neither seen him nor known him. [7]Children, let no one mislead you; the one who makes it a practice to be righteous is righteous, even as Jesus is righteous; [8][Yet] the one who practices sin comes from the devil, because the devil persists in sinning from the beginning. For this purpose the Son of God appeared, [3:8d] that he might destroy the works of the devil. [9]Everyone who has been fathered by God does not practice sin, because God's seed remains in him; and he is not able to sin, because he has been fathered by God. [10]By this the children of God and the children of the devil are made clear; everyone who does not practice righteousness is not of God that is the one who persists in not loving his brother and sister.

[11]For this is the gospel message that you heard from the beginning, namely that we should love one another; [12]not as Cain who was of the evil one [12]and who brutally murdered his brother; and why did he brutally murder Abel? because his deeds were evil, but his brother's deeds were righteous. [13]And so, do not be surprised, brothers and sisters, that the world hates you. [14]We know that we have passed out of death into life, because we persistantly love our brothers and sisters. The one who does not persist in love abides in death. [15]Everyone who persists in hating his brother and sister is a murderer, and you know that no murderer possesses eternal life abiding in him or her. [16]By this we know love, that Jesus gave up his life for us; and that we are obligated to give up our lives for our brothers and sisters. [17]But whoever possesses the resources of the world and whoever percieves his brother and sister with a need and whoever shuts off his heart against him or her, how does the love of God remain in him or her?

[18]Little children, let us not love with word or with tongue but in deed and truth. [19]And so by this we will know that we are of the truth, and that we will convince our heart before him [20]that whenever our heart condemns us, that God is greater than our heart and that he knows all things. [21]Beloved, if our heart does not condemn us, we feel confident before God, [22]and so whatever we ask for we will receive from God, because we persist in keeping his commands and doing the things that are pleasing in his sight. [23]And this is God's commandment, namely that we believe in the name of his Son Jesus, who is the Christ and that we persist in loving one another, just as God commanded us. [24]And the one who persists in keeping his commandments abides with God and this one abides with God; And by this we know that God abides in us, by the Spirit whom he has given us.

[4:1]Beloved, do not believe every spirit, but test the spirits to determine whether they are from God, because many false prophets have gone out into the world. [2]By this you know the Spirit of God; every spirit, who repeatedly acknowledges Jesus to be the Christ who has come in flesh, is from God, [3]but every spirit, who does not repeatedly claim Jesus has come in the flesh, is not from God; and this is the spirit of the antichrist, about which you have heard that it is coming, and which is now already in the world. ⁴You yourselves are from God, little children, and you have overcome these antichrists, because the one who is in you is greater than the one who is in the world. ⁵They themselves are from the world; therefore they speak regualarly from the world's perspective and the world listens to them. ⁶We are from God; the person who knows God listens to us, whoever is not from God does not listen to us. From this we know the spirit of truth and the spirit of deceit.

⁷Beloved, let us persist in love for one another, because love is from God, and everyone who loves has been fathered by God and everyone who loves knows God. ⁸The person who does not love does not know God, because God is love. ⁹By this the love of God was made known among us, that God sent his one and only Son into the world in order that we may live through him. ¹⁰In this is love, not that we loved God, but that he loved us and that he sent his Son to be the atoning sacrifice for our sins.

¹¹Beloved, if God so loved us, then we ourselves are obligated to love one another. ¹²No one has seen God at any time; if we persist in loving one another, God abides in us, and his love is perfected in us. ¹³By this we know that we remain in God and he remains in us, that God has given us a portion of his spirit. ¹⁴And we have seen and testify that the Father sent the Son to be the savior of the world. ¹⁵Whoever professes that Jesus is the Son of God, God remains in him, and he remains in God. ¹⁶And so we have come to know and to believe the love which God has for us.

God is love, and the one who abides in love abides in God and God abides in him. ¹⁷By this, love is perfected with us, so that we may have confidence in the day of judgment, because just as Jesus is so also are we in this world. ¹⁸There is no fear in love, but perfect love expels fear, because fear includes punishment and because the one who fears is not perfected in love. ¹⁹As for us we persist in love because he first loved us. ²⁰If someone says, "I love God," and that same someone hates his brother and sister, he is a liar. For the one, who does not love his brother and sister whom he has seen, is unable to love God whom he has not seen. ²¹And this commandment we have from him, name;y that the one who loves God should love his brother and sister also.

⁵:¹Everyone who persists in believing that Jesus is the Christ has been fathered by God, and everyone who persists in loving the father loves also those who have been fathered by him. ²By this we know that we love the children of God, whenever we persist in loving God and whenever we persist in carrying out his commandments. ³For this is the love for God, namely that we keep his commandments; and his commandments are not difficult to carry out, ⁴because everyone who has been fathered by God overcomes the world; and this is the victory that overcame the world, our faith.

⁵Now who is overcoming the world except the one who believes that Jesus is the Son of God? ⁶This is the one who came by water and blood, Jesus, who is the Christ. Jesus came not by water only but by the water and the blood; and the Spirit is the one who testifies, because the Spirit is the truth, ⁷For the ones that testify are three, ⁸they are the Spirit, the water, and the blood, and these three are in agreement. ⁹If we receive the testimony of men, God's testimony is greater, because this is the testimony of God, that he has testified concerning his Son.

[10]The one who believes in the Son of God has the testimony in himself; [10]the one who does not believe God has made him a liar, [10]because he has not believed in the testimony that God has testified concerning his Son.

[11]And this is the testimony, that God has granted us, eternal life, and this life is in his Son. [12]The one who has the Son has eternal life; the one who does not have the Son of God does not have eternal life.

[13]I have written these things to you, who believe in the name of the Son of God, so that you may know that you have eternal life. [14]And this is the confidence that we have before him: that whatever we ask for according to his will, he hears us. [15]And if we know that he hears us, namely, he listens to whatever we ask, we know that we have the requests that we have asked from him. [16]If anyone sees his fellow follower of Jesus committing a sin not leading to death, he should ask [God], and God will grant life to the one who does not commit a sin leading to death. There is a sin leading to death; I do not say that he should ask about that. [17]All unrighteousness is sin, and yet there is a sin not leading in death. [18]We know that everyone fathered by God does not persist in sin, but the one fathered by God he preserves him and the evil one cannot harm him. [19]We know that we are of God, and that the whole world lies in the power of the evil one. [20]And we know that the son of God has come, and that he has given us understanding in order that we may know the truth; and we are in the true one, in his son Jesus, who is the Christ. This one is the true God and eternal life. [21]Children, guard yourselves from idols.

Selected Bibliography

Although *Translating 1 John Clause by Clause* is not a commentary, it certainly evidences features of a critical commentary in that 1 John's structure and syntax was both explained and interpreted to an extent that even some critical commentaries ignore for one reason or another. Nevertheless, historical issues, text critical discussions, word studies, theological issues were *nearly* non-existent. The focused attention was on the co-ordination and subordination of independent and dependent Greek clauses. So the following are a few sources that might assist in your continual study of 1 John and in some cases books that may assist in helping develop translational and exegetical skills.

Further Reading for Translating Johannine Letters

Bateman IV, Herbert W. *A Workbook for Intermediate Greek: Grammar, Exegesis, and Commentary on 1–3 John*. Grand Rapids: Kregel, 2008.

Bauer, Walter, Frederick W. Danker, William F. Arndt, and F. Wilbur Gingrich. *A Greek–English Lexicon of the New Testament and Other Early Christian Literature*. Third Edition. Chicago and London: University of Chicago Press, 2000. (Abbreviation: BDAG)

Burer, Michael H. and Jeffery E. Miller. *A New Reader's Lexicon of the Greek New Testament*. Grand Rapids: Kregel, 2008.

Culy, Martin M. *I, II, III John: A Handbook on the Greek Text*. Waco, TX: Baylor University Press, 2004.[11]

Further Reading for Developing Exegetical Skills

Bateman IV, Herbert W. *Interpreting the General Letters*. Handbooks for New Testament Exegesis. Edited by John D. Harvey. Grand Rapids, Kregel, 2013.

Interpreting the General Letters consists of eight chapters covering genre, background, theology, interpretation, and communication of the general letters in the New Testament. Of particular significance is the step-by-step approach to interpretation of the letters.

Bock Darrell L. and Buist M. Fanning, editors. *Interpreting the New Testament Text: Introduction to the Art and Science of Exegesis*. Wheaton, IL: Crossway, 2006.

Interpreting the New Testament Text consists of two parts: exegetical methods and procedure and exegetical examples and reflections. The first collection of outstanding articles examines the numerous area of interpretation: grammar, clausal layouts, word studies, validation, biblical theology, the use of the Old Testament in the New, and genre studies. It also provides an excellent collection of articles exemplifying the interpretive process and relevance.

Selected Clause by Clause Commentaries

Brown, Raymond E. *The Epistles of John*. The Anchor Bible. Garden City, NY: Doubleday, 1982.

The AB is a technical/*critical* commentary series whose quality varies depending on the book. The commentary is arranged as a verse-by-verse commentary with interpretive translations, critical notes, and expositional sections. The series is mostly moderate-liberal.

Brown's commentary on the Johannine epistles remains a foundational work for the letters. His translation, his identifying clauses in English, his exegetical notes, and his concluding comments are extremely helpful.

---

[11] Culy, though helpful at times, struggles with syntactical and semantical labels. For instance, he does not provide semantical labels for verb tenses. "I continue to believe," he says, "that such tense labels should be abandoned since the phenomena they describe are at best only partially related to the Greek verb tenses themselves and frequently lead exegetes to think erroneously that an aorist verb, for example, *emphasizes* the beginning of an action." Culy, *I, II, III John* [2004], xxii-xxiii. Consequently, Culy will not entertain semantical classifications of verb tenses. Yet he does recognize the relevance of other syntactical and semantical labels and does engage the text in helpful ways. He is, however, at odds with other intermediate grammarians like Daniel B. Wallace, *Greek Grammar Beyond the Basics*. This translation guide, however, is more in keeping with Wallace and others like him when it comes to classifying verb tenses and entertaining other syntactical and semantical classifications.

Yarbrough, Robert W. *1–3 John.* Baker Exegetical Commentary on the New Testament. Grand Rapids: Baker Academic, 2008.

The Baker Exegetical Commentary on the New Testament is intended to address the needs of the pastor and others involved in preaching and teaching the New Testament. The series is evangelical and contributors come from a variety of theological traditions and yet they share a belief in the trustworthiness and unity of Scripture. It is a *critical* commentary series of great value.

Yarbrough's volume is an exceptional recent complement to Brown. It provides a cause-by-clause examination for the Johannine letters. The interaction with the Greek text clause-by-clause and the interaction with syntactical and semantical issues are extremely helpful.

Made in the USA
Lexington, KY
24 April 2019